Women and Priesthood in the Church of England

Ten Years On

Women and Priesthood in the Church of England

Ten Years On

Ian Jones

Lincoln Theological Institute

Lincoln Institute Research Reports
Editors: Martyn Percy and Helen Orchard

 CHURCH HOUSE
PUBLISHING

Church House Publishing
Church House
Great Smith Street
London SW1P 3NZ
Tel: 020 7889 1451
Fax: 020 7898 1449

ISBN 0 7151 4035 3

Published 2004 by Church House Publishing

Email: copyright@c-of-e.org.uk

Cover design by Church House Publishing

Printed in England by Biddles Ltd, King's Lynn

Contents

List of tables and figures   vii
Acknowledgements   x
Executive summary   xi
Preface by Martyn Percy and Helen Orchard   xiii
Introduction   1

Part I: The First Ten Years

Chapter 1: Setting the scene: the 1992–94 Settlement, before and after   17
1.1   Women and ordained ministry: a very short history   17
1.2   Expectations and contingency plans   20
1.3   Champagne on ice: reactions to the vote   25
1.4   Women deacons and their supporters: preparing for priesthood   34
       Conclusion   36

Chapter 2: Patterns of support and opposition   38
2.1   Diocesan and deanery voting   39
2.2   Overall patterns in the questionnaires for clergy and congregations   41
2.3   How far have clergy attitudes changed?   42
2.4   Attitudes amongst the case study congregations   43
2.5   How far have lay attitudes changed?   44
2.6   Gender-related patterns   46
2.7   Age- and cohort-related patterns   48
2.8   By Church tradition   51
2.9   By experience of women's ministry   53
       Conclusion   56

**Chapter 3: 'Who are we to prevent it?': Anglican popular belief on
women and priesthood**   57
3.1   Some common arguments   58
3.2   Divine intervention and personal calling   61
3.3   Gut feelings   62
3.4   No theological objections?   64
3.5   Gender roles and characteristics   65
3.6   More than just a job?   68
3.7   The icon of Christ?   70
3.8   Division within and without   72
3.9   Social expectation and the demands of mission   73
3.10   The significance of tradition   74
3.11   The biblical witness   77
       Conclusion   79

Chapter 4: Assessing the impact on the Church   82
4.1   *Some popular expectations*   82
4.2   *Parish stories*   90
    Church 1   90
    Church 2   92
    Church 3   93
    Church 4   94
    Church 5   95
    Church 6   96
    Church 7   97
    Church 8   99
    Church 9   100
    Conclusion   102

Part II: Current Issues
Chapter 5: The appointments question   107
5.1   *Patterns of clergy deployment*   108
5.2   *Parishes, chaplaincies and stipends*   113
5.3   *A stained glass ceiling?*   115
5.4   *The appointments process*   121
5.5   *'We'll take a woman, but not yet'*   122
    Conclusion   123

Chapter 6: Communion and cooperation in parish, deanery and diocese   125
6.1   *Working relationships: some general patterns*   125
6.2   *Deanery issues*   130
6.3   *Diocesan occasions*   134
6.4   *Sector ministries*   138
6.5   *Organized support for women clergy*   139
    Conclusion   141

Chapter 7: Opting out of women's priestly ministry: working the provisions   143
7.1   *The uptake of the Resolutions: some general patterns*   144
7.2   *Clergy and lay attitudes to the opt-out provisions*   147
7.3   *Unresolved issues*   157
    a)   *Interpreting the legislation*   157
    b)   *Voting on the Resolutions*   158
    c)   *Unforeseen circumstances*   160
    d)   *Petitioning for extended episcopal oversight*   162
    Conclusion   167

Part III: Looking to the Future
Chapter 8: Coexistence and the future   171
8.1   *The 'reception' of women's priestly ordination*   172
8.2   *The short-term future*   178
8.3   *Four responses to 'anomaly'*   181
    Conclusion   185

Chapter 9: Women bishops, the Act of Synod and the future   186
9.1   *Women in the episcopate*   187
9.2   *The Act of Synod, a third province and the limits of diversity*   195
    Conclusion   201

Summary and conclusion   204

Appendices   213
Appendix I   *Questionnaire for clergy*   215
Appendix II   *Questionnaire for congregations*   227
Appendix III   *The 14 deanery case study congregations*   235

Bibliography   237
Index   246

List of tables and figures

Table 1i	The three main diocesan case studies	9
Table 1ii	The three deanery case studies	10
Table 1iii	Summary of diocesan/deanery case studies	10
Table 1iv	Summary of main case study congregations	11
Table 2i	Percentage of deanery synod clergy and laity voting in favour of the Draft Women Priests Legislation, 1990, by diocese	41
Table 2ii	Levels of agreement with the 1992 decision to ordain women as priests in the main case studies	42
Table 2iii	Percentage support for the 1992 decision to ordain women as priests: clergy report their views of 1992 and 2001/2	43
Table 2iv	Change in attitude to the 1992 decision to ordain women as priests amongst clergy who 'strongly disagreed' and 'disagreed' in 1992	43
Table 2v	Percentage support amongst 22 case study congregations for the Church of England's decision in 1992 to allow women to become priests	45
Table 2vi	My attitude to the ordination of women was/would be influential in my current choice of church/any choice of church I make in the future (% by congregation)	46
Figure 2vii	Combined percentage of clergy 'strongly agreeing' and 'agreeing' with women's ordination as priests, 2001 (by case study diocese)	47
Table 2viii	Percentage 'strongly agreeing' and 'agreeing' (combined) with women's ordination as priests across the 22 congregations (by gender)	47
Table 2ix	Percentage of clergy and lay questionnaire respondents 'agreeing' or 'strongly agreeing' with the decision to ordain women as priests (by age group)	48
Table 2x	Attitudes to the 1992 decision to allow the ordination of women as priests, amongst successive cohorts of those ordained deacon/commissioned deaconess (combined figure for six case studies)	50
Table 2xi	Percentage of clergy 'strongly agreeing' or 'agreeing' with the Church of England's decision to ordain women to the priesthood, by Church tradition (2001)	52

Table 2xii   Current attitudes to women's priesting amongst congregations, by Church tradition (ranked according to levels of agreement/strong agreement)   52

Table 2xiii   Support for women as priests amongst male clergy who have worked in a mixed male/female clergy team, and those who have not (% 'strongly agreeing' or 'agreeing', combined)   54

Table 2xiv   Percentage of churchgoers surveyed who felt 'very' or 'quite' comfortable with different aspects of women's ministry, comparing the views of those who have/have not experienced each aspect   54

Table 3i   Ten common reasons for supporting or opposing the Church of England's decision to ordain women as priests (% support for these statements amongst lay respondents grouped according to their level of agreement with women priests)   59

Table 4i   Responses to some commonly suggested consequences of the decision to ordain women as priests, amongst current diocesan clergy   85

Table 4ii   Responses to some commonly suggested consequences of the decision to ordain women as priests, amongst respondents from the 22 case study congregations   86

Table 5i   Percentage of Church of England clergy who are women, 2002 (by diocese)   109

Table 5ii   Percentages of stipendiary and non-stipendiary clergy who are women, 2002 (by diocese)   110

Table 5iii   Has your gender, or your views on women's priesting, ever been a positive or negative factor in your obtaining a suitable position in ordained ministry? (% 'yes' amongst clergy respondents, by diocese and gender)   112

Table 5iv   Has your gender, or your views on women's priesting, ever been a positive or negative factor in your obtaining a suitable position in ordained ministry? (% 'yes' amongst clergy respondents, by level of agreement with 1992 decision)   112

Table 6i   Have you a) ever, b) in the last six months, been ignored or treated rudely: because they did not believe women should be priests? (women); because you held differing positions on the ordination of women as priests? (men) (% 'yes' amongst current clergy, by gender)   127

Table 6ii   In the great majority of cases, I enjoy good working relationships with a) senior clergy, b) fellow clergy, c) lay people who differ from me on the question of the ordination of women (% 'strongly agree' and 'agree' combined for each diocese, by gender)   128

Table 6iii   Have you ever known a) a fellow member of the clergy, b) a lay person, take the following approaches to communion because/despite the fact that they do not accept a) your priesthood as a woman (women), b) your views on the ordination of women as priests (men)? (% 'yes' for each diocese, by gender)   129

Table 7i   Percentage of parishes passing Resolutions A and B, and petitioning for extended episcopal oversight (EEO) by diocese, 1999   145

Table 7ii   Percentage support for Resolutions A and B, and the petition for extended episcopal oversight, amongst respondents from the 22 case study congregations   148

Table 7iii   Percentage support for Resolutions A and B, and the petition for extended episcopal oversight, amongst lay questionnaire respondents (total sample, by Church tradition, % 'strongly agree'/'agree')   149

Figure 7iv.a How far do you agree that the safeguards offered by the 1992 Priests
(Ordination of Women) Measure were an acceptable consequence of
the decision to ordain women as priests?   151

Figure 7iv.b How far do you agree that the safeguards offered by the 1993
Episcopal Ministry Act of Synod were an acceptable consequence
of the decision to ordain women as priests?   151

Figure 7v Clergy views of discrimination in the 1993 Measure and the Act of Synod
(% 'strongly agree'/'agree')   152

Table 7vi Clergy attitudes to the assertion that there were a) good pastoral grounds,
b) good theological grounds for having provisions in the Measure and
the Act for those who cannot accept the ordination of women as priests
(% 'strongly agree'/'agree')   154

Table 7vii Clergy attitudes to the statement that 'overall, on balance, the provisions are
working well' (% 'strongly agree'/'agree')   155

Table 7viii Clergy attitudes to the statements that the provisions are a) occasionally,
b) regularly being abused to extend the power of one constituency
over another (% 'strongly agree'/'agree')   156

Table 8i Clergy's levels of agreement with nine statements on the theological idea
of 'reception' (overall figure for clergy samples)   174

Table 8ii Clergy attitudes to the use of the concept of 'reception' in the
ordination of women debate, comparing support for the terminology
amongst those of differing views on women's ordination as priests
(amongst total clergy sample)   176

Figure 8iii Alan Aldridge's typology of responses to 'anomaly'   183

Figure 9i Clergy 'strongly agreeing' or 'agreeing' (combined) with women as priests
(1992 and 2001) and women as bishops (2001)   188

Figure 9ii Percentage of laity 'strongly agreeing' or 'agreeing' (combined) with the
Church of England's decision to ordain women as priests and with the idea
of the Church of England ordaining women as bishops   190

Acknowledgements

Many, many people deserve to be thanked for the part they played in helping this report to be written. At the Lincoln Theological Institute, particular thanks go to Martyn Percy on his invaluable guidance when, in the early stages of the project, I was beginning to research this topic from a 'standing start', and to Helen Orchard for her good advice on conducting case study research. Other colleagues Ralph Norman and Caroline Dicker were always full of relevant observations and searching questions. I am also grateful to Rosemarie Kossov, Steve Whitelam, Louise Dyson and Sarah Roberts for their work entering the questionnaire responses onto the database.

Some of the ideas contained in this report received their first outing as papers for conferences, seminars and workshops, and particular thanks are due to the participants in these for their constructive criticisms – particularly at the British-Dutch Church Historians' Colloquium on the 'Pastor Bonus' (Utrecht, 2002); staff and students at Ripon College, Cuddesdon; the Religions and Theology Departmental Seminar in the University of Manchester; delegates to a series of consultations at St George's, Windsor and participants in the CIHEC International Conference in Exeter (2003). Thanks also go to the bishops and diocesan secretaries who provided useful information on their dioceses at the beginning of the project.

Several friends deserve particular thanks for their practical help in reading/testing draft questionnaires and chapters; particularly Janet and Nic Tall, Andrew Knight, Simon Watkins and Peter Webster. Major thanks go to family and friends (too many to mention individually!) who offered their hospitality as I travelled around the country doing the research. I am also grateful to those individuals who agreed to serve on the panel of reference for the project – often despite very heavy workloads of their own. Particular thanks also go to Kathryn Pritchard, Linda Foster, Katherine Davey and others at Church House Publishing for their diligent work on the finished draft, to those who read and commented on the manuscript and to Andrew Mikolajski for his proof-reading. Three final thank-yous go to people without whom this report could not have been written: first, to David Lloyd (and latterly to the Lincoln Theological Institute Trustees and the University of Manchester) for their extremely generous financial support in funding the post. Second, to Alison, for her love, encouragement and reading of drafts, and for agreeing to take on a future husband with an unfinished research project in tow. Finally, to the clergy and congregations featured in this report. The welcome and help I received from them in the course of the research was phenomenal, and I have met some inspiring people along the way. I hope this report does justice to what they shared with me.

Executive summary

1994 saw the very first ordinations of women to the priesthood in the Church of England, amidst considerable public interest and after a heated debate within the Church. The tenth anniversary of these occasions offers a good opportunity to consider the experience of this first decade.

How far had women's priestly ministry been accepted by fellow clergy and congregations? How was the initial impact of women's priesting gauged? What practical challenges had arisen from the 1992–94 settlement and how were these addressed? Looking to the future, how much support existed for the ordination of women as bishops?

Written from the perspective of contemporary history and drawing on extensive original social research, this report maps some of the key contours of the Church of England's experience over the first ten years of women in priestly ministry. Findings are based on:

- Case studies of three Church of England dioceses and three deaneries
- Nine main case study congregations and thirteen supplementary congregational studies
- 933 questionnaire responses from clergy and churchgoers
- 147 in-depth interviews (22 with bishops, 60 with clergy and 65 with lay people)

The main findings are:

1. 81% of clergy surveyed supported the 1992 decision to ordain women as priests, with even higher levels of support in many case study congregations. A significant number of respondents had never been able to understand why women were not priests, but there are also strong indications that support for women's priesting has increased over the past decade.

2. A majority of participants in the study made a positive assessment of the impact of women's inclusion in the priesthood over the first ten years. Whilst some regret was expressed over the division caused by the debate, the most common focus was on the additional gifts and insights that women have brought through their priestly ministry.

3. Although very widely accepted as priests, there was widespread expectation amongst clergy and congregations that women's priestly ministry would look different to men's priestly ministry. However, a majority of participants in the study were also reluctant to generalize too far about the respective qualities and attributes of men and women.

4. Debating the ordination of women is now a less pressing issue for most respondents than attempting to work through the theological and practical challenges of the 1992–94 settlement – particularly for clergy.

5. Key areas of 'unfinished business' identified by clergy were: concern over fair and equal access to clerical appointments; day-to-day working relationships with clergy of different views on women's priesting and the handling of key deanery and diocesan occasions; the practical implementation of the opt-out provisions for parishes not wishing to receive a woman priest.

6. Only 44% of clergy identified a pastoral justification for allowing parishes to opt out of receiving a woman's priestly ministry and only 21% saw good theological grounds. Whilst the existence of the opt-out provisions was sometimes justified by suggesting that the Church was in the midst of an 'open process of discernment' or 'reception' over women's priesting, clergy respondents voiced considerable ambivalence over the idea of a 'period of reception' and 35% felt the term had 'no useful meaning whatsoever'.

7. Looking to the future, 69% of clergy supported the idea of the Church of England allowing women to become bishops. Similar levels of support were also found amongst lay respondents, though there was often wide variation between the case study congregations.

8. The tension that surrounded the 1992 debate has lessened significantly over the decade. 78% reported 'good working relationships' with fellow clergy who had different views on women's priesting (although this owed as much to the ease with which the different constituencies could remain separate, as to genuine engagement and reconciliation). Whilst the 'coexistence project' of the 1992–94 settlement was widely thought viable, some of its elements were found increasingly anomalous.

9. A simple distinction between 'supporters' and 'opponents' is inadequate for reflecting the variety of perspectives on women's priesting. A four-fold model of response featuring 'exclusion', 'accommodation', 'opportunism' and 'indifference' was found to be a more subtle instrument for exploring responses to issues raised by the 1992–94 settlement.

10. Whilst the first ten years of women's priesting have been a time of great change, continuities in attitude and experience must also be emphasized. Notably, it is argued that women's priesting may have been widely accepted partly because of the ease with which women clergy could be incorporated into quite traditional expectations of the clergy (for example, that the good vicar is compassionate and accessible to their parish).

Preface

'At first sight the question of the admission of women to the Christian priesthood might seem to be merely a matter of common sense, which could be resolved in the same kind of way as their admission to other vocations and professions. But the Church is not simply a human institution: it is of divine appointment.'

Hugh Montefiore, *The Theology of Priesthood*, 1978

The debate surrounding the ordination of women to the priesthood in the Church of England is hardly new. It progressed through several decades of the twentieth century, and the debate looks certain to continue well into the twenty-first. In this important and timely study, Dr Ian Jones, Research Associate at the Lincoln Theological Institute (University of Manchester) examines the most recent decade. For some, this has been a turbulent and troublesome chapter in the life of the Church. For others, it has marked a new beginning, flecked with hope and promise. Still for others, the changes have raised new questions, relating to authority and order, as well as the changing nature and identity of the church. Few individuals or congregations have been left untouched by change.

Crucially, this *Report* does not seek to take sides in the debate. Whilst it discusses policies or guidelines for the Church, the origin of the report lies in empirical research. It does not commence from a position of advocacy that reflects a particular slant or interest in the debate. From the very beginning, Ian Jones's research was concerned with the grounded reality of the Church of England, as it has sought to adjust to the advent of women priests within the last decade. The research is balanced, fair, grounded in ethnographic methodologies, sifted through carefully constructed interviews (at all levels: laity, clergy, bishops; parish and diocesan perspectives; 'for' and 'against'; etc), and rooted in a wide range of surveys. The *Report* does not seek to ask if the decision to ordain women was right or wrong. It does not seek to debate the nature of 'divine appointment', or to make assumptions about 'common sense'. Rather, it is concerned with how dioceses and congregations have come to terms with the events of the last decade that were set in motion in November 1992. The *Report* is concerned with how churches have received the priestly ministry of women, and how they now understand their theology, mission and ecclesiology in the light of the last decade.

Research Reports from the Lincoln Theological Institute are committed to a deep engagement with the 'concrete church'. Whilst not in any way wishing to devalue other types of ecclesiology, these *Reports* are grounded in empirical research, and are undertaken by fully funded postdoctoral fellows who have relevant expertise in research methods. In examining the Church and its ministry 'as it really is', each *Report* seeks to excavate hidden but vital data, which in turn reveals something of the actual life and shape of congregations and their dioceses, and of professional ministry and its reception in the contemporary world.

It is our hope that readers will carefully weigh the findings of this *Report*, and begin to reflect afresh on how churches address and cope with change. Clearly, the Church has much to learn from itself as it seeks to understand how it is able to negotiate its way through complex and contested arenas of order and doctrine. By researching the common praxis of the Church in any particular situation, especially one that generates such voluminous deliberation, it should be possible to glean some fresh wisdom that provides a new perspective on the nature of the Church. Research, in other words, can begin to uncover new vistas that illuminate the capaciousness of the Church, even in the midst of one of its most disputed debates.

Martyn Percy and Helen Orchard, series editors

Dr Martyn Percy is Director, and Dr Helen Orchard is an Honorary Research Associate, of Lincoln Theological Institute for the Study of Religion and Society
Department of Religions and Theology
University of Manchester
Oxford Road
Manchester
M13 9PL

Introduction

The Revd Mary Green[1] already had eight years' experience of diaconal ministry when in November 1992 the Church's General Synod met to decide whether to accept the ordination of women to the priesthood. Initially she had been unsure whether God really called women to priesthood, but had quite unexpectedly found a conviction growing within her that this was indeed what God had in mind, and the counsel of others only seemed to confirm this. Indeed, in the months preceding the vote she found herself, quite to her surprise, being invited to speak at meetings and local debates in favour of the measure. Gathered around the television with friends on the afternoon of 11 November 1992, she watched expectantly as the result came through: a majority in favour. Even after their immediate rejoicing, the messages of congratulation did not seem to stop: messages from friends and well-wishers at church on her answerphone, a bottle of champagne left mysteriously on her doorstep, the delight of non-Christian staff in the local school with which she had connections.

At the same time, in a parish two dioceses away, Fr Paul Hopkins was listening to the vote on the edge of his seat. He remembered the ordination of women first being discussed at theological college back in the 1970s, but at the time it had seemed little more than 'a cloud, no bigger than a man's hand', and he doubted anything would come of it in his lifetime. As the diocesan synod vote swung narrowly in favour of women's priesting, Fr Hopkins and like-minded colleagues became increasingly worried, but clung to a gut feeling that in the end, General Synod would not allow the draft Ordination of Women Measure to proceed. The result in favour came as a heavy blow, leaving them facing the coming weeks with a sense of dazed unreality. One of the leading local opponents of the Measure, who was supposed to be visiting Fr Hopkins' church the following Sunday, phoned up to give his excuses, saying he felt too devastated to preach. In the next door parish, where the priest took the same view, all music for the service was cancelled as a mark of mourning over the Church's decision. What, wondered Fr Hopkins, was now going to happen to the Church of England, to its prospects for unity with Rome, and to those who still believed in a male-only priesthood?

In a small town at the other end of the country, the news of the Church of England's vote to ordain women was brought to several very different homes by the television news that evening. Dave and Kate Campbell, members of an independent charismatic fellowship, watched the broadcast with detached concern; their interpretation of several biblical passages led them to doubt whether positions of church leadership were indeed open to women. On the other side of town, Janice Winter registered the news with passing interest, thinking that the Church had at last done something good for women. However, she thought little more of it – church, after all, was not something she had much time for these days. Just a few streets away Margaret Jenkins, a regular attender at the local Anglican church, heard the news with disappointment; ordaining women seemed to threaten the stability of family life by taking women away from their responsibilities to home and children. At least with their male vicar, she reasoned, they would probably not have to face a woman priest in their own parish, in the foreseeable future. By contrast, fellow church member Martin Ford greeted the result with some pleasure. It had for some years seemed odd to him that women were not allowed to become priests, and since women had clearly proved their worth as deacons, why should they not be allowed to exercise their gifts as vicars and rectors too?

---

[1] All names have been changed in this introductory section, to preserve the identities of the speakers.

When I met and interviewed all these speakers between late 2000 and early 2002, almost a decade had elapsed since the General Synod vote to ordain women as priests. Ten years on, how had their views changed and what had their experiences of women's priestly ministry been? The Revd Mary Green was just a few weeks away from retirement, having served her last incumbency in a small working class parish in her home city. She looked back with thanks on the past decade, grateful for the ministry she had been able to exercise and the support she had received from her parishioners. Indeed, the priestly ministry of women seemed so far accepted in her parish that she could scarcely recall any occasion when it had been challenged. Ironically, the few negative comments she had received came from fellow clergy who had objected to the result of the 1992 vote, although by and large they had been able to foster good working relationships across the divide. As one of the senior women clergy in the diocese, however, she had listened to increased expressions of concern from female colleagues, who were beginning to feel frustrated at difficulties surrounding the non-appointment of women to particular parishes and the degree to which, ten years on, female clergy were still being asked not to celebrate their priesthood too loudly lest it upset those who objected.

For his part, Fr Paul Hopkins retained grave doubts about women's priesthood, but after briefly considering converting to Rome he became convinced of the rightness of staying within the Church of England and learning to work with the current situation. His parish had opted out of women's priestly ministry under the terms of the 1992 Priests (Ordination of Women) Measure and he himself had derived some support from belonging to a local 'alternative chapter' for clergy unable to accept women's priesting. He was glad that the Church had avoided worse division over the matter and felt reasonably content to work under the current arrangements (even agreeing to teach a recently ordained female colleague about the celebration of the Eucharist in the Anglo-Catholic tradition). However, he looked with concern at the growing support for women as bishops, feeling that if this came, he might no longer be able to remain in the Church of England without the creation of a third province solely for those who believed in a male-only priesthood and episcopate.

Three years ago, Dave and Kate Campbell found themselves tiring of the long journey to their independent charismatic fellowship and began to worship at the local Anglican parish church, which suited their evangelical tradition. On entering for the first time, they found themselves surprised to see an ordained woman leading the service, at the time a comparative newcomer to the parish. However, through prayer and Bible study they resolved their initial reservations about women in church leadership and when I met Dave early in 2002 he expressed his enthusiasm for the gifts their female vicar had brought to the Church and for the quality of her preaching and teaching. Fellow member of the congregation Martin Ford remained satisfied that the Church of England had taken the right step in ordaining women and had seen several aspects of the parish's work grow under their present incumbent. However, he also regretted the loss of several members of the congregation who felt unable to accept her ministry and expressed concern that a church too dominated by women might begin to put off men. Nevertheless, he thought, if women were allowed to become priests the episcopate should certainly be open to women as well.

Margaret Jenkins continued to harbour reservations about women's ordination. Though she remained part of the Church and on good personal terms with her female vicar, she chose to attend only morning or evening prayer and take communion from a male priest at another nearby church – something she somewhat regretted but had become resigned towards.

Janice Winter, on the other hand, was now a regular and enthusiastic member of the Church. A few years before we met, she had been helped through a major personal crisis by the same vicar, and had rediscovered the faith of her childhood. Firmly convinced that women's ordination was right, Janice spoke particularly of her surprise and delight at the way the clerical profession had been enriched with the distinctively feminine qualities that women had brought to it. Inspired by this example, she herself had now begun to take an active part in her church's ministry of prayer and healing.

Aims

This report has begun with the stories of six individuals actively involved in the Church of England, and their stories about women and priesthood a decade on from the historic vote of 1992. Similar stories may already be familiar to readers through their own experience or that of their clergy or fellow church members. The debate on the ordination of women as deacons and priests that took place in the Church of England from the late 1960s to the early 1990s has been well chronicled,[2] but less has been written about what happened after to the vote. For many Anglicans, the first ten years of women's priesthood remains in the realm of individual experience or anecdote, with little overall sense of how women's ministry is being received. However, the passing of a decade since the first ordinations of women to the priesthood provides an opportune moment to stop and assess the Church of England's experience thus far. This report seeks to offer an independent, research-based perspective on those first ten years, and in particular on what might have emerged as the key trends and issues by the beginning of the twenty-first century. In particular, it asks:

- How far have women been accepted as priests in the Church of England?

- What are the key patterns of support and opposition amongst clergy and laity?

- How have respondents assessed the impact of women's priesting?

- What have been the most pressing unresolved issues arising out of the 1992–94 settlement and how have these been tackled?

- How is the Church of England's current position on women's ordination currently understood, both in terms of the practical viability of the current settlement and in terms of the suggestion that we are now in the midst of a 'period of open discernment' or 'reception' over women's priesting?

- How did respondents view the future – in particular the growing calls for women's inclusion in the episcopate?

In answering these questions, the report draws on a series of case studies across selected English dioceses, using questionnaire surveys to clergy and congregations, and a major programme of in-depth interviews. The report does not in any sense aim to answer the question 'should women be priests?', but does seek to offer an honest assessment of the Church of England's experience ten years on.

As I began to research this report, the question I was most often asked was how far women had been accepted in their ministries as priests. In the Spring of 1994 a majority of the active members of the Church of England stood in favour of ordaining women as priests, but the reality of women's priestly ministry was as yet unknown. There have been several important studies detailing the experiences of this first generation of female priests

---

[2] For the history of the ordination of women debate, see: Sean Gill, *Women and the Church of England, from the Eighteenth Century to the Present* (SPCK, London, 1994); Margaret Webster, *A New Strength, A New Song; The Journey to Women's Priesthood* (Mowbray, London, 1994).

themselves,[3] but much less is known about the way their ministry has been received more widely in the Church (Hilary Wakeman's *Women Priests; The First Years* being an honourable exception[4]), about the proportions of clergy and laity across the Church of England at large who support or oppose women's ordination as priests or about the organizational implications of the decision.[5] This report therefore presents some data to begin to address questions of how women's priestly ministry has been received, what levels of support for women's priesting may exist within the Church of England, whether the extent of support has changed over the past decade and what impact Anglicans seemed to think women's priesting was having. This of course gives significant space to the perspectives of women in priesthood themselves, but sets these alongside the responses of lay Anglicans and fellow (male) clergy. At the conclusion of her important survey of the first generation of women to be priested, Helen Thorne asks how her results would have been different had the views of male clergy and lay churchgoers been included.[6] This report takes up that challenge, as it aims to map a much broader spectrum of Anglican experience.

The story told thus far has tended to focus on the emergence of a division between supporters of the admission of women to the priesthood, and those who oppose it. However, since the first ordinations of 1994, these differences of opinion on the 1992 decision have sometimes been less important in day to day terms than the business of seeking a *modus vivendi* within a church that is still to some extent divided on the question: the Church of England now permits the ordination of women as priests (but not bishops), but also officially seeks to enable a variety of views to coexist within it – even to the extent of providing certain opt-out provisions for parishes that could not embrace the decision. This report seeks to assess how that settlement has been worked out in practice. In 1992, Church and national press alike prophesied that the question of women in priesthood could split the Church. But how far has this division manifested itself in reality? How have clergy and congregations of differing opinions on women's priesting been able to coexist, and what have been the problems and challenges in accomplishing this?

A particular set of issues relates to the interpretation and implementation of the legislative settlement established in 1992/3. For those unfamiliar with the current framework, a brief explanation is in order: the 1992 Priests (Ordination of Women) Measure made provision for women to be ordained as priests, but with certain conditions attached to the exercise of their ministry. First, the Measure expressly excluded women from becoming bishops, mainly because it was not yet felt that sufficient consensus existed to take this step. Most campaigners for women's priesthood reluctantly accepted this condition as the necessary price for securing a place for women in the priesthood in the short-term. Second, the

---

[3] For academic studies, see particularly: Helen Thorne, *Journey to Priesthood; An In-depth Study of the First Women Priests in the Church of England* (University of Bristol, Bristol, 2000); Leslie J. Francis and Mandy Robbins, *The Long Diaconate, 1987–1994; Women Deacons and the Delayed Journey to Priesthood* (Gracewing, Leominster, 1999). Two good collections of personal reflection by ordained women on the first decade of women's priesting are: Christina Rees (ed.), *Voices of this Calling: Experiences of the First Generation of Women Priests* (Canterbury Press, Norwich, 2002); Andrew and Liz Barr, *Jobs for the Boys? Women who Became Priests* (Hodder and Stoughton, London, 2001).
[4] See particularly Wakeman's own article in this collection: Hilary Wakeman, 'What Difference is Women's Priesthood Making in the Pews?' in Hilary Wakeman (ed.), *Women Priests; The First Years* (Darton, Longman and Todd, London, 1996), pp. 1–26.
[5] Although Mark Chaves' study of women's ordination in some of the major denominations in the USA has taken denominational policy and organization as its starting-point (Mark Chaves, *Ordaining Women: Culture and Conflict in Religious Organisations* (Harvard University Press, Cambridge (Massachusetts), 1997), p. 1).
[6] Thorne, *Journey to Priesthood*, pp. 151–2.

Measure contained provisions enabling any parish that disagreed with women's priesting[7] to bar an ordained woman priest from celebrating communion/pronouncing absolution in the parish (Resolution A, in the Measure) or working as an incumbent in that parish (Resolution B).[8] A financial package of assistance was offered to those who felt forced to quit their full-time role in the Church of England over the issue.[9] Furthermore the Measure enabled diocesan bishops already in post who objected to women's priesting to declare that women would not be ordained or licensed in their diocese.[10] There were widespread fears that the Church of England might be split into dioceses that accepted women as priests, and 'no-go' dioceses that did not. But already by 1993, this last clause had been superseded by the Episcopal Ministry Act of Synod. Drawn up by the Bishops' Meeting with the intention of preventing the creation of 'no-go' dioceses and achieving 'the maximum degree of communion between those of differing views',[11] it enabled parishes to seek 'extended episcopal oversight' if they objected to their bishop's decision to ordain women as priests (popularly known as 'Resolution C'). This oversight was to be provided first on a diocesan or regional basis, but failing that through a newly-created system of Provincial Episcopal Visitors (dubbed 'flying bishops' by the press).

For the Act of Synod's architects, these arrangements were the direct product of over twenty years' reflection at Anglican Communion level concerning how to hold differing views on women's priesting together in the same Church.[12] For many grass roots Anglicans, who knew little of official Church reports, the Act seemed a puzzling partial retreat from what had been decided in 1992. Some campaigners for women's priesting (who had only accepted the opt-out clauses in the original measure with reluctance) expressed anger at the extra provisions in the Act, claiming that it encouraged the creation of parallel jurisdictions for 'supporters' and 'opponents' and cultivated the belief that bishops could somehow be 'tainted' by ordaining women.[13] On the other hand, many campaigners for an all-male priestly tradition insisted that the Act was the minimum possible concession that would allow them to remain within the Church of England.

Across the whole spectrum of views, some expressed concern that the terms of the Measure and the Act reduced the question of women's priesting to one of private opinion rather than theological consensus. On the other hand, some claimed that the settlement was right to allow such a large degree of diversity of opinion, in order to keep the Church together. In the event, the Act of Synod was passed by a very large majority in General Synod in November 1993.

---

[7] If the incumbent and a majority of the PCC were in agreement.

[8] *Priests (Ordination of Women) Measure 1993 (No. 2)* (HMSO, Crown Copyright [web version downloaded 27 June 2002]).

[9] *Ordination of Women (Financial Provisions) Measure, 1993 (No. 3)* (HSMO, Crown Copyright [web version downloaded 20 November 2003]).

[10] *Priests (Ordination of Women) Measure 1993*, part 2.

[11] House of Bishops, 'Statement by the House following its Meeting in Manchester, 11–14 January 1993', p. 7.

[12] Mary Tanner traces the idea of communion in diversity over women's priesting to the Diocese of Hong Kong's decision to refer their wish to ordain women as priests to the 1968 Lambeth Conference, rather than choosing to ordain women unilaterally. Meeting in Limuru in 1970, the Anglican Consultative Council (ACC) advised the bishop to proceed should his diocese vote yes, with the ACC itself seeking to ensure continued communion between themselves and other dioceses that did not ordain women (Mary Tanner, 'The Episcopal Ministry Act of Synod in Context' in Paul Avis (ed.), *Seeking the Truth of Change in the Church: Reception, Communion and the Ordination of Women* (T & T Clark, London, 2004), pp. 58–74 (pp. 59–60).).

[13] For the main arguments against the Act, see: Monica Furlong (ed.), *Act of Synod: Act of Folly?* (SCM Press, London, 1998).

The Measure, the Act and its official supporting documentation appear to envisage the 1992-94 settlement as long-term arrangements: a time limit on the opt-out provisions had specifically been removed from an earlier draft of the 1992 Priests (Ordination of Women) Measure,[14] so in legal terms the settlement was set to continue *ad infinitum*. In theological terms, too, the settlement was framed in long-range terms: the House of Bishops' report 'Bonds of Peace', issued in June 1993, states that 'discernment of the matter is now to be seen within a much broader and longer process of discernment within the whole Church under the Spirit's guidance'.[15] Clearly a reception of women's priesthood by the entire Christian Church was not going to come quickly, and in this sense the writers of the documents wished to discourage the idea that this was a stopgap solution. That said, the Measure and the Act in other respects appear to represent a provisional settlement for the Church of England – in fact if not in theory. For some observers, talk of an 'open process of discernment' in itself implied that the 1992–94 settlement was an interim measure only insofar as that process lasted. For others, the existence of the 'opt-out' provisions seemed to imply that women's priesting was still regarded as an optional extra rather than a full part of Church order. For others, the 1992–94 settlement had established a trial period to help discern whether women's ordination as priests would be accepted by the whole Church. For many, permitting the ordination of women as priests but not as bishops had left important business unfinished. One element of the settlement – the Ordination of Women (Financial Provisions) Measure – even came with a time limit attached: any full-time stipendiary priest or church worker wishing to leave the Church of England over women's priesting, and claim financial assistance as a result, had to do so by early 2004.[16] As this deadline approached, some campaigners began to suggest that perhaps the whole settlement should also be up for renegotiation. But how much appetite was there for this?

Additionally, some felt that important questions on the nature of priesthood and the relationship between men and women remained to be debated. Alongside the more theological/theoretical aspects of those questions, dioceses were faced with more practical challenges, at parish, deanery and diocesan level: how would the different sides in the debate be held together, and the integrity of their views respected as far as possible? What did communion and catholicity mean in a divided church? Would the 1992–94 settlement hold together, or would it simply lead to further division over the following decade? How were some of the opt-out provisions and guidelines on implementing the settlement to be interpreted? How would questions of appointments and preferment be tackled? Now that women could be ordained as priests, would they have the same opportunities to progress as their male counterparts, or would they still be disadvantaged when it came to more senior posts? Would objectors to women's priesting become marginalized now that they were clearly in the minority of clergy and parishes? What would be the impact on their participation in diocesan life? This report seeks to outline and investigate some of these key unresolved issues facing the Church in connection with the women priests settlement, at the turn of the millennium. In so doing, it will be found that the usual division of Anglicans into those 'for' the ordination of women and those 'against' is often too crude a tool for understanding the differences of approach to the practical outworking of the settlement. Not only did the Church of England in the late 1990s exhibit a multiplicity of shades of opinion

---

[14] The arguments for and against a twenty-year rule are given in detail in: General Synod November Group of Sessions 1989, *Report of Proceedings No. 20, Vol. 3* (General Synod, London, 1989).

[15] GS 1074 'Bonds of Peace: Arrangements for Pastoral Care following the Ordination of Women to the Priesthood in the Church of England' in *Ordination of Women to the Priesthood: Pastoral Arrangements – A Report by the House of Bishops* (Church House, London, 1993), p. 5. See also: General Synod GS Misc 418, *Being in Communion* (Church House, London, 1993).

[16] *Ordination of Women (Financial Provisions) Measure* (HMSO, Crown Copyright) section 2 [web version downloaded 4 December 2003].

over women's priesting itself, but on the question of how to proceed in the context of a divided church, conflicting approaches to these 'unresolved issues' often created a range of alternative responses that cut across the traditional categories of 'supporters' and 'opponents'.

Methods

In short, the report seeks to offer a map for reading and understanding some of the main themes and issues in the Church of England's experience of ordaining women over the first ten years. Inevitably there are parameters: a map cannot detail every aspect of the landscape that it seeks to describe, but then nor does it mean to; instead a good map displays the sorts of features required for particular modes of navigation. Rather than functioning as an exhaustive investigation of the theology and culture of the Church of England a decade on from the vote to ordain women as priests, this particular map will seek to map some important contours of opinion on women's priesting, and explore some of the most pressing pieces of 'unfinished business' to be identified by clergy and congregations participating in the study at the beginning of the twenty-first century. To this end, the report places particular emphasis on attitudes towards what I have called for shorthand 'the 1992–94 settlement'. The idea of an 'ordination of women settlement' appears frequently in the course of this report, and so it is worth explaining the term briefly here. The 'settlement' here refers specifically to the 1993 Priests (Ordination of Women) Measure, the accompanying Ordination of Women (Financial Provisions) Measure and the 1993 Episcopal Ministry Act of Synod, which together formed the legislative framework for allowing the ordination of women to the priesthood and providing certain 'opt-out provisions' to those who could not accept the move. But the term also refers in a more general sense to the wider project of coexistence that this legislation was designed to embody; the conviction that different views on women's priesting could be found space within the same church, and that the existence of this division of opinion should be in some sense formally recognized as a feature of the post-1992 ecclesiastical landscape. Therefore in addition to being useful shorthand, the term also diverts attention from any suggestion that the 'real problem' is women priests, or the Act of Synod (depending on one's point of view) and recognizes that the changes introduced between 1992 and 1994 come as a package that (however welcome or unwelcome) was formally agreed as part of the same process. Parallels could be drawn here with the so-called 'Elizabethan Settlement' of 1559, which bequeathed the Crown the title of 'supreme governor' of the Church of England, re-established the Edwardine Prayer Book and settled upon Thirty-nine Articles of Religion.[17] Here, a variety of measures were incorporated within a single 'settlement' aimed at resolving a particular religious debate, although it also raised as many questions as it settled, and those affected by it then had to seek to work out how to inhabit the new situation in practice – not unlike with the '1992–94 settlement'. Of course, not every aspect of this settlement can be considered in the space available here; in particular, there is much more to be said about the cultural consequences of the present arrangements. As a result, this report focuses primarily on the general reception of women's priesting by clergy and laity, and on the key pieces of 'unfinished business' arising from settlement, as outlined above. It is hoped that further exploration of the culture of the Church of England since 1992 will be considered further in a subsequent publication. Meanwhile, if the current

---

[17] The comparison with the Elizabethan Settlement is intended to illustrate how the term 'settlement' is used in the context of this report. The idea of the 1992 vote as marking 'a new Elizabethan Settlement' was first raised in: Stephen Trott, *A New Elizabethan Settlement: Priests (Ordination of Women) Measure* (Cost of Conscience, London, 1993) but the use of the term here is not intended to reflect that author's diagnosis of events. It is not intended, necessarily, to imply that 1992 took the Church of England in a similarly 'protestantizing' direction!

report seeks to offer a 'map' of these issues ten years on from the first ordinations of women as priests, it is important to understand what kind of map it seeks to be.

This particular map is drawn up broadly from the perspective of contemporary history and social research. It does not seek to answer the question of whether women should or should not be priests and bishops. Nor, primarily, is the report a systematic study of the academic theological arguments put forward on different sides of the debate. Instead, it deals in the attitudes, experiences and reflections of Anglican clergy and churchgoers in an attempt to explore the Church of England's lived experience over the past decade. To this end, the research derives substantially from case study research in six contrasting deanery and diocesan case studies across the Church of England, making particular use of questionnaire surveys and oral testimony.

There is a degree of suspicion in some quarters of the Church as to whether social research methods such as these can have anything useful to say on the questions of women and priesthood. Some may even object that sociology is an inherently secular discipline (thus out of place in Church matters), and that the only valid map with which to read the terrain is a theological one.[18] Let me attempt to allay those concerns: although the project draws on large amounts of social survey material, and although I doubt whether theology and sociology can be as easily separated from each other as some claim, I do not believe that theological questions can or should be settled solely by *vox pop*. If one hundred per cent of the Church of England believed that women should be priests, this would not necessarily make it God's will (although a growth in consensus and conviction may often be one sign of the guidance of the Holy Spirit). Nevertheless, theologians always begin their work of trying to understand revelation, scripture and tradition from a particular point in history, and the kinds of questions they ask are inescapably shaped by the context in which they work. Therefore as well as trying to understand the 'blueprint', theological enquiry must also take account of its starting point in the concrete situation of the present.[19] If so, our understanding of the issues surrounding women and priesthood may be enriched by a greater appreciation of the current context. This report focuses on the Church of England's experience *as it is*, rather than on trying to create a theological blueprint (a task that has been given extensive attention elsewhere[20]). Therefore to expect this report to offer new theological insights into the nature of gender or priesthood is to misunderstand its aim. That said, if the reader is seeking fuller exploration of some of the theologies both implicit and explicit in the Church of England's experience of women's priesting, it is hoped that more space will be given to this in a future publication.

The data sample

As explained above, the raw material for this report was derived primarily from a series of six contrasting case studies of Anglican dioceses and deaneries conducted between early 2001 and the summer of 2002. In each of these, two questionnaire surveys were distributed, one to clergy (henceforth the 'Questionnaire for Clergy') and one to a selection of regular churchgoers (the 'Questionnaire for Congregations') in selected case study congregations. These were chosen according to strict criteria, including that some were to have experienced women's priesting ministry, some were to have one or more of the resolutions in place, and some were to fall into neither category. The questionnaire surveys were then followed up by a series of in-depth interviews with selected questionnaire respondents who

---

[18] Having said that, the use of social survey data is not confined to any one particular view or campaigning group on women's priesting.

[19] The idea of 'blueprint' theology and ecclesiology derives from: Nicholas M. Healy, *Church, World and the Christian Life* (Cambridge University Press, Cambridge, 2000).

[20] See bibliography for more details.

had indicated their willingness to be interviewed. Interviews were also conducted with the bishop and archdeacons, and a selection of other senior clergy who had some broader overview of the diocese (this included, where relevant, the diocesan adviser for women's ministry and the leading local representative of clergy with reservations over women's priesting). The structure and rubric of the case study research is outlined in **Tables 1i** (the main three diocesan case studies) **and 1ii** (three smaller deanery case studies). In total, the six case studies and two smaller pilot studies yielded 933 completed questionnaire returns, in addition to which 147 clergy and churchgoers were interviewed (mostly from the case studies, but with additional interviews with other senior Anglican clergy).[21] Given the sensitivity of some of the material, all names of dioceses, parishes and individuals have been anonymized, and some details have been omitted to preserve confidentiality. In order to place the case studies in their broader context, the research also included study of a variety of journals and publications that enabled consideration of views from beyond the case study contexts, and which case study participants themselves may have read or drawn upon. However, as this is case study research, each case should be taken primarily as a unique experience in itself, rather than as merely an example of some wider trend. This is important, because although the case studies have been chosen as far as possible to reflect the diversity present in the Church of England, one cannot automatically assume that the issues and trends discussed here were also replicated across the Church of England as a whole.

Table 1i: The three main diocesan case studies				
Case study	Diocese involved (for more details see Table 1iii)	Research methods	Parishes involved (for more details see Table 1iv)	Research methods
1	Diocese A	In each diocese, questionnaires sent to all diocesan clergy, interviews with selected respondents.	Church 1	In each parish, up to 100[22] questionnaires distributed randomly in church, interviews with selected respondents.
2	Diocese B		Church 2	
3	Diocese C		Church 3	

[21] The 147 interviewees were split as follows: 65 active lay Anglicans, 60 clergy and 22 bishops. Excluding the bishops (at this stage an exclusively male group), 61 women and 64 men were interviewed across the sample of clergy and laity.
[22] 'Up to one hundred' because in some churches, the regular congregation was less than one hundred. It was decided to fix a maximum number of questionnaires for any given congregation in order to keep the responses to a manageable and comparable size.

Table 1ii: The three deanery case studies				
Case study	Deanery involved (for more details see Table 1iii)	Research methods	Parishes involved (for more details see Appendix III)[23]	Research methods
4	Deanery D	In each deanery, questionnaires sent to all clergy, interviews with selected respondents.	Church 10 Church 11 Church 12 Church 13	In each parish, up to thirty questionnaires distributed to a cross section of the church, interviews with selected respondents.
5	Deanery E		Church 15 Church 16 Church 17 Church 18 Church 19	
6	Deanery F		Church 20 Church 21 Church 22 Church 23	

Table 1iii: Summary of diocesan/deanery case studies						
Diocese/ Deanery	Province	Type (urban, rural, etc.)	Diocesan bishop ordains women as priests?	% of clergy in diocese who are women	% parishes passing resolutions	Arrange-ments for opted out parishes
A	X	Urban/rural	Yes	Below average	Above average	Diocesan
B	Y	Rural	Yes	Above average	Below average	Provincial
C	Y	Urban/rural	Yes	Above average	Above average	Regional
D	X	Urban/rural	No	Below average	Above average	Diocesan
E	Y	Urban	No	Below average	Above average	Diocesan
F	Y	Mostly rural	Yes	Above average	Below average	Provincial

Even with this number of questionnaires and interviews to work with, it is inevitable that the report cannot cover every angle of the Church of England's experience of ordaining women. With the high degree of diocesan autonomy and variety of approach within the Church of England it would be impossible to select six case studies that would exhaustively cover the difference of experience. As with all data samples, it runs the risk of emphasizing some perspectives, whilst skimming over others. In **Table 1iii** the balance of the case studies is tipped slightly towards one province of the Church of England rather than the other, and the selection also includes a disproportionately large number of dioceses with an above-average percentage of parishes passing the resolutions. There is a slight over-representation of traditionalist Catholic perspectives, and a slight under-representation of evangelicals. Nevertheless, the selection was made carefully and represents a good diversity of contexts and approaches. It should be noted that whilst the information was correct at the time of the case study, some details will subsequently have changed.[24]

---

[23] There is no 'Church 14'. This is because the parish originally involved was forced to withdraw at very short notice and it was not possible to find a replacement.
[24] For example, the percentage of clergy who are female working in a given diocese.

Coverage of lay opinion was particularly problematic, given the difficulty of obtaining an 'accurate' sample of churchgoers in each diocese. A postal questionnaire was considered, but it was finally decided that a parish-based approach would be the most appropriate, given that the parish church provides the primary context through which most lay Christians will have encountered women in priesthood, or those who oppose women's priesting. The results from only three parishes out of a whole diocese should not be taken as either exhaustive or even representative without severe qualification; however, the parish case studies may be understood as 'borehole' sampling (drilling for a richer mine of information in a confined space, rather than merely scratching the surface of the whole diocese), and again, the parishes were selected for their diversity of experience, as **Table 1iv** suggests. Selections were made in consultation with senior diocesan clergy and the incumbents of the relevant parishes, with the final choice taken by me as researcher.

Table 1iv: Summary of main case study congregations						
Church /Dioc.	**Location**	**Tradition**	**Congregation**	**Clergy**	**Vicar's view**	**Resolutions**
1 (A)	Middle class suburb	Central/ Liberal Catholic	Medium-large, most professional	Mixed m/f clergy team, male vicar	In favour	No
2 (A)	Working class suburb	Evangelical (charism. and conservative)	Small-medium, working class	Male vicar	In favour	No
3 (A)	Village	Prayer Book Catholic	Small-medium, socially mixed	Male vicar	Against	Yes
4 (B)	Middle class suburb	Evangelical (various types)	Large, mainly professional families	Male vicar, trainee female OLM	In favour	No
5 (B)	Group of small villages	Broadly Central	Small churches, mixed congs.	Female rector	In favour	No
6 (B)	Group of small villages	Catholic (various)	Small churches, mixed congs.	Male vicar	Against	Yes
7 (C)	Commuter village	Catholic-Evangelical	Large, mainly professional	All-female clergy team	In favour	No
8 (C)	Council estate	Anglo-Catholic	Small, mainly working class	Male vicar	Against	Yes
9 (C)	Working class area in city	Catholic (various)	Large city church, social mix	All-male clergy team	Uncertain, growing more in favour	No

Again in the interests of clarity, some of the particular problems associated with questionnaire- and interview-based research should be acknowledged. Since the questionnaire survey was entirely a voluntary exercise, rates of return varied markedly between parishes: Church 7 returned 62% of its questionnaires, whilst Church 9 in the same diocese returned just 17% (there was some evidence that churches with either experience of women's ministry or of the resolutions were more likely to produce higher returns). The overall average response rate for the Congregations Questionnaire was 42%, but this was largely due to the success of 'targeting' a cross section of the congregation in the smaller deanery studies (the response rate for the main nine case study congregations averaged much lower at 33%). The Clergy Questionnaire returns were better, however, with an overall average return rate of 46%, representing a reliable sample of those surveyed. The main factor in the non-completion of the questionnaire seemed to be the length of the survey combined with lack of time to fill it in. One irate churchgoer allegedly exhorted his fellow parishioners to throw their questionnaires into the bin (!), but this seemed to be an isolated incident, and in general clergy and congregations seemed happy to participate where they could. The voluntary nature of the questionnaires and interviews inevitably means that the responses disproportionately reflect the views of those who have the strongest opinions, or feel they have most to say, but an effort was made – with the interviews in particular – to ensure that a wide variety of different perspectives and degrees of conviction were included.

Some important caveats

However, whilst the report contains a broad spectrum of Anglican views, there are notable qualifications and omissions, of which the reader should be aware. Firstly, the study has time parameters: several good histories and commentaries on the ordination of women debate already exist, and so this report does not seek to cover this same ground again. The study starts with the well worn territory of the 1992 debate and reactions to it, but it does so with the intention of presenting some alternative voices not so clearly heard in previous 'top-down' accounts of the vote, which prioritize the experience of those involved in the organizations campaigning 'for' or 'against' (important though these perspectives are). The study finishes at the time of writing, although it should be remembered that most of the interview and questionnaire material derives from the period between October 2000 and August 2002, and it is inevitable that some interviewees' opinions will have changed by the time of publication. In this sense, the report should be read as a 'marker' of the state of opinion at the beginning of the twenty-first century, rather than as a guide to opinion after that.

Certain groups and sources of testimony are also deliberately omitted or regrettably under-represented. One significant feature is that the study focuses only on those who are actively involved in the Church of England. On one hand this excludes those who left the church over women's priesting. Their testimony forms an important part of the history of the last ten years, but the need to place manageable parameters on the project, and the fact that their experience has been so different from that of those who stayed, meant that in the end this group was excluded from the current study (although it is hoped to say more about them in the second, larger book). Similarly, an important study remains to be done on attitudes to women's priesting amongst the wider population who do not regularly attend church, but this is left for another researcher and another project. The study also has a heavy bias towards parish life, and as such underplays the role of the many Anglican societies and organizations that have influenced the shape of the first ten years of women's priesting. Groups with a direct interest in the issues do feature prominently (for example, WATCH, Forward in Faith, Reform and GRAS), but the limited time available meant that there was little scope for considering the role of patronage organizations, religious orders, societies representing church parties (for example, the Modern Churchpeople's Union or the Church Society) or other organizations in which the issues were heavily debated (for example, the Prayer Book Society or the Additional Curates' Society). Membership of so-called 'para-church organizations' has become an increasingly important aspect of religious belonging in the later twentieth century, and as such a consideration of the role of these organizations would have been welcome (it is hoped to say more on this in a future publication). But given the constraints on the project, it was felt most important to focus on the place where most active Anglicans came into contact with ordained women or alternative positions: the parish. Whilst the case studies reflect a wide diversity of Anglican parish life, it is particularly regrettable that Black and Asian Anglicans are under-represented in the study, because one only of the case studies (Deanery E) was located in a city with a large degree of ethnic diversity. A further case study that might have begun to redress this imbalance ran into a number of difficulties and did not in the end come to fruition. Despite these omissions and qualifications, however, the body of evidence collected here represents a significant breadth of opinion amongst active Anglican clergy and laity, and is arguably the most comprehensive general survey to date.

A third set of qualifications relates to the picture of the Church of England that is presented here. Because the report is primarily concerned with mapping the degree of acceptance of women's priestly ministry, and with identifying key areas of 'unfinished business', some aspects of the report (particularly Parts II and III) place particular emphasis on what continues to divide. This could easily lead the reader to conclude that the Church of England is in a perpetual state of internal conflict over women's priesting. It is not. The great majority of clergy and congregations have accepted women's priesting even to the degree that many were surprised that it warranted any further research.[25] Moreover, women's priesting was neither the only, nor the most important, issue to exercise the minds of committed churchgoers and their clergy. Attendance, finance, mission and community outreach, fabric maintenance and a whole range of doctrinal and ethical questions meant that no single issue could dominate the life of the Church of England for long, however much some imagined that it might. The report must be read with this in mind. Nevertheless, it is scarcely avoidable that a disproportionate amount of space in this report is allocated to considering issues that still require resolution, and on which Anglicans continue to disagree. This should not be allowed to obscure the (often successful) efforts to build consensus and work together despite differing views, over the first ten years of women's priesting. Thus the report also attempts to highlight areas of agreement and efforts to build a workable *modus vivendi* despite continuing differences of opinion.

A final point surrounds the integrity of the research. It is a sadly inescapable fact that any new research on the ordination of women or related issues is championed in one quarter as a reliable piece of scholarship that 'proves' the point of one particular group, whilst being dismissed in another quarter as 'partisan' and therefore unreliable.[26] Given the history of the debate, I do not expect this report to fare any better. However, I wish to underline in the strongest possible terms the *independent* nature of the research that has been undertaken. The project was not commissioned by any campaigning organization either for or against women's ordination as priests, nor by the Church of England itself, but as a piece of academic research conducted under the auspices of the Lincoln Theological Institute. Sole responsibility for the content of the report lies with the author. Some overall project supervision was provided by the Director of the Institute, and generous financial support was offered by the source of funding for the project, but in neither case did this extend to influencing the report's conclusions. To ensure that the different positions on women's priesting have been accurately reflected, and to act in an occasional consultative role, a panel of reference was configured at the beginning of the project, which included a leading academic in the study of religion, an experienced social researcher on church matters, a long-standing campaigner on behalf of ordained women in the Church of England, and a very senior Anglican clergyman who has strong reservations about women's priesting. Whilst their advice has been invaluable, the content of the report remains my own. It should

---

[25] Some evidence for this assertion is offered in Chapters 2 and 3.
[26] Here, one only needs to look at the reception given to Helen Thorne's *Journey to Priesthood* or to the Cost of Conscience-commissioned survey *The Mind of Anglicans* (see: *New Directions* vol. 5 nos 86–8, July-September 2002 for a breakdown of the main results).

also be underlined that whilst I have my own views on women's ordination as priests (and have had the opportunity to develop them in the course of this project), I am not, nor have ever been, a member of any of campaigning group either for or against it, nor an active campaigner on any 'side' of the debate. In 1992 I was still an undergraduate student and only just becoming aware of the wider church outside my own parish; therefore researching and writing about the ordination of women debate has been more an exercise in historical reconstruction for me than the retelling of a story in which I had any personal involvement. That said, I am an active member of an Anglican parish church community and hope for the report to be a constructive contribution to the life of the Church of England; particularly to understanding its recent experience of ordaining women, and how some current issues may be resolved. Presenting a fair reflection of experiences and attitudes of the participants in this study is an important prerequisite to achieving this.

Part I

The First Ten Years

Chapter 1

Setting the scene: the 1992–94 Settlement, before and after

Books will doubtless be written which survey the Christian past and its treatment of women and end with November 1992, but of course the vote is not the end ... the result must now be carried through, given flesh, made incarnate.[1]

In seeing the 1992 vote on women's priesting as the beginning rather than the end of something, this report is primarily concerned with the first decade of women's ministry as priests in the Church of England. However, for those who know little or nothing of what happened before then, and for those who feel their memories need refreshment, this chapter offers a brief historical introduction to the development of a movement to ordain women in the Christian Church and an account of the Church of England's own experience of debating and preparing to ordain women as priests between 1992 and 1994. This represents the starting point and essential context for the 'first ten years' of the report's title, but also identifies some key patterns of response to the debate that remained influential in subsequent attempts to manage the settlement reached (for more on which see Chapters 5–7). The present arrangements have undoubtedly posed significant practical challenges to sections of the Church of England. However, for many clergy and churchgoers, 1992–94 seemed not primarily a time of head-scratching over a knotty problem, but a time of interest, curiosity and some celebration that the church was about to ordain its first ever female priests. Chapter 1 therefore also gives particular space to the experiences of ordained women themselves and their supporters, as they greeted the result of the vote, looked forward to priesthood and began to think about the possible challenges ahead. However, the chapter also recognizes the existence of other perspectives on the vote and so also gives consideration to the experiences of those who could not accept women's priesting and those charged with implementing the settlement in their dioceses.

1.1 Women and ordained ministry: a very short history

When the General Synod met in London on 11 November 1992 to vote on women's ordination to the priesthood, it marked the culmination of decades of formal debate and discussion, and almost a century and a half of wider change in the role of women within the Church of England. In 1845, after more than three centuries of absence from the formally recognized structures of ministry, the establishment of the Anglican Sisters of Mercy reintroduced sisterhoods to the Church of England. In 1861, the first Anglican deaconess was ordained by the Bishop of London, beginning a period of clarification and redefinition of the role lasting for the next 125 years, only to be closed to new recruits in 1987 when the Church of England voted to admit women to the diaconate alongside men.[2] The question of women as priests had first appeared in official Church reports as early as 1919, but it was arguably not until the 1962 report *Gender and Ministry* that the language of official publications began to shift from asking why women should be priests to questioning why it

---

[1] Susan Dowell and Jane Williams, *Bread, Wine and Women; The Ordination of Women Debate in the Church of England* (Virago, London, 1994), p. 113.
[2] Jacqueline Field-Bibb, *Women towards Priesthood: Ministerial Politics and Feminist Praxis* (Cambridge University Press, Cambridge, 1991), pp. 67–162.

had always been assumed that they should not be.[3] By 1975, General Synod had voted that 'there are no fundamental objections to the ordination of women to the priesthood', and despite several unsuccessful attempts to vote on women's priesting over the next nine years, the November 1984 meeting of the Synod voted to 'bring forward legislation to permit the ordination of women to the priesthood in the provinces of Canterbury and York', beginning the drafting process that eventually led to the 1992-94 settlement.[4]

Whilst the Church of England's discussions on women and priesthood go back over a century and more, beliefs about gender and priesthood have a much longer history, partly reflecting wider cultural assumptions about the respective natures and roles of men and women. The all-male priesthood of early Israel was partly shaped by the need for God's chosen people to worship in ways distinct from those of their Middle Eastern neighbours (whose fertility religions – greatly disliked by Hebrew reformers – often featured a female or mixed priesthood).[5] The ministry and teaching of Jesus raised profound questions about the role and status of women, and most scholars agree that women enjoyed a greatly enhanced position in the earliest Christian communities, sometimes including participation in formal offices of worship and service. Increasingly, writers have suggested that at least some leading women in the early church were exercising diaconal and presbyteral (and even episcopal) ministry in the same way as men, although this is still very much a subject for debate. The difficulty of drawing firm conclusions on women's ordained ministry from the biblical evidence results partly from the fact that even by the end of the New Testament period, the threefold order of bishops, priests and deacons recognized by episcopally-ordered churches today was still some way from being settled. However, in the structure of Christian leadership emerging from the late first century, male oversight for communities of believers increasingly became the norm as the Church sought to flourish in the Roman Empire.[6]

By the middle ages the maleness of the priest was underpinned by a sophisticated theological anthropology that drew upon Aristotelian ideas of the respective natures of male and female. For Aquinas, the most influential theologian of that age, women were disqualified from priesthood for being unlike the designated sacramental symbol for priesthood: a man.[7] Even so, women continued to play an important part in the life of the Church: women were often vigorously active at local church level, abbesses wielded some

---

[3] For more detailed accounts of the legislative process itself see Sean Gill, *Women and the Church of England, from the Eighteenth Century to the Present* (SPCK, London, 1994), Chapter 10 and Margaret Webster, *A New Strength, a New Song; The Journey to Women's Priesthood* (Mowbray, London, 1994).

[4] Gill, *Women and the Church of England*, pp. 251–5.

[5] Mary Hayter, *The New Eve in Christ: The Use and Abuse of the Bible in the Ordination of Women Debate* (SPCK, London, 1987), pp. 14–18; Manfred Hauke, *Women in the Priesthood? A Systematic Analysis in the Light of the Order of Creation and Redemption* (Ignatius Press, San Francisco, 1988 [first German ed. 1986]), pp. 214–15. It is notable that here writers of differing views on women's priesting generally concur that this was an influential factor in the shaping of an all-male priesthood for the Hebrew people.

[6] See essays by Constance F. Parvey and Rosemary Radford Ruether in: Rosemary Radford Ruether (ed.), *Religion and Sexism: Images of Woman in the Jewish and Christian Traditions* (Simon & Schuster, New York, 1974), pp. 117–49, 150–83.

[7] See A.J. Minnis, '*De Impedimento Sexus*: Women's Bodies and Medieval Impediments to Female Ordination' in P.A.J. Biller and A.J. Minnis (eds), *Medieval Theology and the Natural Body* (York Medieval Press/Boydell and Bewer, York/Woodbridge, Suffolk, 1997), pp. 109–140. However, it should be acknowledged that there is a long-running debate over the meaning of Aquinas' words here and how they should be applied to the question of women's priesting today (compare, for example: Jeremy Miller, 'A Note on Aquinas and Ordination of Women', *New Blackfriars* 61 (719), April 1980, pp. 185–90 and Michael Nolan, 'The Defective Male: What Aquinas Really Said', *New Blackfriars* 75 (880), March 1994, pp. 156–66).

influence and female mystics such as Julian of Norwich could become recognized as amongst the most creative thinkers and spiritual directors of their age. The European Reformations of the sixteenth and seventeenth centuries signalled major changes for the construction of gender in society and culture. In places where Protestant reform was embraced, women's identity began to be constructed in new ways other than with heavy reference to the 'bad' and 'good' paradigms of womanhood identified in Eve and Mary respectively. Married women could enjoy greater spiritual influence within the family unit. In new radical sects such as the Quakers, women could even enjoy a preaching ministry on roughly equivalent terms to men. On the other hand, the dissolution of religious orders by Protestant authorities and the abandonment of many other practices of medieval Catholic piety deprived many women of the traditional opportunities to express their faith, whilst a renewed emphasis on the Bible tended to reinforce the prevalent interpretation that ordination, preaching and indeed any public office were the province of men, whilst women were assigned the private sphere.[8]

From the nineteenth century women's preaching and ordained ministry were beginning to return to the agendas of many denominations in the Protestant tradition; sometimes partly influenced by much broader changes in gender roles arising from rapid social change and the values of the enlightenment, sometimes in direct contravention of wider cultural assumptions about suitable roles for men and women. The major part played by women in the mission field seems to have been particularly influential in encouraging non-Roman or - Orthodox denominations to reconsider women's ministry in a congregational or parochial setting.[9] Late twentieth-century debates on ordaining women have – at least in the West – been characterized by a backdrop of secularization (real or imagined), the perception of an growing chasm between church practice and changing theological, social and cultural values (particularly over questions of equality), by the growth in 'bottom up' campaigning for women's ordination and by the emergence of organized opposition to it.[10]

Calls for women's ordination in the Church of England emerged out of a much wider growth of interest in female suffrage in the years immediately before the First World War. By 1922, the efforts of campaigners such as Maude Royden had won the right for women to be licensed to preach and lead prayers in church and by 1930 a dedicated campaign organization – the Anglican Group for the Ordination of Women into the Historic Ministry of the Church – had also been formed.[11] Although the cause of women's ordination in the Church of England receded into the background during the middle years of the century, it began to re-emerge onto the agenda from the 1960s onwards in the context of much wider debates about theology and the relationships between the sexes. For some, this implied women priests were a fad of the permissive society; secular in origin and corrosive in effect. For others, it was the rediscovery of an important strand of early Christianity after centuries buried under wider social attitudes to gender that had (at best) questionable Christian credentials. The first motion put forward that women should be ordained on exactly the same terms as men was heard by the Church Assembly[12] in the Spring and Summer Sessions of 1967. Although falling well short of the required level of support, it was the first of a series of votes that brought the prospect of women's ordination as priests

---

[8] For more on the changes of this period as they related to England, see: Patricia Crawford, *Women and Religion in England, 1500–1720* (Routledge, London, 1993).

[9] Gill, *Women and the Church of England*, Chapters 8 and 9; Mark Chaves, *Ordaining Women; Culture and Conflict in Religious Organisations* (Harvard University Press, London, 1997), Chapter 6.

[10] Chaves, *Ordaining Women*, Chapter 7 and p. 148.

[11] This had succeeded the League of the Church Militant and (before that) the Church League for Women's Suffrage (Gill, *Women and the Church of England*, p. 238).

[12] The predecessor of the General Synod.

progressively closer. In 1975, Synod voted for the first time that 'there are no fundamental objections to the ordination of women to the priesthood', although subsequent votes in 1978 and 1986 failed respectively to produce legislation on women priests and permission for women ordained as priests abroad to celebrate in England. Even so, 1985 had seen Synod take an important step in the expansion of women's ordained ministry when it voted to allow women to become deacons, the first candidates being ordained in 1987.[13] And critically (although less dramatically at the time) General Synod had also voted in 1984 that the Standing Committee should 'bring forward legislation to permit the ordination of women to the priesthood in the Provinces of Canterbury and York',[14] beginning a process that came to fruition with the General Synod vote of November 1992.

However, the story of the Church of England's own journey towards ordaining women as priests should not be allowed to obscure the fact that other denominations and other parts of the Anglican Communion had already taken steps towards including woman in their priesthood/ordained ministry. Congregationalist and Baptist Churches had begun to ordain women in the early decades of the twentieth century, and the first women was ordained to the Methodist ministry in Britain in 1974, after a strong vote in favour the previous year. The first of the mainline episcopally-ordered denominations to ordain women were the Evangelical Lutheran Church of Denmark in 1948, followed by its sister church in Sweden in 1960. Within Anglicanism, the difficult circumstances of war in the Far East prompted Bishop R.O. Hall of Hong Kong and South China to ordain Florence Li Tim Oi as the first female priest in the Anglican Communion. Hong Kong could also received the first Anglican women ordained as priests under 'normal' circumstances in 1971 when Bishop Gilbert Baker ordained Jane Hwang and Joyce Bennett. Anglicans in Burma took the same step the following year. From there, the cause of women's ordination within the Anglican Communion gathered pace. Most controversial were the ordinations to the priesthood of eleven female deacons of the Episcopal Church of the USA, which took place in Philadelphia on 29 July 1974 without the formal sanction of their Province (although their ordinations were recognized retrospectively by the Church two years later). Amongst the provinces to join in ordaining women as priests in the following decade were the Anglican Churches in Canada (1976), New Zealand (1977), Kenya (1983) and Uganda (1984). By the time that the Anglican Church of Ireland voted to ordain women as priests in 1990, the Church of England's own legislation was receiving extensive consultation in deanery and diocesan synods around the country.

1.2 *Expectations and contingency plans*

Of course, by this time speculation was already mounting over the possible outcome of such a vote. Many who would be directly affected by the result (whatever it happened to be) had long since begun to consider their different options, depending on the outcome. Ideas on the most appropriate contingency plans also varied within individual organizations: the Movement for the Ordination of Women had always contained a diversity of views and approaches within its ranks (for example, over campaigning methods). Similarly in 1992, some members felt that they would be unable to stay within the Church of England should the legislation fall, whilst a majority resolved to stay and step up the campaign. A similar pattern was seen amongst ordained women in the Church at large: one report by female deacons from Ely Diocese published just prior to the vote suggested that a minority were considering leaving for another denomination, ordination abroad, or another kind of ministry altogether.[15] (Indeed, it is often forgotten that a 'no' vote in 1992 may have

---

[13] Field-Bibb, *Women towards Priesthood*, pp. 159–162.
[14] Gill, *Women and the Church of England*, p. 255.
[15] *After November; Some Possible Responses in the Event of the Failure of the Draft Priests (Ordination of Women) Measure and its Associated Canons – A Report by the Women Deacons of the*

resulted in more candidates lost to the priesthood over the following ten years than actually left as a result of the legislation being passed.)[16] On the other hand, a majority vowed to continue the campaign. Some even raised the possibility of 'irregular' celebrations of communion, or even 'illegal' ordinations.[17] For most women, however, the sense of calling to priestly ministry in the Church of England seems to have been so strong that they saw little option but to stay and continue their ministry whilst waiting, working and praying for their ordination as priests by 'constitutional' means.

For campaigners for a 'no' vote, speculation about the eventual outcome had also prompted discussions of possible contingency plans. Those who were involved in the legislation's early drafting and passage had pushed hard for clauses in the measure that would allow those who could not accept their diocesan bishop because he ordained women to seek oversight from an 'alternative' bishop. By 1989, this idea of 'alternative episcopal oversight' had been officially adopted by the association for traditionalist Catholic clergy *Cost of Conscience*, the organization's agreed statement on the subject receiving the support of around 1000 clergy at a conference in London that year.[18] In July 1991 the organization went a step further, circulating draft plans for the formation of a parallel church structure, including an alternative General Synod, a network of 'traditionalist' bishops, and plans for withholding quota from dioceses.[19] However, this seemed a compromise too far for some members of traditionalist organizations, and a number of individuals made it clear their only option was to leave for Rome, the Orthodox Church, or an evangelical Protestant free church.

Aside from campaigning groups and individuals, those most concerned at the possible outcome of the vote were the decision-makers; the Church's bishops and legislators. From the very beginning of the legislative process it was clear that whatever the final result, a substantial minority would be disappointed, and this would require careful handling; not least because the House of Bishops itself contained a variety of views on the question. Nevertheless, the corporate response of the House of Bishops was to become extremely significant for the eventual shape of the legislative settlement. Whilst some individual bishops were active campaigners for and against women's priesting, the House of Bishops as a whole had initially (in the eyes of many observers) held off from taking a firm line on the question either way, partly through a reluctance to divide the Church unnecessarily, and partly from the conviction that it was a matter for the dioceses to decide. 'We are all in favour of change', remarked the then Bishop of Gloucester regretfully, 'so long as it doesn't

---

Ely Diocese (1992).

[16] Almost 2000 women entered the Church of England priesthood between 1994 and 2001 (Gordon W. Kuhrt (ed.), *Ministry Issues for the Church of England: Mapping the Trends* (Church House Publishing, London, 2001), p. 12). Over the same period, 487 priests accepted compensation under the Ordination of Women (Financial Provisions) Measure, although of these 64 have returned (Archbishops' Council Ministry Division, *Statistics of Licensed Ministers 2001,* General Synod, GSMisc 673 (London, 2002), p. 32). The numbers of priests leaving the Church of England over women's priesting is certainly higher than this, since some took retirement early or through sickness, and some did not accept the financial compensation on offer. Even if we take the view of one leading campaigner against women's priesting that the combined figure should be 'nearer the six hundred mark', [int. cs5:8:112] and suppose that in each year between 1994 and 2001 the Church of England was accepting a third fewer male candidates for priesthood through 'traditionalist' losses (an improbably large figure of 1310), there has still been no net loss in numbers of clergy.

[17] Using overseas or retired bishops, some of whom had already indicated their willingness to participate in such actions.

[18] Cost of Conscience [prepared by Geoffrey Kirk], *Alternative Episcopal Oversight: The Agreed Statement* (Cost of Conscience, London, 1990), p. 9.

[19] Jonathan Petre, *By Sex Divided; The Church of England and Women Priests* (HarperCollins, London, 1994), p. 153.

make any difference'.[20] One Synod member closely involved in drafting the legislation remembered how, through most of the 1980s, it had been extremely difficult to obtain the cooperation of the House of Bishops in furthering the passage of legislation.

However, by 1990 the draft legislation had been passed by most diocesan synods and women's entry into the priesthood was beginning to look a real possibility. The bishops began to think more proactively about the shape of a post-vote Church of England, and with two particular concerns in mind: first, the bishops had become increasingly convinced that the diversity of opinion present within the Church over women's priesting had to be embraced rather than ignored or eradicated. On one hand this view was underpinned by the increasing influence of ecclesiological models emphasizing communion in diversity and the incorporation of division within the same church.[21] On a more pragmatic level, the bishops were also keen to avoid a repetition of the sharp divisions and legal wrangles experienced in the Episcopal Church of the USA (ECUSA) when women's priesting had been confirmed by a single-clause measure. Making provision for the disappointed minority, it was hoped, would head off similar division or the formation of a 'continuing' church for traditionalists, as some were beginning to advocate.[22]

In practice, this meant some form of enhanced safeguards that went beyond the terms already set out in the draft measures, and involved granting some measure of extended episcopal care to those refusing to accept women as priests. One early proposal[23] involved the creation of 'two tier dioceses', where a diocesan bishop of one persuasion would be balanced by a suffragan bishop of a different view, to ensure that each diocese could both ordain women and give episcopal care that was acceptable to those who disagreed with women's priesting. Although this idea was eventually rejected,[24] a subsequent group under the chairmanship of Archbishop of York, John Habgood, met to consider alternative proposals for a revised system of extended episcopal oversight, along similar lines to those that were eventually included in the 1993 Episcopal Ministry Act of Synod, involving a system of shared episcopal care over diocesan, regional and provincial areas.[25] Although at this stage most of these discussions were not widely known, the attention given to opt-out provisions for those objecting to women's priesting left some supporters of the measure with the feeling that the House was more concerned with the feelings of traditionalists than with the priesting of women[26] (although there was an important sense in which opt-out

---

[20] Quoted in the summary of the St George's Windsor Consultation on 'Changing Perceptions of Ministry', January 1993, p. 12.

[21] *Report of the Archbishop of Canterbury's Commission on Communion and Women in the Episcopate* [The Eames Commission] (Anglican Comsultative Council, London, 1994); Stephen Sykes, *The Integrity of Anglicanism* (Mowbrays, London and Oxford, 1978); Stephen W. Sykes (ed.), *Authority in the Anglican Communion: Essays Presented to Bishop John Howe* (Anglican Book Centre, Toronto, 1987). See Chapter 8 for more on this.

[22] General Synod GS 738, *The Ordination of Women to the Priesthood: The Scope of the Legislation* (Church House, London, April 1986), paragraphs 15, 17.

[23] The co-called 'Ripon Report' of 1992, drawn up by a group including David Young and David Hope, then Bishops of Ripon and London respectively.

[24] Partly because few could contemplate a lengthy process of revising the existing draft legislation to incorporate it. On the other hand, many of those whom it was intended to benefit felt insufficiently reassured by the suggestion that the extra safeguards could simply be appended to the measure as a Code of Practice (Petre, *By Sex Divided*, pp. 155–7).

[25] See below and also Chapters 7 and 8.

[26] Certainly the discussion of financial provisions for an uncertain number of clergy and lay workers unable to accept women's priesting only seems to have served to harden divisions between those campaigning for the measure, and those campaigning against it – particularly at a time of financial difficulty for the Church of England (Ivan Clutterbuck, *Marginal Catholics: Anglo-Catholicism – A Further Chapter of Modern Church History* (Gracewing, Leominster, 1993), p. 249).

provisions *had by default* to consider the position of opponents, since the main point of the legislation itself was to permit women to be ordained priests). Even so, it appears that many bishops continue to doubt that the legislation would be passed. Most seem to have expected to spend the weeks after the vote comforting disappointed female deacons, and set time aside in their diaries to do so. Others (again including Archbishop Habgood) began to consider proposals for an enhanced role for female deacons should the legislation fall, including increasing the numbers in pastoral charge of parishes. Some bishops managed successfully to avoid prejudging the situation – the bishop of Diocese B, for example, established a committee composed of both men and women, 'supporters' and 'opponents' to consider both the eventualities of a 'yes' or a 'no' vote. The most optimistic bishops had even begun placing female deacons in key positions ready for priestly ministry should the vote go in favour. However, as a group, the body of bishops (in the words of one observer) 'expected the Measure narrowly to fail, so what the bishops had done was to prepare their continuance plans. Although they had looked at the other possibility, they didn't seriously believe it would happen'.[27]

The expectations and responses of campaigning groups and church leaders undoubtedly had far-reaching implications for the final shape of the legislation and its practical outworking. However, much of this discussion took place at several removes from the experience of many grass roots Anglicans – particularly if no ordained women were on the staff of the parish, or if their priest had no strong objections to women as priests. Clergy and lay expectations of the possible impact of women's priesting per se are considered further in Chapter 4 but briefly here, how did interviewees from the grass roots Church anticipate the vote itself? A majority appeared to view the impending decision with a mixture of interest, curiosity or (in some cases, if there was a more personal stake in the result) nervousness lest the result go the wrong way. For a minority of those interviewed, the impending decision on women's ordination as priests was greeted with mounting alarm. One male priest from a 'traditionalist' Catholic position remembered how the vote on women's priesting seemed to have arrived with indecent haste after a paltry debate that he believed had paid more attention to secular fashion than theology. When the question had first appeared on his horizon in the early 1970s, he had simply dismissed it as 'one of those daft things that Americans do ... I didn't believe it would come over here'.[28]

Indeed, right up to the day of the vote, it seems that a significant proportion of those with objections to women's priesting continued to expect the legislation to fall.[29] Others found the 'turmoil' (either national or local) around the vote itself 'very upsetting'.[30] Nor were all of those sympathetic to women's priesting reassured by the tone of those campaigning for the change: 'they were militant and I thought that with all its existing problems the Church could do well without adding this to them', said one male respondent from Church 5.[31] (Indeed, it was often the case amongst grass roots respondents that a distrust of feminist 'militancy' or 'stridency' was nevertheless accompanied by ready agreement with the principle being campaigned for.) Others remembered feeling that the debate was a distraction from other issues they rated as more important – particularly questions of mission and evangelism.[32] Amongst some respondents (notably amongst evangelicals) there

---

[27] int. 13:p.3.

[28] int. cs2:7:72.

[29] As part of a series of features in the *Church Times* in 2002, to mark the tenth anniversary of the vote, leading campaigner against women's priesting Margaret Brown remembered feeling confident that the measure would be rejected, until the night before the vote, when she realized that the result was too close to call (*Church Times*, 8 November 2002, p. 17).

[30] LQ54, female 20–29, Church 3.

[31] LQ132, male 60–69, Church 5.

[32] Although whilst this could be a genuine concern, Monica Furlong also suggested that the decade of

was genuine uncertainty as to what the proper outcome of the vote should be. One Reader from the evangelical Church 2 in Diocese A remembered how, at one local pre-vote debate, evangelical clergy spoke both for and against and 'people found it very difficult, because [the two speakers] both gave very convincing arguments, and you felt that you could go either way ...'[33]

However, while it is important to recognize the great variety of responses to the impending vote, the most common response amongst interviewees was one of more positive anticipation. Indeed for many women's entry into the priesthood was entirely expected: 'I had always thought that one day women would be ordained', wrote one lay woman.[34] Experience of women's ordained ministry in other denominations appeared particularly significant in encouraging the expectation that women would be priested in the Church of England: one former URC member recalled how when she started attending an Anglican church, 'the C of E having a big issue with women leaders surprised me'.[35] Above all many of the testimonies contained a strong sense that history and the prompting of the Holy Spirit within it were moving slowly but surely in favour of women's inclusion into the three-fold ministry of the Church. A male priest from Diocese F remembered surveying middle school children's views on women as priests in 1991 as part of a school assembly and finding that out of 66 present 65 children were in favour, one was unsure and none were against: 'that made me think: it can't possibly *not* happen!'.[36]

Even so, as the morning of the vote approached, whilst many female deacons shared this conviction that women's priesting would inevitably come, few were so certain that the legislation would achieve the necessary support.[37] One remembered 'I actually had a job getting some of the people [in the parish] to realize that this was something they needed to pray about. If they were for it, they needed to pray that it would go through. They were saying "well, it's a foregone conclusion", and I said "no it's not!".'[38] For most the day was one of anxious waiting: for those who travelled to London to participate in the vote or stand in vigil outside Church House, the experience of solidarity and the support received from passers-by at least provided temporary relief from the waiting, but anticipation was rising all the same. For some of those awaiting the result elsewhere, the day seemed to drag unbearably: one female deacon decided to decorate her house to take her mind off the debate until the result came; another woman training at theological college could not even bear to watch the result on television and went off to do her washing instead.

---

evangelism also sometimes served as a convenient excuse for inaction over women's priesting by the Church – furthermore, an excuse that underestimated the extent to which the Church's treatment of women might have missiological implications (Monica Furlong, *A Dangerous Delight; Women and Power in the Church* (SPCK, London, 1991), pp. 89–128).
[33] int. cs1:13:115.
[34] LQ120, female 70–79, Church 7.
[35] LQ301, female 20–29, Church 7.
[36] int. cs6:3:158. Implicit understandings of history and teleology clearly exerted a major influence on the debate over women's priesting – at both academic and popular level – and it is hoped to explore this theme further in a subsequent publication.
[37] Indeed, one postal survey of female deacons conducted just three years before the vote found only 50.7% of respondents believed the Church of England was likely to ordain women priests before the end of the century! (Alan Aldridge, 'Discourse on Women in the Clerical Profession: The Diaconate and Language-Games in the Church of England', *Sociology* 26 (1) February 1992, pp. 45–57 (p. 52).).
[38] int. cs5:2side2:443.

1.3 Champagne on ice: reactions to the vote

At 10 a.m. on the morning of 11 November, General Synod began final proceedings to accept or reject the draft Priests (Ordination of Women) Measure. The long and at times emotionally charged proceedings have been well documented elsewhere,[39] so need no detailed repetition here. Recollections of those who were present tended to differ sharply between supporters and opponents of the legislation: those who were 'against' often characterized the debate as theologically shallow, whilst those in favour chiefly remembered it as serious and fair. Examining the debate transcripts with a historian's eye, Sean Gill notes the wide range of viewpoints expressed in the speeches, but also the 'set piece' quality of the occasion: the real discussion had already taken place, with the Synod debate itself merely providing an opportunity for summing up.[40] Even so the result was still far from clear. Late in the afternoon Archbishop John Habgood concluded the speeches. A moment of silence for reflection and prayer was called, and Synod began to vote. Some engaged in frantic calculations to gauge whether the necessary two-thirds majority had been achieved. Others simply sat in uneasy silence, overwhelmed by the occasion. Just before 5 p.m. the result was announced: 39 'ayes' to 13 'noes' in the House of Bishops, 176 'ayes' to 74 'noes' in the House of Clergy and 169 'ayes' to 82 'noes' in the House of Laity: the motion had been carried.

For all sides, the emotion of the occasion was palpable as participants and observers realized what had happened. Stories of the scenes of jubilation and despair around Church House have been told on many occasions[41] and need no extensive retelling here, save to highlight the complex mixture of emotions felt by all those who watched or took part. For most writers and interviewees, the dominant image of the day was that of the celebrations of women deacons and their supporters outside Synod. Those sympathetic to the result have focused on the joy and relief of the 'yes' constituency and their inability to keep from celebrating with shouts of joy and bursts of song. Many accounts emphasized how this joy was shared by others, often people without any regular association with church: motorists sounded their horns to signal support to those keeping vigil outside Church House; passers-by congratulated any woman (and some men) wearing a dog collar; answerphones were jammed with messages of congratulation from friends and colleagues; one woman returning to the railway station from Church House was grasped and twirled around in celebration by a respectable-looking city gent with an umbrella.[42] As Canon Wendy Bracegirdle was to recall ten years on, the public reaction constituted 'an astonishing display of awareness of the affairs of the Church. The vote was an event noted and celebrated out there on the streets'.[43]

[39] See especially: General Synod, The Ordination of Women to the Priesthood: The Synod Debate, 11 November 1992: The Verbatim Record (Church House Publishing, London, 1993).

[40] Gill, Women and the Church of England, p. 258.

[41] For accounts of the day of the vote itself from the perspective of women who are now priests, and their supporters, see: Liz and Andrew Barr, Jobs for the Boys? Women who Became Priests (Hodder and Stoughton, London, 2001) and Christina Rees (ed.), Voices of this Calling; Experiences of the First Generation of Women Priests (Canterbury Press, Norwich, 2002). For reactions of those who stood opposed to the Measure, see particularly Petre, By Sex Divided, chs. 11–12 and William Oddie, The Roman Option: Crisis and the Realignment of English-Speaking Christianity (HarperCollins, London, 1997), ch. 1.

[42] int. 9side2:4fwds.

[43] Wendy Bracegirdle, 'Priesthood and Society' in Rees (ed.), Voices of this Calling, pp. 132–4 (p. 132).

For active campaigners for women's priesting, a long-sought objective had now been achieved. At the offices of the Movement for the Ordination of Women (MOW) in London, workers remember being deluged with messages of congratulation and requests for interviews. The only question was how noisily to celebrate. One more radical member of MOW remembered how:

> *we had a council meeting on the Saturday of the week of the vote ... And that day Joyce Bennett [...] she celebrated. And you know, someone came up to me afterwards and said 'you shouldn't have done that'; it's very counterproductive', and I said 'counterproductive to what? We've got the vote! There's nothing to be counterproductive about!'. But you know that was the extreme caution at one end – [that] you must never rock the boat..!*[44]

Those who had sought a 'no' vote have sometimes characterized the scenes of celebration as 'triumphalist' or insufficiently sensitive.[45] Doubtless this criticism was prompted partly by their own sense of shock and disappointment. Additionally it may have been prompted by a gut feeling that such scenes were also somehow 'un-Anglican' in their very public enthusiasm: several churchgoers watching the news reports at home on television recalled (in the words of one), 'they were overjoyed in their own way, but was that a way to carry on? It was a cause of alarm to me that they could[n't] have shown their jubilation, if you like, in a bit more restrained way than that!'[46] However, for others, the outburst of joy was a sign of the rightness of the decision: one woman remembered seeing the pictures of women deacons outside Church House crying with happiness, and realized just how much they wanted to be priests.[47] One female Reader with a passion for football remembered watching the vote on television at home and feeling 'nothing but excitement – it was like watching the 1966 World Cup Final!'.[48]

Nevertheless, the atmosphere was not one of unmitigated joy: Margaret Webster remembers many supporters seeking out their diocesan bishop to thank them for voting the measure through, but some bishops seemed burdened by their decision and were in no mood to celebrate, whilst others had vanished altogether, to seek a quiet place to pray and reflect.[49] For some, the implications of the decision had begun to weigh on their minds: one female deacon recalled her relief at the vote but also knew this meant she had to consider whether she should go forward for priesthood.[50] One male vicar strongly in favour of women's priesting nevertheless found himself surprisingly saddened at the result, realizing on one hand that prospects of unity with Rome had been placed further into the distance, whilst the familiar and comfortable ethos of all-male clergy gatherings was now likely to change for good.[51] For women deacons themselves too, joy at the possibility of priesthood was immediately tempered by fears of what might result from the legislation just passed: in Diocese C, women deacons faced an anxious wait to find out whether their diocesan bishop would agree to ordain women. One couple who had bought a bottle of champagne to

---

[44] int 8:332.

[45] Oddie, *The Roman Option*, p. 20.

[46] int. cs5:4:212.

[47] int. cs3:20:373.

[48] int. cs5:7:384.

[49] Margaret Webster, *A New Strength, A New Song*, p. 185.

[50] int. cs5:6:444. This theme is also noted in: Sue Walrond-Skinner, *Double Blessing: Clergy Marriage since the Ordination of Women as Priests* (Mowbray, London, 1998). She adds that clergy couples could also find that the priesting of the female partner prompted a reconsideration of the roles and identity of husband and wife within the couple.

[51] int. cs3:7:107.

celebrate the result kept it on ice for a year until the future became clearer.[52] In Diocese A (as in many others around the country), women deacons were urged by senior staff to keep their celebrations muted ('we musn't crow about it, because of other people's feelings – that was the attitude', one recalled).[53] In fact women deacons and their supporters from Diocese A appear to have shown remarkable forbearance: one clergyman from the 'no' camp remembered how his female colleagues had not been at all 'triumphalist', whilst some of his own constituency had at times been 'less than gracious'.[54] However, this was by no means always the case: a few who had argued against women's priesting accepted the result immediately as the will of the Church, whilst others who continued to have objections or reservations (like the previous speaker) were known for having been courteous and conciliatory in 'defeat'.

Amongst those hoping for a 'no' vote in 1992, the aftermath of the result was sometimes remembered as a bereavement. Many described the first stage of this as stunned bewilderment. 'I was absolutely devastated', said one senior clergyman; 'I don't think I have ever felt so dumbfounded in all my life'.[55] Several traditionalist clergy remembered instinctively removing their clerical collars and shirts upon hearing the result,[56] a heavily symbolic commentary on their assumption that the Church of England had abandoned the Catholic priesthood now that it had decided to ordain women. Indeed, one talked of feeling a 'huge cultural loss of meaning' that had left him 'a refugee; a stateless person'.[57] In the first weeks after the vote, conducting worship appears to have been a particularly difficult experience. Some worshippers from parishes with a clergyman who had voted against the measure remembered their priest in tears during the service; some worshippers were palpably moved by this and pained at the distress caused to their priest – though others were irritated by what seemed to them a big fuss over nothing.[58] Clergy who had been against the 1993 Measure were particularly likely to recall feelings of disorientation in dioceses where the bishop was a known supporter. Conversely, where the bishop shared their view, sadness was slightly tempered by a feeling of security – at least for the time being.

For some, the next stage was to question what to do next, and a range of different options presented themselves. In his 1997 book *The Roman Option*, William Oddie suggests three main courses of action were open to those disappointed with the result of the vote: first, to leave the Anglican priesthood and seek refuge in another denomination; second, to remain within the Church of England but remain in a position of official opposition to the move, working to continue an all-male priestly tradition; third, to stay put for the short to medium term and watch how the legislation unfolded.[59] The first option was that most favoured by those who regarded the Church's decision as fundamentally heretical. Here again the much-used metaphor of life and death came into play – as one clergyman argued, in the event of bereavement, one should not sit around waiting for the corpse to come back to life.[60] Most of those seeking sanctuary in the Roman Catholic or Orthodox Churches did so as

---

[52] int. cs3:9:260.
[53] Although privately one of the episcopal team who was strongly in favour rang up each female deacon individually to congratulate them on the result (int. cs1:4:50, 86).
[54] int cs1:15:90.
[55] int. 5:p.11.
[56] Oddie, *The Roman Option*, p. 25.
[57] int. 15:274.
[58] Particularly in a small number of cases where the priest in question had shown little compassion to those who welcomed women's priesting, and who were disappointed when the resolutions were passed.
[59] Oddie, *The Roman Option*, p. 25.
[60] Quoted in Oddie, *The Roman Option*, p. 30 although the speaker quoted here did not himself leave the Church of England.

individuals – some 300 clergy had taken this route by August 1994.[61] A small number of congregations began processes of consultation to discern whether they should be received into another denomination together and talk of 'whole ecclesial communities journeying into communion with the Bishop of Rome' was widespread in certain quarters at the time.[62] Nevertheless, such action was extremely rare – particularly given the collapse of hopes for the creation of a separate traditionalist Anglican church under Roman Catholic oversight.[63] Those seeking a move to Rome could also experience opposition from two quite different sources; on one hand, some Roman Catholic bishops who were themselves privately supportive of women's priesting, and on the other hand from members of their congregation (even in strongly Anglo-Catholic parishes, where some clergy were taken aback by the 'naked anti-popery' they perceived amongst their congregation when the question of Rome was raised[64]).

The second and much more popular path for those who objected to the decision to ordain women as priests was to remain an Anglican but adopt a stance of dissent from the official position on women's priesthood. One young evangelical minister remembered thinking at the time of the vote: 'I can't stick around here, can I? I'll have to jack it in and join the Lutherans', but after a period of disquiet and uncertainty, came to the conclusion that even if he was surprised by the result, God would not have been, and would therefore continue to have a plan for the Church of England – and for the speaker as an ordained minister in it.[65] For many in this position, the process of continuing as an Anglican was helped by mutual support amongst like-minded friends, or (in the case of lay people) by moving to a new congregation.

An additional source of support now came from two organizations founded in the aftermath of the vote to speak for those concerned at the direction the Church of England had taken. First, in December 1992, came Forward in Faith, formed by a grouping of (mainly Catholic) traditionalist societies, including Cost of Conscience, Women against the Ordination of Women and the Association for Apostolic Ministry.[66] Its first published statement called for the Church to ensure a succession of bishops who did not ordain women as priests, and for the construction of a parallel organizational framework for those opposed to women's priesting.[67] In some respects FiF was an uneasy alliance of interests, but a proportion of Anglicans (particularly clergy) derived a sense of assurance from its existence,[68] and in addition the presence of such an organization gave clearer expression to one part of the male-only priesthood constituency. Senior clergymen of this position spent considerable time travelling the dioceses, 'rallying the troops', often making contact with sympathetic parishes and clergy through local FiF representatives.[69] In dioceses such as Diocese A, where 'traditionalists' were numerous, this process led to the formation of an

---

[61] Petre, *By Sex Divided*, p. 181.

[62] int. 15:16.

[63] The full story of hopes for a 'Catholic moment' (in which traditionalist Anglicans would again become reunited with the Roman Catholic Church) is told extensively in Oddie's *The Roman Option*.

[64] int. 15:372. The importance of a distinctively 'Anglican' ethos and identity is considered further in the Conclusion.

[65] int. cs5:9:420.

[66] Forward in Faith also enjoyed strong links with much older Catholic Anglican societies such as the Church Union and the Society of the Holy Cross (SSC).

[67] Oddie, *The Roman Option*, p. 60.

[68] One vicar told me: 'we were left to sink or swim, and if it wasn't for FiF and a network of like-minded people supporting each other, who knows what the impact on people's health would have been?' (int. cs2:5:310). Having noted the sense of assurance traditionalist clergy derived from FiF, it is also important to state that lay people also make up a significant proportion of its membership.

[69] int 17side2:404.

'alternative' clergy chapter. By contrast in Diocese B, where traditionalist clergy were much fewer, one experienced rector began to act as *de facto* chaplain to like-minded colleagues.

Although FiF was formed as an umbrella organization for all 'traditionalists', it was largely Anglo-Catholic in inspiration and quickly became more so in ethos. For conservative evangelicals disappointed at the current direction of the Church of England, this seemed symptomatic of the way in which their voice seemed to become lost in the debate.[70] In January 1993, however, a group of conservative evangelical clergy met for a conference on women's ordination at St Helen's Bishopsgate, London. Out of this experience, Reform was born, an organization primarily aimed at evangelical clergy and congregations of a 'reformed' or 'conservative' disposition, aimed at renewing and reforming the Church of England.[71] Women's ordination as presbyters was by no means the sole issue at stake; concern over liberal positions on human sexuality and the payment of quota for questionable diocesan ends were also on the agenda. However, women's role in ordained leadership started and remained a key focus for the organization; its founding covenant including the statement that '... the divine order of male headship ... makes the headship of women as priests in charge, incumbents, dignitaries and bishops inappropriate'. For Reform in its official stance, the opening of ordained leadership roles to women was nothing less than a questioning of the centrality of scripture in the Church of England.[72]

However, in both Forward in Faith and Reform, differences of opinion existed from the beginning as to the aim of the organization. For some, the maintenance of an 'orthodox'[73] position within the Church of England was to be a long-term project, but others preferred to make the third response suggested by Oddie: to play for time to see how the ordination of women legislation and related provisions would work out in practice and whether continued existence within the Church of England was still possible. Certainly initially, leading figures in FiF such as John Broadhurst and George Austin seem to have viewed the organization primarily in terms of enabling the creation of breathing space in which to grow alternative structures for use in the event of a greater level of detachment from the Church of England.[74] On the other hand, some of those most interested in exploring links with Rome felt betrayed by traditionalist bishops in their complicity with the Act of Synod, which to them merely seemed like playing for time.[75] The choice between leaving the Church of England, maintaining opposition to women's priesting within an increasingly distinct 'traditionalist' constituency or playing for more time mirrored a much wider sense in which responses to the 1992–94 settlement did not simply reflect a crude pattern of

---

[70] For example, whilst a small number of evangelicals have been prominent in calling for extended episcopal oversight, the emphasis in the Act of Synod in particular on extended *sacramental* care for clergy and parishes was primarily a concession to disappointed Catholics (and indeed even ten years on only a handful of evangelical parishes have petitioned for extended Episcopal oversight).

[71] Of course, being either 'reformed' or 'conservative' does not imply opposition to women's priesting, and indeed there continue to be a substantial number in *Reform* churches who nevertheless agree with women's ordination as presbyters. However, amongst church activists at least, being a 'conservative' evangelical has increasingly come to be identified with a series of defining issues (opposition to women's ordination being one), as evangelicalism as a whole has diversified.

[72] Mark Burkill, 'Women's Ordination: Why is this a Crisis for the Church of England?' Reform Discussion Paper 2 (Reform, Sheffield, 1993).

[73] 'Orthodox' here does not refer to the Eastern Christian tradition, and nor do I intend it to denote that I consider this constituency to be truer to authentic Christianity than any other tradition. It is used here in brackets as one of the key words used by the male-only priesthood constituency to describe their own position. The attempt by groups on all sides to identify themselves with a historic, authentic Anglican Christian tradition is further explored in Chapters 2 and 8.

[74] Petre, *By Sex Divided*, p. 178.

[75] Oddie, *The Roman Option*, pp. 56–7.

'acceptance' on one hand or 'rejection' on the other. Both principled opposition and pragmatic compromise coexisted within the constituency of those unhappy about women's priesting, and attitudes towards the future often comprised a complex mix of fundamental belief, willingness to tolerate coexistence across disagreement and conception of the most appropriate time to push for further change.[76]

However, William Oddie's study of the responses of traditionalists in the aftermath of the 1992 vote did not consider a fourth option: to accept the result and work with it. One male priest who described himself as a 'not yet' person before 1992, nevertheless decided to accept the result and at the time of interview had a female curate. For him, as for many who changed their minds, this decision had lost him friends, and could also lead to misunderstanding: he recalled occasions when both female deacons and members of Forward in Faith had assumed he was opposed simply on the grounds of his Catholic position.[77] Another remembered:

> *a sense of shock when the vote actually went through ... feeling that suddenly all things had change and we really weren't quite sure where we were – it took a long time for that to work its way through, but it was a sense of 'I am in the Church of England, this is where we belong and we now work with it' and I've been exploring ways of working with it, and just gradually moving to a position of more acceptance, rather than opposition ...*[78]

What of the responses of diocesan bishops and senior clergy? For many, the 1992 result brought private feelings of joy or regret, but also the challenge of how to offer satisfactory pastoral oversight to both those celebrating the outcome of the vote, and to those who were angered or upset by it. Observers have frequently noted how many bishops were quite unprepared for the degree of hurt and anger expressed by those who objected to the result.[79] An immediate action of many diocesan bishops was to meet with groups of clergy who had voted against women's priesting.[80] The success of these meetings appears to have depended very much on the extent of affinity between bishop and clergy and the willingness of both parties to act in a conciliatory fashion. In Diocese A, where the then bishop himself had reservations over women's priesting, the continued unity of the diocese across the different views on the subject had been a major concern for senior clergy from the start: 'we do things together – that was the message', as one recalled.[81] The bishop's assurances of support and fairness appear to have gone some way towards relaxing the atmosphere after a tense diocesan clergy conference the week after the vote. Although some ordained women remembered feeling disappointed that the bishop had asked them to 'lie low' out of consideration for those upset by the result, they also felt that their diocesan had treated them fairly despite his own reservations.

Steps towards conciliation did not go so far in every diocese, however. In Diocese B, where clergy had overwhelmingly voted for women as priests, disappointed clergy were again given the opportunity to meet with the bishop and discuss their concerns. Here however, the occasion only seems to have contributed to traditionalists' sense of isolation as an embattled group. Neither seem to have been entirely innocent: 'opposed' clergy came away from the

---

[76] This theme will be explored further in Part III: Looking to the Future.
[77] int. cs1:28:238–320.
[78] int. cs3:6:40.
[79] Webster, *A New Strength, a New Song*, p. 192 and interviews.
[80] Initially, such meetings had been pencilled in to many bishops' diaries as occasions for meeting and comforting disappointed women deacons in the more expected event of a 'no' vote.
[81] int. cs1:2:185.

meeting with the impression that their diocesan could not offer them any comfort, suggesting that they should accept the result, keep quiet, or leave.[82] Some dissenting clergy do not appear to have helped improve the atmosphere either; one had already written to the bishop informing him that he was no longer welcome in the parish.[83]

The way dioceses handled the 1992 result had important implications for subsequent levels of cooperation between the constituencies over the following decade (a theme considered further in Chapter 6). Where they worked well, meetings between the bishop and groups of clergy acted as a pressure release valve and could begin to rebuild trust. On the other hand, advocates for women's ordained ministry could be left feeling that the bishops were paying more attention to soothing the hurts of 'opponents' than celebrating the new possibilities presented by women's entry to the priesthood. [84] Additionally, post-vote meetings could help to cement a stronger sense of collective identity amongst clergy with objections to women's priesting, often self-consciously distinct from the diocesan 'mainstream'. Some bishops deliberately avoided such meetings, feeling that they encouraged the emergence of a lobby group culture. However, this seems to have been an exceptional view; a majority of bishops seemed to see the work of reconciliation (if only unconsciously) as one of managing the competing claims of two main interest groups ('the women' and 'the opponents') for the sake of those who fell into neither category. Whilst this diagnosis of the situation was in keeping with the House of Bishops' previous attitude to the shaping of the legislation, it risked constructing 'women priests' and 'opponents' as two equally extreme positions, similar in size, to whom concessions had to be made by the 'normal' mainstream.[85]

It is arguable that this assumption was most evident in the development of the additional 'safeguards' for clergy with objections to women's priesting that by late 1993 had become the Episcopal Ministry Act of Synod. Efforts to reconcile the different positions at a diocesan level could prove valuable, but even before the November 1992 vote, most senior figures in the Church of England had come to believe that the project of coexistence must also involve action at national level.[86] Faced with the prospect of hundreds – perhaps thousands – of traditionalist clergy leaving the Church of England unless their requests for additional 'safeguards' of their position were met, the bishops gathered in Manchester in January 1993 to consider the next step. Participants remember a tense meeting, with considerable efforts being made to achieve unanimity on a plan. With reasonably little contention the bishops agreed procedures for discerning the vocations to priesthood of women already ordained as deacons. But the Manchester meeting has become best known for its statement on ensuring 'continued episcopal oversight and pastoral care for all members of the Church of England following the coming into effect of the legislation'.[87]

---

[82] Reports of this meeting are anecdotal and several accounts of it disagree as to what was actually said.

[83] int. cs2:7:354.

[84] E.g., Jean Mayland remembers: 'there were long speeches about the pain of those who were opposed, the desperate situation of the Church of England, the fear of mass defections, and the threat that numerous parishes would not pay their quota. Even those who had supported the ordination of women in the past seemed to be regretting their action and implying that they wished women would crawl back into the woodwork and stay there'. Jean Mayland, 'An Act of Betrayal', in Monica Furlong (ed.), *Act of Synod: Act of Folly?* (SCM Press, London, 1998), pp. 59–75.

[85] I owe this observation to the Revd Dr Judith Maltby. Having said this, clergy on all sides of the debate were themselves sometimes responsible for reinforcing this analysis of the shape of the post-1992 Church of England; notably those who used the language of battle to describe the debate on women's priesting.

[86] The path to the Act of Synod as traced through the official reports of the C of E and Anglican Communion is clearly and concisely outlined in: Mary Tanner, 'The Episcopal Ministry Act of Synod in Context' in Paul Avis (ed.), *Seeking the Truth of Change in the Church: Reception, Communion and the Ordination of Women* (T & T Clark, London, 2004), pp. 58–74.

[87] House of Bishops, 'Statement by the House following its Meeting in Manchester, 11–14 January 1993', p. 1.

In June 1993 these proposals were published in fuller form in the House of Bishops document 'Bonds of Peace', accompanied by a draft 'Act of Synod' and a further theological paper, *Being in Communion*. These acknowledged the diversity of views amongst the bishops and outlined how bishops of differing views would assist each other to provide 'extended episcopal oversight'. For example, 'it will be a mark of continuing communion when a diocesan bishop in favour of the ordination of women to the priesthood invites a bishop who does not accept it to minister to priests and congregations in his diocese who themselves do not accept it'.[88] If possible these arrangements were to be offered internally in each diocese, but failing that on a regional level.[89] If this was not possible 'the Archbishop of Canterbury proposes up to two additional Suffragan Bishops for his diocese and the Archbishop of York one additional Suffragan Bishop for his diocese, to undertake duties across the Province on a similar basis to the Bishops appointed to Act regionally'. These 'Provincial Episcopal Visitors' would 'work with the Diocesan Bishop concerned in enabling extended pastoral care and sacramental ministry to be provided; and… act as spokesman and adviser for those who are opposed to the ordination of women to the priesthood and assist the Archbishops in monitoring the arrangements made for them'.[90]

As the proposals were announced many bishops confessed their relief that a settlement had been reached. As one leading architect of the plans later reflected, it seemed 'a statesmanlike way of obtaining the best thing we could from a situation that promised deep division in the Church'.[91] But among campaigners on all sides the response to the plan was mixed. For many of those who had worked for the cause of women's priesting, the proposals seemed like a betrayal of what had been decided in 1992. Writing later, Monica Furlong castigated the bishops for their 'total inability to identify ... with the women and what they must be feeling as their offering of themselves was debased with insulting concessions given to those who opposed them'.[92] Some raised the question of whether it was acceptable to create suffragan bishops to look after a minority constituency on this issue, when no such similar steps had been taken over any other matter. Moreover, despite denials to the contrary in the Manchester Statement, some speakers suggested that that the proposals seemed to condone the view that male bishops could be 'tainted' by ordaining women. Campaigners for an all-male priesthood were likewise not always pleased with the proposals, with some claiming they did no go far enough.[93] Nevertheless, when Synod came to debate the draft Act of Synod at the November 1993 group of sessions, only a few voices were raised against the plans, and the Act was passed overwhelmingly, with 39 ayes, 0 noes in the House of Bishops, 175 ayes to 12 noes in the House of Clergy, and 194 ayes to 14 noes in the House of Laity.

To the architects of the Act the provision of extended episcopal oversight was entirely consistent with the direction of previous Anglican Communion reports on communion in diversity over the matter of women in ordained ministry. *Being in Communion* argued that in a fallen world communion amongst Christians would inevitably be partial or even impaired and quoted previous Lambeth resolutions calling for respect amongst those of different views

---

[88] 'Bonds of Peace' in General Synod GS1074, *Ordination of Women to the Priesthood: Pastoral Arrangements – A Report by the House of Bishops* (Church House, London, 1993), para. 5. Also in General Synod GS Misc 418, *Being in Communion* (Church House, London, 1993), para. 23.

[89] 'Draft Episcopal Ministry Act of Synod 1993' Appendix B (paras. 3, 4) in *Ordination of Women to the Priesthood: Pastoral Arrangements* and also in the final document.

[90] 'Bonds of Peace', para. 13.

[91] int. 12:300.

[92] Furlong (ed.), *Act of Synod, Act of Folly?*, p. 9.

[93] E.g., some members of FiF had requested that there be seven Episcopal Visitors; the Manchester Statement proposed a maximum of three.

'without such respect necessarily indicating acceptance of the principles involved'.[94] Furthermore, the ordained ministry acted as 'one of the constitutive elements of *koinonia*' and 'bishops have a particular responsibility for maintaining and focusing the internal unity and communion of the Church'.[95] Extended episcopal oversight would be made possible by the bishops' pledge to support the Act despite their differences and by their mutual recognition as part of the same 'college'. However, if the proposals seemed consistent to the minority of people who knew about these documents, they came as a considerable surprise to the majority who did not. As already suggested, most of the groundwork for the Act was done in the two years immediately before and after November 1992[96] and was not widely discussed or reported. As one observer who was intimately involved in the legislative process recalled, 'there was no putting heads above the parapet, over what became the Act of Synod, until after the vote'.[97] In addition to the Act's lineage in previous Anglican Communion documents it is important to emphasize the contingent factors that may have contributed to its passing in November 1993. It undoubtedly received ready support from those Anglicans with objections to women's ordination as priests who still wished to remain within the Church of England. Some bishops who had been expecting to comfort disappointed female deacons found themselves faced with a somewhat different (but no less disappointed) constituency. Some were taken by surprise by the strength of feeling they encountered and this may have added to their sense that further help for opponents of the Measure might be necessary. Some observers have also suggested that by 1993 Synod was tired of debating the ordination of women legislation, leaving little appetite for a protracted struggle over the plans – particularly since the loss of more clergy and congregations through the Financial Provisions Measure at a time of deep financial crisis was hard to contemplate.[98] Most importantly, however, many Synod members appear to have viewed the Act of Synod as an act of fairness towards the dissenting minority. The Church had been 'fair' to women and now it seemed only right to be 'fair' to opponents of women's priesting.[99] If this was the case Synod was not so much changing its mind on women's priesting as acting quite consistently with its previous behaviour on this question.

Having said that, responses to the Act of Synod did not straightforwardly reflect dividing lines between 'supporters' and 'opponents'.[100] Even within MOW itself, attitudes differed widely – not least because the future role and purpose of the organization was also under debate now that its main objective had been achieved. It was a measure of the breadth of its membership that whilst some talked of fighting the Act of Synod and beginning the campaign for women bishops, others even seemed hesitant to celebrate the progress so far and accepted the short-term pastoral necessity of the Act. In the event, MOW continued to make the case that the provisions of the Act of Synod were discriminatory, but once the first

---

[94] *Being in Communion*, para. 18 (Resolution 1 of the 1988 Lambeth Conference).

[95] *Being in Communion*, paras 6, 7.

[96] Although proposals for some form of extended episcopal care were discussed in both the 1986 McClean Report (GS738) and the 1987 House of Bishops report (GS 764) on women's priesting, the balance of opinion amongst the reports' authors was not in favour of adopting a system of extended episcopal oversight at this stage, and it did not find its way into the draft Women Priests measure.

[97] int. 4:p.7.

[98] One interviewee who was a member of General Synod suggested this had been an important issue for at least some of his colleagues. The speaker in question was amongst those who had strongly supported women's ordination as priests in 1992, but also voted for the Act of Synod in 1993 (int. cs2:13:400).

[99] int. 9side3:35f. The speaker ascribed this original interpretation of General Synod's action to long-standing member of MOW and WATCH, Monica Furlong. Notably, some supporters of an all-male priesthood similarly interpreted the result, suggesting that supporters of women's priesthood may have been sufficiently pleased with the November 1992 result to feel that they could afford to be generous to the minority view (int. 17:33).

[100] For more on this, see Chapter 9.

women were ordained priest in 1994, the organization was wound up, with its original objective reached. At a diocesan level, too, more informal groups of women and their supporters continued to meet, but many seemed to have felt these were increasingly superfluous now that women could be priested. Even some of the more radical voices in MOW conceded (partly for strategic reasons) that 'whatever happened in the future, a new organization would have to do it; we couldn't go on being seen to be the same organization that had been working for so long ... some of us who were so identified with it that we needed some others'.[101] By 1996, a mounting sense that the work of supporting women's ministry was far from over led to the creation of Women and the Church (WATCH), formed out of a London-based group of the same name, aimed at supporting and campaigning for the development of women's ministry in the Church of England, whilst monitoring the experiences of the new female priests and the outworking of the legislation.[102] Indeed, many former members of MOW now came to see the years between 1992 and 1996 as a time of lost initiative. As long-standing member Peter Selby wrote, 'those of us who supported the legislation were not... continuing to sustain ourselves as a powerful movement with a well thought-out programme or strategy, and if we now flawed the responsibility for that is one we share' wish to say that the Act of Synod is seriously.[103]

Nevertheless, in the short term, the Priests (Ordination of Women) Measure and the accompanying Ordination of Women (Financial Provisions) Measure received parliamentary assent by an overwhelming majority in the House of Commons on 29 October 1993 and in the Lords four days later.[104] Within weeks, General Synod approved the Episcopal Ministry Act of Synod, which enshrined the plans for extended episcopal oversight developed from the Manchester Statement and existing proposals by Bishop of London David Hope. The legislation went forward for Royal Assent, and Canon C4B, enabling the ordination of women to the priesthood, was finally promulged in late February 1994 after several last minute challenges in the courts had fallen. The first ordinations of women as priests in the Church of England could now finally take place.

1.4 Women deacons and their supporters: preparing for priesthood

For most female deacons and strong supporters of women's ordination as priests, 1992-94 was a period of anxious but excited wait for the first priestings. No story of the two years following the November 1992 vote would be complete without a short account of this, although the first ordinations will not be chronicled in depth here, and have already been done so more fully elsewhere.[105] Since 1992 the bishops had drawn up guidelines for discerning the vocation of those women who were already deacons but wished to be considered for priesthood. The emphasis was placed upon 'discernment' rather than 'selection' or 'testing' to recognize the call that some had felt for years and correspondingly no further training would be required before ordination to the priesthood.[106] For many, the priesting of women held out the promise of fulfilment of a long-held calling. For some, this calling had always specifically been to priesthood. Many had been engaged in extensive

---

[101] int. 8side2:528.

[102] For more on the inception of national WATCH, see: Rees (ed.), *Voices of this Calling*, pp. 9–10.

[103] Selby, 'Working the Act' in Furlong (ed.), *Act of Synod: Act of Folly?*, p. 80.

[104] House of Commons Official Report: Parliamentary Debates (Hansard), Vol. 230, no. 235, Friday 29 October 1993 (HMSO, London, 1993) and Parliamentary Debates (Hansard), *House of Lords: Official Report* Vol. 549, No. 194, Tuesday 2 November 1993 (HMSO, London, 1993). The Commons votes on the Main Measure and the Financial Provisions Measure were by 215 votes to 21 and 195 votes to 19 respectively, with those voting against mainly drawn from the Conservative and Northern Irish Unionist parties, and were mainly Anglo-Catholics, converts to Roman Catholicism, and Free Evangelicals.

[105] See, for instance, Rees (ed.), *Voices of this Calling*, passim.

[106] House of Bishops, 'Guidelines for the Testing and Discernment of Vocation and the Preparation for Ordination to the Priesthood of Women already in Deacons' Orders' (London, June 1993).

Christian service (sometimes as deacons) during which they discerned a further calling to priesthood that could not yet be fulfilled. One female vicar from Diocese C remembered originally supposing her sense of calling to be bound up with her husband's ordained ministry, but gradually realized how she was herself 'doing priestly things' in her own work in the parish.[107] A female curate from the same diocese described how 'Particularly when the vote went forward, it was "Yes ... you've got to go forward – you can't now run away from it, now that it is [possible]".'.[108] Indeed, in a smaller number of cases, the vote itself offered additional food for thought: one woman remembered how, 'during deaconess time, I never imagined priesthood was a possibility, though when in my training I discovered that that was my calling'.[109]

However, despite the novelty of the situation, few of the first generation of women to be priested remembered the discernment of their vocation to priestly ministry as a complicated process. Only two main problems seem to have presented themselves in a minority of occasions: firstly, women's own perceptions of their vocation could sometimes conflict with the expectations of their DDO or selections secretary – and not necessarily in the most obvious ways. Several women's testimonies suggested an eagerness amongst some selectors to recommend women for priesthood when they themselves had initially candidated as deacons: one female deacon considered it unbiblical for her to take a headship role and her church had to write to the Archbishop of Canterbury to ensure she was not priested.[110] Sometimes a further hurdle could be erected by a sponsoring diocese or parish: one female student at Cuddesdon in the years following the vote remembered some parishes dropping their female candidates, whom they would have been happy to accept as deacons, but less certain of accepting as priests.[111] The women deacons of Diocese C faced a further, more agonizing, time as they waited to see whether their diocesan bishop would decide to ordain them. Many ordained women I interviewed in the diocese recounted to me the meeting at which their bishop announced his decision. Tension mounted as he read out his prepared statement, charting his anguished journey of faith on the matter. Only at the end did he finally announce that he would, after all, ordain women as priests. Itching to celebrate, but holding back out of consideration for his feelings, the tension felt by the diocese's female deacons was finally broken only by one of the assembled clergy who suggested that perhaps, after all this, a good cup of tea was in order.

The very first women to become priests in the Church of England were ordained in Bristol Cathedral on 12 March 1994. It had been decided that special ordination services should be held for women who had been waiting for priesthood as deacons; and a slightly heady unofficial scramble then ensued to see who could be the first diocese to do so. In the event, the first woman to receive the laying-on of hands (from Bishop Barry Rogerson of Bristol), Angela Berners-Wilson, remembered the 'weight of expectation and hope, or anger and rejection', the sense of joy at now being able to fulfil her calling, the opportunities and burdens of conducting so many television interviews, and the letters 'ninety-nine per cent ... extremely positive' from well-wishers around the world, who promised to pray for her as she took this step.[112] Generally the ordination services passed off with little interruption, despite fears that protests may take place. Helen Thorne's analysis of the reminiscences of that first generation of women to be priested noted how memories of the occasion were frequently rich in theological significance and religious symbolism; in particular, a sense of

---

[107] int. cs3:9:p.1.
[108] int. cs3:25:15.
[109] int. cs5:3:13.
[110] The Revd Carrie Sandom interviewed in *Church Times*, 08.11.02, p. 9.
[111] int. cs2:10:117.
[112] Angela Berners-Wilson, 'Pilgrimage to Priesthood' in Rees (ed.), *Voices of this Calling*, pp. 181–4.

boundaries being broken down and the Kingdom of God being advanced.[113] These qualities remained characteristic of the recollections gathered in this project. As one of the first women to be ordained in Diocese C remembered, the cathedral was packed on the day of the service itself – so much so that stewards hurried around trying to find extra chairs. All sorts of people seemed to be present, but most striking to her was that the cathedral seemed full of people with disabilities. 'It was almost like a prophetic sign – the poor, the blind and the lame! They were obviously the people women had been ministering to, who had been touched by women's ministry',[114] but it also seemed to her a sign the Kingdom of God was here, as the first generation of women were priested in the Church of England. Now English women could play a new part in the furtherance of that kingdom.

Conclusion

This first chapter has taken a primarily narrative approach to the years of the early 1990s as the legislation to ordain women as priests was prepared, debated and enacted for the first time. It sets the scene for the analysis of current attitudes and experiences that follows, emphasizing the delicate balance of convictions that existed in 1992 but also – most importantly – the atmosphere of celebration that for many surrounded the vote. But it has also raised a number of key themes and issues that are relevant to that analysis: first, though the 1992–94 period was partly a time of watching and waiting to see what would happen after the vote, it was also a period during which patterns of response to the new situation began to take shape: the nature of the legislation and the ways in which individual dioceses responded to the result could often be influential in determining if and how the different positions on women's priesting could work alongside each other in the future. Neither a realignment in institutional church politics nor the role of campaign and lobby groups were by any means new, but the experience of debating the ordination of women arguably added another dimension to this mix. The reaction of the bishops to issues related to women's ministry was powerfully shaped in this period, and their tendency to see resolution in the balancing of two opposing campaigning groups ('women' and 'opponents') also continued to be an important feature in the following decade.

However, the chapter has also suggested that seeing the debate merely in terms of two opposed campaigning groups – 'women' (and their supporters) in favour, 'opponents' against' – is unsatisfactory. Whilst the ordination of women debate became a defining issue for some, it was only a matter of passing interest, sometimes irrelevance, for others. Those generally considered to be 'pro' women priests could differ considerably on their reasons, or their approach to the vote and what happened next. The same was true for those labelled 'anti women priests'. Conversely, some 'supporters' and 'opponents' could share the same hopes and fears for women's priesting, whilst disagreeing over whether it should happen in the first place. Indeed, now that women *had* been ordained, it is arguable that support for, or opposition to, the principle of women as priests/presbyters was now somewhat less important than how one responded to the new, post-1992 environment in the Church of England. If the chapter has suggested that simple categories of 'for' or 'against' are inadequate in tracing the contours of the Church's response to women's priesting, it has also drawn an important distinction between a 'no compromise' response to the result, an alternative response of greater willingness to work with an imperfect solution, a further alternative response of actively attempting to reconcile the different positions, and a fourth, more indifferent response, which ignored or held at arm's length the whole debate. This pattern of responses will be revisited in subsequent chapters before being more fully developed in Part III of the report.

---

[113] Thorne, *Journey to Priesthood*, p. 121.
[114] int. cs3:12:182.

Meanwhile, no sooner had the vote been taken than observers began to consider the meaning and significance of ordaining women as priests. What would the impact of the decision be? How would the legislation work in practice? To what extent would accepting a female priest – or voting to pass the resolutions – have an effect on a parish and its congregation? How, moreover, was the vote itself to be interpreted? Had it been the proper outcome of a growing appetite for women's priesting within the Church of England, or an unwelcome change foisted upon a reluctant church by a minority of enthusiasts. Whilst the history of the national debate has been comparatively well documented, much less is known about the strength of opinion amongst Anglican clergy and laity at grass roots level. Chapter 2 therefore considers the possible patterns of support and opposition to women's priesting amongst the case study dioceses and congregations, as a further part of the 'map' of the debate.

Chapter 2

Patterns of support and opposition

Contentment is not vociferous. The majority of people in the congregations of the Church of England are clearly either very pleased to have women priests, or have taken it in their stride, wondering what all the fuss is about.[1]

As the Church of England begins to reflect upon the significance of the decision to ordain women as priests, there is continued interest in how far the General Synod vote of 1992 was a fair reflection of the views of grass roots clergy and congregations. Throughout the interviewing process, many participants were keen to know what percentage of the Church now accepted women's priesting, how many did not. After expectation was widespread that clergy and churchgoers who had stood out against the decision would either quickly leave or gradually accommodate to the new position. On the contrary, Helen Thorne's interviews with the first generation of women to be priested left her with the impression that 'far from disappearing, opposition to women's ministry is well organized, vocal and growing'.[2] In 2002, one contributor to the *Church Times* letters page even went so far as to suggest that 'the enthusiasm of the vast majority of churchgoers' for women priests was just 'spin'.[3] Any adequate map of the Church of England's experience of women's priesting must therefore give some consideration to the changing levels of support and opposition to the move over its first decade. Chapter 2 seeks to provide this. Drawing on the results of the questionnaires to clergy and congregations and also on some published diocesan statistics, it explores how far Church of England clergy and laity might have welcomed the move to ordain women as priests, whether support is growing or declining and which groups are more and less likely to be in favour.

This comparatively brief survey cannot hope to be exhaustive. Here, the central aim is to investigate clergy and lay attitudes to women's priesting as a fact of the late twentieth-century Church of England. A simple yes/no question such as 'do you agree with women's ordination as priests?' is too probably too general to be of use in the contained environment of a questionnaire survey (not least in that in 1992 a significant minority declared themselves in favour of women's priesting in principle, but unconvinced on matters of timing). Instead, respondents were invited to give their views in the light of the specific decision taken by the Church of England in 1992. Since the results are derived from a series of case studies rather than a cross-sectional model, one should exercise extreme caution in generalizing out from this data about the experience of the Church of England as a whole. Since the completion of the survey was voluntary, it was most likely to be returned by those with strong opinions on the subject, and response rates would inevitably vary from diocese to diocese, church to church. Where 'closed answer' data is used (i.e., where the respondent is invited to tick a box or rate their view along a scale) this can lead to an overly reductive interpretation, and therefore it is important that the patterns outlined in this chapter are read alongside the more qualitative data presented in the rest of the report (particularly Chapter 3).

---

[1] Hilary Wakeman, 'What Difference is Women's Priesthood Making in the Pews?', in Hilary Wakeman (ed.), *Women Priests: The First Years* (Darton, Longman and Todd, London, 1996), pp. 1–26 (p. 1).
[2] Helen Thorne, *Journey to Priesthood; An In-Depth Study of the First Women Priests in the Church of England* (University of Bristol, Bristol, 2000), p. 17.
[3] Letter to the Editor from Joanna Monckton, *Church Times*, 14 June 2002.

Nevertheless, the quantitative data explored here may provide a rough framework for understanding changing patterns in the acceptance of women's priestly ministry, as a prelude to the discussion of more specific issues in the rest of the report. Notably, it may help to shed some new light on the existing (and often conflicting) assumptions about what levels of 'support' or 'opposition' to the 1992 decision exist. Throughout the debate on women's priesting and its implications, statistics have been a highly attractive source of legitimation to several of the different positions on women's priesting – even some who would otherwise reject the suggestion that social science methodology had anything to say on the question. As Nathan Keyfitz has commented, 'numbers provide the rhetoric of our age.[4] Some readers will be fundamentally sceptical about the value of statistics and questionnaire data to a report on women's priesting: does it amount to theology by opinion poll? Here, another word of reassurance is in order: the survey material presented in this chapter is not intended to decide the rightness or otherwise of women's priesting by appeal to popular support. Instead, it simply seeks to provide informative commentary on the current position.

2.1 Diocesan and deanery voting

First then, how far did Church of England clergy and laity support the decision to ordain women as priests? For the period before 1992, very little information exists on grass roots Anglican attitudes. Our best sources of information are diocesan and deanery synod voting figures on motions and draft legislation connected with women's ordination. Deanery synod figures in particular provide fairly reliable data on levels of support amongst clergy, although the number of lay men and women serving on deanery synods represent only a tiny (and unrepresentative) proportion of active churchgoers – so the lay voting figures referred to here should be treated with greater caution. Beginning in 1975, diocesan synods were asked to vote on two related questions: first whether there were any fundamental objections to the ordination of women as priests, and second whether the barriers to women's ordination should be removed in consequence. In the first vote, thirty of the forty-four diocesan synods voted in favour, with average support of 60% of clergy and 70% of laity across the synods. Already sharp differences in levels of support between dioceses were emerging: 81% of clergy in the Canterbury diocesan synod and 89% of laity in the Birmingham diocesan synod voted in favour, whilst Truro's diocesan synod recorded the lowest percentage in favour amongst both clergy and laity: 27% and 43% respectively.[5] However, whilst most diocesan synods agreed that there were 'no fundamental objections to the ordination of women as priests', only eleven of the forty-four synods voted to remove the barriers to legislation.

How had patterns of support changed by the time of the diocesan synod votes on the Draft Ordination of Women Measure in 1990?[6] The figure for lay synod members is almost exactly the same, suggesting that a majority of this constituency was already heavily in favour a decade and a half before the crucial vote. The fact that this figure has not risen substantially may perhaps be a function of the greater mobilization of concerned lay churchgoers by groups campaigning against women's priesting.[7] On the other hand, clergy

---

[4] Quoted in Raymond M. Lee, *Doing Research on Sensitive Topics* (Sage, London, 1993), p. 55.
[5] Of those dioceses whose figures are recorded. See GS Misc 252, *The Ordination of Women: Report of the Standing Committee on the Reference to the Dioceses* (CIO, London, 1975).
[6] All figures in this paragraph are derived from General Synod GS Misc 336, *The Ordination of Women to the Priesthood; Reference of Draft Legislation to the Diocesan Synods, 1990* (Church House, London, 1990), p. 3.
[7] Gill suggests the major mobilization of clergy and lay support for an all-male priesthood only began in the mid-1980s (Sean Gill, *Women in the Church of England, from the Eighteenth Century to the Present* (SPCK, London, 1994), pp. 254–5).

support had risen substantially; perhaps partly because of an equally active mobilization of male clergy who supported women's priesting, and partly because since 1987 women deacons were eligible to become members of the House of Clergy. However, as suggested below, even when these additional factors are taken into account, wider clergy opinion also seemed to have been moving slowly towards support for women's ordination as priests.

The 1990 deanery synod figures give a much clearer insight into clergy (and to some extent lay) opinion across the Church of England (**see Table 2i**): just over 70% of deanery synods gave approval to the draft legislation, with average support of 65% amongst deanery synod clergy and 69% amongst deanery synod laity. Again there was considerable variation between the dioceses, with the highest percentages tending to come in dioceses of the Canterbury province with a predominantly 'middle of the road' Anglican reputation (every deanery synod in Worcester, Bristol, Guildford and St Albans[8] dioceses voted for the legislation). On the other hand, dioceses with a strong history of Anglo-Catholicism tended to return the lowest percentages: in the diocese of Chichester, only one in three deanery synods and only 43% of clergy voted for the legislation.[9] If these figures are compared to those for the 1990 diocesan synod debates, deanery synod clergy tended to be on average *more* favourable than those clergy sitting on diocesan synods (perhaps meaning that the results of the diocesan debates slightly underestimated the degree of support for women's priesting amongst serving clergy as a whole). Conversely, diocesan synod laity voted more heavily in favour of women's priesting than their counterparts in deanery synod. For both clergy and laity, however, the differences in levels of support between diocesan and deanery synods were not greatly significant.

---

[8] Of course, some will suggest that these dioceses have an explicitly liberal (rather than central) tradition, but even if that is true of their leadership, it is much less true of the parishes, which do not as a whole tend particularly strongly in any direction.
[9] Although as in every other diocese, a majority of lay deanery synod members were in favour: the lowest recorded percentage came in the Truro diocese, where 54% of the deanery synods in the diocese voted for the draft legislation.

Table 2i: Percentage of deanery synod clergy and laity voting in favour of the Draft Women Priests Legislation, 1990, by diocese[10]

Diocese	% clergy 'yes'	% laity 'yes'	Diocese	% clergy 'yes'	% laity 'yes'
Bath & Wells	61	70	London	53	55
Birmingham	62	64	Manchester	69	61
Blackburn	52	61	Newcastle	53	61
Bradford	67	69	Norwich	56	69
Bristol	79	71	Oxford	66	67
Canterbury	68	69	Peterborough	57	67
Carlisle	65	73	Portsmouth	55	62
Chelmsford	60	62	Ripon	66	69
Chester	57	56	Rochester	65	69
Chichester	43	61	St Alban's	76	73
Coventry	74	68	St Ed & Ips	62	73
Derby	67	67	Salisbury	69	70
Durham	Figures not supplied		Sheffield	61	58
Ely	64	66	Sodor & Man	Figures not supplied	
Exeter	51	63	Southwark	74	74
Gloucester	63	69	Southwell	72	70
Guildford	68	73	Truro	48	54
Hereford	67	73	Wakefield	62	61
Leicester	58	67	Winchester	65	69
Lichfield	65	63	Worcester	81	78
Lincoln	66	69	York	63	68
Liverpool	72	68	Europe	51	62

2.2 *Overall patterns in the questionnaires for clergy and congregations*

The pattern seemingly already well established by 1992, of greater support amongst laity, a more substantial difference of opinion amongst clergy and a slow increase in support for women's priesthood overall, also seemed evident in the Questionnaire for Clergy and Questionnaire for Congregations circulated to the six case studies in 2001–2. **Table 2ii** provides a comparison of the percentages currently agreeing or disagreeing with the Church's 1992 decision to ordain women as priests, amongst diocesan clergy in the three main case studies[11] and a selection of members of the three case study congregations in these dioceses. With the significant exceptions of Churches 3, 6 and 8 – the three congregations passing resolutions barring women from exercising priestly ministry in the parish – levels of agreement amongst lay churchgoers are at least as high (and levels of disagreement significantly lower) than amongst clergy. The results of the three main diocesan clergy case studies in **Table 2ii** suggest majority support for the Church's decision to ordain women as priests (with the majority of clergy in 'strong agreement'). Not entirely surprisingly, where women constitute a larger percentage of the diocesan clergy sample, support for women's priesting is also higher. Higher levels of support are also generally found in dioceses with below average numbers of parishes passing one or more of the resolutions.[12] For example, Diocese B shows high levels of support for women's priesting, has an above-average proportion of female clergy and few parishes passing resolutions;

---

[10] Based on figures given in: GSS Misc. 336, *The Ordination of Women to the Priesthood; Reference of Draft Legislation to the Diocesan Synods, 1990* (Church House, London, 1990).

[11] Unless otherwise stated, all figures relate to currently serving diocesan clergy, and exclude retired clergy.

[12] Although as discussed below, this does not mean that there is a complete correlation between clergy views on women's priesting and whether or not they work in a parish with one or more resolutions in place.

Dioceses A and C (which show much lower levels of support) have more parishes with resolutions in place.

Table 2ii: Levels of agreement with the 1992 decision to ordain women as priests in the main case studies			
Diocese/church samples	No. of cases	% 'strongly agree' and 'agree'	% 'disagree' and 'strongly disagree'
Diocese A Clergy	90	81.1	16.6
Diocese A Church 1	39	92.1	7.9
Diocese A Church 2	21	80	5.0
Diocese A Church 3	26	61.5	30.7
Diocese B Clergy	115	88.7	9.6
Diocese B Church 4	20	90	0.0
Diocese B Church 5	38	92.1	2.6
Diocese B Church 6	28	25.9	66.7
Diocese C Clergy	99	78.7	16.1
Diocese C Church 7	61	90.2	3.2
Diocese C Church 8	8	12.5	75.0
Diocese C Church 9	19	100[13]	0

2.3 How far have clergy attitudes changed?

Significantly, the percentages of case study clergy *currently* in support are much higher than in the deanery voting figures of 1992 discussed above. Why might this be? In part, it is because a cohort of those who voted against the legislation in 1992 subsequently left the Anglican priesthood or took early retirement, and are thus absent from any later opinion survey such as this one. Current levels of agreement are also much higher because women are more heavily represented amongst the clergy than in the deanery voting figures of 1992, and are with only very few exceptions supportive of the decision to ordain women as priests. However, a change in the demographic profile of Anglican clergy does not by itself explain the apparent change in levels of support, since the evidence also suggests that some of those surveyed had changed their minds in favour of women's priesting since the vote.

In addition to surveying their *current* views on women's priesting, the Questionnaire for Clergy also asked respondents to rate their level of agreement *at the time of the vote*, along the same scale of 'strongly disagree' to 'strongly agree' (effectively inviting them to assess whether their views were now more, less or equally favourable). As **Table 2iii** suggests, a significant minority of clergy may have shifted their views towards stronger agreement. In Diocese A, for example, 22.8% of clergy rated women's priesting more favourably in 2001 than in 1992 (with only 1.1% less supportive). Even in Diocese C, where 4.1% of clergy now took a more negative view,[14] 27.6% had become more favourable. The most significant feature of the data was a clear upturn in the percentage of clergy 'strongly agreeing' with the move. In some dioceses a clear majority of clergy already 'strongly agreed' in 1992, but

---

[13] The sample from Church 9 was a very small percentage of the population and seems to have picked up only those members of the congregation who were in favour of women's priesting. However, it is known that a range of opinions existed within the congregations of Church 9, to the extent that senior diocesan figures even believed the parish may have been close to passing resolutions A and B at one stage in its history (although it had moved further away from that position in recent years). This stands as a further warning that questionnaire data must always be handled with caution and ultimately interpreted alongside other sources of evidence. Evidence from the other eight churches offers no reason to suppose that the questionnaire results from these are also skewed in this way, or in the opposite direction.

[14] The highest percentage by some way in any of the diocesan case studies.

by 2001 they had been joined by many who had previously rated their view as 'agree' or 'neither agree nor disagree'. In Diocese B, for example, 68.7% of clergy now 'strongly agreed' with women's priesting in 2001, compared with only 53% in 1992.

	Strongly agree		Agree		Neither agree nor disagree		Disagree		Strongly disagree	
	1992	2001	1992	2001	1992	2001	1992	2001	1992	2001
Diocese A	53.9	68.9	18	12.2	7.7	2.2	6.7	2.2	14.6	14.4
Diocese B	53.0	68.7	21.7	20.0	13.0	1.7	5.2	2.6	7.0	7.0
Diocese C	45.9	64.6	21.4	14.1	11.2	5.1	6.1	3.0	15.3	13.1
Deanery D	30.8	30.8	30.8	38.5	7.7	7.7	7.7	7.7	23.1	15.4
Deanery E	52.0	61.5	12.0	23.1	20.0	0.0	4.0	7.7	12.0	7.7
Deanery F	60.0	90.0	10.0	10.0	20.0	0.0	10.0	0.0	0.0	0.0

Table 2iii: Percentage support for the 1992 decision to ordain women as priests: clergy report their views of 1992 and 2001/2

Table 2iv: Change in attitude to the 1992 decision to ordain women as priests amongst clergy who 'strongly disagreed' and 'disagreed' in 1992 (numbers, in total sample)

Numbers of clergy moving from 'strongly disagree' to:		Numbers of clergy moving from 'disagree' to:	
Strongly disagree [i.e., no change]	34	Strongly disagree	2
Disagree	3	Disagree [i.e., no change]	5
Neither A nor D	3	Neither A nor D	2
Agree	0	Agree	6
Strongly agree	1	Strongly agree	4

What of clergy who disagreed with women's priesting in 1992? The data suggests that most continued to disagree. Only 2.7% of the total clergy sample had moved from a position of outright disagreement to one of outright agreement (although significantly, none had moved in the opposite direction). Those who 'strongly disagreed' in 1992 were most likely to remain of the same opinion (**Table 2iii** suggests the size of this group did not change much over the 1990s). However, as **Table 2iv** suggests, a small proportion of those with objections/ reservations over women's priesting had become more favourable by 2001. Despite this, the main trend appeared to be towards a strengthening of conviction at either end of the spectrum: a greater number of clergy in 'strong agreement', a largely unchanged minority in 'strong disagreement' and a shrinking number of respondents adopting one of the intermediate positions ('agree', 'neither agree nor disagree', 'disagree'). This suggests at the very least that experience of women's ministry as priests and the 1992–94 settlement has tended to resolve uncertainty on the question, and perhaps even suggests a growing degree of polarization in clergy opinion.

2.4 *Attitudes amongst the case study congregations*

What of the views in the case study churches? Congregations Questionnaire respondents were asked: 'overall, how far do you agree with the Church of England's decision in 1992 to ordain women as priests?'. **Table 2v** presents a breakdown of the responses from the nine main case study congregations[15] and from thirteen further congregations from the three deanery case studies.[16] Although only a portion of each congregation was therefore surveyed (and the results must be treated with caution as a result), several important patterns emerge: first, just as with Anglican clergy, the weight of opinion amongst lay respondents surveyed is strongly in favour of the Church of England's decision to ordain women as priests. No overall percentage of support for women's priesting amongst the lay sample is provided because it would be meaningless to try and extrapolate a more generally representative figure from such a small selection of case studies. However, it may be significant that most of the congregations exhibited higher levels of agreement with women's priesting than the 64% figure suggested by the Cost of Conscience Survey, 'The Mind of Anglicans'.[17]

On the other hand, the results of the Congregations Questionnaire also reflect the spectrum of opinion that is present in almost every church.[18] Congregations with the resolutions in place all included regular churchgoers who supported women's priesting (e.g., Church 15), whilst the 1992 decision did not receive universal acceptance even in congregations with a female incumbent (e.g., Church 5). However, support for women's ordination as priests is particularly strong in parishes with an ordained woman on the staff team (e.g., Churches 1, 7, 13 and 22) and notably weak in parishes with one or more resolutions in place (e.g., Churches 6 and 8). Support is particularly low where a parish has to some extent acquired a reputation in its local area as a 'safe haven' for those who regret the Church's decision to ordain women. However, it is wise not to generalize too far; several of the case study congregations with no experience of women's priestly ministry also returned high levels of support (e.g., Churches 4, 11 and 23).[19] And in Church 3, a majority of respondents agreed with women's priesting despite what the Congregation's Resolution A and B status might otherwise suggest.

---

[15] Where up to 100 questionnaires were distributed randomly amongst attenders. Churches 1, 2, 4, 5, 6, 7 and 9 each received 100 (in each case representing a lesser or greater proportion of the regular congregations. Churches 3, 6 and 8 received 60 questionnaires, since they were smaller congregations).

[16] In these, four to five congregations were chosen and thirty questionnaires were distributed to selected churchgoers, as far as possible in proportion to the demographic profile of the congregation.

[17] Robbie Low, 'The Mind of Anglicans' [part of a digest of the full survey, presented in:] *New Directions* vol. 5, no. 86, July 2002, pp. 17–19.

[18] Only Church 9 shows 100% support for the decision amongst respondents to the questionnaire. However, a very low return rate for this congregation almost certainly obscures the variety of opinions on women's priesting that were known to be present amongst members of the regular congregation.

[19] Although it should be added that Church 4 has for many years enjoyed the ministry of a female lay pastoral assistant who at the time of the study was undertaking ordination training. Experience of women's ministry did not necessarily need to mean women's *priestly* ministry to encourage a more receptive attitude to the ordination of women to the priesthood.

Case	Strongly agree	Agree	Neither agree nor disagree	Disagree	Strongly disagree	Numbers returned
Table 2v: Percentage support amongst 22 case study congregations for the Church of England's decision in 1992 to allow women to become priests (shaded area shows most common answers for each church)						
1 (A)	81.6	10.5	0	2.6	5.3	39
2 (A)	50	30	15	5	0	21
3 (A)	26.9	34.6	7.7	19.2	11.5	26
4 (B)	75	15	10	0	0	20
5 (B)	47.4	44.7	5.3	2.6	0	38
6 (B)	7.4	18.5	7.4	11.1	55.6	27
7 (C)	70.5	19.7	6.6	1.6	1.6	62
8 (C)	12.5	0	12.5	25	50	8
9 (C)	83.3	16.7	0	0	0	19
10 (D)	47.1	41.2	0	0	11.8	18
11 (D)	65.3	17.4	4.3	4.3	8.7	23
12 (D)	23.5	29.4	23.5	17.6	5.9	17
13 (D)	78.6	14.3	0	0	7.1	15
15 (E)	0	10	20	10	60	20
16 (E)	47.8	34.8	4.3	4.3	8.7	23
17 (E)	9.1	36.4	18.2	13.6	22.7	22
18 (E)	42.9	14.3	28.6	14.3	0	7
19 (E)	53.8	34.6	7.7	3.8	0	26
20 (F)	50	35.7	7.1	0	7.1	14
21 (F)	14	28.6	28.6	0	23.6	8
22 (F)	77.3	22.7	0	0	0	22
23 (F)	66.7	8.3	8.3	8.3	8.3	12

2.5 How far have lay attitudes changed?

The strong support shown for women's ordination as priests in many congregations begs the question of how far lay attitudes have changed over the first decade of the new settlement. Here, the answer is more complicated than for the clergy sample, since no comparable question was asked about the respondent's view in 1992 (interviews confirmed that lay respondents were in general less likely to recall in detail their views of ten years previously). Instead, participants in the Congregations Questionnaire were asked if their opinion had changed over the time since the decision was taken, whether their views on women's priesting had been a factor in choosing a church in the past, and whether they might become so in the future. In response, very few participants said that their views had changed (less than 10% of respondents from most congregations, although in Church 7 – a largely evangelical congregation with a female incumbent – over 18% acknowledged a change of mind. The reasons for this are discussed further in Chapter 4). Moreover, as **Table 2vi** suggests, only a minority of respondents said their current choice of church *had* been influenced by their views on women's ordination as priests. Significantly, more respondents believed their views on women priests would influence their choice of church in the future. The largest shifts in attitude here tended to come amongst members of evangelical congregations (for example, Churches 2, 4, 11 and 16)[20] once again highlighting

---

[20] Curiously, Church 7 was the major exception to this trend – at least according to the questionnaire data. In fact, interviews with church members revealed a considerable degree of politicization over issues of women in ministry. Some, for example, were angry at the apparent inability of senior clergy to find stipendiary posts

the extent to which the climate of opinion in Anglican evangelicalism may have been crucial in the outcome of the 1992 debate (and may still be in relation to women in the episcopate, as Chapter 8 will suggest). Interestingly, respondents from parishes that had passed the resolutions did not always think their views on women's priesting would be influential in any future choice of church they made: in Churches 3, 6 and 8 around a third of the congregation thought this might be relevant, whereas in Churches 15 and 21 (both of which receive extended episcopal oversight) respondents were much less likely to think their views on women's priesthood influential. It is worth remembering that people belong to churches for a wide variety of reasons, and even very strong opinions on women's priesting were not necessarily significant considerations for a majority of churchgoers when searching for a new place of worship and fellowship.

Table 2vi: My attitude to the ordination of women was/would be influential in my current choice of church/any choice of church I make in the future (% by congregation)

Church	Current	Future	Church	Current	Future
1 (A)	23.8	19.2	12 (D)	6.8	38.0
2 (A)	6.8	26.2	13 (D)	4.5	22.7
3 (A)	10.0	32.7	15 (E)	16.5	15.7
4 (B)	4.0	30.0	16 (E)	8.6	41.4
5 (B)	10.0	18.4	17 (E)	15.3	14.9
6 (B)	13.3	28.6	18 (E)	14.3	14.3
7 (C)	16.6	3.2	19 (E)	6.8	35.3
8 (C)	4.0	37.5	20 (F)	4.9	48.3
9 (C)	15.8	16.2	21 (F)	4.5	0.0
10 (D)	4.5	17.1	22 (F)	8.6	17.8
11 (D)	8.2	16.4	23 (F)	4.9	28.3

2.6 Gender-related patterns

Within these overall patterns, which clergy and laity were most and least supportive of the Church of England's 1992 decision on women as priests? As **Figure 2vii** suggests, one of the key variables was gender – at least for clergy. Female clergy were overwhelmingly in favour of women's priesting,[21] whilst support amongst men was somewhat lower (although even in areas reputed to be strongholds of traditionalism, with few female clergy – such as Diocese D – two thirds of clergy questioned in the selected deanery were in favour). Given that male clergy seem less likely to support women's priesting than their female colleagues, can the growth in support for women's priesting amongst clergy therefore be attributed to the greater number of women now working as clergy? Again, the results suggest that if this is partly true, it is by no means the whole story. If we compare the attitudes of male and female clergy in the current sample for 1992 and 2001, we find that support has risen amongst men as well as women. Indeed, given that most of the female respondents to the clergy questionnaire were already in favour in 1992, one could even say that it is amongst male clergy that attitudes to women's priesting have changed most.

---

within the diocese for women who were former members of the congregation who had gone forward for ordination.

[21] The less than 100% support amongst female clergy from Diocese C can be accounted for by one respondent who ticked 'neither agree nor disagree'. She regretted the loss of time with her family and had been upset by the rudeness of some of her male colleagues.

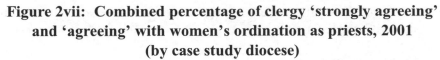

Figure 2vii: Combined percentage of clergy 'strongly agreeing' and 'agreeing' with women's ordination as priests, 2001 (by case study diocese)

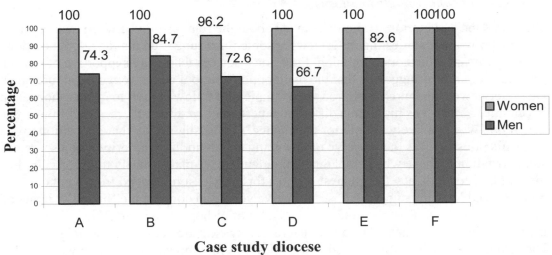

Table 2viii: Percentage 'strongly agreeing' and 'agreeing' (combined) with women's ordination as priests across the 22 congregations (by gender)					
Church	**Female**	**Male**	**Church**	**Female**	**Male**
1 (A)	85	100	**12 (D)**	70.0	28.6
2 (A)	78.6	83.3	**13 (D)**	92.3	100
3 (A)	60.9	66.6	**15 (E)**	16.7	0
4 (B)	85.7	100	**16 (E)**	85.7	77.7
5 (B)	93.1	88.9	**17 (E)**	42.8	50.0
6 (B)	31.8	0	**18 (E)**	66.7	50.0
7 (C)	92.7	85.7	**19 (E)**	92.9	83.4
8 (C)	16.7	0	**20 (F)**	83.3	100
9 (C)	100	100	**21 (F)**	50.0	0
10 (D)	83.6	100	**22 (F)**	100	100
11 (D)	87.5	71.5	**23 (F)**	66.7	100

Whilst in the clergy survey dissent from the 1992 decision was most likely to come from men, popular opinion expected a different pattern when it came to the laity. Conversations with both clergy and churchgoers revealed a widespread perception that the strongest opposition to women's priesting came from lay *women* rather than lay men. However, the results of the Questionnaire for Congregations presented in **Table 2viii** suggest no straightforward gender-related patterns amongst lay respondents. The results from the resolution parishes ran particularly contrary to popular expectation, since here, male members of the congregation were most likely to disagree with the ordination of women as priests (in Church 6, for example, 31.8% of women 'agreed' or 'strongly agreed', but 0% of men[22]). However, although men seemed most likely to be opposed in congregations officially opting out of women's priestly ministry, this should not be taken as representative

---

[22] The other two resolution parishes are Church 3 and Church 10. Church 10 may be regarded as an exceptional case here, since although it has Resolution B in place, it also had a female curate.

of the views of male churchgoers in general: a very rough aggregate of the survey samples suggested 76% of women and 74% of men 'strongly agreed' or 'agreed' with the move – not a particularly significant difference (although of course aggregate figures of this kind should be treated with particular caution).

2.7 Age- and cohort-related patterns

Alongside the assumptions sometimes made about the relationship between gender and support for women's priesting, interviewees sometimes suggested that age or generation were significant indicators of opinion. First, interviewees who were supportive of women's priesting sometimes suggested that the main opposition to it came from older churchgoers. One interviewee in Church 3 offered the example of a fellow church member who was 'in his eighties… that puts him into a different generation… a different era… and I think that generation was less likely to vote for the change'.[23] This suggestion that opposition to women's priesting was the preserve of an ageing and dwindling minority was a source of some irritation to those who campaigned to defend an all-male priestly tradition.[24] In the view of this constituency the greatest support for the Measure derived from a cohort of ordained and lay campaigners whose formative years had come in the 'liberal' climate of the 1960s:[25] at the time of the vote 'you had a lot of bishops who were fifties, sixties men…', reflected one priest from a parish receiving extended episcopal oversight in Diocese B.[26] As such it was implied that enthusiasm for women's ordination would only be a passing phase. (This construction of women priests as 'yesterday's fashion' by some defenders of an all-male priesthood presupposed a much larger set of beliefs about the direction of the Church of England in the twentieth century.)[27] But did the questionnaire responses suggest a more hesitant attitude to women's priesting amongst the oldest age groups? Conversely, was support for women's priesting most common amongst those whose formative years came in the 1960s?

Table 2ix: Percentage of clergy and lay questionnaire respondents 'agreeing' or 'strongly agreeing' with the decision to ordain women as priests (by age group)				
	Clergy % (no. of cases in brackets)		**[Laity][28] (no. of cases)**	
Under 20	n/a	(0)	[80][29]	(5)
20-9	100	(4)	[69.2]	(13)
30-9	76.4	(41)	[72.7]	(33)
40-9	84.3	(104)	[79.1]	(67)
50-9	88.1	(144)	[82.6]	(98)
60-9	75.3	(91)	[72.7]	(128)
70-9	77.8	(36)	[71.4]	(105)
80+	71.4	(7)	[67.6]	(34)

---

[23] int. cs1:7:204.

[24] 'Do not permit our detractors to say that traditionalists in the Church of England are all above a certain age!' said one report on a Forward in Faith youth event in *New Directions* 1 (11) April 1996, p. 10.

[25] 'Liberal' here is placed in inverted commas in order to avoid the common over-generalization that the 1960s were only to be characterized by liberal radicalism. A much richer picture of that decade is presented in: Arthur Marwick, *The Sixties: Cultural Revolution in Britain, France, Italy and the United States, c. 1958–1974* (Oxford University Press, Oxford, 1998).

[26] int. cs2:5side2:575.

[27] It is hoped to explore this further in a future publication.

[28] Appears in square brackets to indicate that the figure should not be taken as resulting from a representative sample of Anglican congregations.

[29] Only 5 lay respondents under 20 returned questionnaires, so here the sample is too small to be of much value.

Table 2ix breaks down clergy and lay support for women's priesting by age group, this time including the responses from a number of retired clergy from the three main case study dioceses, who were also surveyed. The results should be treated with care, since the questionnaire responses came disproportionately from those aged between 40 and 70,[30] with comparatively few responses from younger people. In particular, whilst the clergy sample offers a reasonably accurate breakdown of opinion, the lay sample is based upon only a small selection of congregations, and a different selection would have resulted in very different results.[31] Nevertheless, the responses suggest some tendency for older respondents (both clergy and lay) to be less likely to agree with the decision to ordain women as priests. In both cases, the 80+ age group was less enthusiastic about the change, with levels of support increasing amongst those in mid-adulthood and (amongst the laity) in the under-20s age group. Amongst clergy, the picture was slightly different, with the 40-59 age group slightly more in favour. This may in part reflect the slightly greater preponderance of female clergy in middle age but this trend was also evident where the views of male clergy were considered by themselves. If the cohort of clergy currently in middle age were most heavily in favour of women's priesting, the influence of a 'post-1960s generation' in calling for women's ordination as priests should not be completely discounted. However, the actual result of the 1992 debate owed just as much to clergy and laity now in their sixties and seventies who have since retired from office; a group which (according to these results at least) were slightly less likely to support women's ordination as priests than younger age groups. Far from suggesting that enthusiasm for women's priesting was merely a passing fad of the 1960s, then, the result of the 1992 vote rested equally on the views of those who came after.

An alternative approach to the question of cohort difference is to examine not biological age but date of entry into the ordained ministry. If the experience of selection, training and first curacy was an important formative period for clergy of any age, it might be asked whether clergy ordained before, during or after the ordination of women debate show any differences in levels of support for the 1992 decision. **Table 2x** compares clergy attitudes (with retired clergy included here) across four cohorts of ordinations to the diaconate.[32]

- Those ordained before 1975 (at which point the Church's General Synod voted that there were 'no fundamental theological objections' to women's ordination as priests.
- Those ordained between 1975 and 1986 inclusive (after 1975 any man entering ordained ministry in the Church of England should have been aware that women's ordination was now a theoretical possibility, although until the vote to ordain women as deacons in 1986 it remained as such).

---

[30] Although this to some extent reflected a wider bias towards middle age and upwards amongst active Anglicans as a whole, the questionnaire responses were more than usually weighted towards the older end: 68% of the Congregations Questionnaire respondents were aged between 50 and 79, and two thirds of clergy respondents were aged in their forties and fifties. The comparative lack of teenagers and young adults answering the questionnaire may be explained partly by the lower response rates from evangelical churches (where these age groups are disproportionately to be found) and partly because respondents in early adulthood were widely considered to be 'time-poor' and thus less likely to fill in what was in fact quite a lengthy survey.
[31] Even so, 9.5% of the questionnaire returns came from congregations with resolutions in place and no women working as priests in the parish – a figure very comparable to the 9.6% of Church of England parishes with one or more of the resolutions in place.
[32] Date of ordination to the diaconate is used in preference to date of priesting, since this allows the inclusion of women entering ordained ministry before 1994.

- Those ordained between 1987 and 1993 (during which women were first ordained deacon, the women priests debate was at its height, but as yet priests could only be male).
- Those ordained after 1994 (from whence women and men followed the same path to ordination as deacons and priests, and after which all clergy had to accept the reality of women in priesthood, whether they agreed with it or not).

Table 2x: Attitudes to the 1992 decision to allow the ordination of women as priests, amongst successive cohorts of those ordained deacon/ commissioned deaconess (combined figure for six case studies)

	% 'strongly agree' and 'agree'			% 'disagree' and 'strongly disagree'		
	Female	Male	Overall	Female	Male	Overall
1975 and before	None[33]	73.1	73.1	None	23	23
1976–1986	100	78.4	79.4	0	15.7	15
1987–1993	97.7	89.5	93.2	0	10.6	5.9
1994 onwards	100	67.7	86.1	0	25.8	11.2

Table 2x suggests growing support for women's priesting across the oldest three cohorts. This is partly due to the increased numbers of women in successive cohorts, almost all of whom were in favour of the 1992 decision. However, the proportion of male clergy in favour drops amongst the post-1994 cohort. Does this signal a possible swing away from support for ordaining women amongst the rising generation of clergy? The signals are mixed: on one hand, leading campaigners for women in the Church sometimes expressed concern that the 1992–94 settlement allowed traditionalists to nurture vocations and train new clergy in virtual isolation from female candidates and the arguments for ordaining women. Certainly some theological colleges had acquired reputations for appealing to ordinands of one view or another, even if this was not always reflected in reality. On the other hand, few Diocesan Directors of Ordinands perceived a rise in vocations from resolution parishes. Nor (as already suggested) did clergy appear to be changing their minds *against* women's priesting (if anything, the reverse was true).

With a comparatively small number of cases considered here, the result may also be a statistical fluke. However, it seems unlikely that the figures contained in **Table 2x** reflect a rise in support for a male-only priesthood. For one thing, the pre-1994 cohorts of clergy represented here are now without those men who left the Church of England as a result of the 1992 vote. The first three rows of the table therefore possibly underestimate the numbers of those objecting to women's priesthood in the original cohort of ordinands.

The post-1994 cohort of clergy may also be without some supporters of an all-male priesthood who decided not to offer themselves for ministry as a result of the vote, but probably not in the same proportion as those who left from previous cohorts. Indeed, unlike their immediate predecessors, post-1994 ordinands with reservations or objections about women's priesting have decided to enter the Church of England fully knowing the current situation, benefiting from the existence of the 'safeguards' and prepared to work with (or in spite of) a situation they would not have chosen. However, in the last analysis, differences in levels of support between different age groups and clergy cohorts should not be overemphasized; at least two thirds of respondents in each age group either 'agreed' or

---

[33] Coincidentally, none of the responses came from women who had been ordained deaconess before 1975, although a few were present in each diocese.

'strongly agreed' with the Church's decision on women in priesthood. In this context, the disparities between younger and older respondents and different generational cohorts seem comparatively slight.

2.8 By Church tradition

Alongside the assumption that age and gender were significant, it was frequently suggested that Church tradition was a strong indicator of opinion. Traditionalist publications frequently suggested that women's priesting had been ushered in only with the ascendancy of a 'liberal agenda'[34] and that right-thinking Catholics and evangelicals would naturally advocate an all-male ministerial priesthood. Conversely, women in priesthood often reported most opposition to their ministry came from 'the black-shirted brigade'.[35] Others suggested that opposition to women's priesting was the preserve of 'Anglo-Catholics and Conservative Evangelicals' (indeed, very occasionally interviewees dropped the 'conservative' and implied that most evangelicals were against women's priesting). How far were these common assertions reflected in the questionnaire data? Clergy and lay respondents were asked to tick which of eight traditions most nearly corresponded to their own and their attitudes to the 1992 decision were analysed according to these designations. Again the results should be interpreted with caution, given that these are self-ascriptions and a significant minority of respondents could not (or would not) assign themselves any churchmanship. Others questioned the use of such labels altogether or preferred to leave the boxes blank and instead declare themselves 'Church of England', 'Christian', or 'Central'.[36] Nevertheless, the results provide a useful approximation of opinion amongst those who to some extent identify themselves with a particular tradition within Anglicanism.

Table 2xi summarizes the percentage of those of different traditions 'agreeing' or 'strongly agreeing' with women's priesting amongst male and female clergy, in the three main case study dioceses.[37] Agreement with the Church's 1992 decision seems most likely to come from those who placed themselves somewhere along the 'liberal' part of the spectrum, from Catholic to evangelical.[38] At the other end of the scale, clergy describing themselves as 'Anglo-Catholic' were least likely to accept the decision to ordain women as priests, although significantly this was almost exclusively due to the very low levels of support given by *male* Anglo-Catholic clergy. (There was some anecdotal evidence that female clergy from the Catholic tradition distanced themselves from the label 'Anglo-Catholic' because it was assumed to imply opposition to women's priesting.)[39] However, it was

---

[34] For example, int. cs1:3:427; int. cs3:25:150.

[35] Denoting Anglo-Catholic churchmanship from the common attire of many Anglo-Catholic clergy. Of course a black clerical shirt was not the exclusive preserve of Catholics, nor of those with reservations over women's ordination as priests. For more on the symbolic significance of clerical dress see Chapter 6.

[36] The question of 'central' churchmanship is an interesting one. Although a style of worship and participation we could designate 'middle Anglican' clearly exists (particularly in rural communities), it is much more difficult to define accurately. It was also occasionally suggested in interviews that the 'central' churchmanship formerly characteristic of many Anglican parishes was fast disappearing, to be replaced by more definitely evangelical, liberal or Catholic approaches. Despite the keenness of many respondents to identify themselves as 'central', the temptation to include a 'central' box on the questionnaire was strongly resisted since it was anticipated that respondents of very different traditions would want to identify themselves with the 'authentic middle ground' of the Church (see Conclusion for more on this). This suspicion proved well founded.

[37] Again, in several columns the numbers of cases referred to are less than five, so the results should be treated with caution.

[38] Here, 'Liberal-Evangelical' does not refer to the liberal evangelicalism of early twentieth-century American theology but to a more English kind of open evangelicalism. The difficulties of using any label were amply demonstrated where interviewees sometimes wished to identify themselves as 'Liberal' on women priests, but not on other doctrinal or ethical issues – or vice versa.

[39] Over a half of female clergy identified themselves as 'Liberal-Catholic' compared to around a third of

notable that Anglo-Catholic clergy were the only group not to show majority support for the decision to ordain women as priests.

Table 2xi: Percentage of clergy 'strongly agreeing' or 'agreeing' with the Church of England's decision to ordain women to the priesthood, by Church tradition (2001)								
	Diocese A			**Diocese B**			**Diocese C**		
	f	m	all (n =)	f	m	all (n =)	f	m	all (n=)
Anglo-Cath.	100	33.3	39.1 (23)	100	38.5	46.7 (15)	N/A	18.8	48.3 (24)
Lib.-Cath.	100	100	100 (35)	100	96.8	97.9 (47)	100	95.2	97.1 (34)
Liberal	100	100	100 (7)	100	100	100 (16)	100	100	100 (13)
Lib.-Evan.	100	100	100 (4)	100	100	100 (8)	N/A	100	100 (5)
Evangelical	100	66.6	80 (5)	N/A	100	100 (6)	N/A	100	100 (5)
Charis.-Ev.	N/A	100	100 (4)	100	80	83.3 (6)	100	71.4	77.8 (9)
Cath.-Evan.	100	100	100 (4)	100	71.5	77.8 (9)	100	66.6	75 (8)
Cons.-Evan.	N/A	66.6	66.6 (3)	N/A	100	100 (1)	100	0	66.7 (3)

By contrast, evangelicals were much more likely to have been supportive of the decision. Indeed, when ministers' current views (as presented in **Table 2xi**) were compared to their views at the time of the vote, evangelical respondents were most likely to have become more favourable to women's priesting over the first ten years. This lends further statistical weight to the popular theory that increased evangelical acceptance of women's ordained ministry in the early 1990s may have been a crucial factor in the legislation achieving the necessary support. Certainly in interview, several leading figures in the conservative evangelical group *Reform* conceded that they had been unable to rouse evangelical opposition to the women priests legislation, and that even a majority of evangelical laity of a 'conservative' persuasion were largely untroubled by the prospect of women's ordination.[40]

Table 2xii: Current attitudes to women's priesting amongst congregations, by Church tradition (ranked according to levels of agreement/strong agreement)[41]		
Church tradition (n=)	**% strongly agree/ agree**	**% strongly disagree/ disagree**
Liberal-Evangelical (14)	92.9	0
Liberal (50)	92.0	2.0
Liberal-Catholic (32)	84.4	12.6
Evangelical (68)	83.8	4.4
Conserv.-Evangelical (54)	81.4	7.4
Catholic-Evangelical (9)	77.8	11.1
Charism.-Evangelical (24)	75.0	20.8
Anglo-Catholic (161)	57.1	32.9

male clergy. A quarter of male clergy identified themselves as 'Anglo-Catholic', but only around one in twenty female clergy did so.

[40] Although, as shall be suggested in Chapter 8, conservative evangelicals were somewhat more likely to express reservations about the consecration of women as bishops.

[41] Includes five questionnaire responses from the pilot study.

Indeed, the results of the Questionnaire for Congregations suggest similar patterns of support for women's priesting amongst active lay members of different church traditions. Evangelical congregations such as Churches 4, 7 and 11 display very high levels of support for the 1992 decision, although where a more conservative evangelical tradition predominates the congregation is often more divided; for example in Church 12 in Diocese D (a parish with links to *Reform*, where both vicar and curate strongly believe in a doctrine of male headship for local congregations). Conversely, levels of support for the Church's decision to ordain women as priests was often at its lowest in Anglo-Catholic congregations.[42] This is not to say that Anglo-Catholic laity were mainly opposed to women's priesting; as **Table 2xii** suggests, 57% of respondents labelling themselves Anglo-Catholic (drawn from across both resolution and non-resolution parishes) agreed or strongly agreed with the 1992 decision. A more unexpected result was the higher level of support for women's ordination as priests amongst 'conservative evangelicals' than amongst 'charismatic evangelicals'. Conservative evangelical clergy were sometimes heard to lament that the charismatic renewal's emphasis on spiritual experience and personal calling had encouraged evangelicals to accept the case for women's ordination in the face of apparent biblical evidence against it.[43] In the current sample, however, 'charismatics' seemed slightly less commonly in favour than 'conservatives' (although the difference was only 6%, and a different selection of congregations might well have yielded very different results). The difficulties of plotting patterns of support and opposition to women's ordination as priests by church tradition suggests observers should not expect attitudes to be dependent upon any single variable, and instead should encourage a proper awareness of the complexity of factors involved, including gender, church tradition, individual and congregational attitude to the resolutions, and experience of women's ministry itself.

2.9 By experience of women's ministry

The last of these variables forms the focus for the final section of this chapter: did personal experience of ordained women's ministry encourage greater acceptance of women's priesting more generally? Interviewees generally assumed that it did (a belief that to some extent politicized the question of clergy appointments and deployment[44]). However, research by Edward Lehman suggests that if it increased acceptance of the ordained woman in question, it did not necessarily increase acceptance of women's ordination as priests more generally.[45] What did the results from the current survey suggest? Some evidence already points to the importance of experience: as already suggested in section 2.2, clergy opinion seems to have shifted in a more favourable direction since the vote, whilst in section 2.1 it was noted that congregations with experience of a woman's priestly ministry were amongst the most supportive of the 1992 decision. On the other hand between 10 and 15% of clergy remain strongly opposed to women's priesting and certain congregations contain a significant number of lay respondents who also continue to express reservations or disagreement. These were mostly from resolution parishes, although sometimes very high levels of support for the ordination of women as priests could exist even where the parish had no experience of a woman in that office.

[42] Although there are notable exceptions: Church 10 in Diocese D, an Anglo-Catholic congregation with Resolution B in place, nevertheless has a very popular female curate, and almost 90% of respondents agree or strongly agree with women's priesting.
[43] For example, in int. cs4:1:460.
[44] See Chapter 5.
[45] Quoted in Leslie J. Francis and Mandy Robbins, *The Long Diaconate, 1987–1994; Women Deacons and the Delayed Journey to Priesthood* (Gracewing, Leominster, 1999), p. 11.

Women and Priesthood in the Church of England

	Previous or current experience of working in a mixed clergy team (no. of cases in brackets)	No previous or current experience of working in a mixed clergy team (no. of cases in brackets)
Diocese A	89.2 (28)	50 (24)
Diocese B	89 (50)	66.7 (32)
Diocese C	89.3 (38)	32.8 (29)
Diocese D	100 (4)	20 (5)
Diocese E	92.9 (12)	62.5 (10)
Diocese F	100 (3)	N/A (0)
Whole Sample	92.3 (135)	46.9 (100)

Table 2xiii: Support for women as priests amongst male clergy who have worked in a mixed male/female clergy team, and those who have not (% 'strongly agreeing' or 'agreeing', combined)

Nevertheless, further results from the questionnaire support the idea of a relationship between a positive view of women's priesting and experience of women in ministry. For the clergy, **Table 2xiii** compares levels of support for women's priesting between male clergy who have worked with (or currently work with) a female colleague who is a priest, and male clergy who have no such experience.[46] The table clearly shows a relationship between attitude to the 1992 decision on women's priesting and the respondent's experience of working in a mixed clergy team.

Table 2xiv: Percentage of churchgoers surveyed who felt 'very' or 'quite' comfortable with different aspects of women's ministry, comparing the views of those who have/have not experienced each aspect

	Have	Not
Having a woman as vicar/rector of your church	91.8	66.6
Having a woman as curate of your church	93.5	71.5
Having a woman as deacon of your church	95.2	75.1
Having a woman as reader at your church	97.2	82.4
Women clergy occasionally preaching at your church	92.4	68.5
Visiting women clergy occasionally presiding at communion	96.8	69.8
Receiving a visit from an ordained woman chaplain at work, hospital, etc.	92.3	83.8
Being present at a service led by a priest who is a woman	88.9	57.4
Taking communion from a priest who is a woman	93.9	59.0
Being baptized (either you or your child) by a priest who is a woman	98.3	78.7
Meeting women in priesthood regularly through mutual involvement in a church group	93.9	75.1
Having a female friend who is a priest/training for priesthood	91.1	77.7
Your new vicar having been ordained by a woman bishop	None	54.3

[46] Figures for female clergy are not given here, since all have worked in mixed clergy teams, and all but two or three support women's priesting.

54

The Congregations Questionnaire results also suggest a similar pattern. Respondents were asked to indicate a number of different ways in which they had encountered women's ministry, and evaluate how far they had felt comfortable with this experience (or how comfortable they thought they *might* feel, if they had not actually experienced it yet).[47] **Table 2xiv** shows the combined percentage of those who were 'very' and 'quite' comfortable with their experience of a priestly ministry being conducted by a woman.[48] The 'have' column indicates the percentage agreement amongst those who have already experienced women's ministry, whilst the 'not' column details the responses of those with no such experience, and how far they thought they would feel comfortable with women in these roles.[49] The results suggest a clear difference may indeed exist between those who have experience of a woman's ministry and those who have not: consistently over 90% of those who had experience of a woman in priesthood felt they had been 'very' or 'quite' comfortable with the experience. Those who had no such experience seemed much less likely to be comfortable, and expressed particular reservations over accepting a woman as vicar or rector of their parish, or attending a service led by a female priest. On the other hand, feeling comfortable with women's ministry was not specifically dependent on experience of a woman's *priestly* ministry. Having a female deacon or reader in the parish was often enough to encourage congregations to look favourably on the idea of women as priests.[50]

It is important to remember that these figures only help us to establish a relationship between experience of women's priesthood and acceptance of it; they do not in themselves tell us about the nature of that relationship. Some clergy and congregations may indeed arrive at a more positive view of women's priesthood through their experiences of it, but the results may also reflect the fact that those who have reservations or objections about women's priesting may deliberately seek to limit their contact women in priesthood (particularly, though not exclusively, when this involves sacramental worship).[51] Nevertheless it is noticeable that the final option – having a vicar ordained by a female bishop – attracts considerably less support overall.[52] This could be because women in the episcopate represented a step too far for some, or it could be further evidence of uncertainty over that which has yet to be experienced (this is explored further in Chapter 5). Whichever is the case, there is sufficient evidence to suggest that women's ordination as priests is most often accepted by those who have some experience of a woman's ministry in the wider sense.

---

[47] For some, the question of feeling 'comfortable' with women in priestly roles is either insulting or irrelevant; particularly if decisions on women and priesthood are to be taken on theological, rather than emotional, grounds. However, the questionnaire needed to take into account the fact that for a significant proportion of people it was experience of women's ministry, of feelings about it, that were more significant determinants of their view than ideas. Thus the Questionnaire for Congregations offered participants the chance to rate their degree of comfort with women in priesthood as well as their beliefs about it.

[48] Includes five questionnaire responses from the pilot study.

[49] In each case, the respondents whose views do not appear in the table are those who were uncertain of their reactions, or rated the experience as 'not very' or 'not at all' comfortable.

[50] Writing before the 1992 vote, Alyson Peberdy also concludes that experience of women working as deacons led many Anglican laity to question why women were not also priests (Alyson S. Peberdy, *A Part of Life; A Study of Lay People's Responses to Women's Ministry in the Church of England* (MOW, London, 1985), p. 23).

[51] This should not be taken to imply that all of those with reservations over women's priesting practise a 'theology of taint'; simply that it is relatively common human behaviour to disassociate oneself from anything that is considered to be wrong. The question of 'taint' is explored further in Chapter 7.

[52] Although within this overall figure, nearly 95% of those who 'strongly agree' with women's priesting were 'very' or 'quite' comfortable with the idea, compared to just 2% of those who 'disagreed' or 'strongly disagreed'.

Conclusion

This chapter has suggested that a clear majority of clergy and lay respondents in the current survey agree with the Church of England's decision of 1992 to ordain women as priests. In the case studies considered here, agreement/strong agreement with women's ordination as priests consistently runs above seventy per cent of clergy (and in some deaneries clergy support is virtually unanimous). If the surveys of the case study congregations are at all representative, levels of agreement amongst Anglican laity are very often even higher. What is more, the current generation of Anglican clergy appears to have moved increasingly towards agreement with the 1992 decision, over the first decade of women's priestly ministry. However, if those who were uncertain of their position in 1992 have generally tended to move towards strong agreement with the decision, a significant minority (perhaps fifteen to twenty per cent in some cases) continue to remain firmly unconvinced that the right step was taken. This wider division of opinion was to some extent reflected at parish and deanery level, where congregations almost always contained a diversity of views on women's priesting, and deanery chapters frequently did. It should probably therefore be concluded that whilst clergy and laity were becoming increasingly certain over whether the 1992 decision should be welcomed or regretted, it was also important to recognize the limits of polarization at different levels in the Church of England.

However, the vote to enable women to be ordained priest did tend to receive greater acceptance from some quarters than from others. One of the most significant factors for both clergy and laity was the church tradition of the respondent, with Anglo-Catholics significantly more likely to have been against the decision and evangelicals crucially tipping the balance in favour of women's priesting. For clergy in particular, there were strikingly different levels of support for women's priesting between women and men (although this is scarcely surprising given that the vast majority of the clergywomen surveyed had themselves been ordained priest). For lay respondents, however, support for the 1992 decision seemed to depend less on traditional demographic indicators such as age and gender, and more on a complex blend of local circumstances such as the dominant tradition of their local church, personal experience of women's ministry (not necessarily as priests) and their parish's official stance on the matter (for example, whether or not the resolutions were in place). The importance of this local dimension is explored further in Chapter 4, where the stories of the nine main case study congregations are considered in greater depth. However, if the case studies could differ greatly, the overwhelming trend remained towards large-scale acceptance of the vote to ordain women to the priesthood amongst both Anglican clergy and laity. Of course, this conclusion currently rests only on the answers to a handful of closed answer responses on a questionnaire, and it itself says little about the *degree* of acceptance of women's priesting or the most significant reasons *why* the decision to ordain women might have been welcomed, or how these statements of support or opposition might be qualified. Chapter 3 therefore explores the question in greater depth, focusing on the justifications given by grass roots clergy and laity for their views on women's ordination as priests.

Chapter 3

'Who are we to prevent it?': Anglican popular belief on women and priesthood

> *If a woman is called to serve God in their way, who are we to prevent it?*
> (LQ 75, male 60-69, Church 2)

The debate on women's ordination as priests amongst academic theologians and church leaders has long been a multifaceted affair, going beyond questions of mere eligibility for office to questions about the nature of God and the Church, the correct interpretation of scripture, tradition, reason and experience, theological understandings of gender and the nature of ministry, and the extent to which doctrine may develop. But whilst the discussions bishops, councils and synods have been well documented,[1] less is known about attitudes to women and priesthood amongst 'grass roots' clergy and laity who make up the majority of the Church. This chapter seeks to redress that imbalance, by taking as its frame of reference the issues and questions that preoccupied clergy and laity at the grass roots of the Church of England as they sought to explain their views on women and priesthood in the interviews and questionnaires.

The relationship between the formal debate and popular perception is a complex one.[2] 'Popular' here should not be taken to imply an absence of theological reflection. Gut responses and assumptions of course feature in grass roots discussion of women's priesting, but even the most learned theologian must acknowledge the impossibility of producing a purely rational and objective argument on the matter. 'Formal' and 'popular' debates on women as priests have also influenced each other throughout (for example, most older churchgoers had heard their clergy speak on the subject and many had read up on the issues in 1992) – although issues that were central to the 'learned' debate have not necessarily figured prominently in popular discussion – and vice versa. Seeking to understand grass roots attitudes may not necessarily yield many new insights into the key theological questions at hand, but helps to enrich our understanding of the first ten years of men and women in priesthood in the Church of England, and may provide important clues as to the likely response towards a move to admit women as bishops.[3] Moreover, if 'reception' is partly to be understood as the acceptance of a development in doctrine or order by the whole Church, a brief survey of popular beliefs on women and priesthood may provide useful insights into the nature of that reception process in one particular part of the worldwide Church.

---

[1] For the Church of England's debate see: Sean Gill, *Women and Priesthood in the Church of England, from the Eighteenth Century to the Present* (SPCK, London, 1994) and the verbatim transcript of the November 1992 debate: General Synod of the Church of England, *The Ordination of Women to the Priesthood: The Synod Debate, 11 November 1992: A Verbatim Record* (Church House Publishing, London, 1993). See also: Margaret Webster, *A New Strength, A New Song; The Journey to Women's Priesthood* (Mowbray, London, 1994); Jonathan Petre, *By Sex Divided; The Church of England and Women Priests* (HarperCollins, London, 1994); Susan Dowell and Jane Williams, *Bread, Wine and Women; The Ordination of Women Debate in the Church of England* (Virago, London, 1994).

[2] For the interdependence of 'learned' and 'popular' religion in recent religious history, see for example: Ellen Badone (ed.), *Religious Orthodoxy and Popular Faith* (Princeton University Press, Princeton N.J., 1990); S.C. Williams, *Religious Belief and Popular Culture in Southwark, 1880–1930* (Oxford University Press, Oxford, 1999).

[3] For which see Chapter 9.

The structure of this chapter seeks to reflect the multilayered character of most individuals' beliefs and assumptions about women's ordination as priests. Few participants claimed their views were informed by one single consideration, and even those who did displayed a whole range of hopes, concerns and assumptions in their responses to the questions, even if they were not always consciously aware of these. Most individuals' attitudes to women's priesting arose from a combination of worldview, life experience, gut feeling and reasoned theological argument. The role of gut feeling is particularly recognized in section 3.3 of this chapter, although it is acknowledged that the assumed, the unsaid and the subconscious are very difficult to reflect accurately in a contained piece of social research such as this, particularly where only interview and questionnaire material are used.[4] Given the evidence available, then, this chapter focuses particularly upon more explicitly held beliefs and values that in some way arose from the conscious desire to make sense of evidence on women's priesting from within the treasury of faith. On all sides of the debate there was a shared conviction that if the question of women's ordination as priests was to be decided properly, this must be achieved through convincing theological argument. Not all that stood outside this realm was ruled as inadmissible evidence, as the discussion of personal calling and divine guidance in section 2.2 seeks to suggest. First, however, section 3.1 sets the scene by considering how some of the most common arguments for and against women's ordination as priests were weighted by respondents to the Questionnaire for Congregations.

3.1 Some common arguments

After participants in the questionnaire survey were first given space to outline their views in their own words, they were then presented with ten statements on women and priesthood and asked to indicate how far they agreed with each.[5] The results are set out in **Table 3i** and are arranged to show how differing levels of support for women's ordination as priests tended to lead to differing levels of agreement with the statements.

---

[4] Participant observation and ethnography would afford more opportunity to investigate actions and assumptions that are less consciously articulated, but the constraints of the project did not allow for this.
[5] These were written after a review of some of the published material from the debates and an initial round of interviews, and were designed to reflect some of the key aspects of the debate in the late 1980s/early 1990s.

Table 3i: Ten common reasons for supporting or opposing the Church of England's decision to ordain women as priests (% support for these statements amongst lay respondents grouped according to their level of agreement with women priests)					
	% support amongst laity 'strongly agreeing' with women as priests	% support amongst laity 'agreeing' with women as priests	% support amongst laity who 'neither agree nor disagree', etc.	% support amongst laity who 'disagree' with women as priests	% support amongst laity who 'strongly disagree' with women as priests
The ordination of women was right because it enables us to move closer to other churches that have ordained women for many years.	84.7	74.0	33.3	7.4	3.6
The Bible speaks of man being the head of the woman, just as Christ is head of the Church. Therefore it is not appropriate for ordained women to have seniority over men.	2.0	17.9	51.3	62.9	50.0
Men and women are fundamentally the same, and therefore it was right to allow women to become priests.	92.0	87.0	46.2	7.4	0.0
Women do not have the necessary character attributes and psychological attributes to be priests.	3.6	13.8	22.1	33.3	42.9
The Bible speaks of how in Christ, there is neither Jew nor Greek, neither slave nor free, neither male nor female. Therefore it is just as appropriate for women to be ordained to the priesthood as it is for men.	89.4	91.8	64.1	3.7	5.4
The ordination of women in the Church of England was wrong because it distances us from other churches that do not currently ordain women.	2.0	8.2	35.9	62.9	69.6
Were Jesus alive on earth today, he would surely have included women amongst his apostles, therefore women should also be priests today.	94.8	90.2	58.9	25.9	1.8
Many women feel called to be priests, but their understanding of their calling must have been mistaken.	1.2	12.2	12.8	40.7	64.3
For a priest to truly represent Christ at the altar, the priest must share Christ's humanity; gender is not important to the function of the priest.	94.3	91.1	69.2	18.5	8.9
Whilst the whole church is still in the process of deciding whether women can be priests, it was wrong for the C of E to go ahead and ordain women unilaterally.	6.0	13.8	48.7	96.3	85.8

The results presented here give some insight into the considerations were important for respondents who agreed with women's priesting, which were important for those who did not, and which were popularly regarded as most and least persuasive. Disappointingly, respondents seem to have tended to agree with any statement that could lend weight to their overall view, and to disagree with any statement that could be construed as undermining their position. Nevertheless, the *degree* of agreement between the statements could differ sharply.

To those who 'strongly agreed', 'agreed' or 'neither agreed nor disagreed' with the 1992 decision, the two most important considerations were i) that the Bible speaks of how 'all are one in Christ Jesus' and ii) that the gender of the priest is less important than his/her humanity. Both arguments share a sense that priesthood and membership of the Church were meant to be inclusive of the whole of humankind, and that women's ordination as priests seemed consistent with this vision. On the other hand, lay respondents who 'disagreed' or 'strongly disagreed' were most likely to support the assertions that it was wrong 'for the C of E to go ahead and ordain women unilaterally' and 'because it distances us from other churches that do not currently ordain women'.[6] So for lay members of the Church of England with objections/reservations over the 1992 decision, questions of consensus and timing were felt to be more convincing than *a priori* arguments citing something in nature or theology that made women's ordination as priests either unsuitable or heretical. Indeed, suggestions that women 'do not have the necessary character attributes or psychological attributes' for priesthood, or that 'their understanding of their calling must have been mistaken' attracted little support across the board. The suggestion that 'men and women are fundamentally the same ...' was also widely seen as less important or less convincing. Meanwhile, the biblical evidence on ministry, and the need to avoid division in the wider church if possible, attracted generally higher levels of support, regardless of the respondent's overall view on women's priesting. This is important, because it suggests that – far from 'supporters' and 'opponents' of women in priesthood emphasizing entirely different arguments – some factors were commonly accorded greater weight than others. If these results are at all representative of the wider picture, one might conclude that the majority of Anglicans in England share some underlying assumptions about the question of women and priesthood, regardless of their overall view of the rightness of the 1992 decision: little appetite for 'impossibilist' arguments;[7] a desire to accord the Bible greater authority than any theories about gender characteristics (although such theories were still influential); a preparedness to accept women's sense of calling as genuine; a regret over anything that might split the Church; but also a sense that gender was of less soteriological or ecclesiological significance than humanity. These became common themes in the interview and questionnaire testimony, as the rest of the chapter will suggest.

---

[6] Although it was notable that the ecumenical argument seemed to work negatively for many respondents: the damage to relations with Rome and the Orthodox Churches was generally rated higher than the positive benefits of moving towards churches that currently ordained women. This may reflect a desire to avoid division *per se*, rather than a particular desire to draw closer to Roman Catholicism and Orthodoxy, especially given what is discussed in Section 3.8.

[7] Although it is accepted that sometimes, objections to women's priesting according to 'the ecumenical argument' could seem more socially acceptable than insisting that it was always wrong to ordain women to presbyteral ministry.

3.2 Divine intervention and personal calling

As candidates for ordained ministry are often reminded, a sense of vocation must begin and end with God. For many, this remained paramount in deciding on the rightness or otherwise of the move to ordain women to the priesthood. The views of a minority of clergy were shaped decisively as a result of direct spiritual or mystical experience. One ordained woman from Diocese C remembered how:

> *I felt initially called to be a deacon; I didn't feel that women should be priests at that time.*

[IJ: What made you change your mind?]

> *God! I was reading 'The Christian Priest Today' by Michael Ramsey, I was in the kitchen, at my house, and I was reading bits about the priest at the altar with people on your heart ... and it was as if there was an electric shock in the book, and it was so real that I was wary of it, walking around [it], sort of thing! – 'I'm not touching you again!' ... and it came to me as it happened, 'I want you to be a priest' ... so that changed my mind a bit, really! You can't argue with that one!*[8]

Likewise, several male clergy from the Catholic tradition had also come to accept the rightness of women's priesting through a profound spiritual experience at the time of first receiving communion from an ordained woman; some even describing it as 'a conversion experience'. Most reflections of this kind came from those who were (or had become) supportive of women's priesting, although occasionally a contributor to *New Directions* cited spiritual experiences that had led them to conclude that the move towards ordaining women had a more malevolent inspiration. According to one of the most strongly opposed clergy interviewees, the division arising from the debate was 'the work of the devil, actually'.[9]

For a majority of respondents, however, supernatural guidance over women's priesting was more beneficent, less spectacular and equally convincing. One female curate from Diocese C told of how 'the call just never, ever went away; ... my friends told me 'you've got everything you want', but I was just never satisfied [...] particularly when the vote went forward, it was 'Yes ... you've got to go forward – you can't now run away from it, now that it is [possible]'.[10] Likewise some male clergy had also been forced to change their minds in the face of a female colleague's sense of calling, ordination, or first steps in ministry: 'I just remembered Peter's words', one said; 'who am I to withstand God? And I felt that God had called them, just as he called me'.[11] By contrast, those with objections/reservations about women's priesting rarely mentioned the question of vocation, although in a more personal interview situation some did express their misgivings: as the results of **Table 3i** suggest, a few denied altogether that women could possibly have heard a call to priesthood, since the priesthood was only for men. Some were suspicious at what they saw as the large numbers entering priesthood in their late fifties onwards, 'who seem to see it as a nice little hobby for their retirement – I mean, that's probably very unfair to them, but I have heard it said by some of them, and they certainly talk about career moves and things like this, which I think is awful ...'[12] Others imputed the growth of female vocations

---

[8] int. cs3:3:435.
[9] int. cs2:7:286.
[10] int. cs3:25:15.
[11] int. cs5:5:85.
[12] int. cs1:10:412.

to a feminist-driven desire to reform the Church as the last bastion of patriarchy.[13] Doubtless some women offering themselves for priesthood did so with these motives: Leslie Francis' and Mandy Robbins' survey of the 'waiting' women deacons of the 1987–94 period suggested 17% had sought ordination partly to 'change the sexist nature of the Church', but this number was dwarfed by the 97% who came forward 'because I believed God wished me to be ordained'.[14] Stories of strong and direct calling also featured prominently in Helen Thorne's study of the first generation of women to be priested.[15]

How did those with doubts over women's ordination as priests/presbyters interpret women's sense of calling? Sometimes it was accepted as genuine but misplaced. This view was most common amongst conservative evangelicals with objections/reservations, who were often happy to accept the possibility of a direct individual call, but suggested that women were only called to diaconal or presbyteral roles subordinate to a male vicar or rector.[16] More commonly, some felt that 'calling' had become too heavily dependent on subjective personal experience; women's sense of calling was mistaken because it did not match up to the biblical pattern, in which only men were called to exercise presbyteral ministry.[17] Certainly inner conviction was a significant theme of respondents' arguments in favour of women's priesting. In one sense this is hardly surprising, given the wider shift in the locus of moral decision-making away from the public sphere and towards the private in late twentieth-century society.[18] Even so, it was more common for respondents to support women's priesthood out of a belief that this was consonant with their understanding of God for both men and women to experience a call to priesthood, rather than out of regard for individual autonomy *per se*. Indeed, women's own sense of calling was the single most common reason given by clergy supporting women's priesting (particularly amongst women themselves), and the third most common answer amongst the laity. As one member of Church 10 responded, the Church's decision was right 'because I believe that a woman, in the same way as a man, is called to the priesthood by God'.[19]

3.3 Gut feelings

More difficult to chart is the impact of gut feelings in individuals' responses. As early as 1973, Dame Christian Howard's report *The Ordination of Women to the Priesthood* recognized that 'On both sides, much of the debate will be conducted at the level of feeling', and that 'any attempt to meet such feelings with logical argument will probably fail, because the person with whom one is arguing is not being met at the real level at which they need to talk'.[20] Correspondingly, clergy and laity from all sides of the debate sometimes suggested that the opposing view was partly underpinned by deeply-held

---

[13] Competing interpretations of feminism were another important feature of the responses, about which it is hoped to say more in a future publication.

[14] Leslie J. Francis and Mandy Robbins, *The Long Diaconate; Women Deacons and the Delayed Journey to Priesthood* (Leominster, 1999), p. 52.

[15] Helen Thorne, *Journey to Priesthood: An In-depth Study of the First Women Priests in the Church of England* (University of Bristol, Bristol, 2000), pp. 85–91.

[16] A number of pamphlets published by the *Reform* organization illustrate this position well. See, for example: *Dogged by the Collar? Getting Women's Ministry Right in the Church of England* (*Reform* Discussion Paper 13, Sheffield, 1996) whose contributors include two female permanent deacons.

[17] int. cs5:9:460.

[18] Gerald Parsons, 'Between Law and Licence: Christianity, Morality and 'Permissiveness', in Gerald Parsons (ed.), *The Growth of Religious Diversity; Britain from 1945* Vol. II: *Issues* (Open University/ Routledge, London, 1994), pp. 231–266 (p. 253).

[19] LQ255, female 50–59, Church 10.

[20] General Synod GS104a, *The Ordination of Women to the Priesthood; A Summary of the Consultative Document presented to the Anglican Consultative Council* (Church Information Office, London, 1973), p. 17.

subconscious feelings (although it was less common for individuals to admit to those feelings themselves). Amongst those that did, gut feeling was acknowledged as important in weighing up the balance of evidence. As one retired male priest and *WATCH* member explained: 'the Jesus I worship, the Jesus that I follow, the Jesus that I study, is not the sort of person who would have turned down women for ordination. How do I know? I feel it'.[21] Respondents who had changed their minds in favour of women's priesting frequently spoke of the tension between head and heart, with one preceding the other into acceptance of the decision. Often this tension was resolved by a first-hand experience of women's priesting. Sometimes, however, a similar combination of intellectual and intuitive reservations could lead to a rejection of women's priesting. As one ordained male member of *Reform* reflected, 'instinctively I felt it was wrong – but I didn't know why, and I thought, well, it must be because it's something new, because I'm male, prejudiced, so I began to read around the subject a lot, obviously all those in favour, and those against, and the more I read, the more disturbed I became.'[22]

More controversially, individuals of one view occasionally suggested that the opposing view owed more to unarticulated gut feelings than to the reasoned arguments they actually gave. Here the most sensitive issue of all was that of sexuality. One male vicar from Diocese A suggested, 'most of the resistance [to women priests] has come from traditionally-minded male priests who have got the whole thing caught up with their own psychological problems about sexuality [...] I've probably over-simplified it ... undoubtedly I have, but I think there's more in that ... than has tended to be acknowledged in the kind of official things that you read ...'[23] In particular, some suggested that a fear of female sexuality could be traced to unresolved issues in a person's own sexuality. This is *not* to suggest opposition to women's priesting was to be linked with a homosexual orientation. One recently ordained woman described how at her theological college (which stood within the Anglo-Catholic tradition[24]), openly gay students had been amongst the most accepting of women's call to priesthood. But others 'lead a very split life ... but officially to not register as gay ... and they're the ones who are not likely to talk to women – or get very nervous'.[25] Members of *Forward in Faith* were insistent in denying any link between repressed homosexuality and a fear of women as priests, even accusing those who made the accusation in public of implicit homophobia.[26] Interview and questionnaire research do not yield the right kind of evidence to come to any objective judgement on this question, and so no firm conclusion is attempted here. However, in off the record conversations, at least three senior figures in the traditionalist constituency acknowledged that a small portion of those with objections to women's priesting may have been driven in part by gut feelings of this kind. It has become fashionable in some quarters to repeat the suggestion that opposition to women's priesting partly derives from the continued influence of pre-modern pollution taboos that surrounded women's bodies and female sexuality.[27] As with any stock explanation, it should not be accepted uncritically.[28] However, it is difficult to ignore

---

[21] int. 14:120.

[22] int. 3:10.

[23] int. cs1:3:427.

[24] The suggestion that homosexual Christian men were attracted to Anglo-Catholicism in unusually large numbers is raised in most of the major studies on the tradition. See: Francis Penhale, *Catholics in Crisis* (Mowbray, London and Oxford, 1986), pp. 147–8; W.S.F. Pickering, *Anglo-Catholicism; A Study in Religious Ambiguity* (Routledge, London, 1989), pp. 184–206; John Shelton Reed, *Glorious Battle: The Cultural Politics of Victorian Anglo-Catholicism* (Nashville, 1996).

[25] int. 10:333.

[26] For example, in a letter by the Revd John Richardson in: *Church Times*, 02.11.01.

[27] For the most often used analysis of the pollution taboos surrounding the female body in 'primitive' societies, see: Mary Douglas, *Purity and Danger* (Routledge and Kegan Paul, London, 1966).

[28] Although of course fashionability alone does not render a statement untrue.

several reported instances (particularly early on in the debate on women priests) where clergy objected to women's priesting on the grounds that an ordained woman could not possibly be acceptable when celebrating communion during menstruation or pregnancy. One lay woman admitted she was unsettled by the sight of a female body in clerical robes.[29] However, in the absence of large-scale, irrefutable evidence in either direction, it is probably fair to conclude that whilst it would be grossly misleading to ascribe all opposition to women's priesting to unresolved psychosexual problems, issues related to sexuality may be influential in a minority of individual cases.[30]

However, 'gut feeling' could relate to more than sexuality. Several interviewees explained how, for them, it simply did (not) 'feel right' for women to be ordained. 'I don't know, really; it just feels OK', said one woman from Church 10,[31] whilst a fellow member of her congregation wrote, 'I think men ought to be priests, not women ... Don't look or sound right. I don't feel like I've been to church'.[32] Of course, such statements could disguise more private or unspoken feelings on the issue, but it is also important to recognize that a minority (particularly amongst the laity) found it extremely difficult to articulate their attitudes on the question and found themselves reaching for the language of feelings rather than ideas to outline their position. As already suggested, much of the learned debate was underpinned by an assumption on all sides (in theory at least) that the issue must be decided by good theology and ecclesiology rather than feelings (which some regarded as inadmissible as evidence in the debate). However, whilst this was in some senses a legitimate expectation, it failed to reflect the way in which the question of women's priesting was actually approached. As one retired clergyman reflected, 'all the reasonable theologians are saying there are no theological objections; all the reasonable sociologists are saying there are no sociological objections, but there's a woman in my housegroup who says "it just doesn't feel right" ... and we need more work doing on that. To say logic matters and emotion doesn't is a very masculine way of running things ...'[33] Many would disagree with the 'masculine = logical/feminine = emotional' equation implied in this statement, but the Church would nevertheless do well to acknowledge the role of gut feeling in popular beliefs on women's priesting – both 'for' and 'against'.

3.4 No theological objections?

Another factor in popular beliefs and attitudes that has received less attention thus far, but remained important, was the widespread failure to understand the arguments of those who took a different view. Around two thirds of lay questionnaire respondents gave no indication that they had ever doubted the rightness of women's priesting, and a significant number of clergy and laity simply responded that 'I can see no reason why not' or that 'I could see no theological objections which should prevent the ordination of women'.[34] Some responses were more robust, with one bishop even suggesting that:

---

[29] int. cs5:13:87. For more on this case, see: Ian Jones, 'Earrings Behind the Altar? Anglican Expectations of the Ordination of Women as Priests', *Dutch Review of Church History Vol.83 (2003)*, pp. 462–76. The importance of clothing in lay Anglicans' first memories of women as priests is also noted in Hilary Wakeman, 'What Difference is Women's Priesthood Making in the Pews?' in Hilary Wakeman (ed.), *Women Priests: The First Years* (Darton, Longman and Todd, London, 1996), pp. 1–26 (p. 16).

[30] This paragraph has not discussed attitudes to female sexuality in relation to support *for* women's priesting, but this was not a particular feature of the interview testimony.

[31] LQ181, female 60–69, Church 10.

[32] LQ185, female 60–69, Church 10.

[33] int. cs1:18:430.

[34] CQ142, male vicar, 40–49.

> *I don't think there was an argument to be had – I think I found all the arguments against so totally incomprehensible, actually, even though I recognize, of course, that they were deeply held.*[35]

Indeed, some implied that the burden of proof now fell upon opponents of women's priesting to justify why the change should not be made. Less commonly, respondents with strong objections to women's priesting suggested that the weight of evidence was not even sufficient to have required that the matter be debated. Several believed that the key theological questions (particularly on the nature of priesthood and nature of gender) had simply not been discussed, and that a genuine debate on the theological issues would have looked very different: as one vicar from Diocese B commented:

> *... [if] the debate happened now, I think the proponents' argument would be blown out of the water. I don't think it would even leave dock, because the particular planks on which it was built were an illusion.*[36]

In an important sense, Mary Douglas' observation on the 1992 ordination of women debate remained true: a lack of real engagement or empathy between the most vehement positions in the debate has to some extent resulted in 'supporters' and 'opponents' speaking *past* each other, rather than *to* each other.[37]

3.5 Gender roles and characteristics

A further layer to popular beliefs on women's priesting was the often complex blend of attitudes and assumptions about gender that respondents brought to their views on women's priesting. In the interview and questionnaire testimony, four key questions emerged: i) Were women and men intrinsically different? ii) Did either faith or reason demand that men and women played different social roles? iii) In what sense was it correct to say that women and men were equal? iv) Did any of the answers to the first three questions dictate that women were ineligible for priestly office? (In actual conversation, these potentially quite separate issues often became merged.) First, how far did respondents speak of men and women as intrinsically different? The relative characteristics of men and women were certainly widely discussed by participants, but not all justified their views on women's priesting with reference to innate gender differences. Occasionally such views would be expressed; for example, that women were too 'bossy' or insufficiently authoritative to make good clergy, or on the other hand that women should be ordained alongside men precisely because the sexes *were* different and a complementarity of perspectives within the priesthood would be enriching. Women's tendency towards particular gifts or aptitudes[38] was a common theme of the testimony; for example one member of Church 5 commented, 'women, on the whole, are good listeners and communicators, and being female, I relate to them well'.[39] However, attempts to define the innate characteristics of men and women almost inevitably reflected popular assumptions about male- and female-ness. Even those who sought to build their case on purely doctrinal grounds could find themselves reaching for generalizations: one minister from Diocese E sought to explain why biblically, only male congregational oversight was authoritative. When asked why a woman preaching a sermon could not also be authoritative if her words were biblically orthodox, the speaker

---

[35] int bpcs1:74.

[36] int. cs2:5:123.

[37] Mary Douglas, *Risk and Blame; Essays in Cultural Theory* (Routledge, London and New York, 1992), Chapter 15: 'The Debate on Women Priests' (pp. 271–294), p. 272.

[38] This is also noted in: Alyson Peberdy, *A Part of Life: A Study of Lay People's Response to Women's Ministry in the Church of England* (Movement for the Ordination of Women, London, 1985), p. 15.

[39] LQ127 female 60–69, Church 5.

replied, 'Because it would be inappropriate for a woman to be doing that, in that she would be being less of a woman. It's a trite answer, but it's not what it means to be feminine'.[40] Indeed, Edward Lehmann Jnr's research on US clergy also noted a tendency for churchgoers to expect certain qualities from their clergy because of their gender – which in turn shaped the way they assessed their minister's effectiveness.[41]

However, whilst some respondents were keen to ascribe innate gender characteristics to their clergy, it was more common to emphasize how the crucial distinction lay in men's and women's different life experiences, which gave them different insights or opportunities in ministry. One female respondent from Church 9 described how her first contact with the Church had come not long after being raped. She had found the support of female members of the congregation invaluable in helping her work through her experience, but added that 'a woman priest would have been useful as well, it might have been easier to open up and I think a lot of women in similar problems, i.e. abuse or even problems with children, would feel the same'.[42] Some respondents were reluctant to make any generalizations, regarding these as a distraction from the individual gifts or aptitudes clergy brought to their ministry.[43] As one diocesan bishop remarked, 'we ought to move beyond the stage somehow where we expect somehow to see this radical difference between men and women *per se*... for me there isn't something amongst the women which you can say 'that's what women's ministry is about'...'[44] It was regularly pointed out that male clergy could be just as skilled and sensitive pastors as women. Some clergy cited research into clergy personality profiles by Leslie J. Francis, which has concluded that female clergy tended to exhibit more traditionally 'male' character attributes than women in general, whilst male clergy were more likely to display traditionally 'female' characteristics than men in general.[45] Even so, despite a general reticence to ascribe men and women innate characteristics of personality or aptitude on the grounds of gender, the feeling remained that men and women were not simply 'the same', that certain characteristics were to be found amongst more women than amongst most men, and that to refuse to ordain women would be depriving the Church of those qualities and experiences.

Second, how far did the question of distinct *roles*[46] for men and women inform the different positions on women's priesting? Whilst a belief in innate gender characteristics could be found amongst both 'supporters' and 'opponents' of women's priesting, the conviction that role was an important concept tended to be found more often amongst those with objections or reservations over women in ordained ministry. As one member of Church 15 responded:

> ... *any woman who wanted to ... be a priest, would be a bit startling, really, just like if a man wanted to be a midwife ... Possible, you know, competent, you could train to do it, but what a strange thing to want to do!*[47]

---

[40] int. cs5:9:385.

[41] Edward C. Lehman Jnr., *Gender and Work: The Case of the Clergy* (State University of New York Press, Albany, 1993), pp. 175–7.

[42] LQ282, female 30–39, Church 9.

[43] This was also reflected in discourse on gender difference in interviews with female priests themselves (Helen Thorne, *Journey to Priesthood: An In-depth Study of the First Women Priests in the Church of England* (University of Bristol, Bristol, 2000), p. 126).

[44] int. 13:517.

[45] Leslie J. Francis, 'The Personality Characteristics of Anglican Ordinands: Feminine Men and Masculine Women', *Personality and Individual Differences* 12 (11) 1991, pp. 1133–40.

[46] Sometimes understood as based on innate gender differences; sometimes as a social concept, implying a God-given station in life or a pragmatic division of labour set in place regardless of personal qualities or characteristics.

[47] int. cs5:16:71.

From a different angle, the views of Margaret Jenkins on p. 1 were representative of a bigger constituency who feared that women in priesthood might be caught in between the competing demands of family and parish life, to the detriment of one or both. Similar attitudes were occasionally expressed throughout all levels of this constituency: one bishop who did not ordain women suggested that married female priests were 'not at the disposal of their parish as men are' and thought it not coincidental that many of the women offering themselves for ordained ministry were single, widowed or divorced.[48] (In fact, Helen Thorne's research suggested only 5% of her sample were divorced – considerably below the national average – although 83% of the total sample had no dependent children.[49]) Notably, however, there was an almost total absence of complaints from parishes with women clergy that their vicar or curate was neglecting the parish in their attempt to balance work and family life. In fact, interviewees were more likely to be admiring of the way they had been able to do both. Moreover, women clergy themselves often suggested that the traditional image of the parish priest who worked every waking hour was not necessarily a healthy model for their congregations to follow in any case.[50]

Churchgoers also occasionally noted that family commitments had often been an issue for ordained men as well as women: one long-standing member of Church 9 remembered a male curate who had rearranged the times of church meetings to enable him to spend time with his children.[51] Most comments acknowledged that the balance between ministry and family commitments needed careful planning, but felt that with due consideration family responsibilities were largely irrelevant to the question of women's ordination. In part this reflected a wider shift away from ascribing pre-defined roles to certain groups within modern western society as a whole,[52] in favour of an emphasis on individual merit: 'Entry to the priesthood should be on grounds of religious conviction and not of sex', wrote one male churchgoer from Church 9; 'There is no reason why a woman could not do the job'.[53] As section 3.11 suggests, many respondents also thought they identified a biblical sanction for this view, in that the teachings of Jesus and the early Church were felt to militate *against* the imposition of roles rather than reinforce them.

A third aspect to discussions of gender was the question of equality. Amongst those indicating their agreement with women's ordination as priests, 'equality' was one of the most common justifications given in favour. This may sound obvious, but as Mark Chaves reminds us, the link between gender, ordination and equality was only forged in the later nineteenth century; previously ordination for women had been considered according to other criteria.[54] For late twentieth-century clergy and laity, equality was a fundamental point

---

[48] int. 2:209, 319.

[49] Helen Thorne, *Journey to Priesthood; An In-depth Study of the First Women Priests in the Church of England* (University of Bristol, Bristol, 2000), p. 68. The small number of women with dependent children may be an unusual characteristic of the first generation of women to be priested, a significant proportion of whom had waited a long time for the opportunity and were older than the average for ordinands, meaning that many of their children would already have left home. More research would be needed to confirm this suggestion, however.

[50] For one thing it encouraged parishioners to think that the life and work of the church was the sole responsibility of the vicar; for another it might be seen to negate the value of rest time if taken to extremes.

[51] int. cs3:18:140.

[52] Robert Towler, 'The Social Status of the Anglican Minister', in Roland Robertson (ed.), *Sociology of Religion* (Penguin, London, 1969), pp. 443–50.

[53] LQ265, male 50–59, Church 9.

[54] Mark Chaves, *Ordaining Women: Culture and Conflict in Religious Organisations* (Harvard University Press, Cambridge, Massachusetts, 1997), p. 66.

of discussion, but what precisely did equality mean? As already suggested, few thought that equality implied 'sameness' or complete interchangeability between the sexes in every respect. Rather, 'equality' was used to denote three main ideas: first (particularly amongst clergy), 'equal status before God of both men and women'.[55] Second (the most frequent answer), that women were equal to men in terms of the gifts they could bring to the Church through ordained ministry: 'it was a natural process of change that recognized the gifts that women bring to the Church', wrote one female member of Church 7, whilst another woman from Church 9 simply responded that 'Women are as capable as men in doing this job'.[56] Third came a common appeal to more general notions of equality or 'natural justice': if there was no overwhelming reason *not* to ordain women (as many believed) it would be unfair to deprive them the opportunity of serving as priests. 'It is a justice issue, God does not discriminate' wrote one male churchgoer from Church 1.[57]

Thus equality and justice were considered not only to be important human values, but also reflective of something of the character of God. Amongst those who offered reasons against ordaining women as priests, attitudes to equality were more complex. A few appeared to discount the relevance of equality *per se*, but once these views were unpacked at greater length in an interview situation, the major concern seemed to be that equality was a concept with secular roots and emphasizing it risked disregarding innate or God-given gender roles and identities: one member of Church 8 feared that sexual equality and sexual identity had been confused, arguing that 'there *can* be subordination and submissiveness, but within an equal partnership'.[58] Indeed, clergy with objections to women's priesting sometimes sought to counter the suggestion that they supported inequality by underlining their commitment to a more general social equality. Nevertheless they would often add, 'except when it comes to ministry, it's not a question of equality – it's all this talk of rights that, although it's OK in the secular world, which when it's applied to holy orders, raises further questions for me, because I don't think ordination's a question of rights…'[59] Supporters of women's priesting sometimes responded by agreeing that no one had the *right* to be ordained, but that did not mean denying them an equal *opportunity* to serve as a priest, in the absence of any compelling argument to the contrary. For a majority of those who expressed a view on this, equality did not neutralize or erase gender difference; it simply implied that some differences between men and women were irrelevant to certain rights, responsibilities or opportunities – including the chance to be a priest. As **Table 3i** suggests, there was wide support for the idea that humanity was a more important qualification than gender.

3.6 More than just a job?

The relevance or otherwise of gender as a qualification for ministry presupposed the question about what women and men were actually being ordained to. Theological understandings of priesthood have been contested throughout the history of the Christian Church, but have been the subject of renewed debate in the twentieth century; particularly given the declining social status of the clergy,[60] the loss of some traditionally clerical roles to the emerging 'secular' professions,[61] a reconsideration of the role of the laity in church[62] and a renewed interest in

---

[55] CQ139, male vicar, 50–59, Diocese B. See also section 3.11.

[56] LQ271, female 30–39, Church 9.

[57] LQ30, male 50–59, Church 1.

[58] int. cs3:18:339.

[59] int. 3:140.

[60] Anthony Russell, *The Clerical Profession* (SPCK, London, 1984).

[61] Robert Towler, 'The Social Status of the Anglican Minister', in Roland Robertson (ed.), *Sociology of Religion* (Penguin, London, 1969), pp. 443–50; Ian R. Boyd, 'What are the Clergy For? Clerical Role Uncertainty and the State of Theology', *Theology* XCVIII (783), May/June 1995, pp. 187–96 and Russell, *The Clerical Profession*, passim.

ecclesiology in the later twentieth century. More generally, organizations experiencing profound cultural change tend to seek stability and unity in the reassertion of power through key roles.[63] An underlying question in debates over women's ordination has been whether ministry is primarily to be understood in functional terms (as the recognition of an individual's licence to perform a special task) or whether priesthood had a distinct ontological status, rendering comparisons between priestly ministry and 'secular' work meaningless. A majority of relevant responses in this study framed ordained ministry primarily in functional terms.[64] This was not taken to imply a negation of the divine calling, or a rejection of the idea that clergy were 'set apart' for a distinctive kind of service of God; simply that ordained ministry was primarily understood as a job, albeit of a special kind. As one male respondent from Church 7 wrote, '[I] do not consider gender to be an issue, the priority is that the job is conducted correctly'.[65] Moreover, the frequent references to ordained ministry as a 'job' exemplified the way in which it was commonly assumed that the clergy should not be exempted from any of the more widely accepted values governing the world of work, e.g. in criteria for selection and training. (This tension between seeing priesthood as a 'task set apart' and the practical need to address the terms and conditions of working within the Church as an organization also became important in the discussion of appointments in Chapter 5.)

By contrast, eligibility for priesthood was popularly located in the personal qualities of the individual, rather than any particular demographic variable or ascribed role:[66] as one female member of Church 11 wrote, 'I believe gender is not the important factor, only the need to serve God in an obedient and humble way with compassion, which I believe men and women can do the same'.[67] Arguably this stood in direct continuity with long-standing expectations of the 'good clergyman' in English society and the church.[68] Moreover, as suggested in section 3.5, women were widely thought more likely to display the desired pastoral qualities than most men.[69]

Assuming a functional understanding of priesthood was in no sense coterminous with support for women's ordination as priests, just as objections to women's priesting were not always underpinned by a belief in the ontological distinctiveness of the priesthood. Some clergy from the Catholic tradition could accept an ontological understanding of priesthood whilst believing there were no justifiable grounds for excluding women, whilst from a more conservative evangelical perspective the idea of 'priesthood' could be rejected altogether whilst continuing to argue that only men should exercise congregational oversight.

---

[62] Exemplified within Roman Catholicism by the Dogmatic Constitution on the Church *Lumen Gentium*, 21 November 1964, para. 33.

[63] Charles Handy, *Understanding Organisations* (Penguin, London, 4th edition 1993), p. 185ff.

64 Also noted in Hilary Wakeman, 'What Difference is Women's Priesthood Making in the Pews?' in Hilary Wakeman (ed.), *Women Priests: The First Years* (Darton, Longman & Todd, London, 1996), pp. 1-26 (p. 10).

[65] LQ232, male 40–49, Church 7.

[66] For differences between an externally ascribed concept of priesthood and one generated internally, see also: Paul Yates, 'The Priesthood of Women: Resourcing Identity in the Anglican Church', *Oral History* (Autumn 1996), pp. 59–65.

[67] LQ263, female 50–9, Church 11.

[68] For attitudes to the clergy in post-war England, see, e.g.: R.H.T. Thompson, *The Church's Understanding of Itself; A Study of Four Birmingham Parishes*, Studies in Ministry and Worship (London, 1957), pp. 33, 48, 62, 76. Churchgoing respondents to Thompson's survey consistently expressed a preference for 'a man of great human understanding' over great sanctity, powerful oratory or organizational skills. The suggestion that in the later twentieth century traditionally 'feminine' traits might have become the social ideal is made in Edward C. Lehmann Jnr, *Gender and Work: The Case of the Clergy* (Albany, 1993), p. 181.

[69] This point is expanded further in Ian Jones's article, 'Earrings Behind the Altar?'.

Nevertheless, a proportion of traditionally-minded Catholic clergy continued to believe that the Church of England had not ordained women with due consideration to the theological distinctiveness of priesthood. As one priest from a resolution parish suggested:

> *Some of the time some people seem to suggest that it's a job like any other job – 'women in the jockey club, women on the high court bench; they can say the words can't they? What's the problem?' And I think a lot of the debate ... is on that level.*[70]

In this view, the original conception of the priestly task had been lost in a headlong rush to reflect wider social values within the Church.[71] Amongst clergy who agreed with the 1992 decision, it was more commonly assumed that the priestly task itself took priority over questions of eligibility. As one male priest from Diocese A observed, 'if your concern is to defend the priesthood, you can have all kinds of rules about who can be a priest, but if your concern is actually how people have access to the Eucharist, then all sorts of people can be ordained, can't they?'[72] In response to this, those who described themselves as 'impossibilists'[73] on women's priesting pointed out that the maleness of the priest was not merely an optional selection criterion for clergy but fundamental to the office, and that the Eucharist itself became of doubtful validity when performed by someone whose orders were in question. This is explored further in the following section.

3.7 The icon of Christ?

As suggested in **Table 3i**, a majority of lay churchgoers surveyed were sympathetic with the view that the priest took on a representative role by virtue of his/her humanity, rather than because of gender. This meant that *a priori* arguments about the necessity of the priest being male were frequently greeted with bemusement by ordinary churchgoers, and many clergy. This was particularly relevant to the argument that the priest needed to be male in order to function properly as the icon of Christ at the Eucharist. Although the idea of the priest as God's representative was on the wane in popular religious culture by the nineteenth century,[74] the 'icon of Christ' argument continued to be a common theme of Catholic theological argument against the ordination of women as priests[75] and its refutation a central feature of literature supporting women's ordination.[76] However, by 1992 (and certainly in the current sample) this argument had lost some of its former centrality. Few amongst the clergy or laity offered the 'male priest as icon of Christ' argument as one of their key reasons for opposing women's priesting (and for conservative evangelicals the 'icon' argument was of

---

[70] int. cs5:15:158.

[71] The idea of a church 'giving into the secular world' was a key underlying debate in the Church since the late 1950s, and its significance to the experience of debating women's ordination is to be explored further in a future publication.

[72] int. cs1:28:141. Here the speaker was recalling a conversation with a Roman Catholic priest that had greatly influenced him in his eventual acceptance of the 1992 decision.

[73] In the 'impossibilist' view it is not, and will never be, right to ordain women as priests because it is actually impossible. In the Catholic tradition this usually takes the form of a belief that the sacrament of holy orders is only valid when conferred upon men. Therefore to speak about 'women in priesthood' is oxymoronic.

[74] James Obelkevich, *Religion and Rural Society: South Lindsey, 1825–1875* (Oxford University Press, Oxford, 1976), pp. 274–5.

[75] See e.g.: E.L. Mascall, 'Some Basic Considerations' and Kallistos Ware, 'Man, Woman and the Priesthood of Christ' in Peter Moore (ed.), *Man, Woman and Priesthood* (SPCK, London, 1978), pp. 9-26, 68–90.

[76] See e.g., Lydia Speller, *Theological Objections?* (MOW Occasional Papers 1, London, 1980); Richard Norris, *The Ordination of Women and the 'Maleness' of Christ* (MOW Occasional Papers 2, London, 1982).

doubtful relevance anyway). Indeed, as **Table 3i** suggests, only those in strong disagreement with the move firmly believed that gender had any bearing on the nature and function of the priest.

The 'icon of Christ' argument appeared most often amongst those who adopted an 'impossibilist' position, whilst most of those with milder reservations considered the argument irrelevant or felt (as in the case of this bishop who did not ordain women) that 'whilst it is not determinative of whether the priesthood should remain male, it is a pointer towards that'.[77] However, outside those with strong objections on grounds of Catholic doctrine, the idea of priest as 'icon of Christ' cut little ice. One lay couple in their 60s from Church 22 remembered their priest explaining the doctrine to them, but as the woman remembered, 'I couldn't get to grips with that and therefore I had no problems about women because I thought, no, no, you're [Revd X] standing there – you are our priest, you are there bringing God to us, Jesus to us – but Jesus there? No'.[78]

In part the 'icon of Christ' argument may have foundered on a much wider and longer-term reluctance amongst English churchgoers to see their clergy in sacerdotal terms: traditionalist Catholic clergy occasionally lamented that the debate had been reduced to a discussion of 'women vicars' rather than 'priesthood', whilst broad church and evangelical clergy sometimes remarked upon how few Anglicans had talked of 'priests' until the ordination of women debates of the 1980s and 1990s.[79] None of this is to suggest the existence of a popular 'anti-Catholicism' in the sense that historians generally use the term, but it may suggest that Catholic understandings of priesthood continued to impact only lightly upon the majority of the Church. This did not mean that the idea of the priest as representative or liturgically symbolic was unimportant – female clergy in particular placed some emphasis on the representative role of the priest. For many ordained women the presence of both men and women in ordained ministry was powerfully representative of the inclusiveness of God and the diversity of a gathered humanity – although there was less reference to standing in the place of Christ at the Eucharist or acting as emissary of God.[80] 'The Church would be stronger and more representative of the wholeness of God with men and women in the priesthood', wrote one female vicar.[81] Traditionally it was assumed that men could carry this representative role on behalf of all humanity, but the responses from the current survey suggested that a majority now felt it possible – even important – that women took their place alongside men in fulfilling this function: the ministry was 'incomplete without full participation of women', wrote one female chaplain.[82]

3.8 Division within and without

As suggested in section 3.1, the most convincing argument for delaying women's priesting in the questionnaire survey was that of the potential division within the Church that might result. Concern over division had two main components (although these were not equally weighted for most respondents): first, the potential erosion of common ecclesiological ground and good relations with other denominations; second, the possible effects of disunity within the Church of England itself.

---

[77] int. cs4:10:180.
[78] int. cs6:1:375.
[79] It has, of course, a much longer heritage in the Anglican tradition.
[80] For more on the conflicting ideas of the 'representativeness' of the priest at the Eucharist in the ordination of women debate, see: Douglas, *Risk and Blame*, p. 279.
[81] CQ340, female vicar, 50–59.
[82] CQ153, female chaplain, 40–49.

Where the ecumenical implications of the vote were discussed, this was almost always in relation to Rome or the Orthodox Churches. As **Figure 3i** has already suggested, relations with (mainly Protestant) churches that already ordained women were not felt to be an overriding consideration (either for or against women's priesting). At first sight this may appear to be surprising, given the suggestion in section 3.7 that many respondents were not greatly influenced by Roman Catholic theology or felt a strong attachment to the Roman Catholic Church, and given current proposals for closer union with the Methodist Church. Instead, it was more common to imply that 1992 had to some extent problematized relations with Rome whilst having little effect on relations with the free churches. A significant number of clergy from the Catholic tradition (particularly those expressing objections/reservations over women's priesting) expressed concern about how ordaining women might 'put us out of step with the majority of Catholic Christendom, Roman and Catholic'.[83] Some even spoke of the Church of England's decision leaving it 'separate from Christendom',[84] indicating the degree to which a minority of Catholic clergy still appeared to harbour strong reservations about the orthodox credentials of Protestant denominations, or else to suggest that the English free churches were small and struggling, and that their views were therefore unimportant.

However, more important than a cultural attachment to the idea of Christendom (a long-cherished concept within Anglo-Catholicism) were particular concerns about the prospects for institutional unity with Rome, and the possible effects on the status of Anglican orders. Many clergy and laity from the Catholic tradition were prepared to concede that women's priesting might theoretically be theologically acceptable, but felt that the Church of England had approached the matter in the wrong way: 'General Synod did not have the authority to do it (Holy orders were not ours – we received them)', as one male vicar wrote.[85] Many believed the only appropriate way to solve the question would be through a General Council, of the kind that had set down the Creeds in the early Christian centuries: as one interviewee from Church 8 reflected, '...if the whole Church, around the world, accepted that women could be priests, I probably wouldn't accept it, but I'd go along with it. But unfortunately the way that this has come about is completely and utterly wrong... because who on earth is the General Synod?'[86]

Even amongst those who supported Synod's decision, the ecumenical dimension was often a cause for concern: 'I had some reservations about how the ordination of women might affect relations with the Church of Rome', wrote one male curate from Diocese B, but 'the present backward-looking attitude of the Vatican renders ordination or non-ordination of women in the C of E irrelevant'[87] – particularly as it was regularly pointed out that Anglican orders were not currently recognized by the Roman Catholic Church anyway. For a majority, the ecumenical dimension remained relevant, but could not remain the controlling factor, and disagreement between the two churches over women's priesting was felt to be an insufficient reason for inaction. One male incumbent from Diocese B recalled his disappointment in 1992 because 'I didn't think priesthood was ours to do with as we wish' and 'we belonged to a western Catholic tradition; would the ordination of women sever this (already weak) link?'. Today, however, 'who is to deny that [women's ordination as priests] might be a moving up of the Spirit and a call to the church to look afresh at its ministry and life? Ministry does properly belong to all'.[88]

---

[83] CQ89, male vicar, 60–69, Diocese A.
[84] int. 2:25.
[85] CQ263, male incumbent, 30–39.
[86] int. cs3: 26:24.
[87] CQ151, male curate, 60–9, Diocese B.
[88] CQ185, male vicar, 40–9, Diocese B.

A second source of concern was the potentially divisive impact of the 1992 vote on the Church of England itself. Writing this in late 2003, observers have frequently commented upon how the ordination of women debate seemed harmonious in comparison to that taking place across the worldwide Anglican Communion on homosexuality. However, in the late 1980s and early 1990s, the prospect of serious schism over women's priesting looked very serious indeed. Catholic and Conservative Evangelical clergy with particular concerns on church order again argued that the Church of England now no longer had an ordained ministry based on a mutual recognition of orders. This seemed particularly damaging as an interchangeable ministry was widely regarded as one important building-block in holding the Church together. However, in the eyes of many clergy in favour of women's priesting, traditionalists simply seemed unable to accept what the Church of England had decided through the proper process. Nevertheless, there had also been a much more general concern at the level of distraction and ill-feeling generated by the debate. One evangelical clergyman from Diocese C remembered receiving criticism from female colleagues in 1992 for feeling that all ecclesiological issues (in which he included women's priesting) were of 'secondary concern' compared to 'kingdom issues, social issues... missions'.[89] Others expressed concern that the debate was being conducted in a divisive spirit, owing more to a lobby group mentality than a slow movement towards consensus (this was all a matter of perspective, as others suggested that the local debates were constructive and well conducted). Disunity in church structures was a more marginal concern to many lay interviewees, but as Chapter 4 will suggest, there was much more awareness of the possibility of division within the local congregation. Nevertheless, whilst few welcomed the prospect of division and disunity, few thought it was a sufficient cause to delay the ordination of women as priests.

3.9 Social expectation and the demands of mission

As Chapter 1 has already suggested, debates on women's ordination in the twentieth-century West were partly distinguished from their predecessors by the wider social expectation that the Church should be ordaining women as priests as a matter of justice. Not surprisingly therefore, many respondents noted the wider climate of opinion in their responses. 'Culturally it had become a nonsense for the Church to be the only organ in society discriminating against women', said one female chaplain[90], whilst one lay woman wrote, 'As a society/culture we are ready to accept women in leadership – who refuses help from a woman doctor when they are in pain?'[91] As this quote implies, many respondents felt that society was moving in the right direction over the treatment of women, and that the Church, too, should move away from its 'unenlightened' past.

Many of those who wished to retain an all-male priesthood were irritated by this view; and implied that the past provided a better guide to life and belief than the present or the future (this is explored further in section 3.10). 'The church was jumping on a bandwagon of political correctness without sufficient consideration', wrote one male vicar; 'pressure group policies are seldom sound policies'.[92] To many who shared his view, the 1992 decision exemplified a more general 'selling out' by the Church to secular values. However, a notable number of supporters of women's priesting were reluctant to draw such a hard and fast line between 'secular' trends and 'religious' ideas. Moreover, as the final two sections will suggest, many believed women's priesting was worthy of support because it seemed

---

[89] int. cs3:10:101. The speaker in question was now firmly supportive of the decision to ordain women as priests.
[90] CQ4, female chaplain, 50–59, Diocese A.
[91] LQ 101, female 50–59, Church 4.
[92] CQ331, male vicar, 60–69, Diocese C.

consonant with scripture and tradition, regardless of 'the world's' values. And whilst respondents did frequently express concern over the Church's future in a secularizing society, there was widespread pleasure that in ordaining women, the Church had done something that was, for once, both theologically acceptable and socially welcomed.

However, if society appeared to many to be pointing the Church back to a more authentic form of ministry, there were also more pragmatic considerations: several respondents wrote of how they hoped women's priesting would make the Church more intelligible to society, and ease the path of mission and ministry. 'I felt that if the Church was to minister to British Society in the twentieth century then women needed to be fully involved and not relegated to a supporting role', wrote one female chaplain from Diocese E.[93] Again some voices raised against women's priesting disputed this, suggesting that relevance was useless if it was conceded at the expense of orthodoxy. However, few who advocated women's priesting suggested to me that doctrine was expendable; simply that a change that was both right and relevant seemed a welcome bonus.

3.10 *The significance of tradition*

As the preceding section has hinted, some of the most passionate observations were reserved for the subject of tradition: the 1992 decision was 'a total break with Christian tradition', according to one male priest,[94] whilst one female member of Church 3 supported the move because 'we have moved on in 2000 years – (in fact we no longer send little boys up chimneys with brushes!)'.[95] However, it would be a gross over-simplification to suggest that supporters of women's priesting favoured a complete abandonment of tradition whilst those who came down against the move were enslaved to a rigid and unchanging tradition. Certainly a few lay respondents believed that 'tradition' was always the enemy of the Gospel, whilst on the other hand a small minority of (usually Catholic) clergy argued that orthodoxy was, in the words of St Vincent of Lérins, 'what has always been believed, everywhere and by all'; a dictum that came close to denying the possibility of any doctrinal change whatsoever. Nevertheless, a majority of clergy and laity surveyed here sought a middle path, insisting that tradition was important but contained some room for development. Lay respondents were more likely to suggest that tradition was either the sole reason for retaining a male-only priesthood or a complete irrelevance to the debate. However, clergy (perhaps because of their formal grounding in theology and church history) were more likely to regard tradition as one amongst several authorities that required consideration. For some, tradition acted as the primary consideration, whilst for others its significance was outweighed by other factors.

When those with objections/reservations over women's priesting talked of tradition, what did they mean? For a minority, the Church's tradition on priesthood derived entirely from the pattern set down at the beginning of the Christian movement by Jesus and the apostles (for which, see also section 3.11), with no room for change. One bishop who counted himself an 'impossibilist' explained how, for him, women's priesting was ruled out by the fact that only men were present at the Last Supper: 'now that was a significant decision by our Lord, and the upper room was where I believe the priesthood was instituted ... I do believe it was our Lord's intention'.[96] However, clergy who disagreed with women's priesting more commonly regarded tradition as normative rather than determinative, and saw the study of tradition in the ordination of women debate as a search for legitimate precedent. As such, theologizing about women's priesting was primarily an exercise in

---

[93] CQ280, female chaplain, 40–49, Diocese E.
[94] CQ263, male incumbent, 30–39, Pilot Study.
[95] LQ61, female 50–59, Church 3.
[96] int. 11:123.

historical reconstruction to provide a justification or refutation of a new development. One priest remembered 'being pretty well convinced' on the ordination of women to the diaconate 'from the Patristic evidence and the Scriptural evidence that I read at the time' but he remained unsure on the question of women's ordination as priests, ' ... on the ground of acceptability to the whole church and conformity to precedent. And if it's not conforming to precedent, there needs to be a wider agreement to depart from what has been the precedent'.[97]

As this perspective suggests, tradition was often felt to have a consensual element; each generation inherited the officially agreed position, and making a change demanded a similar level of official agreement. By contrast, change itself was frequently felt to be disordering. One male churchgoer from Church 6 wrote that he strongly disagreed with women's priesting because of 'tradition – [women's priesting] divides the church and weakens it'.[98] It was notable that in publications such as *New Directions* magazine, the word 'innovation' almost always carried negative connotations. In fact, contributors saw themselves as critiquing *unwarranted* innovation, but it was interesting that the first word (or any equivalent qualification) seldom appeared, leaving the impression that orthodox Christians should be suspicious of 'innovation' in itself. Indeed for some, doubts over a lack of historical precedent were accompanied by a wider, more aesthetic or intuitive sense that the past was a more reliable guide than the present or the future: 'where there is uncertainty and things are contraverted, the ancient traditions of moral theology encourage us to hold to the course that is more certain', wrote Bishop Geoffrey Rowell on the tenth anniversary of the vote.[99] For others, objection to women's priesting was in part informed by the sense that a more stable and familiar way of life was disappearing: one woman who found it difficult even to accept female servers explained that:

> *In a way, somehow, I don't want to get rid of all the tradition – the old way, as it were – just the same as the Bible; I like readings from the Bible, instead of the New Bible and the Alternative Service ...*

[IJ: Right – do you prefer the Authorized Version?]

> *Yes, the Authorized Version – I think it's so much nicer, the language is so much better, and why change for change's sake?'*

[IJ: And you would see it as change for change's sake?]

> *I would ...* [100]

There are some potentially intriguing connections here between some of the opposition to women's priesting and a more generally conservative ideological orientation – although the complexity of the issue and the fact that this connection was by no means universally made means there is insufficient space to explore it fully here.[101] Nevertheless, it should be acknowledged that arguments from 'tradition' against women's priesting could draw upon a variety of sources and take very different forms.

---

[97] int. 7:p.4.
[98] LQ165, male 70–79, Church 6.
[99] *Church Times*, 8 November 2002.
[100] int. cs2:19:281.
[101] It is hoped to consider this in greater detail in a subsequent publication.

When supporters of the decision to ordain women as priests discussed the subject of tradition, what did they mean? Most common was the insistence that respect for tradition should not mean an absence of change. 'Tradition has always evolved', wrote one female curate from Diocese B; 'if we do not continue to grow and be transformed, as a body, what kind of Church will we be, and what kind of message will we be giving?'[102] Lay interviewees in particular sometimes ventured the likely outcome if every aspect of 'traditional' teaching were retained (the most commonly used example being that women would still cover their heads for worship). Indeed, it was occasionally suggested (in the words of this male member of Church 3) 'that the arguments against women's ordination were not Biblical but part of traditional roles of women in society'.[103]

Clergy were particularly likely to suggest that objectors to women's priesting had placed excessive importance on a somewhat limited understanding of 'tradition'. One Anglo-Catholic priest who described himself as 'agnostic' on women's priesting argued that 'we've got other things to worry about [...] in a parish like this, where what's important is what we need for the journey, to talk about orders is highly academic, a luxury ... '[104] Some interviewees were uneasy of the way that references to 'tradition' appeared to brook no argument or discussion. Indeed, a key characteristic of a living tradition is that it rarely requires explicit defence until it is strongly challenged. Traditions are most potent when assumed or inhabited unconsciously.[105] Although a significant minority continued to feel that women's priesting was self-evidently wrong because it was not traditional, a much larger majority felt the need to rationalize or explain the relevance of tradition (either 'for' or 'against'). That tradition became contested territory in this way strongly suggests that belief in a male-only priesthood was already on the defensive long before the 1992 vote itself.[106]

Although arguments from tradition were rarely the *most* important consideration for those agreeing with women's ordination as priests, clergy and laity nevertheless felt it important to engage in the debate about the evidence and precedent for the move. Negatively, it was frequently noted that women's priesting was 'not contrary to scripture or tradition'. Here, they found common ground with some who had voted against in 1992: one male priest from the Catholic tradition who had moved towards acceptance of women's priesting over the past decade reflected how 'contrary to what some people would say, it seems to me that the tradition doesn't teach anything about this [...] If you're a Catholic both doctrinally and emotionally, precedent matters hugely'.[107] Likewise, one bishop who did not ordain women concluded that whilst women's priesting was certainly not 'contrary to scripture', he could find nowhere in the Bible that demanded it either.[108]

---

[102] CQ177, female curate, 50–59, Diocese B.

[103] LQ83, male 50–59, Church 3.

[104] int. cs4:2:146.

[105] Dan Sperber, quoted in: Jonathan Spencer, 'Rethinking Symbolism' in Alan Barnard and Jonathan Spencer (eds), *Encyclopaedia of Social and Cultural Anthropology* (Routledge, London, 1996), pp. 535–9. See also: Zygmunt Baumann, 'Morality in the Age of Contingency' in Paul Heelas, Scott Lash and Paul Morris (eds), *Detraditionalisation* (Blackwell, Oxford, 1996), pp. 49–58 (p. 49).

[106] It is notable that most of the literature defending the concept of an all-male priesthood emerges in the period from the early 1970s onwards.

[107] int. cs1:28:141.

[108] int. cs4:10:180.

More positively, some had been led to conclude that it was right to ordain women as priests because it seemed to be 'rediscovering ancient tradition'.[109] Several cited archaeological evidence from the early Christian centuries of women apparently involved in priestly functions.[110] But as the final section of this chapter will suggest, most arguments for women's priesting from precedent turned back to the Bible itself for support.

3.11 The biblical witness

As suggested in section 3.1, the Bible provided most respondents an important point of reference when considering the question of women's priesting. Whilst the 'learned' debate has been discussed elsewhere,[111] how did grass roots clergy and laity use scripture in formulating their positions on women and ordained ministry? The most common approach amongst clergy was a hermeneutical one, seeking to discern underlying biblical principles. This was felt to be particularly important because most stated or implied that the Bible did not speak directly of Christian priesthood (except of Christ as High Priest and the 'royal priesthood' of believers). Clergy who took this approach tended to focus particularly on the values of justice and inclusiveness they identified within the Christian faith, regarding them as central to the question of whether women should be ordained as priests. Clergy who felt the Bible clearly ruled out the possibility of women's priesting were often suspicious of the hermeneutical method, suggesting that it enabled a biblical justification for any number of new ideas that did not reflect a traditional interpretation of the texts. In practice, however, a hermeneutical approach was not the preserve of one 'side' of the debate or the other, and 'fundamentalist' readings of the Bible were rare. A few clergy from the reformed evangelical tradition spoke of the need to submit to 'the plain meaning of scripture', but many respondents recognized that in some sense, the biblical message required some measure of interpretation. Amongst lay respondents, there was less interest in abstracting underlying principles from the Gospel message than in reading the Bible as a vital source of clues on the teaching of Jesus or the practice of the early Church.

Which biblical passages were felt to be most relevant? Evangelical clergy with objections to women in congregational oversight often put forward 'arguments from creation' based on the first chapters of Genesis. One male curate from Diocese D explained how for him these offered a blueprint for the divine ordering of gender relations before the Fall, a pattern itself based on the Godhead:

> *'the Son and the Spirit do the Father's will, but nowhere does the Father do the will of the Son or the will of the Spirit – so there's some sort of assymetry in their relationships there, but not in their status'. 'Now that assymetry is mirrored, I think, in creation. There is a role for Adam, which there is not for Eve'.*[112]

He continued that refusing to recognize the different roles and natures of men and women would result in a 'disordering' of creation as God had intended it, echoing the convictions expressed in sections 3.8 and 3.10 that women's priesting would be (respectively)

---

[109] CQ237, female curate/hospice chaplain, 60–69, Diocese B.

[110] The word 'priest' as applied to Christian ministers appears to date from the end of the second century, although the link between 'presbyter' and 'sacerdos' is not widely noted until the time of St Cyprian (d. 258). See the entry for 'priest' in F.L. Cross and E.A. Livingstone (eds), *The Oxford Dictionary of the Christian Church* (Oxford University Press, Oxford, 1997), pp. 1235–6.

[111] For a good introduction to this, see: Mary Hayter, *The New Eve in Christ; The Use and Abuse of the Bible in the Debate about Women in the Church* (SPCK, London, 1987). Hayter's conclusions are favourable towards the ordination of women but much space is also given to the arguments of those who doubt that the Bible supports women's priesting.

[112] int. cs4:1:416.

ecclesiologically 'disordering' and disorientating to adherents of 'tradition'. However, few respondents believed that women's priesting was 'disordering', arguing that if this was so, it would surely have visible (and not just metaphysical) results. But as Chapter 4 will suggest, a majority of respondents saw more benefits than problems from women's priesting.

Whereas arguments from creation interested a minority (usually of clergy), most respondents focused on the *New* Testament, with the example of Jesus particularly central for lay participants: 'The scripture says that women followed Jesus in his itinerant teaching 'and ministered to him', wrote one man from Church 14,[113] whilst a female churchgoer from Church 7 suggested that '...traditionally disciples were male, 200 years ago things were very different but Jesus never once excluded women'.[114] For others, Jesus' actions suggested a very different conclusion: 'Jesus Christ was eager to change the old order, and including women amongst his apostles could have been part of this, but he decided otherwise', wrote one man from Church 15[115], whilst another respondent argued, along slightly different lines, 'I never want women as priests. Jesus Christ chose men to be his disciples'.[116] Whilst these views were derived directly from the text, more speculative comments were also to be found amongst the questionnaire and interview testimony: 'I am sure that today Jesus would have welcomed women as his apostles – to play a more proactive role than ... allowed 2000 years ago', wrote one respondent from Church 1.[117] A few others argued that priests should be male because all those present at the Last Supper were men.[118] Although neither of these arguments would be decisive in a learned theological debate on women's priesting, it is nevertheless important to acknowledge their presence in the popular debate, and the conviction with which they were held.

Third, respondents often turned to the New Testament epistles for further guidance. Experienced observers of the debate will not be surprised that Galatians 3:28 regularly featured as a key text: one student from Church 16 wrote of her support for women's priesting because of 'the biblical statement that in Christ we are freed and equal, Jew nor Greek etc. A statement that leads us to all be equal'.[119] Respondents seemed to take seriously the message of freedom and inclusivity they identified in the Christian faith. Clergy seemed particularly likely to point out the significance of common baptism in the New Covenant: as one male vicar argued, a 'gender-free sacrament of initiation into [the] people of God should govern eligibility for ordained ministry'.[120] Indeed, several respondents repeated one of the Movement for the Ordination of Women's key maxims; 'if you will not ordain women, do not baptize women'.[121] By contrast, for those who believed the biblical witness demanded a male-only priesthood/ presbyterate, the so-called household codes of the later New Testament letters contained more relevant guidance:

---

[113] LQ404, male 50–59, Church 14.

[114] LQ228, female 20–29, Church 7.

[115] LQ319, male 70–79, Church 15.

[116] LQ118, female 80+, Church 6.

[117] LQ31, female 50–59, Church 1. Although as Figure 3.i suggested, the 'If Christ were alive on earth today' argument was accorded a much lower priority by the majority of churchgoers supportive of women's priesting than other arguments.

[118] In fact the Gospels do not say whether Jesus and the Twelve were the *only* ones present at the Last Supper, although they are the only ones mentioned.

[119] LQ348, female 20–29, Church 16.

[120] CQ37, male vicar, 50–59, Diocese A.

[121] CQ50, male vicar, 30–39, Diocese A.

> *Theologically, for me, the clincher was passages in scripture – particularly in Paul's writings – 1 Timothy 2, 1 Corinthians 11… in a sense it would have been a lot easier to dismiss them or reinterpret them – time and again I come back to them, and say I hold those to be dear, and they seem to be pretty clear.*[122]

Indeed, the 'headship' argument was amongst the most common put forward by evangelicals with objections to women's ordination (although many added that their concern was not with ordination or the celebration of communion *per se* but with men in positions of teaching authority within the Church). Even so, there was some difference of opinion as to how far male headship applied. The vicar and curate of Church 12 differed over whether it related only to Episcopal roles or also to oversight of the local congregation. For the speaker above, there was a genuine question over whether women should take on *any* role that placed them in oversight of men.[123]

However, it was striking how few evangelical respondents found women's priesting problematic on scriptural grounds. A majority instead seemed quite willing to accept that the Bible must be read in context, with some patterns of ordering more relevant to the first century than to the twenty-first.[124] One ordained woman (whose first sermon after her priesting was – quite by chance – on the text 'women keep silent'!) remembered a heated discussion with a member of her current church on why supporters of women's ordination seemed to 'pick and choose' passages that supported their views, 'to which I was tempted to reply to him about the things he probably didn't do which in the Old Testament men should do!'[125] Concerns that reading the Bible 'in context' might open the door to the removal of core doctrines were regularly expressed by evangelicals and Catholics with objections to women as priests, and some lay respondents in particular found this a formidable problem: 'Ignoring the parts of the Bible that offend me (and they do), is a slippery slope', wrote one female member of Church 16, adding that in relation to women bishops, 'it sounds pompous (and woolly), but I really cannot find scriptural authority for it, without feeling that I am mentally editing out important passages'.[126] Even so, most responses stated or implied that the Church had to accept the inevitability of some measure of change, even if the way ahead was difficult to discern. More positively, the Church needed to be alert to God's prompting in a new generation: as one lay woman from Church 3 responded, 'God often chooses women to do very important work for him', citing 'the nativity, at the resurrection, the Samaritan woman at the well, Judith (apocrypha)'.[127] Here, many found that in the combination of biblical witness and personal calling, two of the most powerful arguments for women's priesting in the popular debate appeared to support each other.

Conclusion

Anglican popular belief on the ordination of women was a complex and multilayered affair, blending elements of the learned debate, personal experience, 'common sense' observation and sometimes more inexpressible feelings. The articulated responses considered here also rested upon deeper, underlying assumptions about the nature of God and humanity, the direction of history and the Church's proper relation to the 'secular' world, at which it has only been possible to hint in this chapter.[128] Generalizations are difficult: first, the dividing

---

[122] int. cs5:9:76.
[123] int. cs4:1side2:340.
[124] Indeed, the need to discern between Gospel commands and that which is merely 'cultural' is a classically evangelical way of framing the question.
[125] int. cs5:2:182.
[126] LQ338, female 30–39, Church 16.
[127] LQ56, female, 50–59, Church 3.
[128] See below for more on the ideological and teleological orientations of Anglican clergy and laity in the

line between those 'for' the priesting of women and those 'against' was often blurred as clergy and laity of one constituency often shared with those of another view similar assumptions about what was theologically important – even if they drew different conclusions from these. Second, the focus upon formally expressed beliefs and attitudes (rather than unarticulated assumptions) perhaps also underestimates the degree to which carefully worded responses could mask a range of more private – even unconscious – feelings on the matter (although this is also true of any debate; not just 'religious' ones). However, despite these caveats, several conclusions may be drawn. The high levels of support for women's priesting exhibited in many dioceses and parishes in Chapter 2 rested upon strong convictions women were being called to ordained priestly ministry, that this calling was entirely consistent with the Bible, that women were no less equipped than men to fulfil it, and that a priest's representative role was possible by virtue of being human, rather than being male. However, if women were widely accepted as priests in theory, it was not on exactly the same terms as men: respondents frequently emphasized the distinctive gifts and roles an ordained woman could offer and few discounted gender difference altogether.[129] There was widespread concern at the divisive potential of the vote, but whilst the drawbacks were keenly felt, few believed that division represented an overriding reason for declining to ordain women. Indeed, few lay respondents could see *any* compelling reason against allowing women to become priests. Even though this had sometimes been a difficult journey, keeping an all-male priesthood seemed to many to create even more moral, doctrinal and missiological problems.

The chapter raises several issues that may be relevant to future debates on women and ordained ministry: first, the responses suggested sharply differing views (and much confusion) over what priesthood and ordained ministry actually were, and some conviction amongst a proportion of clergy that these issues had not been adequately debated in the course of the 1980s and 1990s. Might more theological reflection on this subject generate further dialogue and the establishment of more common ground between the positions?

Second, values of fairness, equality and justice were common themes in the responses, but there was some difference over how these values intersected with the issue of women's priesting, and even how their Christian basis might be formulated. Might the Church benefit from further reflection here too?

Third, if the debate on women's priesting is anything to go by, the Bible will feature heavily in discussions on women in the episcopate (for which see Chapter 9). Amongst the most difficult issues of interpretation were whether the Bible represented a blueprint for all time, and whether New Testament patterns of Church ordering were relevant to today. Some further attention to these issues might help greatly.

Fourth, how can the Church better appreciate the complex nexus of feelings, experiences and assumptions that informed beliefs on women's priesting, and which ran deeper than reasoned argument? An awareness of the place of feelings and assumptions allows us to move beyond seeing faith in purely intellectual terms and may enable greater pastoral sensitivity to be shown to those who are wrestling with the intellectual issues but still maintain that women's priesting 'just doesn't feel right'. On the other hand, an uncritical acceptance of any 'gut feeling' may open the door to some attitudes that are morally or doctrinally questionable. So how is the place of feeling and intuition to be viewed within the realm of theological argument?

---

context of the ordination of women debate.
[129] For more on this, see Chapter 4.

Fifth, the research seems to suggest much continuity between current attitudes to women's priesthood and more long-standing historical attitudes to the clergy *per se*. If so, how far should these historic tendencies be subject to critical scrutiny, and how far may they be affirmed?

Finally, it should be understood that this chapter has only considered popular clergy and lay attitudes to women's priesting *in theory*. Although a majority of respondents had settled their views before the vote itself, a significant minority remained undecided; some reckoned their views provisional until they had actually seen women's priesthood in practice; others found their attitudes to women in priestly ministry very different in practice than in theory; and some even changed their minds after the vote. As this chapter has suggested, so much was expected of women's priesting in the early 1990s, but how was its impact assessed a decade on? It is to this question that Chapter 4 will now turn.

Chapter 4

Assessing the impact on the Church

Whilst most Anglicans agreed that the decision to ordain women should be taken primarily with reference to principle rather than expediency, the 1992 decision also had to be accepted *in practice* as well as in theory. But what would the implications be and what would a Church of England that ordained women as priests look like? This chapter explores how that impact appeared to clergy and congregations ten years on from those first ordinations. This can inevitably only provide a 'story so far'; when I explained to one senior clergyman that the project was partly concerned with the impact of the decision, he looked at me quizzically and replied: 'You expect to assess the effects of women's priesting on the Church after *only* ten years?' He has a point: the long-term impact of the decision (particularly on questions of doctrine and gender relations) remain too far into the future to assess at this stage and is left to historians of future generations. Even many of the short-term consequences remain too close in time to discern with any clarity. However, a report on the first ten years of women in priesthood in the Church would seem incomplete without some reflection on the impact of the decisions that were taken. As with Chapter 3 this chapter cannot offer an exhaustive assessment of the impact of women's priesting ten years on, but confines itself to outlining the views of grass roots clergy and congregations, dealing with some of the possible consequences of ordaining women and the way this was given legislative expression, and also with their actual experiences of women's ministry as priests. Unresolved issues arising out of the legislation and key current issues for clergy and their dioceses are given special treatment in Part II of this report and are not therefore considered in detail here. Instead, the chapter considers perceptions of the overall impact of the 1992–94 settlement on the Church and gives particular space to the experiences of the nine main case study churches.

4.1 Some popular expectations

One useful starting point for this survey is to revisit some of the most common expectations of the pre-1992 period about what the ordination of women as priests would bring. As Chapter 3 has suggested, strong advocates of women's ordination confidently looked forward to the benefits that would ensue: at the most fundamental level, women's priesting would signal a shift away from a patriarchal past, a theological injustice would be righted and the Church would be returned closer to the biblical vision of the Kingdom of God in which there was 'neither Jew nor Greek, slave nor free, male and female'. More prosaically, supporters expected women to be able to pursue the priestly task every bit as well as men; individual women would be enabled to fulfil their calling and their gifts would be released in new ways for the service of the Church and society. Women, in particular, could benefit from the listening ear of a priest who could personally relate to some of the problems women faced. For some, women's ordination also promised a new style of priesthood because of the experiences, perspectives and characteristics that women would bring *as women*. The presence of women in priesthood would end the 'old boy network' that seemed to dominate the clerical profession. If indeed women more naturally worked in a relational and collaborative manner, and that hierarchy was a function of patriarchy, female priests and deacons would encourage new ways of being church that empowered the laity and broke through old systems of power relationships.[1] Whether women would model an inherently

---

[1] For some women's writers, women's historic experience of marginalization from the levers of power had bequeathed them a greater awareness of power's potentially harmful effects (Helen Thorne, *Journey to Priesthood: An In-depth Study of the First Women Priests in the Church of England* (University of Bristol, Bristol, 2000), pp. 107–09).

different style of priesthood simply because they were women was a matter of some internal difference amongst their supporters (just as debates over essentialist and constructivist understandings of gender run through feminism itself).[2] Most could agree, however, that the presence of an ordained woman might also serve as a role model to other women in the Church, giving them more confidence to use their own gifts. Finally, in a wider social context in which the Church was beginning to look repressive and (ironically) un-Christian by not ordaining women, it was hoped that the arrival of women in the priesthood might cause the person in the street to look more favourably upon the Church, opening further avenues of ministry and mission.

For those with reservations about women's priesting, several negative consequences seemed in prospect. For those who believed that ordaining a woman as a priest was simply invalid, a woman at the altar would be unable to celebrate communion or pronounce the absolution, bringing doubt and confusion to the Church of England's sacramental ministry.[3] Others feared women's ordination to the presbyterate would take the Church of England outside a Biblical pattern of ministry.[4] Many expressed concern over the possible impact on prospects of closer union with Rome or the Orthodox Churches. Anglo-Catholic clergy with reservations feared that women's priesting would push the Church of England further towards becoming a Protestant sect and further from the true Church of God. Anglo-Catholic and conservative Evangelical voices could also unite in fearing that 'women priests' might be the thin end of a much larger liberal wedge,[5] opening the door to a whole range of heretical beliefs and suspect moral positions – particularly feminism.[6] Some feared that admitting women to the priesthood would further reinforce the folk belief that the Church was an organization for women, worsening the existing shortage of churchgoing men. Others feared that women would be too tied up with home and family life to make the necessary time and sacrifices for the role, de-professionalizing the ministry and damaging parish life. Even those with the mildest objections feared that the whole debate over women's priesting would cause the loss of good clergy to the Church, and create an unhelpful climate of division and ill-feeling that would detract from more important matters. Moreover, on each side of the debate was the fear that defeat in 1992 might result in their marginalization from the mainstream of Church life.

---

[2] The difference between wishing to see women included in the priesthood as currently constituted, and seeking to transform priesthood completely through the inclusion of women, is also noted in the analysis of the Roman Catholic debate on women's ordination in: Mary Douglas, 'The Debate on Women Priests' in Mary Douglas (ed.), *Risk and Blame; Essays in Cultural Theory* (Routledge, London and New York, 1992), pp. 271–94 (pp. 290–91).

[3] Kallistos Ware, 'Man, Woman and the Priesthood of Christ' in Peter Moore (ed.), *Man, Woman and Priesthood* (SPCK, London, 1978), pp. 68–90; Graham Leonard, 'The Priesthood of Christ' in James Tolhurst (ed.), *Man, Woman and Priesthood* (Gracewing Fowler Wright Books, Leominster, 1989), pp. 1–22.

[4] Georg Gunter Blum, 'The Office of Woman in the New Testament' in Michael Bruce and G.E. Duffield (eds), *Why Not? Priesthood and the Ministry of Women* (Marcham Manor Press, Abingdon, 1972), pp. 63–77; Roger Beckwith, 'The Bearing of Holy Scripture' in Moore (ed.), *Man, Woman and Priesthood*, pp. 45–62.

[5] This point has most recently been made in the *Mind of Anglicans* survey conducted for Cost of Conscience by Christian Research, which appears to show lower levels of agreement with a selection of doctrinal and ethical statements amongst ordained women and liberal male clergy than amongst representatives of Reform and Forward in Faith (see: Robbie Low and Francis Gardom, *Believe it or Not! What Church of England Clergy* Actually *Believe*, Christian Research and Cost of Conscience, London, 2003). However, the result are difficult to interpret given that full details of results and methodology were as yet unavailable at time of writing.

[6] See e.g.: G.E. Duffield, 'Feminism and the Church' and Michael Bruce, 'Heresy, Equality and the Rights of Women' in Bruce and Duffield (eds), *Why Not? Priesthood and the Ministry of Women*, pp. 9-25, 40–55.

In separate research by Leslie J. Francis and Mandy Robbins, the first generation of women to be ordained as priests were invited to assess their attitude to several of these possible scenarios. Amongst the most significant were attitudes to the ecumenical impact of the 1992 decision. In response to the statement that 'The Priests (Ordination of Women) Measure strengthens the Church of England's relationship with other churches in Britain that already ordain women', 88% of female deacons agreed, with 10% unsure and just 2% disagreeing. In response to a similar statement that the Measure 'has had a detrimental effect on the Church of England's relationship with the Roman Catholic Church', just 19% of respondents agreed, with 35% unsure and almost half (46%) disagreeing.[7] In addition, Helen Thorne's study of the first generation of women to be priested asked a range of questions about the working styles of female clergy, and concluded that over three quarters of women favoured a 'synergistic approach' to ministry, whilst much of the interview testimony suggested a strong concern for the empowering of the laity.[8] Evidence from the USA also suggested that women clergy were more likely than their colleagues to prioritize congregational empowerment, with churchgoers taking the same view – although this was more true for women acting as senior ministers in clergy teams than for 'solo' pastors.[9] But if similar questions about the impact of women's priesting were asked across the board, to samples of both male and female clergy, to lay as well as ordained, what kinds of answers would result?

---

[7] Leslie J. Francis and Mandy Robbins, *The Long Diaconate, 1987–1994; Women Deacons and the Delayed Journey to Priesthood* (Gracewing, Leominster, 1999), p. 213.

[8] Helen Thorne, *Journey to Priesthood: An In-depth Study of the First Women Priests in the Church of England* (University of Bristol, Bristol, 2000), Section 3 of the questionnaire and pp. 102–06.

[9] Edward C. Lehman Jnr, *Gender and Work: The Case of the Clergy* (State University of New York Press, Albany, 1993), pp. 79, 181, 184.

Table 4i: Responses to some commonly suggested consequences of the decision to ordain women as priests, amongst current diocesan clergy[10] [SA/A = % 'strongly agree' or 'agree'; NAND = 'neither agree nor disagree'; D/DS = % 'disagree' or 'strongly disagree']			
The Ordination of Women as Priests has...	*SA/A*	*NAND*	**D/DS**
1) Had a detrimental effect on the C of E's relationship with the Roman Catholic Church	31.0	27.6	41.3
2) Enriched ordained ministry through the gifts and experiences that women have brought to it	75.9	13.8	10.3
3) Done nothing to change the over-institutionalized nature of the Church	48.3	24.1	27.5
4) Strengthened the relationship with other churches in Britain that already ordain women	51.8	40.7	7.4
5) Strengthened ordained ministry by creating a truly representative priesthood	69.0	10.3	20.7
6) Been a setback for the development of a permanent diaconate	24.1	31.0	44.8
7) Raised the credibility of the C of E in the eyes of the general public	55.2	31.0	13.8
8) Weakened ordained ministry by bringing doubt about the validity of orders	21.4	3.6	75.0
9) Brought about a more relational/collaborative style of pastoral leadership	32.9	35.7	21.4
10) Undermined the authority of the ordained ministry by going against biblical principles of male headship	13.7	6.9	79.3
11) Led to a less hierarchical style of priesthood	34.4	37.9	27.5
12) Led to an empowerment of the laity	31.0	31.0	37.9

Drawing directly from the questions asked by Thorne, Francis and Robbins, but also from published theological contributions to the debate and conversations with participants in it, two questions were drawn up inviting respondents to indicate their level of agreement with some of the most common suggestions made about the potential impact of women's ordination as priests. The question to clergy comprised twelve statements (six 'positive' consequences, six 'negative') that respondents were asked to rate on a five-point scale from 'strongly agree' to 'strongly disagree'. The question for churchgoers was simpler, comprising nine statements (five 'positive' consequences, four 'negative'), again to be rated on the same five-point scale. **Table 4i** shows levels of agreement amongst all the current diocesan clergy surveyed. **Table 4ii** shows the equivalent results for lay respondents, but this time the results are broken down into three groups: 1) responses from churches with experience of women's priestly ministry; 2) responses from churches with resolutions in place; 3) responses from churches that come into neither category.[11] In both tables, the figures usually add up to less than 100% because the remainder ticked 'neither agree nor disagree'.

---

[10] Statements 1 and 4 are taken from Francis and Robbins, *The Long Diaconate*, p. 213.

[11] An overall percentage agreement figure for clergy is meaningful, in that diocese-based clergy samples are fairly representative of the cross section of Anglican clergy as a whole. Aggregating Congregations Questionnaire responses into an overall percentage agreement figure for churchgoers is not meaningful, because the selection of congregations (whilst reflective of the diversity of experience in the Church of England) is not a scientifically representative sample of lay opinion as a whole.

Possible consequences	WP	Res.	Neither
1) Chances of unity with the Roman Catholic Church have been badly damaged	34.3	59.4	37.9
2) We now have a more representative clergy	87.5	44.0	77.9
3) Women's distinctive style of ministry has led to a less clericalized church	42.0	28.3	30.1
4) The Church of England has become badly divided	20.6	64.3	24.0
5) Fairness has been achieved, and equal opportunities advanced	75.2	39.8	68.1
6) Doubt has been introduced into the validity of Anglican priestly orders	8.5	46.9	17.0
7) Women's gifts have been released for use in ordained ministry	89.0	45.5	82.8
8) The Church of England has turned itself into a sect by acting unilaterally on this issue	2.9	33.6	7.5
9) The Church now seems more intelligible to the person in the street	60.4	30.7	51.1

Table 4ii: Responses to some commonly suggested consequences of the decision to ordain women as priests, amongst respondents from the 22 case study congregations [**WP** = amongst respondents from parishes with experience of women's ministry as priests; **Res.** = amongst respondents from parishes with resolutions in place; **Neither** = amongst respondents from parishes with neither female clergy nor resolutions][12]

The results should be read with caution: those agreeing/strongly agreeing with the 1992 decision tended to focus on the positive consequences of ordaining women, whilst those disagreeing/ strongly disagreeing with the change tended to highlight its negative consequences. In this respect, the results may reflect levels of support for women's priesting as much as they represent individuals' objective assessments of the consequences. Nevertheless, if read in conjunction with interview testimony and responses to the open-ended questions on the surveys, the results suggest that several key consequences were widely identified. On the positive side, a significant majority of clergy and churchgoers felt the decision to ordain women as priests had restored something that was previously lacking from the Church and its ministry: one male vicar spoke of 'a sense of justice – not merely "fairness" but to do with acknowledgement of [one's?] relationship with God'[13] whilst one member of Church 3, a resolution parish in Diocese A, wrote that 'it feels more inclusive and complete, but as far as significant results go – I don't know'.[14] Lay women seemed particularly likely to feel it important that both sexes were represented within the ministry. As the following speaker commented in relation to worship, 'the whole picture's up there now, rather than just half the picture – what's on stage is also off-stage'.[15] Moreover, far from expecting priests to constitute a kind of 'third gender' (as popular religious attitudes had sometimes traditionally implied[16]) or for only one sex to be capable of representing the other, the presence of both male and female in ordained ministry was felt not only acceptable but perhaps even important: 'the priesthood has become more complete', wrote one retired clergyman; 'the gifts of male and female together complementing each other in a way that was impossible before'.[17]

The most popular response was that the first ten years of women's priesting had more generally enriched the life of the Church: 'It has provided us with numbers of richly gifted

---

[12] Note that Church 10 has both a female curate and Resolution B in place, and so results from this case study congregation are included in the overall figures for *both* columns 'WP' and 'Res.'.
[13] CQ145, male vicar, 50–59, Diocese B.
[14] LQ79, female 60–69, Church 3.
[15] int. cs1:22:233.
[16] For popular attitudes to the clergy as a 'third gender' in modern religious history see: Hugh McLeod, *Secularisation in Western Europe, 1870–1914* (Macmillan, Basingstoke, 2000), p. 137.
[17] CQ371, retired male vicar, 70–79.

women ready and willing to serve God', wrote one lay woman from Church 7.[18] This was also often acknowledged by those who had reservations about women's priesting: 'I don't deny at all that God is working in them, in a certain way of grace', explained one male priest, 'and people are brought by them too, just as much as with male priests, to an understanding of Him…'[19] (although he added the qualification that this was in the form of a 'general' rather than 'particular' grace, or that it remained a fundamental departure from orthodoxy). Did respondents have particular gifts in mind when they thought of the impact of women's priesting? Generally not. In line with the discussion of the differences between men and women in Chapter 3 (section 3.5) the difficulties of identifying particular attributes that women brought to the priesthood *as women* were widely noted. Some suggested that 'women bring gifts of greater compassion and greater care',[20] whilst others (particularly clergy) found new insights in worship led by female priests: one male priest recalled seeing a woman elevate the host at the Eucharist for the first time and found himself thinking of a mother cradling her child.[21] Some also noted a more relaxed atmosphere at worship. However, it was more common for respondents to suggest that the Church and its ministry had been enriched less by any intrinsic capabilities that women brought *as women* than 'a wider spread of gifts available to the Church and the world. Not necessarily to do with masculinity/femininity', as one female curate from Diocese C wrote.[22] Female clergy were particularly likely to suggest that women's priesting had also helped to enrich the ministry of ordained men. One recalled leading a deanery workshop on 'women priests' and asking her male colleagues to consider also what it might mean to be a man in ordained ministry. Many of her male colleagues looked surprised, confessed they had never thought of it in this way but proceeded to have good discussion on the subject. If women were thought to offer a distinctive contribution by virtue of their sex, this was most often said to be through their life experiences as women, which offered an alternative (though overlapping) perspective to the life experiences of men. More generally, the addition of women to the body of clergy was widely felt to be a breath of fresh air: 'Clerical gatherings here [are] "loosened up" and also "sharpened up", wrote one retired clergyman; 'There fresh and different minds at work'.[23]

In several important respects, then, the arrival of women as priests in the Church of England was regarded as a very welcome development. However, fewer believed that all of the positive expectations raised in the pre-1994 period were being fulfilled. For one thing, **Tables 4i and 4ii** showed much ambivalence towards suggestions that women's priesting would precipitate a revolution in ministerial style and approach, and in the character of the Church as a whole. The suggestion that women's ordination had 'led to a less hierarchical style of priesthood' was supported by just over half of ordained women, but less than thirty per cent of male clergy.[24] Even those who were in strong agreement with the 1992 decision were almost evenly divided over whether this had taken place, and also over whether women's priesting had brought about 'an empowerment of the laity' or 'changed the over-institutionalized nature of the Church': 'My only criticism of the last 20 years is that it has continued to focus on the ordained priesthood as the main ministry in the Church', wrote one male priest in his sixties; 'It has retarded the development of lay people as real

---

[18] LQ209, female 60–69, Church 7.

[19] int. 7:p.4.

[20] LQ105, female 50–59, Church 4.

[21] int. cs1:16:295.

[22] CQ293, female curate/chaplain, 40–49, Diocese C.

[23] CQ14, retired male vicar, 70–79.

[24] It should be added that some male clergy who had strong reservations on women's priesting believed that hierarchy was implicit in the divine ordering of both creation as a whole and the Church in particular, and was thus not something to be desired from ordaining women.

decision-makers and providers in parish life'.[25] One male archdeacon wrote of his 'disappointment about the hoped for enhancement to the priesthood at stipendiary level – women are not making the contribution many of us hoped for. Is this because their opportunities are limited or because there is a shortage of female professional "career" priests willing to be deployed?'[26] For some this lack of progress was due to a reluctance in some quarters to embrace women's priestly ministry fully. Some members of the first generation of women in priesthood felt that some of their female colleagues had become too comfortable with the establishment now that they were a part of it. One recent study also suggested that whilst female ordinands were more likely to prioritize pastoral aspects of ministry than men, the busy realities of parish work tended to push liturgical and administrative roles further up the agenda of most clergy.[27] For most it would simply take time for such large-scale changes to take place. However, some respondents did suggest they perceived a definite change of style, particularly in parishes with experience of women's ordained ministry: 'I feel women priests can be seen as being more approachable than men, particularly by other women and therefore offer additional gifts to the church', wrote one woman from Church 19 in Diocese E.[28]

However, whilst clergy and laity were divided over suggestions that women's priesting was ushering in a new style of ordained ministry, and new ways of being church, there was much greater consensus that the debate had been a divisive experience: amongst both clergy and laity the suggestion that relations with Rome had been badly damaged received the highest level of agreement of any of the 'negative' consequences listed.[29] This was particularly regretted by Anglo-Catholic clergy with Ultra-Montane[30] sympathies; one male priest from Diocese B described how 'one of the things that was most important to me was the joining together of the Catholic Church in this country ... and when I was ordained it seemed that we were getting close to possible union and the Catholic Church would be one again in this land ...'. However, 1992 was 'a disaster, because it totally closed the door to any Catholic unity within this country'.[31] Dashed expectations of unity were a common theme amongst clergy who expressed their disappointment at the Church of England's decision to ordain women as priests, and the experience certainly seemed to have made more acute the ambiguity of identifying as a Catholic priest, but within the Anglican Church.[32] However, some questioned the validity of this reading of history: one senior Anglican clergyman of the 'traditionalist' constituency with extensive ecumenical experience reflected: 'I would want to check out quite how realistic we were in our aspirations for a more corporate communion ... just round the corner ... There was some unrealism about how substantial the agenda actually was'.[33] Indeed, several voices of

---

[25] CQ302, male priest-in-charge, 60–69, Diocese C.

[26] CQ417, male Archdeacon, 40–49.

[27] Mandy Robbins and Leslie J. Francis, 'Role Prioritisation amongst Clergywomen: The Influence of Personality and Church Tradition amongst Female Stipendiary Anglican Clerics in the UK', *British Journal of Theological Education* 11 (1), August 2000, pp. 7–23.

[28] LQ482, female 50–59, Church 19.

[29] This represented a higher level of agreement than amongst women deacons in Francis and Robbins' 1999 survey – even amongst ordained women (Francis and Robbins, *The Long Diaconate*, p. 213).

[30] Meaning that they considered it important to look towards Rome (literally 'over the mountains' towards Italy). In a technical historical sense, the label 'Ultra-Montane' was applied to those Roman Catholic clergy who favoured a centralization of authority around the Vatican rather than national or diocesan autonomy, although it has now achieved the much wider usage employed here.

[31] int. cs2:7:22.

[32] Indeed, several admitted to feeling that they were probably in the wrong church. There is much more to be said about the place of Catholic and Protestant identity in the ordination of women debates in some future publication. For more on the experience of ambiguity experienced by Catholic Anglican clergy, see: W.S.F. Pickering, *Anglo-Catholicism; A Study in Religious Ambiguity* (Routledge, London, 1989).

[33] int. 18:114.

caution from within the Catholic Anglican tradition doubted whether Rome was immediately contemplating unity and expressed doubt over whether the majority of the Church of England could have accepted this at that point. It was suggested that the series of strongly worded pronouncements against women's priesting from the Vatican in the post-1992 period were intended to quell calls for a similar move from within the Roman Catholic Church as much as to express disappointment at the Church of England's decision.[34]

In addition to the wider ecumenical scene, internal division was also a commonly noted issue: around one in three respondents to the Questionnaire for Congregations agreed that 'the Church of England has become badly divided' (with a further 29% neither agreeing nor disagreeing). This was felt particularly keenly by those with objections to women's priesting, some of whom had decided to leave their previous congregations as a result. One respondent from Church 6 pointed to 'unnecessary divisions causing great sadness and in some cases turmoil'.[35] There was also widespread regret that some clergy and some laity had felt it necessary to leave the Church of England altogether. Even those otherwise supportive of the decision could recognize the price: 'personally, I feel it has enriched the priesthood, but regret the divisions it has caused in the C of E', wrote one woman from Church 19.[36] However, the root cause of the division was interpreted differently, with many of those objecting to women's priesting regretting that the debate had taken place at all, whilst others blamed divisions at local congregational level on the refusal of some groups to accept what the Church had decided, or 'the rigid line taken by their vicars'.[37]

All of this led some to reflect upon what society at large might make of the Church's continued division: 'we have been consumed by an irrelevant issue to the detriment of church growth', wrote one male chaplain from Diocese A; 'the people outside the church have another reason for seeing us as silly'.[38] However, most clergy and lay respondents seemed to feel that the decision to ordain women as priests had made a positive difference to the Church's image: 'the C of E now has much more goodwill and credibility in secular society',[39] wrote one female chaplain from Diocese E. Others were more measured, and there was a particular feeling that it would take a lot more than women's ordination to change the Church's negative image in society as a whole. Even so, there was a widespread conviction that it might have been worse. As one male clergyman from Diocese C put it, 'I think if we *hadn't* ordained women we'd have put ourselves alongside the men's club, the masons, those sorts of institutions that young people have no desire to be engaged with, and no credibility'.[40] In a sense, far from women's priesting being an extraordinary, visionary thing, many clergy and laity simply felt it had made the Church seem more normal.

Indeed, whilst change has been an important theme of the chapter so far, it is also important to emphasize the continuities in experience noted by many Anglicans. One male vicar from Diocese A thought he identified 'not as much impact in general (both good & bad) as I thought it would have',[41] whilst others noted that 'most of the other changes in the C of E – especially in terms of its self-identity and attitudes to mission and ecumenism – actually owe very little to the ordination of women'.[42] It was sometimes noted, for example, that a

---

[34] int. 18:85.
[35] LQ178, age and gender not given, Church 6.
[36] LQ424, female 60–69, Church 19.
[37] LQ266, female 60–69, Church 9.
[38] CQ2, male chaplain, 60–69, Diocese A.
[39] CQ279, female chaplain, 60–69, Diocese E.
[40] int. cs3:10:295.
[41] CQ37, male vicar, 30–39, Diocese A.
[42] CQ140, male development officer, Diocese A.

more collaborative, less hierarchical style of ministry[43] had already begun to be modelled by some male clergy even before women were allowed to come forward for ordination – though they also tended to agree that women's priesting had undoubtedly sped this change. The 1992 decision was also widely reckoned to be less divisive than had been feared: amongst the majority of respondents (who welcomed women's priesting), prospects for unity with Rome had never been immediate in any case, and for many, cooperation and good relations (which were still maintained in many respects) were far more important than organic unity.[44] Finally, whilst the arrival of a parish's first female priest was often initially greeted with curiosity and trepidation, most congregations quickly found her ministry reassuringly normal. As already suggested in Chapter 3, this was partly because women's priesting seemed to demand few departures from what had traditionally been expected of ordained ministry. The following section suggests that this theoretical acceptance was also borne out by experience – although women's priesting was perhaps also not accepted in practice on exactly the same terms as that of men.

4.2 Parish stories

Despite challenges to its hegemony, the congregation arguably remains the pre-eminent focus for participation and belonging in organized Christianity – and for experiencing women's priestly ministry. The following nine short accounts suggest something of how Anglican congregations have received the ordination of women as priests in practice. The Church of England is nothing if not diverse, and such a comparatively small number of case studies cannot mirror the full range of Anglican experience since 1992. However, focusing in on individual case studies can offer an important antidote to generalization, and a fruitful way of exploring the impact of women's priesting at grass roots level. The nine featured here are drawn from both urban and rural contexts, northern and southern dioceses, from Catholic, evangelical, broad and liberal church traditions. At the time of the research, three of the congregations (Churches 1, 5 and 7) had current experience of women's priestly ministry; three more (Churches 3, 6 and 8) had one or more of the resolutions in place and the final three (Churches 2, 4 and 9) had only male clergy, and no resolutions in force.

Church 1

Church 1 is found in a largely (though not exclusively) middle class city suburb in Diocese A, has a regular Sunday attendance of between one and two hundred, tending towards older adulthood but with a good spread of age groups. Its church tradition is predominantly central-Catholic. The largely professional congregation appreciate a thought-provoking sermon and 'high standards' of music, and the church also supports a small number of community projects. A male incumbent leads a mixed male and female clergy team (all of whom support women's priesting). 92% of those who returned the questionnaire supported the 1992 decision (most of those ticked 'strongly agree'), with only 8% against. Until the 1980s, certain roles were reserved for men (to the extent that 'it was considered quite unacceptable that women could be servers'[45]), but since the early 1990s Church 1 has had almost continuous experience of women in orders, dating back to the placement of a fondly remembered female theological college student. Even so, the priesting of women was vigorously debated at the time of the vote: the church was about to receive a female deacon to work in the parish, and the vicar of the day felt strongly that it

---

[43] Particularly in comparison to a proportion of clergy from the 'traditionalist' constituency, who had acquired reputations as doggedly lone operators.

[44] It is important to add that for the significant proportion of clergy and laity who were evangelical, or were broad church/Catholic and had reservations over the authority of the Pope, complete institutional unity with Rome would not have been welcomed in any case.

[45] int. cs1:3:84.

would be wrong to accept her as a deacon if, six months later, the congregation felt unable to accept her as a priest and asked her to leave. As it happened, most of the congregation seem to have been untroubled by the idea, though a small but significant minority of the congregation found themselves unable to accept it. Of these, the younger element left to attend another church, whilst the older members (about four or five individuals in all) decided to stay. As a concession to these, the celebrant is identified for each communion service on the rota, enabling those who have difficulties over women's ordination to avoid those occasions featuring a female celebrant.

During my visit, members of Church 1 regularly suggested to me that women's priestly ministry was now an integral part of the fabric, and most found it difficult to see what the fuss was all about. Some members of the church had already experienced women's ministry whilst attending churches of other denominations (this fluidity in denominational belonging[46] appears to have been important in speeding the acceptance of women's ministry in the Church of England). Indeed, two women from the church have come forward for ministerial training since 1992, with the overwhelming support of the congregation: the first of these was remembered as 'so well regarded that any remaining scruples were overcome at that point'.[47] However, acceptance had not come easily for everyone: some older members of the congregation recalled apprehension at the thought of women clergy leading the service: there were several comments about the unfamiliarity of voice or appearance when the first woman came to preach (a common theme in the responses), and one interviewee remembered fearing that a female voice might be too shrill, and lack reach or authority, to deliver a good sermon.[48] But it seems that for most members of the congregation who still harboured reservations, such concerns were quickly dissolved: one representative respondent in his eighties expressed himself 'quite uncertain as to how I would react beforehand, but quickly became used to the idea of women priests'.[49]

Looking at the wider Church of England, some alluded to the division that the ordination of women debate had caused, but interviewees were unanimous that it had ceased to be an issue for all but four or five individuals within their congregation. This smaller group continued to feel unhappy about the decision, but had quietly worked out a way of continuing to belong, and this was respected by the majority of the congregation. However, many respondents favourable to women's priesting were less sympathetic with those who continued to shout their disagreement loudly in the wider church. By contrast, there was much praise for the 'quality' of the women clergy who had served in the parish, a much valued attribute for a largely professional congregation used to high standards of service at work and leisure more generally. Indeed, few seemed to hope or expect that women's priesting would change the Church in any revolutionary way, and their ability to deliver 'normal service' on the same level as men was a sign of the rightness of the decision.

Nevertheless, many also thought they perceived an enhanced pastoral dimension to women's priesthood. Several (mainly older) respondents felt that their female curates had tended to take a more nurturing rather than directive approach to priesthood; this link with images of motherhood was another popular theme across the case studies.[50] Even though there was still some difference of opinion between the responses over whether women

---

[46] Not by any means a new phenomenon.

[47] int. cs1:22side2:590.

[48] int. cs1:22side2:330.

[49] LQ4, male 80+, Church 1.

[50] Although a younger female curate at the church observed that she may have been less easy to pigeonhole, being too young to fit the 'mother' stereotype and the wrong sex to be treated as a surrogate son, in the way that many younger male curates experienced.

necessarily brought an inherently different approach to priesthood, testimony from Church 1 was strongly marked by a sense that whatever their gifts, it was an offence against Christian morality and natural justice to deny women an equal chance for priesthood. Many referred to the equality in standing and opportunity accorded to women and men in their own workplace. As one simply commented, 'I do not find women in executive positions at work a problem and have always been [for] "equal opportunity" ... What's the beef?'[51]

Church 2

Church 2 is a group of small to medium-sized congregations in a traditional working class suburban part of Diocese A. Most of these fall broadly into the evangelical tradition, though charismatics also rub shoulders with conservative evangelicals and traditional 'low church' Anglicans. At the time of researching, the parish had one male vicar and one female reader, and had not as yet experienced a woman's priestly ministry. Parish stories I heard frequently suggested that on several occasions in recent history, the role of women in the life of the parish had been expanded, resistance had been expected, but hostility had rarely materialized. The previous vicar but one had been firmly opposed to women preaching or taking oversight roles in the congregation on headship grounds. Church 2's female reader remembered how, on being appointed church warden, 'I wasn't sure how it would be received', but found that 'the fact that I was a woman didn't seem to be an issue'.[52] Some suggested that the effective ministry of a female parish lay worker some years ago had done much to prepare the ground for the acceptance of ordained women.

In 1992, several respondents recalled considering the issue of women's priesting carefully, and attending a local debate at which two evangelical clergy spoke; one for and one against. This apparently left some of the congregation feeling that the arguments were finely balanced, with little to choose between them. However, at the time of the study, 80% of respondents to the questionnaire either agreed or strongly agreed with women's priesting, with only 5% disagreeing (the other 15% were uncertain). An ordained woman had recently led the parish's weekend away (although did not celebrate communion), seemingly with no opposition. The current vicar (who supports women's priesting) intends to invite an ordained woman to preach in the parish in due course. He expressed confidence that the parish would take this in its stride, although speculated that some regulars might find it more difficult to accept a woman in overall pastoral charge.

This seemed an accurate assessment, given the comments of other members of the congregation. Those who had already experienced the ministry of ordained women, through visiting other churches, generally seemed positive: one wrote, 'I didn't mind that it was a woman it was what she talked about and how she talked that I was comfortable with',[53] whilst another felt 'very comfortable, the lady concerned took the funeral of a dear relative'.[54] Ordained women were not quite accepted on the same terms as men, however: one interviewee expressed her support for women's ordination but harboured reservations about accepting a female incumbent ('but I don't think that's anything biblical – it's just me') and some respondents seemed less keen on the idea of women as bishops on grounds of male headship. Even so, at the last interregnum no one on the PCC had asked for the parish profile to include a request for a male priest, or for the resolutions to be voted on. Respondents from Church 2 said little about the wider impact of the 1992 decision: few believed that women's priesting had yet had much direct impact on their parish, and there was some awareness of the extent of division within the wider church as a whole, but most

---

[51] LQ14, personal details not supplied, Church 1.
[52] int. cs1:13:28.
[53] LQ5, female 60–69, Church 2.
[54] LQ6, male 60–69, Church 2.

focused their responses on the beneficial release of women's gifts into new aspects of the church's life and work, and a more general sense 'that justice has been done'.[55]

Church 3

Church 3 serves what many of its members described as a traditional village community, in a rural part of Diocese A. The regular congregation numbers around sixty, mainly older adults, but with a growing number of young families under the current, highly popular vicar. The church's Catholic tradition (though of a Prayer Book Anglican rather than Anglo-Catholic or Romanizing variety) is typical of many parishes in this part of the diocese. Church 3 passed resolutions A and B under a previous incumbent, though most seem to have accepted the ministry of a female parish deacon some years ago. The current vicar has reservations about the priesting of women although he is not a member of Forward in Faith. Despite the parish's resolution status, however, 61% of respondents to the questionnaire 'agree' or 'strongly agree' with women's priesting, with 31% 'disagreeing' or 'strongly disagreeing'.

This current division of opinion reflected a much longer-term split in the congregation over an issue that had at times been painful for the church. In 1992 many of the congregation had reservations about the move (and the woman speaking in favour of the measure at the deanery debate on the subject seems not to have endeared herself to many members of the congregation). However, it was also felt that the previous incumbent had at the time placed unfair pressure on the PCC to pass the resolutions, stating his position would be untenable if they were not in place.[56] The PCC had relented, feeling that 'we didn't need a major row in the village, and particularly in the church, because that was divisive, it seemed to be the best solution was to keep the status quo ... and we did, and we voted against women priests'[57] – but even this decision stirred up a certain amount of ill-feeling. The circumstances of the local debate had only added to a sense amongst some members that the ordination of women had been divisive for the Church of England as a whole, and had opened the door to a much larger tide of liberalism sweeping over the Church. Some interviews were marked by a strong sense of pessimism about the future.

Ten years on, the divisive experience of voting on the resolutions had to a significant extent been overcome, not least because the current incumbent had been able to motivate the congregation in several new initiatives, leaving the issue of women in priesthood 'way, way down the list of priorities for the church'.[58] Even so, it was clear that strong currents of feeling still ran under the surface. For one thing, there was apprehension that at some point the church might enter an interregnum and have to debate the resolutions again. Most interviewees suspected that the experience would not be any easier this time around, even though (with new members joining and long-standing members leaving or dying) the congregation would probably be more supportive of women's priestly ministry than it once had. Several also suggested that the debate had also made them more conscious of their theological distance from some of the surrounding parishes. (Church 3, it seems, had some history of disagreement with the rest of the deanery over other issues, and some of this had been reactivated by the decision to pass the resolutions.) Nevertheless, few believed Church 3's resolution status had much practical isolating effect, since there were at that time no ordained women in the deanery in any case.

---

[55] LQ8, female, 70–79, Church 2.
[56] int. cs1:6:p.1.
[57] int. cs1:7:60.
[58] int. cs1:7:228.

In recent years the church had also been clustered with two neighbouring parishes, one of which had expressed strong support for women's priestly ministry, meaning that those of opposing views were increasingly called upon to work together despite their differences. In addition, whilst deanery links remained an important focus for local church activity, Church 3 had no strong connection with Forward in Faith or any other similar grouping that might have focused as an alternative pole of identity.[59] In the early 1990s some church members had accepted an invitation to a regional Forward in Faith event. However, it seems that the parish's representatives had been unable to identify with the organization, largely owing to the fact that the strongly Anglo-Catholic flavour of the worship had seemed alien to Church 3's own Prayer Book Catholicism. The current incumbent was philosophical about this, on the one hand reflecting that Forward in Faith might have denied themselves greater support by aligning themselves so closely to one particular style of churchmanship, on the other hand suggesting that perhaps it was as well to resist the formation of new church parties whilst the process of reception was still under way.[60]

Church 4

Church 4 is a situated on a post-war housing estate with a mixture of working class and middle class households. A focal point for charismatic renewal in the 1970s, the church attracts a mainly evangelical congregation from a variety of backgrounds and traditions (some of them non-Anglican). The large Sunday congregation attracts a significant number of children, teenagers, and parents in their thirties and forties. At time of researching, the church had no experience of an ordained woman as either vicar or curate, although the church's leadership team (headed by a male incumbent) comprised both men and women. In addition, a local hospital chaplain who was female had occasionally celebrated at the church and a full-time female lay worker was currently training for ordained local ministry. The latter appeared to be much valued by the congregation, and several members of the church's leadership team suggested that her contribution to the life of the church over some years had made it considerably easier for the more sceptical in the congregation to contemplate having an ordained woman on the staff.[61]

Previous experience of women's ministry in other forms certainly seems to have prepared the ground for an easy acceptance of women in ordained roles. One respondent wrote how her first experience of women's priestly ministry had been 'quite comfortable, having already been involved with a church that had a Deaconess'.[62] This ready acceptance seemed to come partly because of a strong conviction typical of evangelical congregations that priesthood was not an elevated or ontologically distinct order, but rather an institutional expression of congregational leadership, itself part of a much longer continuum of ministries to which individuals were called and given gifts to pursue. As one respondent wrote, 'I have no problem with a woman having an ordained ministry – either then or now. If God has called them into this type of ministry who am I to argue with his decision?'[63] As was often the case across the case study selections, members of Church 4 seem to have been particularly persuaded of the rightness of women's priesting on the evidence of women's calling and gifts.

---

[59] This is not to say that Forward in Faith officially encourages parishes to isolate themselves from other local churches; some individual clergy *have* pursued an active policy of isolation, whilst others have sought to ensure the parish remains integrated with the rest of the diocese. The history of Church 8 suggests that parishes could easily move from comparative isolation to comparative integration (or the reverse) under the influence of different clergy or PCCs.
[60] int. 6:p.2.
[61] int. cs2:11:p.3 and int. cs2:23:250.
[62] LQ116, female 40–49, Church 4.
[63] LQ112, female 40–49, Church 4.

90% of respondents from Church 4 expressed support for the 1992 decision, with 10% uncertain and none disagreeing (although the present incumbent thought there would probably still be a few church members who had reservations about women's ordination, but principally on questions of congregational headship or women in the episcopate[64]). Apart from one person who had been closely involved in the wider debate in 1992, respondents from Church 4 tended to say little about the wider impact of women's priesting on the Church as a whole (perhaps reflecting the closer individual involvement of many of the congregation in pan-denominational evangelical networks, rather than in the institution of the Church of England). Where an assessment of the impact of women's priesting was given, Church 4 respondents often seemed to feel that – regardless of what women personally brought to ministry – a serious wrong had been righted: 'women are now socially considered equal (as well as in the eyes of God)', wrote one man.[65] Several commented on the biblical evidence for women in positions of congregational leadership, whilst others suggested that ordained ministry had been enriched as a result of the decision and was better able to reach out to the whole of society. Even so, the possible differences between men and women also remained a subject for comment; two key female members of the congregation noted how difficult it was to sign up men for either prayer ministry or the coffee rota, whilst the technical/set up team was entirely male, and the role of verger was always assumed to be for men.[66]

Church 5

'Church 5' was not one church but a group of several widely dispersed parishes under a female rector, in one of the most rural parts of Diocese B. Many of the individual churches are situated in villages with populations of under 200, and attract comparatively small congregations on a normal Sunday. Most of the churches are located in the central stream of Anglicanism and regular attenders happily see their churches as 'traditional' (by which was meant not so much doctrinal conservatism[67] as an attachment to a particular ideal of the church at the centre of the village community, a commitment to maintaining long-standing religious customs (harvest was still a major local event) and a sense that under normal circumstances, continuity was preferable to change).

In keeping with this, many respondents from Church 5 recalled feeling apprehensive at the impending arrival of their first female priest. One male churchgoer remembered feeling 'uncertain, as at the time I knew some women who belonged to the Movement for the Ordination of Women. They were very militant and I thought that with all its existing problems the church could do without adding this to them'.[68] Some also seem to have feared that a woman might be more likely than a man to sweep away long-standing traditions. However, by and large church and village people seem to have decided that having a female priest was better than no priest at all, and so it was right to give her a chance. Most initial hesitancies were quickly dispelled, however; one man describing himself as 'a little hesitant and unsure to start with, but quickly realized that the teaching, sermons etc. would be the same'.[69] Indeed, at the time of the research, 92% of respondents to the questionnaire agreed or strongly agreed with women's priesting, with only 2.6% of respondents against.

---

[64] int. cs2:11:p.3.
[65] LQ100, male 40–49, Church 4.
[66] int. cs2:23:170. The interviewee implied that this was because the role involved heavy lifting duties.
[67] Although many took this for granted.
[68] LQ132, male 60–69, Church 5.
[69] LQ139, male 50–59, Church 5.

For Church 5, the impact of women's priesting was much more tangible than for most: for some years the group had undergone a long and difficult interregnum, only to end in the arrival of a part-time clergywoman. Although the priest in question has long since moved on, responses from Church 5 were dominated by observations that, because of the vote, 'we now have a priest'. Indeed, when I asked senior diocesan clergy why they thought women's priesthood had been so quickly accepted across much of their diocese, most replied to the effect that in the current difficult climate for rural church communities, most parishes simply wanted an ordained minister and any conscientious candidate (male or female) would be welcomed and make a difference.

That said, Church 5's general support for women's ordination as priests did not derive solely from the solution it brought to their staffing problem (and across the whole survey notably few respondents thought the ordination of women had in any way come about through declining numbers of male clergy). Interview testimony suggests that at the time of the 1992 vote, very few in the parish had raised an objection to women's priesting. What was more, the current female rector was widely welcomed ('our very own Vicar of Dibley', as several commented[70]). Some PCC members thought they detected a rise in Sunday attendance since the arrival of the current incumbent (in one church it seemed to have doubled over the time).[71] Some voiced their appreciation for her work in livening up family services; even if the innovations were not quite to some church members' tastes, there was widespread delight that more children were attending the church than for some years.[72] Others made the by now common suggestion that their female priest showed a more compassionate side than many of their previous male clergy, and was certainly less 'starchy'. Even so, one PCC member observed that their ordained women were still not quite accepted as priests on exactly the same terms as men, since many of the congregation continued to expect higher standard from them, as if to prove their worth.[73] Helen Thorne's study of the first generation of women priests suggests that this was a pressure felt by many during their first decade in ministry.[74]

Church 6

Like Church 5, Church 6 is also a group of rural parishes in Diocese B. A range of traditions are represented between the different centres, although the churchmanship of the incumbent and the main parish church are firmly Anglo-Catholic. The male vicar does not agree with women's ordination as priests, but the parish has two female readers. Resolutions A and B are in force and would seem to be supported by the majority of worshippers (two thirds of respondents either 'disagree' or 'disagree strongly' with women's priesting, whilst only a quarter are definitely in favour). There were indications, however, that this opposition might not be shared to the same extent by the smaller village congregations.[75] There are some connections with Forward in Faith, but these do not appear to play a large part in the life of the parish.

In giving their views on the question of women's priesting, the most important considerations for the congregation appear to have been the extent to which priesthood was

---

[70] The significance of the popular BBC comedy in presenting positive images of women in priesthood was also recognized by women clergy themselves (e.g. int. cs2:1:p.1). See also: Hilary Wakeman, 'What Difference is Women's Priesthood Marking in the Pews?' in Hilary Wakeman (ed.), *Women Priests: The First Years* (Darton, Longman and Todd, London, 1996), pp. 1–26, p. 15; Andrew and Liz Barr, *Jobs for the Boys? Women who Became Priests* (London, 2001), pp. 257–8.

[71] int. cs2:9side2:503; LQ143, male 70–79, Church 5.

[72] int. cs2:8b:195.

[73] int. cs2:14:92.

[74] Thorne, *Journey to Priesthood*, p. 131.

[75] int cs2:18:46.

a traditional male role, and the extent to which change was both permissible and necessary: 'Jesus founded the church with his twelve disciples and that is the way things should have remained', wrote one respondent,[76] whilst another suggested: 'women are not suitable and there are plenty of other roles for them'.[77] Many of the current congregation are long-standing parishioners, but the resolution status of Church 6 is also well known in the area, and the main congregation in particular has acquired several new attenders who left their previous parish nearby after a woman was appointed.[78] In effect, the churches in the area had become much more sharply polarized between the majority (where women's priesting was largely accepted) and the minority (such as Church 6), which increasingly catered for those who wanted to retain an all-male priesthood. This proved to be a common trend across the case studies, raising important questions about the practical impact of 1992–94 legislative settlement on local Anglican life (these are explored further in Chapter 7).

Despite this, few from Church 6 felt that the 1992 decision had had any real impact on their parish, with some hints that regulars felt their church was now 'immune' from any influence – although significantly, several members of the congregation recorded that they had encountered female clergy through hospital visits, baptisms, weddings or funerals. Some had become more favourable to women's ministry as a result, whilst others remained in disagreement. More commonly, respondents expressed disappointment that the priesting of women had meant the loss of good male clergy from the church, and there was also some resentment that the whole issue had been highly divisive for the Church of England. On the other hand, a minority of regulars at Church 6 were supportive of women's priesting, and felt disappointed at the church's decision to pass the resolutions. One interviewee commented sadly that Church 6 was unlikely to attract a significantly younger element to its services whilst the official view was against women's priesting. However, for the moment, Church 6 remained an important haven for those with traditionalist views.

Church 7

Church 7 is a large congregation situated in a commuter village of Diocese C. It stands predominantly within the evangelical tradition, but with a firm emphasis on the Eucharist and contains a significant minority of older, long-standing parishioners whose preference is for a central, Prayer Book Anglicanism. The church, which has an all-female clergy team, offers a variety of services and study group activities and attracts a wide spread of ages. The current vicar is Church 7's first female incumbent, successor to a dynamic and highly regarded male vicar. During the previous interregnum, there seems to have been no appetite for passing Resolutions A or B, though many interviewees remembered feeling that a man would be the most natural choice for the job: the previous team of male incumbent and female assistant had seemed to work well and few thought it likely that the diocese would sanction an all-female team (interestingly, no similar qualms were expressed anywhere about the prospect of an all-male clergy team). Nevertheless, representatives from the parish had few doubts that the single female candidate on the shortlist was the best qualified, and so she was appointed.

Her first service seems to have etched itself on the minds of many respondents: one male churchgoer described himself as 'challenged! This was something new and outside my experience and comfort zone. It meant I had to think about the challenge and satisfy

---

[76] LQ170, female 70–79, Church 6.

[77] LQ156, female 80+, Church 6.

[78] Some of these seem to have left immediately on hearing their new vicar was a woman, whilst others seem to have clashed over inclusive language in services and differing ideas on the allocation of time to various aspects of ministry: one wrote that she 'found our woman far too bossy. Wouldn't listen to her congregations. Was lazy. Spent far more time in down and out shop in [local town]' (LQ153, female, 50–59, Church 6).

myself'.[79] A female member of the congregation wrote of how she had been 'curious', but 'the church was packed and the woman vicar was well received. I was reassured by the woman vicar preaching an excellent, in depth, sensible, humorous sermon'.[80] A small number of older churchgoers remained unable to dismiss their reservations/objections and opted to attend only non-Eucharistic services, whilst a handful (most estimates suggested around ten) left altogether. Nevertheless, as with the two speakers above, most hesitations were quickly dispelled. By the time of the current survey in 2001, 90% of respondents from Church 7 'agreed' or 'strongly agreed' with women's priesting, with 7% uncertain and 3% disagreeing/disagreeing strongly. Those who continued to disagree did so privately, and since the current incumbent's arrival there seemed to have been few tensions over the issue. The clergywoman in question remembered her reception as 'wonderful! Not just in the first few months, but also more recently'.[81]

In trying to assess the impact of women's priesting on their parish and the wider church, respondents and interviewees were particularly voluble about the gifts their ordained women clergy had brought to the church. Some of these were specific to the individuals: one of their clergy, for example, was recognized as having a profound spirituality and a passion for encouraging others in prayer. It was also commonly suggested that the church's female clergy had been influential role models for some of the women in the congregation (several of whom had taken major steps in Christian service in recent years). But there was also a particularly strong tendency amongst respondents from Church 7 to emphasize distinctive contributions made to the congregation by the two ordained women themselves, as the following responses suggest:

> *... Our vicar has proved to be super. She seems to serve from a place of 'feelings' ... enabling us to become a church of tears and laughter. Our healing or laying on of hands ministry has grown greatly.*[82]

> *... I liked our male vicar and thought we'd lost a gem. I was surprised at how she'd replaced him with (for me) much more empathy and spirituality and sheer liveliness – not to mention the healing services ... [etc.] ...*[83]

As already suggested in Chapter 3, reflections on the distinctive qualities men and women brought to the priesthood may have been lent weight by the *expectation* that women's priesthood would look different to that of men. Members of Church 7 may have been particularly easily disposed to look for such differences because of the previous shape of the parish's clergy team, where an ordained man and an ordained woman worked side by side, dividing the work between them in ways that to some extent reflected traditional expectations of men's and women's roles (the man acting as leader and chief preacher, the woman devoting particular attention to pastoral work[84]). In other respects too, a proportion of the congregation viewed men's and women's ordained ministry differently: Church 7's incumbent remembered being told after her appointment 'things like "if we'd got to have a woman, you're fine", or "looking at all the others, you were the best man for the job"!'[85] Moreover, a minority expressed a fear that with an all-female clergy team, and more women

[79] LQ200, male 40–49, Church 7.
[80] LQ192, female 70–79, Church 7.
[81] int. cs3:1:255.
[82] LQ209, female 60–69, Church 7.
[83] LQ210, female 50–59, Church 7.
[84] As far as I understood it, this was not done out of any suggestion that these were the proper roles for men and women, but more as a reflection of the gifts of the individuals concerned.
[85] int. cs3:1:255.

entering into positions of lay leadership within the church, men might begin to feel marginalized.[86] Some even suggested that a female clergy team needed to be 'balanced up' with a man – although it was interesting that fewer participants in the study also suggested that an all-male clergy team was equally 'unbalanced'. That said, a common strand to the interview and questionnaire testimony from Church 7 was the suggestion that a mixed male and female clergy team was the ideal. One younger member of the congregation wrote of her experience that initially:

> *The fact that the different approaches adopted by men and women (brought about by cultural influences of modern society) means that having ministers of both genders provide many more options for people to find Christ, they have options and choices.*[87]

Testimonies such as this suggest once again that if women have been enthusiastically accepted as priests by the majority of Anglicans, this is not exactly on the same terms as men.

Church 8

Church 8 is situated at the centre of a large housing estate in a highly urbanized part of Diocese C. Its sixty or so regular attenders are mainly drawn from the local area, which comprises a mixture of former council housing and larger properties. The church stands firmly within the Catholic tradition, of a more Anglo-Catholic kind in recent decades. Church 7's current (male) vicar does not agree with the Church of England's decision to ordain women as priests. Under a previous incumbent the parish passed Resolutions A and B, and petitioned for extended episcopal oversight, an arrangement that continues today. Only eight members of the congregation returned their questionnaire survey, so generalizations about the views of the congregation are hazardous, but the fact that six of these indicated their disagreement with women's priesting may indicate a substantial majority within the church who believe the priesthood should be confined to men.

In 1992, regulars at Church 8 appear to have been more evenly divided on the question, and long-standing members of the church concurred that the debate had been a difficult and divisive one for the congregation. The incumbent of the time left almost immediately to convert to Roman Catholicism, and a number of the congregation quickly took the same path.[88] Others who supported women's entry into the priesthood also left when it became clear that the dominant position of the congregation was going to be one of opposition to women priests. A second wave of withdrawals hit the congregation over the debating of the resolutions eighteen months later. As one interviewee put it to me, 'some left because they didn't agree with the resolutions, and others left because they thought that if we needed to pass resolutions at all, things must be bad'.[89] There was general agreement that at that point, relations with the diocese had been at their lowest ebb: the incumbent of the day would not

---

[86] This fear of a 'feminization of the Church' was also expressed by a number of clergy interviewees with objections to women's priesting, across the diocesan case studies. Adherence statistics certainly suggest that women outnumber men in Anglican churches by almost two to one, although a similar pattern has been in evidence for several centuries. Ironically, however, the Church of England's decision to ordain women as priests came *after* the long-standing connection between piety and femininity had been weakened in the cultural revolutions of the 1960s and 1970s (for gender and church attendance, see: Callum G. Brown, *The Death of Christian Britain: Understanding Secularisation, 1800–2000* (Routledge, London, 2001)).

[87] LQ228, female 20–29, Church 7.

[88] int. cs3:19:78.

[89] int. cs3:11:113.

organize any formal trips to diocesan events, and any wider contact with the church outside the parish came through the local Forward in Faith network.

Ten years on, the parish remained firm in its Resolutions A, B and 'C' status, and its lay leadership was arguably more firmly committed to this than ever (the original PCC vote on the resolutions had been 7:5 in favour, whilst the last interregnum had seen the resolutions reaffirmed by 12:1). However, time, and a new incumbent, had healed some of the rifts: first, women's ordination seemed to be raised only rarely within the life of the church; second, the church's identity as a Forward in Faith-affiliated congregation was now assumed rather than articulated on a regular basis, as several interviewees suggested it had once been. In addition, the congregation had begun to participate again in a number of diocesan projects and the current incumbent was on good terms with the diocesan bishop. Top priority for the congregation was the maintenance of church life and worship in a challenging parish situation, and the development of a new community facility run from the church building. In these senses, Church 8 mirrored the experiences of other resolution parishes that participated in the study; experiencing a time of considerable upheaval and upset at the time of the vote, seeing some join the congregation as a result of their new resolution status whilst others left, and settling down into a period of consolidation and rebuilding, sometimes at arm's length from the rest of the diocese and at other times more closely involved.

Even so, the A, B and 'C' status of Church 8 has meant important differences to the congregation, quite apart from the divisive experience of voting in the safeguards: first, regulars were much more conscious than in Churches 3 and 6 (the other two with resolutions in place) of being different to their neighbouring parishes. Although relations with other churches were by no means bad, some considered that surrounding (non-resolution) parishes had probably sold out their faith. Second, the parish's comparative isolation had left some parishioners with a sense that the Church of England was now more polarized than it actually was; for example, one regular attender was surprised to learn that a majority of Anglican parishes still have neither a female priest nor any resolutions in place. Third, the parish's relationships with its bishops are more complex than would usually be the case: Church 7 members greatly appreciate the extended episcopal care and regular visits given by the PEV, feeling it to be considerably better than that previously received by their diocesan bishops. Nevertheless, the diocesan bishop is still invited to preach (but not celebrate) and whilst some regulars have little problem with this, others deliberately avoid receiving communion distributed from his hands, and a few absent themselves from church altogether when he visits. Fourth, many parishioners seemed unusually pessimistic about the future of the Church of England: when in interview I reached my standard question about women in the episcopate, some appeared to express genuine dread that the Church would have to put itself through the potentially divisive process of debating women's ministry again.

Church 9

Church 9 is a medium to large city church with two smaller worship centres in the parish (both of which were included in the study). It is situated in a mainly working class area of Diocese C (with pockets of extreme urban deprivation), although its eclectic congregation travel from near and far to attend. Church 9 situates itself in the Catholic tradition, although some of its services are more Anglo-Catholic than others. The parish has no experience of women's priestly ministry, although a female deacon worked in the parish some years ago. The current clergy team contains a variety of views on women's priesting, although no resolutions are in place. The current incumbent was unhappy with the 1992 result but has since felt 'a growing acceptance. If I am to be part of [the] C of E and wish to remain in the place I feel called to be I have no choice in the end than to accept'.[90] Church 9 shall be discussed only briefly given that comparatively few questionnaire returns were received from the congregation and those who replied were all in favour (the congregation is known to contain a variety of views on women's priesting, so the sample cannot be said to reflect this accurately). As with many other congregations, the two issues that dominate respondents' assessments of the impact of women's priesting were (positively) the principle of equality between men and women in the eyes of God, the release of women's gifts to the church and (negatively) the division that the debate had caused in the wider church (Church 9's deanery contains a disproportionate number of the diocese's resolution parishes).

Although no women currently work in the parish, female theological college placement students have generally been welcomed, and interviewees experiencing women's ministry elsewhere have been pleased by their energy and approachability: one long-standing member recalled being invited to the wedding of a family friend, at which a female priest was due to preside, 'and I was so anxious to see the service, because I'd never seen a woman take the wedding service, and I wasn't quite sure… what the difference [would be]… and after watching that service, I thought "this is a good thing"…' She added that the bride had been extremely complimentary about the advice she had received from the clergywoman in question, and had since become a regular church attender – 'there's no better reference than that!'[91]

As far as the parish itself is concerned, the ordination of women and the debate on the resolutions seem to have caused some disagreement that still lingers under the surface; at the last interregnum a difficult discussion was resolved by agreeing that the next incumbent should be a man, without the church committing itself to passing the resolutions. This was accepted by the diocese.[92] Church 9 was one of several parishes that seemed to be saying 'yes, but not yet' to women's priestly ministry, leaving senior clergy the difficult dilemma of whether to insist the parish pass the resolutions until it was felt able to accept a female priest, or whether to expect that if no resolutions were passed, the parish would consider both men and women on an equal basis – at the risk of alienating that portion of the congregation that continued to object. (This dilemma is explored further in Chapter 5.)

Several interviewees also suggested that in the most traditional of the three congregations, women's participation in church life had even taken a retrograde step since 1992: one or two members of the congregation not only disagreed with women's priesting but had now also refused to take communion from the hands of a female server; something that they 'never used to do'.[93] (Such cases were extremely rare across the research sample, but were not unknown. The overwhelming majority of Anglicans who objected to women's priesting saw no theological problem whatever in receiving communion distributed by a woman and would have balked at the suggestion that it was wrong. However, the very few exceptions to this remind us that support/opposition to women's priesting was not always based on the purely rational or theological arguments.)

Generally, however, women's priesting rarely seemed to arise as a topic of debate amongst the congregations, and for the small proportion of the congregation who replied to the questionnaire survey, it seemed like an eminently logical and self-evident development of women's existing contribution to the life and mission of the church. That said, some

---

[90] CQ325, male vicar, Diocese C (age not given so as to protect speaker's anonymity).
[91] int. cs3:13:450.
[92] int. cs3:6:312.
[93] int. cs3:13:131.

conceded that whilst a female curate or deacon would be comparatively easily welcomed by many, the prospect of a female incumbent might be viewed differently (one interviewee suggested that the parish's size and the extent of its social problems might place it beyond the experience of any ordained woman at present). As was sometimes expressed elsewhere across the case study congregations, a minority continued to feel that although women and men were equally eligible for ordination, in status before God and in gifting, they still lacked experience (or even an edge of authoritativeness or natural leadership). Most who thought this way (including as many 'supporters' of women's priesting as 'opponents' of it) felt that it was only a matter of time before women acquired the necessary skills and experience, but in the meantime, ordained women and men were not quite regarded as being on a wholly equal footing. In Church 9, this theory remained an untested prospect.

Conclusion

Making generalizations about the impact of women's priesting on the Church of England just twelve years on from the vote is made particularly difficult because, as this chapter has shown, the implications of the 1992–94 settlement were still being worked out across the Church, and each congregation has encountered the ministry of women in priesthood to very different extents. Local histories and contexts could also shape the perception of change across the whole of the Church of England. However, several provisional conclusions are possible.

- First, a large majority of respondents felt that the decision to open the priesthood to women had been a beneficial one. At very least a wrong had been righted, regardless of whether anything else positive had come out of the move. The release of women's gifts into ministry and mission was regularly noted, as was a sense that the priesthood now reflected more fully both the diversity of humanity and the inclusiveness of God.

- Second, however, the consequences of the debate were not regarded as universally positive: just as some who regretted the decision nevertheless appreciated the gifts of the first generations of women to be priested, so some who had welcomed the 1992 decision also regretted the division and bitterness it had caused, and the way in which the Church of England had become more distanced from the Catholic and Orthodox churches. Several case study churches had been forced to cope with tension and disagreement within their own congregations, some of which was still palpable.

- A third important trend at local level was the heightened perception of a dividing line between different sorts of parishes. As the case studies suggested, it was not uncommon for parishes to gain or lose attenders when a new incumbent arrived with different ideas on women's priesting (or was herself a woman). Those who could not accept their church's position then cast around for a congregation that better reflected their opinions.

Of course, church shopping is a centuries-old phenomena: differences between congregations, and between congregations and their dioceses, have always emerged on a wide variety of matters. But the ordination of women debate seems to have lent an added dimension of choice to matters of congregational identity and belonging. In the eyes of some, it had been the spur for many Anglicans to find a more natural spiritual home; for others, it polarized congregations, further reduced faith to a matter of private opinion and created unnecessary disruption.

- Fourth, division and polarization could just as easily result from votes on the resolutions as from differences over the question of women's priesting itself. Indeed, across all twenty-two churches surveyed, those from congregations with the resolutions in force seemed more likely to offer pessimistic diagnoses of the first ten years and the prospects for the future.

- Fifth, however, it would be wrong to conclude that isolation and polarization were the primary features of congregational belonging after the women priests vote; all of the congregations discussed above contained a variety of different views within their ranks, and all to some extent participated in the wider life of the diocese.

- Sixth, the perspectives collected here generally agreed that the worst divisions had eased with the passage of time; the question of women's priesting (and its related issues) did not now occupy the congregation as much as it had a decade previously. Indeed, for most of the case study parishes, the question rarely if ever emerged. Ordained women and their supporters may find this point partly reassuring, but also partly concerning: a lack of discussion of women in priesthood may imply a high degree of acceptance of women's entry into the priesthood, or it may suggest a lack of awareness of some of the ways in which ordained men and women continued to have very different experiences of ministry, and of some of the continued tensions and unresolved issues within the life of the Church.

- Amongst the most significant of these to arise from the current set of case studies are: did parishes always act in the right way when resolutions were passed? How should parishes and clergy of different views on women's priesting be encouraged to work together and contribute to the life of the diocese? How were questions of appointments handled? Where a diocese agreed to allow parishes to appoint only a male incumbent but did not wish to pass any resolutions, was this admirable pastoral sensitivity, or a shameful denial of equal opportunity? These questions and more will be considered in greater depth in Part II of the report, which follows this.

- Eighth, overwhelming acceptance of women's priesting in theory could sometimes mask very different attitudes towards women's ministry in practice. Interviewees sometimes readily insisted that women should be admitted to the priesthood on grounds of equality, whilst expressing concern that women should not nevertheless be allowed to 'take over' the church, or suggesting that a woman's ministry was often best balanced with a man's (similar concerns about male clergy were expressed much more rarely). Moreover, as the discussion of women as bishops in Chapter 9 will go on to suggest, occasional reticence remained (even amongst a minority of supporters of women's priesting) over the question of women in senior leadership positions. Lay interviewees in particular often continued to expect that the ministry of an ordained woman would look somehow different to that of a man (often in line with quite traditional expectations about the respective attributes of men and women).

- Ninth however, it was also clear that many Anglicans were able to accept women's ministry as priests so easily partly because it appeared strikingly similar to the kind of ministry long provided by men. For some, this is a reassuring conclusion: many of those who had previously feared the fragmentation of the Church of England, a triumph of secular feminism or a discarding of long cherished traditions found that their deepest concerns were unfounded. As one priest from Diocese D wrote, 'the great iconoclasm has not happened!'[94] For others, this conclusion was a disappointing one: many who supported women's ordination to the priesthood before 1992 had expected a radical reshaping of church and ministry in the wake of the decision, and the surveys suggested

---

[94] CQ114, male vicar, 30–39, Diocese D.

little consensus amongst clergy and laity over whether this had actually taken place. For ordained women themselves, this presented something of a dilemma. As Helen Thorne has noted, many of the first generation of women to be ordained priest felt themselves faced with an almost impossible task; to prove that their ordination has benefited the Church whilst simultaneously demonstrating that their presence has not fostered radical change'.[95] However, if such a compromise was difficult for many women to bear, it seemed to have been significant in speeding the acceptance of their priestly ministry in practice.

---

[95] Thorne, *Journey to Priesthood*, p. 134.

Part II

Current Issues

Chapter 5

The appointments question

The problem for the Church today is how to deal with change in the light of continuity. The move into a new era has not meant leaving the old behind. So, for example, the present appointments system remains rooted in the ancient parochial system and the patronage arrangements of Anglo-Saxon England. [1]

I just wish I could knock people's heads together, really, and say 'don't you see?' [...] Why aren't the powers that be seeing the giftedness that's sitting there? [2]

When it comes to appointments, people are heard to ask 'Is the Bishop going to play fair?'... [3]

In reflecting on the Church of England's experience of ordaining women to the priesthood, clergy and laity offered not only their views on the principle of women's ordination and its impact on the Church, but also identified a series of current concerns and unresolved issues arising out of the practical implementation of the 1992–94 settlement. Clergy, who generally had to work within the institutional structures of the Church much more closely than their congregations, were particularly aware of the practical challenges involved in implementing the legislation (here, not primarily the priesting of women itself, but the wider project of working in a church containing a diversity of opinions on it). Part II of this report explores three of the most important themes to emerge: the deployment and appointment of clergy, the experience of communion and cooperation in deanery and diocesan life, and the implementation of the provisions designed to allow parishes to opt out of women's priestly ministry.

The three quotations from interviewees that begin this chapter convey in just a few words the degree to which – for clergy in particular – difficulties over the matter of clerical appointments became a key unresolved issue in the practical outworking of the 1992–94 settlement. This was acknowledged from very early on: a gathering of experienced male and female clergy at St George's House, Windsor, in 1993 warned that the development of women's priestly ministry was still far from complete despite the vote of the previous year, and senior clergy would have to exercise care to ensure that women were enabled to enter a range of ministerial appointments on exactly the same terms as men.

Ten years on, this chapter explores aspects of the appointments issue that concerned questionnaire respondents and interviewees in the course of the research. It begins with an overview of the patterns of appointments of female and male clergy and considers four particular areas of interest. As the chapter is driven by those issues participants themselves felt were important, this is not inevitably an exhaustive survey of the appointments process. For example there was comparatively little comment on the small numbers of women so far appointed archdeacons or cathedral deans (although it remained of significant concern to

---

[1] Gordon W. Kuhrt (ed.), *Ministry Issues for the Church of England: Mapping the Trends* (Church House Publishing, London, 2001), pp. 28–32 (p. 31). The point derives from a summary of a paper on the history and theology of ordained ministry given by Anthony Russell to the Ecclesiastical Law Society in 2000.
[2] int. cs3:22side2:44 (female churchgoer, Church 7).
[3] int. cs3:11:332 (male incumbent of a resolution parish, Diocese C).

some), so this subject is only considered briefly along with other 'senior appointments' here. The role of the patronage system also needs further consideration. Conversely, some aspects of the appointments issue have received good coverage elsewhere (for example, the experiences of clergy couples in Sue Walrond-Skinner's *Double Blessing*[4]) and so are not explored extensively here. Nevertheless, the chapter outlines some key concerns over appointments in the context of the Church's experience of ordaining women, and some ways in which dioceses have attempted to address these concerns. In so doing it seeks to provide relevant material for reflection for those involved in any aspect of appointment and deployment of clergy.

5.1 Patterns of clergy deployment

Across the Church of England by 2002, women accounted for approximately 19% of all ordained clergy [5] and given that 49% of those in training for ordained ministry were women,[6] it is not unreasonable to expect the overall percentage of women in the Church of England's ordained ministry to increase in the foreseeable future. However, within this overall figure of 19%, there is considerable variation between the dioceses, as **Table 5i** suggests. Generally, it seems true that dioceses with a history of strong support for women's priestly ministry by senior clergy appoint a higher than average percentage of women (although this is not a hard and fast rule). This is partly due to the tendency for bishops to attract clergy sympathetic to their views. So, for example, recent bishops of Lincoln and Hereford have tended to be strong supporters of women's priesting whilst Chichester, London, Blackburn and Truro (all with amongst the lowest percentages of women clergy) have historically been characterized[7] as strongholds of a more traditional Anglo-Catholicism and either have, or have recently had, bishops who do not ordain women as priests or would have opposed such a move.

---

[4] Sue Walrond-Skinner, *Double Blessing: Clergy Marriage since the Ordination of Women as Priests* (Mowbray, London, 1998).
[5] All overall figures in this section – including those for Figure 6.i – exclude clergy on part-stipends, for which the gender breakdown is not given in the Church of England's summary of ministry figures, Ministry Division of the Archbishop's Council, *Statistics for Licensed Ministers 2002* (GS Misc. 721, Church House Publishing, London, 2003). However, anecdotal evidence suggests women also make up a significant percentage of part-stipend clergy.
[6] 2002/03 figures. If this figure is broken down further by method of training, 32% of those at residential theological colleges were women, compared to 62% on non-residential schemes and 59% on ordained local ministry training schemes.
[7] With a greater or lesser degree of accuracy.

Table 5i: Percentage of Church of England clergy who are women, 2002 (ranked by diocese)[8]

Diocese	Clergy who are women (%)	Diocese	Clergy who are women (%)
Hereford	30.8	Newcastle	19.1
St Alban's	28.0	York	18.0
Portsmouth	26.9	Rochester	17.9
Oxford	26.7	Carlisle	17.8
St Ed. And Ips.	25.6	Norwich	17.6
Southwell	25.5	Birmingham	17.6
Southwark	24.7	Chelmsford	17.6
Guildford	24.3	Bath and Wells	17.6
Salisbury	23.9	Winchester	17.3
Coventry	23.6	Durham	17.1
Lincoln	23.2	Peterborough	16.7
Bristol	23.0	Sheffield	16.2
Worcester	22.2	Truro	16.2
Ely	21.8	Chester	15.8
Ripon and Leeds	21.2	Derby	15.4
Wakefield	21.1	London	15.1
Leicester	20.9	Exeter	12.0
Canterbury	19.9	Bradford	11.5
Manchester	19.6	Blackburn	10.9
Lichfield	19.6	Europe	8.6
Gloucester	19.5	Chichester	7.0
Liverpool	19.2	Sodor and Man	0

That dioceses could acquire a reputation for a particular stance on women's priesting was sometimes a source of regret amongst diocesan bishops themselves: two suggested to me that they would be keen to employ a greater number of female clergy but the reputations of their dioceses as 'traditionalist strongholds', combined with popular beliefs about the bishops' own views on the question, tended to mean that few women applied for posts there. Second, although there were exceptions, dioceses with large numbers of parishes passing resolutions tended to attract proportionately fewer women clergy – not least because of the smaller number of available parishes in which a woman could exercise her priestly ministry. This was a particular problem for Diocese A: in 2001 senior clergy regularly suggested to me that they would soon face both a surplus of women clergy for the number of parishes who would accept them,[9] and a severe shortage of candidates who would be acceptable to the minority of parishes with resolutions in place.

The wide variation in the gender breakdown of clergy in different dioceses is made more complex by the fact that over the first ten years of women's priesting, women and men have not been equally (or even proportionately) represented in different kinds of posts. Across the Church of England in 2002, women accounted for:

- 7% of incumbents;

- 21% of priests-in-charge;

---

[8] Based on figures in: Archbishop's Council Ministry Division, *Statistics of Licensed Ministers 2002* General Synod publications, GSMisc 721 (London, 2003).

[9] Although this was less an issue of 'too many women' and more a consequence of the fact that senior clergy were reluctant to appoint female clergy to any parish without previous experience of women's ordained ministry unless there was a substantial consensus in favour (for more on this, see sections 5.3 and 5.5).

- 31% of stipendiary curates;

- 44% of non-stipendiary ministers (NSM);

- 47% of ordained local ministers (OLM).

Women were also disproportionately to be found in sector ministry positions, whilst constituting only 6% of non-episcopal 'dignitaries' (cathedral deans and residentiary canons, archdeacons, etc.[10]).

Table 5ii: Percentages of stipendiary and non-stipendiary clergy who are women, 2002 (by diocese) [**Inc**. = % of incumbents/team vicars/priests-in-charge who are women] [**Cur**. = % of stipendiary curates who are women] [**NS** = % of non-stipendiary ministers or ordained local ministers who are women]							
Diocese	**Inc.**	**Cur.**	**NS**	**Diocese**	**Inc.**	**Cur.**	**NS**
Bath and Wells	12.3	20.0	40.0	London	7.0	23.08	31.8
Birmingham	9.7	30.6	52.6	Manchester	11.1	34.1	36.6
Blackburn	3.4	28.2	45.8	Newcastle	11.5	40.0	40.9
Bradford	9.0	25.0	28.6	Norwich	8.9	17.9	44.4
Bristol	12.5	43.5	50.0	Oxford	12.5	36.4	45.5
Canterbury	8.8	31.8	45.5	Peterborough	12.8	30.0	36.8
Carlisle	8.8	37.5	40.6	Portsmouth	9.1	16.7	68.2
Chelmsford	11.5	22.2	43.3	Ripon and Leeds	14.1	46.4	30.0
Chester	9.3	29.2	42.3	Rochester	11.1	23.5	55.5
Chichester	1.9	10.2	31.5	St Alban's	16.8	40.8	53.0
Coventry	10.2	57.1	72.7	St Ed. and Ips.	10.9	45.0	50.0
Derby	9.9	13.8	41.2	Salisbury	11.4	28.6	49.4
Durham	8.5	32.4	57.7	Sheffield	13.4	24.1	30.8
Ely	15.0	36.4	46.2	Sodor and Man	0	0	0
Exeter	5.7	25.0	31.0	Southwark	14.8	29.0	40.0
Gloucester	11.6	24.0	39.6	Southwell	18.2	23.1	57.1
Guildford	12.6	42.5	38.6	Truro	4.8	50.0	41.2
Hereford	17.1	58.3	57.9	Wakefield	11.9	45.5	42.9
Leicester	14.2	34.6	44.4	Winchester	5.4	28.9	54.2
Lichfield	11.8	32.8	46.2	Worcester	15.0	40.9	55.5
Lincoln	16.0	39.1	45.2	York	9.9	39.4	41.0
Liverpool	10.7	34.9	42.2	Europe	0.0	12.5	34.5

Table 5ii also shows considerable variation in the proportions of women obtaining stipendiary/non-stipendiary posts across the forty-four dioceses. Here it is much more difficult to spot a clear pattern in the differences between dioceses. Once again the most even spread of women throughout the different types of clerical positions has often come in dioceses with a history of strong clergy support for women's ordination as priests, whilst in many dioceses identified as historic centres of support for a male-only priesthood, women have tended to remain disproportionately in curacies, non-stipendiary and sector ministry posts. As much as anything else, the variations between the individual dioceses seem to rest partly on the level of scrutiny the diocese's senior staff team gives to the question of women's appointments, partly on how many ordained women already work in the diocese, and partly on what levels of experience individuals are perceived to have.

---

[10] If bishops are included, women constitute only 4% of 'dignitaries' as defined by *Statistics of Licensed Ministers*.

The patterns presented here have caused concerns to campaigning groups from a variety of different positions: even respondents with diametrically opposed views on the rightness of women's priesting could be heard to agree (at least in principle) that if women were to be ordained they must be allowed to proceed in ministerial service on exactly the same basis as men (excepting the parishes that have formally opted out). Clergy interviewees who supported an all-male priesthood have also added that official statistics seldom revealed the problems facing 'traditionalist' clergy attempting to secure new or more senior positions. Some respondents suggested that it was too soon for women to expect to be appointed to clerical positions of greater responsibility, given their comparatively recent entry into priesthood. On the other hand, those who were supportive of women as priests and bishops argued that some dioceses neglected to grasp opportunities to appoint women to more senior posts where they could, implying a failure to make good the commitments to even-handedness adopted when women were ordained as priests in 1992. Female clergy themselves were sometimes heard to talk about a 'postcode lottery' when it came to appointments. In 2002, the Group for Rescinding the Act of Synod (GRAS) even published a League Table detailing the record of each diocese on the deployment of female clergy, according to a system of points awarded for the proportion of women present at each level. The worst five were consigned to a 'hall of shame' at the foot of the league![11]

The case must not be overstated. The number of instances where individuals felt personally disadvantaged from obtaining a suitable position on grounds of their gender or their views on the question of women's priesting seem to have been comparatively few. If the responses to the Clergy Questionnaire of 2001/02 are at all representative, only 10% of women claimed their gender had been a negative factor in applying for particular posts (this statistic is broken down by diocese in **Table 5iii**). It fact, it was clergy with objections to women's priesting who were more likely to feel that their views had been a negative factor in obtaining a suitable position (16.7%) but even this represents only a small proportion of that constituency. (See **Table 5iv** for comparisons.) How should these figures be interpreted? An optimistic assessment might emphasize that only a minority of clergy reported being disadvantaged over appointments. Most felt that their gender or views on women's priesting had been neutral factors in the selection process. A more negative assessment might argue that the number of clergy encountering problems in gaining appointments over questions of gender/women's priesthood represents a sizeable minority. Assessing the scale of the difficulties over appointments is doubly problematic since a comparatively small number of 'problem' cases could become widely known, fuelling the perception that some dioceses regularly did not 'play fair' over questions of appointments. This may mean that whilst bad practice in making appointments is by no means rife, it is a sufficiently common problem to warrant serious attention by church leaders.

---

[11] M. Threlfall-Holmes, 'Diocesan Equal Opportunities League Table 2001' (GRAS, 2002). A score of 100 points would indicate equal numbers of men and women at every level amongst the clergy, excluding bishops. Southwark emerged as the highest scoring diocese with 35 points (denoting women in 16% of senior posts and 19% of other posts) whilst Sodor and Man, which had no women clergy at all, scored 0.

Table 5iii: Has your gender, or your views on women's priesting, ever been a positive or negative factor in your obtaining a suitable position in ordained ministry?[12]
(% 'yes' amongst clergy respondents, by diocese and gender)

Factor: your gender				Factor: your views on women as priests			
Diocese	Positive	Negative	Neither	Diocese	Positive	Negative	Neither
Diocese A				**Diocese A**			
Women	43.5	8.7	47.8	Women	30.4	4.3	65.2
Men	29.4	4.4	66.2	Men	32.4	1.5	66.2
Diocese B				**Diocese B**			
Women	40.0	13.3	46.7	Women	30.0	10.0	60.0
Men	34.1	5.2	59.1	Men	32.9	4.3	63.5
Diocese C				**Diocese C**			
Women	60.7	3.6	35.7	Women	35.7	0	64.3
Men	52.8	8.3	37.5	Men	50.7	9.9	39.4
Deanery D				**Deanery D**			
Women	50.0	0	50.0	Women	0	0	100
Men	46.2	7.7	46.2	Men	23.1	7.7	69.2
Deanery E				**Deanery E**			
Women	100	0	0	Women	66.7	0	33.3
Men	43.5	4.3	52.2	Men	43.5	13.0	43.5
Deanery F				**Deanery F**			
Women	25.0	50.0	25.0	Women	25.0	25.0	50.0
Men	50.0	0	50.0	Men	50.0	16.7	33.3

Table 5iv: Has your gender, or your views on women's priesting, ever been a positive or negative factor in your obtaining a suitable position in ordained ministry?
(% 'yes' amongst clergy respondents, by level of agreement with 1992 decision)

Factor: your gender				Factor: your view of women as priests			
Current view of 1992 decision	Positive	Negative	Neither	Current view of 1992 decision	Positive	Negative	Neither
Strongly agree	43.4	5.8	50.4	Strongly agree	39.3	2.9	57.9
Agree	37.7	8.2	54.1	Agree	34.4	3.3	62.3
Neither A nor D	50.0	10.0	40.0	Neither A nor D	10.0	20.0	70.0
Disagree	38.5	0	61.5	Disagree	15.4	23.1	61.5
Strongly disagree	46.3	4.9	48.8	Strongly disagree	42.5	15.0	42.5

If so, what were the most common issues to arise, and what examples of good and bad practice can be identified? The research suggested four main areas of concern, and these are considered in turn in the rest of the chapter.

---

[12] These questions derived from questions asked in Helen Thorne's survey of the first generation of women to be priested (Thorne, *Journey to Priesthood*, Q.20).

5.2 Parishes, chaplaincies and stipends

First, it was regularly highlighted that ordained women were disproportionately found in non-stipendiary parish posts and sector ministries, rather than in full-time stipendiary incumbencies and curacies; a trend reflected in the statistical evidence given in the previous section. Again there are wide variations between the case study dioceses: in Diocese B, where the percentage of stipendiary women was well above the national average, female priests regularly showed awareness of this national pattern, but rarely reported any problems from their own diocese. However, in Diocese C, where women also made up an above average percentage of diocesan clergy, an unusually large number were to be found in non-stipendiary posts. Several ordained women had raised this discrepancy with their bishop over the previous few years, noting in particular a lack of stipends for female curates. As one interviewee commented: 'You'd have to go back to 1998 to find a stipendiary woman being ordained [in this diocese]. Since then, stipendiary women have only been released from the diocese. So how are there going to be women incumbents in the diocese if there aren't full time stipendiary curates?'[13] Women clergy in Deanery D felt that the problem for them was more fundamental: a lack of ordained women in the diocese per se. On the other hand, in Dioceses A and E the problem was identified primarily as one of deployment; certain deaneries contained strong contingents of women clergy, whilst others were regarded as virtual 'no-go areas'.

Whilst identifying the main patterns is comparatively straightforward, explaining why women were disproportionately present in non-stipendiary posts is more difficult. Interviewees offered a variety of interpretations, suggesting both 'push' and 'pull' factors were involved: many ordained women believed senior clergy were too often reluctant to take gender inequality seriously. A more general atmosphere of financial retrenchment meant that stipendiary posts were increasingly hard to obtain in any case. In one parish in Diocese C, which had produced several female ordinands in recent years, members of the congregation occasionally expressed their disappointment and frustration that the diocese had been unable to find them suitable stipendiary positions, leaving each of them little choice but to seek posts in the neighbouring diocese. 'Why are they throwing away all these really gifted people who could give so much?!' asked one interviewee.[14] Helen Thorne's 2000 survey of the first generation of women priests suggested that perhaps a quarter of those who had moved dioceses since their ordination had done so because of difficulties with clergy in their own diocese, or because of difficulties gaining a suitable position there.[15] Family circumstances also appeared to be an important factor: interviewees from Diocese A reported several cases of women encountering difficulties in securing a stipend if their husband was also ordained.[16] Across the Church of England, only 20% of clergy couples received two stipends.[17] This might perhaps have been accepted as a financial necessity in the current climate had it not been for the fact that in the majority of one-stipend clergy couples, the stipendiary post was assigned to the husband – in as many as 85% of cases according to one survey.[18] It was also suspected that dioceses sometimes found it easier to place women in sector ministry posts if a significant percentage of

---

[13] int. cs3:1:371.

[14] int. cs3:22side2:239.

[15] Thorne, *Journey to Priesthood*, p. 80.

[16] Thorne suggests ordained women married to other clergy were also significantly more likely to be in receipt of a part-stipend (Thorne, *Journey to Priesthood*, p. 73). For more on the particular issues facing clergy couples, see: Sue Walrond-Skinner, *Double Blessing: Clergy Marriage since the Ordination of Women as Priests* (Mowbray, London, 1998).

[17] Lesley Bentley, 'Two-clergy Couples' in Gordon Kuhrt (ed.), *Ministry Issues in the Church of England: Mapping the Trends* (Church House Publishing, London, 2001), pp. 208–10.

[18] Quoted in Bentley, 'Two-clergy Couples', p. 208.

parishes had passed resolutions or were hesitant to receive a female priest. Certainly ordained women seeking paid positions often found chaplaincy posts more readily available (a historic trend dating back to the years of the deaconess order). In addition, women working in sector ministries noted that the climate of trust and acceptance in chaplaincy jobs often exceeded that in a parish/diocesan situation. 'Working for an organization like the NHS, equality means equality', said one female hospital chaplain from Diocese E; 'My gender, my colour, did not come into it; it wasn't important; it was whether I could do the job'.[19] A female colleague from the same diocese, also with hospital chaplaincy experience, expressed similar sentiments: 'women are totally accepted. My manager at the hospital could not see what the problem was. He couldn't believe what was happening out there in the church when I was a senior member of the hospital team'.[20]

Against suggestions that dioceses had been lax in tackling the lack of stipendiary posts for women, senior diocesan clergy sometimes responded that, in fact, many women had entered non-stipendiary ministry out of choice rather than by default: if women were disproportionately more likely to candidate for non-stipendiary ministry, it was not surprising that male clergy took up more full-time stipendiary posts. This is to some extent borne out by the Church of England's own figures: whilst only 29% of male candidates in training in 2002/03 had entered on the 'permanent NSM' track, 47% of women had taken this route. This even led some priests with objections or reservations over women's ordination to assume that women were less committed to the priestly task (which in turn led them to suggest that the 1992 decision had therefore been a mistake). Certainly some ordained women did choose part-time or non-stipendiary work in greater numbers: perhaps 17% of female clergy chose to delay moving to a new post in order to strike the best balance between ministry and family commitments, according to Helen Thorne.[21] 'There are points in the journey when it is more sensible to create chaos amongst one's family!' suggested the female incumbent of Church 7, who herself had had experience of a variety of different working patterns.[22]

Whilst it was expected that many would be disappointed with a clergyperson who did not give every waking hour to the parish, in fact a majority of interviewees seemed admiring of clergy (both male and female) who worked hard *and* gave time to their home life. Nevertheless, although many women chose to work as part-time or non-stipendiary because of their personal circumstances, it would be too simplistic to conclude that personal preference was the only factor influencing this. One recent survey of ordained women in clergy couples suggested that perhaps 10% were 'NSM other than by choice';[23] a small but significant proportion. Indeed, some interviewees suggested that women coming forward for ordination were sometimes being influenced to pursue a permanent non-stipendiary track even before training, or were disproportionately being placed in non-stipendiary roles when they had candidated for stipendiary/ non-stipendiary ministry.[24] There was insufficient

---

[19] int. cs5:3side2:584.

[20] int. cs5:6:211. A similar point is made in Thorne, *Journey to Priesthood*, p. 79.

[21] Thorne, *Journey to Priesthood*, p. 77. A further 12% said they had made a positive choice to enter non-stipendiary ministry for other reasons. Thorne also found that amongst the first generation of women to be priested, those with dependent children tended to be concentrated in more junior posts (p. 69) although it is not known whether this simply because more senior posts were more likely to be filled by older women, or because selectors were more reluctant to hand senior positions to women with dependent children than to men in the same circumstance.

[22] int. cs3:1:140.

[23] Bentley, 'Two-clergy Couples', p. 208. Thorne's research suggested that perhaps 23% of women had not chosen to pursue NSM (Thorne, *Journey to Priesthood*, p. 77).

[24] A similar situation seems to have occurred during the first decades of women's ordained ministry in the US Episcopal Church (see: Paula D. Nesbitt, 'Dual Ordination Tracks: Differential Benefits for Men and

space to investigate these suggestions in-depth in the current report, and the factors involved in pushing women towards non-stipendiary ministry are also already being investigated elsewhere.[25] However, a proper assessment of the issues relating to appointments will have to consider not just the experiences of clergy once in ministry but also the process of calling, selection and training that preceded it. It may be that more procedural flexibility is needed at this earlier stage so that women (and men) are enabled to move more easily between stipendiary/non-stipendiary and permanent non-stipendiary ordination tracks.[26] Indeed, Diocese C was already beginning to address this question as a matter of diocesan policy.

5.3 A stained glass ceiling?

Just as women were disproportionately present in non-stipendiary and sector ministry, so they were also under-represented as incumbents and in more senior clerical posts.[27] Lesley Bentley's survey of women's ministry in Gordon Kuhrt's Ministry Issues in the Church of England identified this as one of the most significant sources of concern amongst women in priesthood.[28] But what were the reasons for this pattern? Again, often conflicting interpretations were offered. A minority of those with objections to women's priesthood suggested that this was only to be expected, since generations of churchgoers had implicitly expected their clergy to be male and so were more likely to seek a male priest: 'I think if you've spent most of your time as a worshipper believing that the priesthood is male, and the priest stands there as did Christ at the Last Supper, I can see why some people can be a bit disturbed.'[29] A small number suggested that women would never be fully accepted as leaders in church because churchgoers instinctively knew that leadership was not a woman's role – although it should be remembered that this was not a majority view; comparatively few (those with objections/reservations about women's priesting included) thought that women were simply not designed for the job.

Senior clergy also frequently defended themselves against the suggestion that the lack of women in senior appointments had in any way resulted from their own policies. A few suggested that because more women had trained on non-residential ministerial training courses, they had not received the intellectual formation that would equip them for preferment.[30] It was more common to suggest that women would of course one day be appointed on the same terms as men, but not yet:

> *In two or three years' time, things will look very different ... I know some of the women would like me to move faster than I probably would have done, but I take the long view, and the women incumbents thing I don't think can be cracked by appointing jazzy archdeacons and deans, because I think if you make provocative appointments you often retire them.*[31]

Women Clergy' in William H. Swatos (ed.), *Gender and Religion* (Transaction Publishers, London, 1994), pp. 27–44 (p. 40).).

[25] Research currently being commissioned by GRAS.

[26] In fact, the categories to which candidates for ordained ministry are allocated were already under review at time of writing.

[27] For example, as residentiary canons, deans and archdeacons.

[28] Gordon W. Kuhrt and Lesley Bentley, 'Women and Ordained Ministry' in Kuhrt (ed.), *Ministry Issues in the Church of England*, pp. 234–9 (p. 237).

[29] int. 12:566.

[30] There was a widespread perception that residential theological training was of superior quality to non-residential schemes. It is not the place of this report to judge whether this was in fact the case; the observation is merely reported as one of the factors identified by some clergy as to why ordained women were less likely to be selected for more senior posts.

[31] int. cs3:4:424.

Some suggested women clergy should be more patient until such time as the sensitivities of the past decade had died down and appointing a woman to a parish for the first time would be a less remarkable matter. A much more common suggestion (from laity as well as clergy) was that some parishes were inappropriate appointments for women in any case, because of their socially challenging circumstances; for example, the perceived impropriety of appointing a single woman to an inner city parish where her personal security might be at risk. Most significantly, it was suggested that the main reason women were not being appointed to senior incumbencies was not because their applications were being rejected, but because they were *simply not applying* in great numbers.[32] One archdeacon even quoted some recent figures in support of his point: a large parish had recently begun searching for a new incumbent, indicating on the advertisement that they would 'welcome applications from a woman'. One hundred and forty clergy visited the vacancies web site, thirty-five downloaded the application form, twenty-five ordered an application pack over the telephone, and of the six who applied, all were male.[33] Were women simply not applying for such posts? Certainly some evidence from other provinces and denominations pointed to a similar picture: despite over forty years of women's priesting in the Church of Sweden, 42% of male priests became vicars but only 8% of women. Many of the latter seemed to have eschewed the lure of leading a 'big parish' in order to concentrate on missionary and pastoral work.[34] However, one influential study from the USA concluded that this was not a significant consideration amongst American clergywomen.[35]

Female clergy responded to suggestions such as these in a number of ways. In answer to claims that they lacked the necessary experience, many ordained women argued that their years of diaconal service were being discounted, and their experience only measured since their priesting after 1994 (even in the case of some women who had served as deacons-in-charge of parishes, or had taken positions of responsibility in a cathedral setting).[36] As one interviewee from Diocese C complained, 'You get told that you don't have the experience for a certain job, but how can you gain the experience if you're not given a chance to gain it?'[37] Citing lack of experience was generally felt to be an excuse for not taking a more proactive approach to the matter of more senior appointments for women. Most ordained women seemed to accept that the current pattern of appointments was not exclusively the fault of the bishops: more women had chosen to enter permanent non-stipendiary ministry and were therefore effectively removing themselves from consideration for some more senior posts. Others suggested that many women lacked the confidence of their male counterparts to put themselves forward for the bigger jobs.

Female clergy whose husbands were incumbents were often unable to take up vicar/rector posts in their own right because they were required to live in the parish; something that would mean splitting the family. There was no a priori reason why clergy couples were prevented from taking it in turns to take up an incumbency (and in some cases, this was exactly what had taken place) but in many cases – as with the question of stipends considered above – the husband's job often took precedence. Likewise, with stipendiary

---

[32] Partly because, as already suggested, it remained more common for the husband's job to take precedence.

[33] int. cs3:7:294.

[34] Brita Stendahl, *The Force of Tradition; A Case Study of Women Priests in Sweden* (Fortress Press, Philadelphia, 1985), p. 102. Conversations with two clergy conversant with the current situation in the Church of Sweden suggests that this pattern continues.

[35] Jackson W. Carroll, Barbara Hargrove and Adair T. Lummis, *Women of the Cloth: A New Opportunity for the Churches* (Harper and Row, San Francisco, 1983), pp. 133–5.

[36] See also: Kuhrt and Bentley, 'Women and Ordained Ministry', p. 237.

[37] int. cs3:3:97.

posts at a premium, women who elected not to uproot their entire family to a new diocese in order to obtain an incumbency were thus faced with a reduced pool of available posts to fish from.[38] This pool was further reduced by the additional existence of a number of team parishes that – although they had no resolutions in place – found it difficult to contemplate appointing a woman as team rector or team vicar if one of the parishes objected to women's priestly ministry.

Of course, some women were content to develop their ministries through a series of curacies and team posts (and worried that some of their female colleagues had been seduced by the lure of running a large, successful parish[39]). But in several dioceses it was sometimes suggested that women were disproportionately handed the less challenging posts. As one senior clergyman from Diocese B suggested:

I think there is a danger women end up with the jobs men won't take…

[I.J.: do you mean the difficult parishes?]

No, no – you'll often find men taking on the difficult parishes; it's the boring parishes – vast tracts of lovely, lush agricultural land, with super communities, but heavily depopulated, so you can have a parish which will stretch seven, eight, nine, ten miles, a group of parishes, and in there might live two and a half thousand people. And there comes a limit to know what you do as a parish priest once you've visited those who are vaguely interested … what do you do tomorrow? And my fear is … my concern is that we take very competent women, and we bore them.[40]

As this comment suggests, such views were not only expressed by women. One diocesan bishop recalled how the first women appointed as priest-in-charge or incumbents in his previous diocese 'took on parishes that were at a very low ebb… they were willing to take posts that many men would not have done. […] the chances of succeeding are considerable, and it was certainly true ... that the first women appointed to parishes often increased congregations, and were seen to be successful. That began to alter the way in which they were perceived ...'[41] Clearly if such parishes sometimes offered less of a challenge, they could also offer additional opportunity. More seriously, many women thought they perceived a reluctance on the part of some dioceses to appoint women to parishes where the weight of opinion was not heavily in favour of their priestly ministry. Some senior clergy acknowledged that this was generally the practice in their diocese. On one hand this could be interpreted as admirable concern for consensus over clerical appointments, and a strong desire to minimize division and ill-feeling. On the other hand, such a practice begged significant questions about whether it was ethical (or even legal) to allow parishes without resolutions in place to say 'yes, but not yet' to a woman's priestly ministry. Parishes in this position are considered further in section 5.5, but meanwhile this difficulty may be noted as a further of example of the way in which women had been widely accepted as priests but not perhaps yet on exactly the same terms as men.

Ordained women were not, however, the only clergy to feel that obtaining a new post had been made more difficult by the 1992–94 settlement and the climate surrounding its

---

[38] Although of course this could also be a factor for male clergy, it seems in practice to have been a more significant factor for women, who were more likely than men to follow their spouse's job.
[39] int. cs2:1:p.3b.
[40] int. cs2:12:335.
[41] int. 13:500.

operation. One of the most common complaints from clergy with objections to women's priesting was that they were consistently passed over for senior appointments. At the time of interviewing, it was regularly commented that with the exception of the current Bishop in Europe, no member of the male-only priesthood constituency had been made a diocesan bishop since 1994.[42] Certainly the Church of England's 2001 report *Working with the Spirit: Choosing Diocesan Bishops* (chaired by Baroness Pauline Perry) noted that 'expressions of concern that candidates opposed to the ordination of women to the priesthood are unfairly discriminated against have been the most numerous'.[43] Although the report added that whilst opposition to women's priesting did not in itself make a candidate unsuitable for Episcopal office, certain views against women's priesting were very difficult to reconcile with the work a diocesan bishop would have to do. (Indeed, the emphasis placed on the bishop as a symbol of unity in his diocese arguably worked in favour of candidates from the centre ground of the Church of England – to the relief of some and the disappointment of others.) The Perry Report acknowledged, however, that the diversity of the episcopate was not being helped by the tendency for diocesan bishops to be chosen from amongst suffragan bishops, who were themselves the personal appointees of their diocesans (and therefore often of similar views). It is conceivable that this could have hindered the progress of 'traditionalist' candidates to the episcopacy, although Lady Perry herself emphasized that the Commission's investigation had found 'general confidence that the system is demonstrably fair, robust and effective'.[44] It should also be added that of course, at this stage, women were not eligible for consideration as bishops at all.

Clergy with objections to women's priesting also voiced concerns about the distribution of parish level appointments to candidates from their constituency. The most common theme here was that resolution parishes and parishes with evenly divided congregations were allegedly being given to men who supported women's priesting with the deliberate intention of 'softening up' the parish in preparation for the rescinding of the resolutions and the possible eventual appointment of a female priest.[45] Traditionalist clergy in Diocese B were particularly insistent that this was a deliberate policy of their bishops – and this issue will be explored further in Chapter 7. In addition, some clergy in resolution parishes suggested that too often they were only being offered priest-in-charge status, rather than incumbent status. Some clergy interviewees in Diocese A alleged that this was a deliberate policy by senior clergy to enable them to be moved on to another parish more easily. It is notable that both Forward in Faith and Reform have campaigned forcibly for the defence of freehold, feeling that a move to more finite terms as priest-in-charge may strengthen a diocese's ability to 'crack' traditionalist parishes.[46]

Such was the degree of concern over appointments amongst some 'traditionalist' clergy that a few even used the language of 'persecution' or 'ethnic cleansing' to describe their experience. Of course, sometimes the issue of women's priesting could simply add an

---

[42] This was before the appointment of the Ven. Nicholas Reade as the new Bishop of Blackburn in August 2003 (*Church Times*, 8.8.03). The Rt Revd John Hind, Bishop in Europe since 1993, was translated to Chichester in 2001. Several clergy who did not favour women's ordination as priests have also been made suffragan bishops since 1994.

[43] Review Group of the Archbishop's Council, *Working with the Spirit: Choosing Diocesan Bishops* (General Synod GS 1405, Church House Publishing, London, 2001), section 2.27 (p. 26).

[44] Statement by Lady Perry, 09.05.2001 [http://www.cofe.anglican.org/cgi-bin/news/item_frame.pl?id= 128, viewed 11.11.2003].

[45] int. cs2:7:529 and 'Thirty Days' column in *New Directions* 1 (6) November 1995, p. 16.

[46] Reform even published an 'alternative churchwarden's handbook' detailing how to steer a course through the difficult area of appointing the right incumbent. As the Revd Steve Donald wrote in the first edition of *Reform Newspaper*, it was 'easy to feel vulnerable or cowed by the powers that be…Forewarned is forearmed' (p. 4).

additional layer onto an existing disagreement (for example, the persecution of Romanizing or High Church clergy has become an integral part of the Anglo-Catholic historical memory. A traditionalist view on women priests, it was believed, gave a liberal or evangelical bishop just one more reason to seek their removal. Several clergy from resolution parishes in Diocese E were particularly scathing about their former bishop's attitude to Anglo-Catholics, and interestingly a female Anglo-Catholic priest from the same diocese reported a similarly difficult experience of the same bishop[47]). Even traditionalist clergy who placed greater trust in their senior diocesan clergy could sometimes feel that there were still unresolved problems: some felt that the 1992–94 settlement had left them pigeonholed as clergy who would only work in resolution parishes, even where this was not the case. One male vicar from Diocese C recalled how in his previous parish, he had been largely successful in uniting a congregation divided over women's priesting, without either inviting a woman to celebrate or passing any of the resolutions. However, on leaving the parish he had found it difficult to get an interview anywhere that had not passed resolutions A and B. In his view, 'A and B' clergy like himself were in a doubly difficult position: non-resolution parishes doubted his willingness to be affirming of women's ministry in any form, whilst parishes that received the ministry of the PEV regarded him as 'insufficiently kosher' because he was happy to receive communion from his diocesan bishop and had theological objections to extended episcopal oversight.[48]

Just as with the questions surrounding the deployment of women clergy, so senior diocesan clergy were also often keen to refute accusations that 'traditionalists' were being marginalized. One noted that increased power of appointment now resided with parish representatives to the extent that it was almost impossible for a bishop or patron to force a candidate on an unwilling parish. Others suggested it was unrealistic to expect more senior appointments to be given to clergy with objections to women's priesting: as the Bishop of Diocese B observed, 'every senior appointment we make they accuse us of not taking the traditionalists seriously but in a diocese where ninety-five per cent of parishes are for the ordination of women I can't really honestly appoint an archdeacon for this five per cent…'.[49] With regard to parish appointments, it was also argued that the numbers of clergy who disagreed with women's priesting were so small that some parishes with resolutions in place would have to accept a male priest who was 'in favour' if they were to have a priest at all. Occasionally it was suggested that it was simply a question of merit; that there were too few 'traditionalist' clergy of sufficient calibre and experience to warrant large-scale appointments to senior positions (an argument that clergy against women's priesting particularly disliked). One of the most problematic areas for senior clergy was making appointments to team parishes or multi-benefice parishes where one congregation did not support women's priesting and the others did. Here, several bishops noted that it was particularly difficult to find a candidate who had the right theological credentials to satisfy the parish *and* who would also be happy to work in a team situation that would almost certainly include clergy supportive of women's priesting, and possibly ordained women themselves.[50]

---

[47] These remarks, it should be said, related not to the Diocesan Bishop but to another bishop in the diocese.

[48] int. cs3:24:314.

[49] int. cs2:4:271. Once again, this seemed to reflect a wider assumption that an important aspect of the appointments process was the need for senior posts to be representative of the different traditions and interest-groups within the diocese.

[50] This was a particular problem for Church 21 in Diocese F, which at the time of research was in the midst of a lengthy interregnum whilst a mutually acceptable candidate was sought.

It is nevertheless important not to overstate the extent of the problem. As the first part of this chapter suggested, less than one in five clergy had ever felt their gender, or their views on women's priesting, had been a negative factor in obtaining a suitable position. In some dioceses, senior clergy were greatly respected across the board for managing the question of appointments sensitively and enabling the different constituencies to feel included (for example, hardly anyone had a bad word to say about the bishop with pastoral responsibility for the case study deanery selected in Diocese E). Moreover, whilst unresolved issues were frequently raised, it is also important to acknowledge the ways that some dioceses were seeking to tackle them. In Diocese C, for example, senior clergy had actively taken steps to encourage promising candidates lacking in education or experience to undertake some further ministerial education or development. Such a process implied no guarantee of future preferment, and was primarily to be understood as continuing ministerial development rather than as a stepping stone to promotion. However, bishops and archdeacons sometimes realized that the more promising clergy were afforded such opportunities, the larger the pool of local talent they would be able to select from when the next vacancy for an archdeacon or dean was announced. In many organizations 'continuing professional development' is accepted as an integral part of the organization's activity, but it was clear from the case studies many dioceses were not giving this matter sustained reflection. This should perhaps be reconsidered. In addition to growing a better educated, better equipped body of clergy, according development opportunities to more clergy (of all perspectives on women's priesting) might help to defuse some of the mistrust surrounding the question of more senior clerical appointments discussed here. National networks supporting women's ministry had begun to discuss ways in which senior male and female clergy could help to resource and mentor women applying for their first incumbencies, enabling them to feel more equipped to apply for parishes and eventually more senior positions. Eventually it was hoped that this might result in a database of suitable candidates for positions of responsibility (the so-called 'Isabella's List'[51]).

With regard to appointments of 'traditionalist' clergy, some diocesan bishops in this study had built up good relationships with the relevant Episcopal Visitor, so that when resolution parishes entered a period of interregnum, the two worked collaboratively to draw up a shortlist of possible incumbents.[52] More than any of these specific measures, however, dioceses had begun to learn by getting their fingers burned: in one notorious case, one diocese had advertised a key diocesan adviser's post (in theory open to both men and women) that was tied to a half-time appointment in a resolution A and B parish. No sooner had the advertisement been published than the diocese received a number of angry complaints that women were effectively excluded from applying for the adviser role. In interview, the bishop in question freely admitted that the diocese had failed to realize the error, and vacancies were now drawn up with greater attention to the implications for women. On one hand, the fact that this had become an issue at all illustrates the extent to which an extra set of new issues had been added to the appointments process by the shape of the 1992–94 settlement, bringing extra tension to the already often tricky business of clerical appointments. On the other hand it was clear that gradually, dioceses were beginning to adapt to the sensitivities of the current situation, with the added result that more transparent approaches to appointments were beginning to be explored – to the potential benefit of all clergy.

---

[51] After Isabella Gilmore, a pioneer of the deaconess order in the Church of England.

[52] This reflected one recommendation of the Blackburn Review report (House of Bishops Standing Committee, 'Episcopal Ministry Act of Synod 1993: Guidelines for Good Practice Emanating from the Report of the Working Party of the House of Bishops Chaired by the Bishop of Blackburn' ('The Blackburn Report'), GS1395' (7 March 2001), point 13).

5.4 The appointments process

This was also true in relation to the application and selection process itself, although here female clergy often felt that dioceses still had some way to go. In particular, several clergy commented on dissonance between the increasingly developed recruitment and selection procedures they had experienced in their working life prior to ordination, and the Church's own procedures that seemed to many to be regulated primarily by the assumption that the interviewers would have the best intentions of all concerned at heart. Some experienced female clergy suggested that one of the main problems with the current system was the level of trial and error involved in finding a new post. With no central database of vacancies, some posts became vacant and were filled without many suitable candidates even being aware of the job's existence. Of course, any difficulties with the current system of advertising vacancies affected men as well as women, but there was a strong suspicion that an 'old boys' network' still operated within the Church, to the detriment of female applicants – particularly for senior posts. Several also criticized interviewing and selection procedures at parish level – for example female applicants being asked questions about their personal lives that did not directly relate to their ability to do the job. Amongst those who had objections to ordaining women, the most common complaint was that the women priests question too often became the defining topic of conversation in the interview: 'I think in so many situations now…it's the one question they can ask you: "Father, what's your view on the ordination of women?"…'[53] Of course, without further research into individual cases it is difficult to be sure of the circumstances surrounding any bad experience of the appointments process. Failure to secure a new position could arise from one of several potential sources (not being the best candidate for the job, not being the 'best fit' for the parish, even a clash of personalities or church traditions) and was not necessarily a function of discrimination. However, whilst accepting that a combination of factors could work against an applicant, there was sufficient concern that failures in the appointments process were affecting women to suggest that improvements need to be made.

Certainly some parishes seemed ill-schooled in the business of advertising for and interviewing for new clergy. In one of the most controversial cases encountered, a parish with no resolutions in place had advertised for a new incumbent and invited two candidates for interview – one female and the other male. The female candidate seemed to most of those on the interview panel to be clearly the best choice, and at the end of the day she was led to believe that, barring the formalities, an offer would be made within the coming week. The letter never arrived. When senior clergy asked what had happened, one of the two parish representatives responded that they had had second thoughts, and decided that the church might find it difficult to accept a female incumbent at that stage. The female candidate was left feeling angry and badly let down, whilst the bishop and archdeacon expressed exasperation that the parish representatives had allowed the interview process to reach such an advanced stage without mentioning this consideration.[54] As a result, at the time of researching, the diocese in question was engaged in drawing up enhanced procedures for the writing of parish profiles, including a more in-depth consultation between archdeacon and parish representatives. It was hoped these measures would ensure that parishes were clearer about their preferred choice of incumbent from the beginning.

Senior clergy in the diocese were also beginning to consider making it standard procedure for unsuccessful candidates to receive feedback on why they had not been chosen for the post.

---

[53] int. cs3:24:279. The speaker in question was asked 'which chrism masses have you attended in the last five years' – presumably as a way of testing out his allegiance to a particular theological tradition.

[54] In fact most of those who recounted the story suggested that a majority of the congregation had been quite willing to accept a female incumbent, with the reservations coming from a small number of influential figures in the parish.

Whilst such measures are not yet mandatory within the Church of England, they are standard practice in many other contexts. This diocese seems to have been unusual in contemplating such measures, but other dioceses might also benefit from exploring similar processes.

5.5 'We'll take a woman, but not yet'

If parish profiles are to give clearer statements on the congregation's views on male and female clergy, it will also become essential to address the question raised in this final section of the chapter: whether it is acceptable for a parish to consider only male clergy when no resolutions are in force. As already hinted, the most difficult issues raised by the 1992–94 settlement were *not* those explicitly covered by the terms of the legislation. Parishes that were enthusiastic to receive a female priest, and parishes that had passed the resolutions, were often comparatively straightforward cases. Amongst the most difficult decisions came when parish representatives indicated that the congregation had no desire to pass the resolutions, but did not think the time was right to invite a woman to be the incumbent. Across the case studies included here, there seemed to be no clear consensus over whether it was acceptable to allow a parish to say 'yes' to women priests, but also 'not yet'. For some, such as this senior clergyman from Diocese B:

> ...*my line is very simple: if they want to pass the resolutions, the Measure enables them to make their case. If they're not able to pass that, they must consider women, because women have no rights under the Measure – it's a balance of rights. I'm not happy with that fudging, saying 'oh, well, you know ...', because I think that is an agenda being hijacked by very few in a congregation; not the majority. If they were confident, they'd go to the resolutions.*[55]

However, a former colleague of the speaker took a different line, suggesting that he had been prepared to allow parishes to say 'we don't want to pass a resolution, but don't want to have a woman this time', appointing female clergy only to parishes he knew that would overwhelmingly accept them.[56] Given the lack of consensus within this one diocese, it was little surprise that practices also varied from diocese to diocese.

A second layer to the problem was whether it would be better to draw up standard guidelines for working with 'yes, but not yet' parishes, or whether the flexibility to treat parishes on a case by case basis was most important. In recent decades the church has seen a remarkable growth in what Norman Doe has termed 'ecclesiastical quasi-legislation'; resolutions, procedures and guidelines without the force of law but carrying the moral authority of the bishops and/or Synod.[57] (The 2001 House of Bishops' guidelines for the implementation of the Blackburn Review of the Act of Synod offers a relevant example of this.) Attempts to standardize practice across the dioceses have the merit of openness and consistency and promise a straightforward method for adjudicating on matters of dispute. But a trenchant critique of the 'McDonaldizing' force of such guidelines and procedures has come from Richard H. Roberts, who points out that such approaches too often enforce conformity at the expense of developing solutions that build trust and consensus.[58] Amongst senior clergy interviewed here, the balance of opinion was also in favour of a case by case

---

[55] int. cs2:12:182.

[56] int. cs2:6:515.

[57] Norman Doe, 'Ecclesiastical Quasi-legislation', in Norman Doe, Mark Hill and Robert Ombres (eds), *English Canon Law; Essays in Honour of Bishop Eric Kemp* (University of Wales Press, Cardiff, 1998), pp. 93–103.

[58] Richard H. Robers, *Theology, Religion and the Human Sciences* (Cambridge University Press, Cambridge, 2002), pp. 40, 60.

approach to 'yes, but not yet' parishes (despite the suggestion of some that this opened the system to abuse and legal challenge). However, if dioceses *are* to be left free to pursue their own resolutions for such cases, serious thought will need to be given to what kinds of factors constitute a 'reasonable' justification for a parish to say 'yes, but not yet' to women's priesting. Just as clergy of all different positions recognized that resolutions were sometimes passed for reasons other than those for which they were intended,[59] so parishes and senior clergy should work carefully to ensure that parishes saying 'yes but not yet' are doing so for reasons that were generally regarded as acceptable. The case also raises a second question that requires careful consideration: if a parish is to be permitted to say 'yes but not yet' because it might be less divisive to accept a female incumbent next time around, how long is it acceptable to allow the parish to continue in that position? Should dioceses allowing parishes breathing space to accept what was decided in 1992, or are they prepared to allow 'yes, but not yet' to become a much longer-term position? It was here that the wider debate about the 'reception' of women's priesting[60] became most relevant at parish level. What remains clear is that the case of parishes that choose not to appoint a female priest *and* decline to pass a resolution requires serious investigation if a climate of trust between the different constituencies and diocesan authorities is to be built.

Conclusion

Concern for an equitable deployment of female and male clergy was important to many interviewees, but the appointments issue arguably acquired even greater significance because of the widespread belief that experience of women in ordained ministry was key to their acceptance as priests.[61] Even where the incumbent was male, it was widely acknowledged that his views on women's priesting might exert a wider influence on congregational opinion – perhaps towards welcoming a female priest or conversely towards passing the resolutions. (As Chapter 4 illustrates, both could happen.) In the minds of those with the strongest views in either direction, appointing a favoured candidate could even acquire strategic importance. In one sense there is nothing new in this: clergy have always (consciously or unconsciously) sought to leave their mark on their parish – for example, in 'raising' or 'lowering' the churchmanship of the church. Popular suspicion of 'the bishop's man' or 'the patron's candidate' also have a long history. Concerns over the appointment of clergy with particular views on women's priesting simply added a new dimension to that wider picture. However, because women's ordination could often become a defining issue in particular cases, it became much easier for different groups to feel marginalized over questions of appointments. This discourse of marginalization permeates much of the discussion of current issues in this part of the report, and arguably made it easier for senior clergy to regard the project of coexistence as a matter of trying to balance the interests of different 'sides'. Indeed, it was not unknown for a senior clergyman to remark that if the diocese was receiving equal numbers of complaints from ordained women and from traditionalist clergy, they had probably got the balance about right. In one sense this is true: an organization can never wholly meet the needs of all its members, and only a balance of interests can enable most individuals and groups to be satisfied most of the time. However, too great an emphasis on the existence of different 'integrities'[62] or 'constituencies' and the

---

[59] See Chapter 7, Section 8.3c.
[60] For more on the question of 'reception', see Chapter 8.
[61] Lehman suggests that congregations tend to become more favourable to women's ordained ministry as the result of a clergywoman being appointed to their own church, although this does not necessarily increase support for women's ordained ministry as a whole (quoted in Leslie J. Francis and Mandy Robbins, *The Long Diaconate, 1987–1994; Women Deacons and the Delayed Journey to Priesthood* (Gracewing, Leominster, 1999), p. 11).
[62] The House of Bishops' Manchester Statement and *Being in Communion* argued for the need to allow the integrity of the different views on women's priesting to be respected. Over the following decade, this

need to balance their competing claims could at times reinforce this sense of polarization. This was ironic since, as Chapter 2 suggests, the boundaries between 'supporters' and 'opponents' were sometimes more blurred than has generally been supposed.

As this chapter has sought to suggest, one way of beginning to tackle residual suspicion over appointments is to develop procedures that can be generally accepted as fair, open and honest. This might include:

- working with parishes to develop profiles that are clear about the priest they want and to provide guidance and training on how to interview candidates fairly and thoroughly;
- working with promising candidates for senior appointments who may yet lack sufficient experience to encourage them to pursue opportunities for further development;
- consulting widely on appointments to parishes whose circumstances are specially sensitive;
- developing clearer policies on parishes that do not wish to pass a resolution but that also do not want a female priest this time around (this will include deciding what count as legitimate and illegitimate reasons for saying 'yes but not yet', and also deciding whether a uniform policy for each diocese is more or less helpful than allowing a degree of flexibility over particular parish situations);
- devising a more open system of appointments to senior positions including (where appropriate) the use of common human resources procedures; e.g., an open applications process, use of CVs and references, less reliance on word of mouth to hear about opportunities and provide information on possible candidates, feedback for unsuccessful applicants. The very positive response given on all sides to *Working with the Spirit* (which recommended applying various aspects of HR good practice to the choosing of diocesan bishops) suggests that measures of this kind could also be extended to other senior positions.

Of course, such practices always have limitations, and it would be inadequate for the Church simply to attempt to 'manage' its way through division. Such developments are merely sticking plaster unless they are reinforced by a determination on all sides not to regard appointments as a way of gaining territorial advantage over another constituency (a trap into which individuals on *all* sides of the debate sometimes fall). However, beginning to address such practical issues may help to build trust and address some of the concerns surrounding the appointments question, freeing the Church to focus on its wider mission, ministry and theological understanding.

---

language metamorphosed so that some clergy and laity began to talk of the existence of 'the two integrities'.

Chapter 6

Communion and cooperation in parish, deanery and diocese

'I have not really come across these problems. Nearly all clergy and lay mix well and are supportive' (Q272, female, associate vicar/chaplain, 50–59)

'We're all doing a lovely Anglican dance to ensure that no one's been put in an awkward position ...' (Interviewee 2, Diocese D)

Alongside the specific issues of the appointments process (Chapter 5) and the opt-out provisions (Chapter 7), clergy also identified a more general set of unresolved issues around the daily business of working and worshipping alongside colleagues with differing views on women's priesting. After the drama of the 1992 debate had subsided, church life still had to carry on. If the incumbent and congregation shared similar views, the question of women's priesting rarely became contentious, and (as already suggested in Part I) ordained women for the most part found their ministry readily accepted. With most respondents having comparatively little involvement in the institutional structures of the Church of England outside their own parish, encountering members of another constituency was comparatively rare, and seldom posed a challenge greater than handling a personal difference of opinion. However, for clergy (who were – at least theoretically – required to participate in wider church life outside the parish on a more regular basis) the 1992–94 settlement presented a larger number of occasions when working and worshipping together with other clergy with different views on women's priesting became necessary. Often such encounters were entirely unproblematic, with the old dividing lines over the ordination of women as priests hardly registering as a source of tension. However, some occasions could become more difficult, and this chapter seeks to identify those aspects of post-1992 deanery and diocesan life that required more care and attention, exploring both the problems and some of the ways in which these were addressed.

Four main areas are considered: first, the general temperature of working relationships between clergy; second, specific issues arising within a deanery context; and third, participation in wider diocesan occasions. Sector ministry is also briefly considered, before the chapter concludes with a review of the changing support given to women clergy themselves through diocesan support groups and advisers in women's ministry. Throughout, particular attention is given to the role of the bishops and their attempts to act as foci for unity and managers of conflict in their diocesan contexts. An extended conclusion reflects upon the key themes and challenges to emerge. Once again, much of the evidence is necessarily anecdotal and must be treated with caution, since it may say as much about clergy perceptions of the current degree of communion and cooperation as about what is actually taking place. Nevertheless, as Chapter 5 has already suggested, perception could play a crucial role in shaping reality.

6.1 Working relationships: some general patterns

A good starting point for this chapter is to take a rough measurement of the temperature of working relationships across the whole clergy sample. On the Clergy Questionnaire, respondents were invited to indicate if they believed their working relationships had been affected by the experience of 1992–94. The question was included because many clergy recalled a tense atmosphere at deanery and diocesan occasions in the aftermath of the vote. In Diocese A, where the diocesan clergy conference had taken place just a week after the result, one male vicar remembered 'people going off into huddles, to lick their wounds',[1] whilst one senior diocesan clergyman with reservations about women's priesting called it 'the most awful week I've had'.[2] Female clergy often recalled how, after the vote, and particularly after their own priesting, deanery and diocesan colleagues who had voted against the Measure sometimes began to ignore them, or express their hostility more openly. This seems only rarely to have manifested itself in direct verbal attacks, but could involve snide comments or asides: one senior female priest in Diocese A recalled her rural dean introducing business with 'Ladies and Gentlemen ...', upon which one fellow chapter member muttered that as far as he was concerned, 'there are no ladies here'.[3] Such stories of rudeness should not be allowed to obscure the many occasions on which those of differing opinions congratulated or commiserated each other on the result and continued to work well together as colleagues. Nevertheless, the strain placed on some working relationships after the vote has become part of the emergent oral tradition on the early 1990s, and has been documented in a number of other studies.[4] But how widespread were such experiences?

In the Clergy Questionnaire, respondents were asked to reflect on their experiences of being ignored/treated rudely by fellow clergy over this issue, the extent to which their working relationships with lay and clergy had been affected, and whether this had manifested itself in a refusal to participate in communion. In each case, respondents were asked to comment on their own experience, leaving aside the question of whether they had known others encounter similar problems. This allows us to move a short distance beyond the realm of anecdote and draw some conclusions as to the pervasiveness of the problem. Table 6i compares the responses of female and male clergy to the first of these areas. If the responses summarized here are at all representative, it seems that a significant minority of clergy have experienced some personal opposition as a result of their views on women's priesting – particularly in the case of ordained women. Nevertheless, such experiences do not seem to be a regular occurrence; as the second column of figures suggests, only a small percentage of respondents had been ignored or treated rudely by fellow clergy over this cluster of issues in the six months prior to their completion of the questionnaire.

I raised this disparity with several more experienced clergy, asking whether they thought this might indicate a warming of relations between the different constituencies, or alternatively whether it simply meant that such experiences had always been comparatively rare. There was general agreement both that tension *had* eased, and that in the majority of cases, such incidents had always been more exceptional than normal.[5] However, this did not necessarily suggest a real reconciliation of the different positions; in the words of one, 'all that's happened is that I don't think we've had the discrimination because I don't think we've been together as much'.[6] A possible trend in this direction will become an important theme of the chapter as a whole.

---

[1] int. cs1:25:25.

[2] int. cs1:15:80.

[3] int. cs1:25:49.

[4] See for example Helen Thorne, *Journey to Priesthood: An In-depth Study of the First Women Priests in the Church of England* (University of Bristol, Bristol, 2000), pp. 94–5.

[5] This conclusion is also broadly supported by Lesley Bentley, 'At the Grass Roots: The Act in the Parishes' in Monica Furlong (ed.), *Act of Synod: Act of Folly?* (SCM Press, London, 1998), pp. 101–114 (p. 101).

[6] int. cs1:25:412.

Table 6i: Have you a) ever, b) in the last six months, been ignored or treated rudely:
because they did not believe women should be priests? (women);
because you held differing positions on the ordination of women as priests? (men)
(% 'yes' amongst current diocesan clergy, by gender)[7]

Diocese	By fellow clergy?				By lay people?			
	Female clergy		Male clergy		Female clergy		Male clergy	
(no. of cases[8])	Ever?	L 6 M	Ever?	L 6 M	Ever?	L 6M?	Ever?	L 6 M
Diocese A (87)	76.2	50.0	34.8	19.6	65.0	30.8	29.7	15.2
Diocese B (112)	60.0	22.2	20.7	11.4	48.3	14.8	22.0	7.7
Diocese C (95)	80.0	46.7	31.4	20.9	44.4	27.8	20.3	9.0
Deanery D[9] (11)	100	100	22.2	0	100	100	12.5	0
Deanery E (24)	100	100	28.6	4.8	66.7	0	23.8	13.6
Deanery F (10)	100	0	33.3	33.3	75.0	0	33.3	33.3

Having said that, it would be wrong to conclude that working relationships between clergy were anywhere near breakdown. In the same set of questions, respondents were asked to comment on their working relationships with lay people, fellow clergy, and senior clergy who differed from them on the question of women's ordination as priests. As **Table 6ii** suggests, the vast majority agreed or strongly agreed that for the most part, these working relationships were good. Of the rest, a majority responded that they 'neither agreed nor disagreed', and very few disagreed/strongly disagreed with the statement.[10] Clergy-lay relations were least likely to be seen as problematic, whilst the most common difficulties arose in relationships with senior clergy. This was particularly true for male clergy, probably reflecting the perception amongst many of the 'traditionalist' constituency that they were marginalized by bishops and archdeacons apparently resentful of their dissenting ways. The results presented in this section must be treated with caution, since they are based only on self-reporting. It was notable how often interviewees (of all positions) seemed at pains to construct their own position as one of normality and moderation and not of incendiary extremism. This may have encouraged respondents to emphasize the harmony of any situation in which they were involved. Nevertheless, there is no reason to suppose that the results are without foundation, and certainly the impression gained from the interviews is of occasional problems and tension rather than an unrelenting atmosphere of hostility.

[7] These questions are based on questions asked in Helen Thorne's questionnaire sent to the first generation of women to be priested (Thorne, *Journey to Priesthood*, Q.20).
[8] The number of cases on which the percentages are based changed slightly from question to question. Here, the number of cases relating to the left hand column of figures is provided, to give a rough idea of the size of the samples.
[9] Figures for Deaneries D, E and F are based on only a very small sample of clergy, and therefore results are probably less reliable than for the three main case study dioceses.
[10] This conclusion is in line with Francis and Robbins' survey of the 'waiting' women deacons before 1994, in which – although 43% reported 'some trouble with colleagues', 73% felt their 'clerical colleagues are always very supportive of me' whilst 84% thought their congregations were 'always supportive of me' (Francis and Robbins, *The Long Diaconate*, pp. 108, 116).

Table 6ii: In the great majority of cases, I enjoy good working relationships with a) senior clergy, b) fellow clergy, c) lay people who differ from me on the question of the ordination of women (% 'strongly agree' and 'agree' combined for each diocese, by gender)						
Diocese (no. of cases[11])	Working relationships with senior clergy of different views		Working relationships with fellow clergy of different views		Working relationships with lay people of different views	
	Female clergy	**Male clergy**	**Female clergy**	**Male clergy**	**Female clergy**	**Male clergy**
Diocese A (92)	79.2	85.3	87.5	85.3	79.1	87.1
Diocese B (99)	64.0	58.1	65.5	81.7	69.0	85.4
Diocese C (96)	59.3	66.7	66.7	87.7	74.1	90.4
Deanery D (13)	100	72.7	50.0	90.9	100	90.9
Deanery E (25)	100	65.2	100	65.2	100	82.6
Deanery F (9)	66.7	83.4	75	83.4	75	83.4

Where tensions existed between clergy over their differing views on women's priesting, these often became focused on the question of communion. At the most basic level, this was not unexpected: Christians of a variety of traditions have found communion a particularly intimate experience, and a particularly cherished part of worship.[12] If it is true that conflict tends to coalesce around whatever is held to be most important (in any group or organization), it is perhaps not surprising that communion should become a key node of tension for disagreements over women's priesting. At another level, many clergy who had objections to women's priesthood laid great importance on the authenticity of their orders – without which (in some theological traditions) a valid communion service could not performed. A variety of other clerical roles contained no such sacramental dimension and even the firmest of opponents of women's priesting could therefore accept a woman performing them (for example, the office of rural dean). However, since the Eucharist had to be celebrated by a validly ordained minister, communion could become a key source of tension for Catholic clergy in particular, if they expressed doubts about the authenticity of women's orders (conservative evangelical clergy rarely had a problem with women celebrating communion since it was primarily an act of memorial).[13] On another level still, communion was that that was supposed to bind the Church and its ministry together, and those who felt that women's priesting had taken the Church several steps away from doctrinal orthodoxy could therefore find it difficult to contemplate taking communion with or from those they regarded as schismatic (although this was not a problem for all). The questionnaire therefore also asked about clergy's experience of the ordination of women debate as an issue at communion.[14] Female respondents were asked whether anyone had refused to take communion from them because they were ordained priests. Male clergy were asked whether anyone had refused communion from them because of their views on women's priesting. Both men and women were also asked if anyone had accepted

---

[11] As with Table 6i, the number of cases varied slightly from question to question. To provide a rough guide to the sample size, figures are given for the number of responses to the question on senior clergy.

[12] Ian Jones, 'The "Mainstream" Churches in Birmingham, c. 1945–98; The Local Church and Generational Change' (University of Birmingham PhD Thesis, 2000), Chapter 6.

[13] For conservative evangelicals with this objection to women's ordination as presbyters, the question of a woman's authority to preach or have headship of a local congregation was much more important. Eucharistic presidency only became problematic for evangelicals where it was taken to be symbolic congregational headship.

[14] These are based on questions in Helen Thorne's 2000 survey of ordained women (Helen Thorne, *Journey to Priesthood: An In-depth Study of the First Women Priests in the Church of England* (University of Bristol, Bristol, 2000), Q20).

communion from them despite their differing views on women's priesting. **Table 6iii** summarizes the responses:

Diocese (no. of cases[15])	Experience of clergy refusing to take communion from you over differences		Experience of laity refusing to take communion from you over differences		Experience of clergy accepting communion from you despite differences		Experience of laity accepting communion from you despite differences	
	Female	Male	Female	Male	Female	Male	Female	Male
A (87)	59.1	20.0	81.0	10.8	31.8	62.1	66.7	63.1
B (113)	43.3	9.6	63.3	8.5	20.7	60.5	58.6	65.9
C (98)	48.1	19.7	69.2	11.3	38.5	62.5	46.2	65.8
D (16)	50.0	16.7	100	18.2	50.0	72.7	100	72.7
E (22)	100	31.6	100	30.0	66.7	47.4	66.7	75.0
F (10)	100	50.0	100	50.0	100	50.0	100	33.3

Table 6iii: Have you ever known a) a fellow member of the clergy, b) a lay person, take the following approaches to communion because/despite the fact that they do not accept a) your priesthood as a woman (women), b) your views on the ordination of women as priests (men)? (% 'yes' for each diocese, by gender)

Here the proportion of respondents who had experienced such difficulties was considerably higher, as many as four in five women had encountered a lay person refusing to receive communion from them for this reason.[16] In the experience of many, this had been most common in the early years of women's priestly ministry, and on the first occasion that a church had experienced a woman celebrating communion. Often this proved a temporary difficulty, however. One female curate remembered how on her arrival as the parish's first female priest, just two members of the congregation voiced their objections to women's priesting. In order to respect their views, the clergy team ensured that at least one communion service every week would be taken by a man. In addition to taking advantage of these, the two women with reservations also began to attend communion services celebrated by the female speaker, simply opting not to come forward to receive the bread and wine. However, one day, without a word, they quietly came to the front and took part in the whole act of worship. It was 'quite a touching time when they did that for the first time', remembered the speaker.[17] Of course, not all churchgoers changed their minds. Church 10 in Diocese D was a traditional Anglo-Catholic parish with Resolution B in place but where the ministry of a female curate had also been accepted. Here, two elderly women from the regular Sunday congregation continued to feel uncomfortable with the ordination of women as priests and once again the communion rota was arranged to ensure they had the opportunity to receive from a male priest each week. The female curate observed, 'I think I'm OK about that – there would have been a time in my life when I'd have played merry hell about that'. I asked why the change of mind.

[15] As with Table 6ii, the number of cases varied slightly between the questions. To offer a rough guide to the sample sizes, the number of responses given relates to the left hand column of figures.
[16] In the smaller deanery cases studies, every female priest who responded had experienced such a situation, but because of the smaller size of these samples it is probably preferable to take the three diocesan case study figures as more reliable indicators of the wider picture.
[17] int. cs1:12:90.

> *It's the fact of this lady, who's struggled with it so conscientiously – when you know somebody that's in that situation, and you know that they'd struggled with the issue, and that they've tried to come to terms with it, and do so decently, I wouldn't want her to be receiving anything at home that she wouldn't be happy to receive, if she knew.*[18]

Here again it seems that a majority of lay respondents with hesitations over women's priesting either resolved their difficulties and accepted the new circumstance, or else quietly avoided any situation with which they would have been uncomfortable. This reflected a much wider trend throughout the case studies for the most problematic experiences of communion to come in all-clergy gatherings. For most of the bishops attempting to implement the 1992/93 settlement, it was imperative that clergy and laity remained 'in the highest possible degree of communion' with each other, even if this fell short of individuals from the different constituencies actually sharing bread and wine together. In some quarters, the current state of affairs was referred to as 'impaired communion', whilst others asked whether refusal to participate in the Eucharist (as the primary reflection of a wider *koinonia*) could really be described as 'communion' at all. As will be explored through the rest of this chapter, and further in Chapter 7, the place of communion remained a key underlying question for the whole of the 1992–94 settlement.

6.2 Deanery issues

Despite the fact that most Anglicans identify the parish and diocese as the two primary units of church organization, the practical implementation of the 1992–94 settlement appears to have caused particular challenges for clergy at *deanery* level. Deanery chapter meetings often provided the context for stories of both rude and reconciliatory behaviour. On the negative side, one female curate from Diocese C spoke of the exasperating experience of being one of the few female clergy in the midst of a deanery heavily populated with resolution parishes:

> *[it] make[s] chapter meetings dire ... I mean, I've got to the extent where I don't go any more, and the Archdeacon has actually chided me for that; said it's not going to change unless you do go [...] you go to chapter lunches, and it's like there's a line down the middle. There's the black-suited brigade, and then there's three or four that talk to me ... and a couple of others who are out on a limb – strange! [...] I started working in industry back in 1970, and I feel like I'm running through the same experiences and battle as I had then!*[19]

However, this speaker's situation was exceptional, and I could find few other ordained women who would absent themselves from deanery chapter because of the tense atmosphere there. Much more common was for male clergy with objections to women's priesting to withdraw from deanery chapter – sometimes even before the arrival of the first woman to be priested in the deanery – or to attempt to maintain a measure of distance when they attended. Several female clergy recounted how, earlier in the decade, they had occasionally arrived at deanery events occasions, gone to robe for the service, and were told that the room was for priests only (or sometimes – more obliquely – a changing room for men only; an unusual concept given that robing did not usually involve the removal of any existing item of clothing that would leave naked flesh on display): 'you lined up, and you could see them all shuffling, so that they didn't have to go in with you, and it's awful, to

---

[18] int. cs4:7side2:456.
[19] int. cs3:25:138, 279.

130

feel that nobody wants to walk in with you'.[20] Conversely, those with the strongest objections to women's priesting could also feel marginalized in a setting where they were in the minority; several told of being passed over for the position of rural dean, apparently because of their views. (Indeed, others complained that initial promises to ensure a balance of male and female clergy, and a diversity of views on women's priesting, at deanery level, had not been met. Clergy against women's priesting observed that in some rural areas in particular, lay respondents who could not accept a female priest might have to travel miles to receive communion consecrated by a man. Conversely, it was noted that in a small number of areas every parish had a resolution in place, and the community was effectively being deprived of the opportunity to experience a woman ministering as a priest.[21])

However, deanery clergy meetings could also become sites of reconciliation: one deanery had benefited greatly from the existence of a guild for Catholic clergy, which ran in addition to the clergy chapter, and that attracted Anglo-Catholic priests of a variety of different positions on women's priesting. As one member of the group explained, 'the aim of that group was very much about not just being those opposed, or those in favour, but how do we try and understand what the Catholic identity is within the Church of England across – in inverted commas – "the divide" ... I think in the early days, that helped us feel like we belonged'.[22] In a different deanery of the same diocese, one female priest recalled with pleasure how every member of her deanery chapter attended her induction service and congratulated her on her appointment, even though some of them had reservations about her orders.[23] With openness and respect, a good deal of cooperation could take place: one priest from a parish receiving extended episcopal care told of his good working relationship with the woman appointed to the neighbouring parish, and had invited her to preach on one recent occasion.[24] The priest he had invited (who was also interviewed) concurred that their differences of opinion posed few practical problems – except for the disappointment of not being able to share communion ('but I don't go looking for trouble').[25] The overall impression from interview testimony and the questionnaire responses was that relations at deanery level between clergy of differing views on women's priesting had become discernibly less tense as the decade had progressed. Instances of outright hostility had largely faded, although this was often because many of those with the strongest objections to women's priesting had long since ceased to attend chapter. These withdrawals were a source of much disappointment to many clergy regardless of their views on ordaining women; if the tense atmosphere of the early 1990s had largely dissolved, this was a hollow victory if this had only been achieved through creating a measure of distance between clergy, rather than by real engagement with individuals and issues. Of course, disagreement with fellow clergy or absence from deanery chapter were not new phenomena, arising purely from the debate over women's priesting. Some clergy had always been 'solo operators' out of preference, and the Church of England has a long history of groups

---

[20] int. cs1:25:473. This was despite the fact that the Code of Practice accompanying the 1993 Measure insisted that 'when the clergy of an area, or the holders of particular offices such as that of rural dean or canon, are invited to robe, the invitation will apply in all cases without discrimination as to gender' (House of Bishops, 'Priests (Ordination of Women) Measure 1993: Code of Practice' (Church House, London, 1994), para. 30). The significance of clerical attire, and its symbolic value in constructing identity in the midst of the first decade of women as priests, is a fascinating area of its own and one hopefully to be explored further in a future publication.
[21] The need for cooperation at deanery level to ensure 'a proper diversity of pastoral ministry' had been emphasized as early as 1993 in the House of Bishops' 'Statement by the House following its Meeting in Manchester' 11–14 January 1993, p. 6.
[22] int. cs3:6:86.
[23] int. cs3:10:146.
[24] int. cs2:5side2:378.
[25] int. cs1:p.4.

occasionally withdrawing from deanery and diocesan life over other issues (for example, the Birmingham Anglo-Catholic parishes of the 1920s that had protested at Bishop E.W. Barnes' views over the reservation of the sacrament[26]). In this sense, disagreements over women's priestly orders merely added another layer to a pre-existing pattern.

However, clergy also pointed to three *new* issues that had arisen from the coexistence of differing views on women's priesthood. One of these was the provision of cover for services during an interregnum. Indeed, in Diocese A the handling of interregna was one of the most contentious issues to arise from the 1992–94 settlement for clergy at deanery level (although in Dioceses C, D E and F the question was hardly mentioned, once again reflecting the way in which diocesan context played an important part in determining experience and perception of the whole). Covering during an interregnum was a duty that normally fell to deanery clergy (and particularly the rural dean) to arrange between themselves. Under the terms of the 1993 legislation, women were clearly not permitted to celebrate communion in any parish with Resolution A in force. This was rarely challenged,[27] but could sometimes present logistical problems – particularly in a deanery with large numbers of female clergy and also large numbers of resolution parishes, where the duty of cover was left to a comparatively small number of male clergy.

The vicar of Church 1 in Diocese A regretted the time lost to his own parish through spending several Sundays a month taking communion at his neighbouring (Resolution A and B) parish church when otherwise this duty could have been shared with his female curate. However, in Diocese A, covering resolution parishes turned out to be less contentious than providing cover for parishes with no resolutions in place and no previous experience of women's priestly ministry. Here, several priests with the most serious doubts about women's orders seem to have complained vehemently that senior clergy were using the interregnum to introduce a parish to a woman's priestly ministry, thus attempting to 'turn' a parish towards accepting a woman in the future.[28] This had prompted senior clergy to draw up a policy whereby a parish should *not* be introduced to a woman's priestly ministry during an interregnum if a woman had not previously celebrated communion at the church.[29] According to senior clergy in the diocese the policy had been a necessary mechanism for building up trust and had been accepted with 'huge grace and goodwill' by senior ordained women.[30] Nevertheless, it was far from clear that all clergy in the diocese knew of the policy, and amongst those that did the solution was not universally welcomed. Indeed, whilst male clergy who supported women's priesting had initially been prepared to work with the policy, there were signs of a change of attitude: several male interviewees increasingly felt uncomfortable about covering resolution parishes in place of their female colleagues, feeling that to do so would be to implicitly condone the view that women's ministry as priests was invalid. Some had gone so far as to choose not to provide cover for resolution parishes, and even for parishes whose support for women's ministry was regarded as suspect. The tension this issue created in Diocese A should not be exaggerated (indeed, this was the only diocese where interregna proved problematic for this reason), but the episode had nevertheless certainly not helped relations between the different positions.

[26] See: Adrian Hastings, *A History of English Christianity, 1920–1990* (SCM Press, London, 3rd Edition 1991), pp. 202–03. I am grateful to Dr W. M. Jacob for reminding me of this example.
[27] Although see Chapter 7, section 7.3b for suggestions that some senior clergy were using interregna as a time to urge parishes to rescind their resolutions.
[28] int. cs1:10:245.
[29] It is possible that senior clergy found their justification for this policy in paragraph 22 of the 'Priests (Ordination of Women) Measure 1993: Code of Practice' (House of Bishops, January 1994). This states that 'During a vacancy in a benefice the practice which obtained prior to that vacancy will be continued, unless a resolution is passed by the PCC under the provisions of Section 3 of the Measure'.
[30] int. cs1:15side2:470.

A more common development in deanery clergy life since 1992 was the establishment of parallel structures for those who could not accept women's priesting. 'Traditionalist' chapters had originated from a variety of circumstances, but often followed the pattern described by this clergyman: 'it came about in the aftermath of the vote, I think was formed either the next year or the year after ... really as an association of those clergy who were opposed to the ordination of women, and initially, perhaps, particularly felt isolated in their own deanery chapters, or felt for various reasons they couldn't go to their deanery chapters'.[31] Subsequently some (though not all) of these had developed links with Forward in Faith's structure of regional deans.[32] Dioceses varied in their approaches to these alternative chapters: in one diocese the 'traditionalist' chapter was placed on the same footing as normal deanery clergy chapters in all except legal status. Its clergy were encouraged to attend their usual deanery chapter, some chose to participate only in the 'alternative' chapter, and its dean was invited to attend rural deans' meetings. In Diocese A, the equivalent chapter existed primarily as an *additional* support network, with clergy expected to attend their existing deanery clergy meetings too (again, some did and others did not). Other senior clergy preferred to discourage such gatherings, fearing they would only breed discontentment and polarization. For many clergy, the emergence of alternative chapters was not a major source of difficulty, but was a disappointing sign of the polarization of the different positions within the Church of England.

Third, aside from the question of 'alternative' chapters, clergy also identified regular deanery clergy chapter meetings as potential sites of difficulty; particularly over communion. Catholic clergy with objections to women's priesting generally took the decision not to receive communion when this was celebrated by a woman, and this could lead to potential difficulties at clergy chapter meetings, since these often began with communion. Here, however, clergy chapters across the case study dioceses seem to have been able to find ways of working together as far as possible despite differing views (though a variety of approaches were taken). In some cases, clergy reached a mutual agreement that those who could not accept women's orders would not attend when a woman celebrated, but would otherwise play a full part (as one ordained man from Diocese B put it, 'I think it's far better, it seems to me, if they're not actually at the service, and everybody knows why. But to actually go to the service and not actually take communion I think is divisive'[33]).

In other cases, clergy with reservations/objections about women's priesting attended and participated in the service in every respect except for receiving the bread and wine. As the female incumbent of Church 7 suggested, it was better to gather corporately and only travel so far, than to meet without some of the deanery present, as if nothing was the matter.[34] Some of the most creative solutions came where the differences of opinion over women's priesting prompted an extensive rethinking of the purpose of the chapter meeting itself. The vicar of Church 3 in Diocese A explained how clergy in his deanery had taken the arrival of the first female priests as an opportunity to re-examine the whole *raison d' être* of the deanery clergy chapter. After discussion it was generally concluded that sharing worship

---

[31] int. 7:p.18. These tended to appeal primarily to Catholic clergy. Evangelical clergy with reservations about women's ordination as presbyters were less likely to belong to such structures – partly through lack of interest in institutional church structures *per se*, and partly because existing fellowships for evangelical clergy provided a ready-made alternative network.

[32] Developed in 1995 in order to bolster the work of Forward in Faith and provide a support network for clergy opposed to women's priesting (Stephen Parkinson, 'Pastors and Friends', *New Directions* 1 (2) July 1995, p. 5).

[33] int. cs2:2:end.

[34] int. cs3:1:472.

and news, and taking time away from the parish, were the most important elements. The question of celebrating the Eucharist at clergy chapter did not even arise, and so it was simply agreed to start meetings with a time of prayer, followed by discussion and chat over a pub lunch in the host parish. Church 3's vicar explained that currently all of the clergy in the deanery were male, but should a female priest be appointed to one of their parishes in the future, the issue of sharing/not sharing communion at chapter meetings would simply not arise, and therefore even those with the strongest objections to women's priesting need not absent themselves.[35]

A majority of clergy who referred to similar kinds of arrangements acknowledged that these were ultimately compromise measures, and Catholic priests in particular regretted that regular communion with one's fellow clergy had become a casualty of the settlement. Some clergy still refused to participate in deanery or diocesan events regardless of any attempt at compromise; in one of the most extreme cases, a priest from Diocese B had locked the doors of his church when his diocesan bishop had tried to visit.[36] However (as with the example from Church 3) it was generally the case that where clergy were open and honest about their differences of opinion but committed to working together as far as possible, the most strained of relationships could be improved considerably. For many clergy, the atmosphere in deanery chapter meetings ten years on from the vote could perhaps be summed up by the following two perspectives from Deanery E:

> *Generally [in this deanery] it's settled down to a situation where women priests are very much accepted – we haven't got any of the nastiness, people turning their backs on women or walking out when they're there, or whatever – obviously when it's a eucharistic issue, or something around there, people just aren't present.*[37]

> *I haven't come up against difficulties with male colleagues, but I don't go looking for it [...] I tend to take things at face value, and if people treat me OK, I just assume they're OK unless or until I hear a contrary view expressed.*[38]

Given the way in which tight financial resources are beginning to place renewed emphasis on the deanery or cluster as a unit of mission and ministry, those dioceses with outstanding issues arising from the 1992–94 settlement at deanery level would probably do well to redouble efforts at strengthening working relationships at this level.

6.3 Diocesan occasions

Having said that, involvement in the wider diocesan context still remained one of the most common ways in which clergy with differing views on women's priesting rubbed shoulders. As already suggested in Chapter 1, diocesan clergy conferences in the first months after the 1992 vote were sometimes tense affairs, and whilst the high emotion of the first few months gradually subsided, clergy continued to identify several aspects of diocesan life that presented outstanding issues. The most common was the ordination service. Some (although by no means all) clergy who had not supported the decision to ordain women as priests felt that it was inappropriate for candidates of their persuasion to be ordained priest alongside a female candidate, and from the beginning had called for separate ordination services. As a justification for this, some simply suggested that because they did not believe women

---

[35] int. cs1:6:p.7.
[36] int. cs2:7:354.
[37] int. cs5:1:96.
[38] int. cs5:2:393.

should be priests/presbyters it was wrong for them to be ordained alongside women because to do so would be to implicitly condone what the Church of England had decided. Others said that their objections were primarily on grounds of sacramental theology; that if ordination simply did not 'take' when conferred on women, why participate in an empty ritual? Some had further doubts as to whether – by ordaining women – the bishop had placed himself outside mainstream orthodoxy, fracturing the unity of the threefold order of ministry and making it necessary for 'traditionalist' candidates to seek ordination from those whose actions they regarded as unimpeachable. As a result of these objections, diocesan bishops were obliged to consider the best way of conducting ordination services in order to cater for the differing views. As with many of the other unresolved issues, very different problems in each of the case study dioceses led to very different solutions.

In Diocese A, where a significant minority of clergy supported an all-male priesthood, ordinations were variously characterized by interviewees as 'still a live issue', 'very tricky' or (in one case) 'a nightmare'. Since 1992 the policy of senior diocesan clergy had been to seek to keep the diocese together, as far as possible providing its own alternative arrangements in order to minimize the need for any parish to petition for extended episcopal oversight. Unwritten tradition had dictated that when it came to ordinations, candidates could expect *either* their deaconing or priesting service to be held in the cathedral, with the other service in their new parish. After 1992, this was modified so that all ordinations to the diaconate (over which there were very few objections) took place in the cathedral, whilst priestings (the more controversial element) were held either individually or in small groups in a parish church setting.

In practical terms, this seemed largely to have worked, although a minority of men refused to be ordained deacon alongside female candidates,[39] and in a couple of instances, priesting services had attracted too many attenders to fit inside parish churches. However, a small handful of male candidates had refused ordination from their diocesan bishop, and the bishop himself remained dissatisfied that the current arrangements adequately expressed the unity of the priesthood. As the research was under way, a new policy of ordaining priests in the cathedral was about to be implemented, but it was not known how successful this proved to be. It is worth adding that – just as with the issue of interregna – complaints about ordination services did not only come from women or from 'traditionalist' men; male clergy supportive of women's priesting were amongst the most discontented, some arguing that they did not wish to be ordained alongside a 'traditionalist' if this meant that their ordained female friends were forbidden from laying hands on them at the ordination 'scrum'.

Across the case studies, the key dilemma for the diocesan bishop was how to remain a focus for unity in ordination whilst respecting the views of the candidates *and* maintaining the integrity of his own position. It quickly became apparent that different bishops had different ideas of how to do this, as will be seen if one compares the differing approaches of Diocese A to that of Diocese D. In both cases, a diocesan rather than provincial solution was possible, but the arrangements looked quite different. In Diocese D, ordinations to the diaconate had traditionally been performed together in the cathedral, by the suffragan bishops, with priesting services happening individually in the parishes. However, the diocesan bishop at the time of the research had come to the conclusion that this was unsatisfactory.[40] In recent years, therefore, the policy was revisited, with the diocesan

---

[39] The 'Code of Practice' accompanying the Measure suggested that 'In the case of ordinations to the diaconate, it would be inappropriate to exclude candidates of one sex from a particular ordination service, or to arrange separate services for ordinands opposed to the ordination of women to the priesthood' (para. 14).
[40] int. cs4:9:93.

bishop now ordaining all candidates to the diaconate, and with two separate diocesan services being held for ordinations to the priesthood – one led by a bishop who ordained women and the other led by a bishop who did not (thus obviating the need for an official 'alternative' ordination service taken by the Provincial Episcopal Visitor). However, although both priesting services were officially regarded as diocesan services, the unspoken assumption was that one of these services was primarily intended for those who disagreed with women's priesting, whilst the other was for those who had no objections. An additional problem was the need to settle upon the right service for each candidate; not only for themselves but also for their incumbent. On one or two occasions when ordinand and training vicar had differing views on women's priesting, this could prove difficult.

In other dioceses, ordinations were less problematic: in Diocese B the scarcity of new clergy who were opposed to women's priesting meant that the issue of ordinations rarely achieved such levels of contention. Where a male candidate refused to be ordained alongside a woman, the ordination was conducted by the PEV.[41] An earlier attempt at a joint ordination service with the diocesan bishop and the provincial visitor presiding was not continued, owing to the feeling of some senior clergy that the service had become a opportunity 'for waving the Forward in Faith flag'.[42] In Dioceses C and E, the most significant initial problems had arisen when, not long before the ordination service, candidates who believed in an all-male priesthood discovered that their priesting was due to happen alongside that of female candidates, and requested a separate service. In both instances this was granted, but not without generating some ill-feeling amongst other male and female candidates who supported women's priesting, and not without some exasperation amongst senior clergy who asked how the candidate could have got this far through the ordination process without realizing he might be priested alongside a female colleague. In both cases, this led to changes: in Diocese C the bishop began to write to all candidates in advance of ordination to ascertain their views, so that suitable arrangements could be made in advance. In Diocese E the question was covered at an early stage of post-ordination training, to allow views to be aired well before ordination to the priesthood.

However, although for the most part the early difficulties surrounding ordination services were being addressed, many clergy supportive of women's priesthood expressed their frustration at the logistical gymnastics required to satisfy the needs of all concerned, and their exasperation that anyone should feel the need for an ordination service separate to women at all:

> ... *people who were already in ministry when that happened, and who didn't have much of a choice ... you don't want to say well, you've got to change your views or get out. But I still find it more difficult that people can still say we disagree with that, and opt in, since the vote ... refusing to be ordained in the same service as woman, and things like that – I find that very difficult ...*[43]

Similar views were expressed in relation to other diocesan occasions with a sacramental element. Alongside separate ordination services, the first decade after 1994 saw the emergence of alternative Chrism masses. Taking place during Holy Week and appealing primarily to clergy from the Catholic tradition, the Chrism service saw the blessing of the oils for baptism, for the sick and for various solemn blessings, including confirmation and

---

[41] int. cs2:2side2:560.

[42] int. cs2:2side2:510. In order to maintain the anonymity of each diocesan case study, PEVs were not asked to comment on specific cases, and so it was not possible to gauge an alternative view of the occasion.

[43] int. cs5:2:501.

ordination. In time, the service also came to function as the occasion on which clergy could gather to renew their ordination vows. Here again (as with communion) the very occasions that were supposed to symbolize unity and reconciliation became the most sensitive points of possible conflict. When asked to explain the need for an alternative Chrism service, clergy who attended them argued that women's ordination as priests had fractured the unity of the ordained ministry. It would be strange, they argued, to renew their ordination vows with women whose orders they believed to be invalid in the first place. Some respondents added that by ordaining women, the diocesan bishop was placing himself outside the community of the orthodox and therefore a question mark hung over the Chrism oil he had blessed. Just after the vote had been taken, one priest from Deanery E remembered how:

> *I went to one [Chrism Eucharist] in the cathedral and the bishop made a point of thanking me for being there, said 'so good of you to come'. And I said, 'but you haven't done it [ordained a woman to the priesthood] yet, father! But assuming you have by next year, I shall not be here'. And I said it in a very calm and measured way, so that he realized what he was doing ... that he was actually cutting himself off from me'.*[44]

Whereas most dioceses made alternative arrangements for ordination services, fewer provided alternative Chrism eucharists. Diocese D was an exception here. As its bishop explained, the primary reason for holding two such services was to maintain consistency with the policy of providing diocesan rather than provincial arrangements where possible. This had certainly enabled those with objections to women's priesting to renew their vows at diocesan level, even though the bishop acknowledged that the existence of *two* separate Chrism services in some sense missed the point of the occasion. It could also lead to ill-feeling: one female priest interviewed from another diocese that held two Chrism services said that 'because they decided to hold two services, one for those who could not accept women renewing their vows as priests in the same service, I thought "I am not going to either of those services, if they are going to hold these separatist services" ...'[45]

In most cases, however, the diocesan bishop held one Chrism Eucharist only, and those who could not accept this would generally attend a regional or provincial alternative provided by the relevant Episcopal Visitor. Sometimes this seemed to accentuate the sense of polarization felt between the different constituencies. Even so, several considerations prevented the issue of Chrism masses becoming truly contentious: first, many clergy seem not to have placed a high priority on Chrism services to begin with (the service itself – whilst claiming roots back into early Christianity – was not a major feature of mainstream Anglican liturgy for much of the modern period).

Second, where the meaning of the service was reconsidered, a new occasion could emerge that had potential appeal across the divides of opinion on women's priesting. In Diocese C, for example, senior clergy had reconfigured the Chrism Eucharist as a blessing of the oils and 'a commitment to ministry, in all its forms and all its glory and I think that is a sensitive way of both enabling people to make a commitment and not forcing people to say things they don't feel able to do'. To avert the possibility of tension over robing, only the altar party donned liturgical dress.[46] This had the added effect of placing clergy and lay

---

[44] int. cs5:12:394.

[45] int. cs5:2:531.

[46] int. cs3:6:223. Such a development was in keeping with the recommendations of the Blackburn Review (House of Bishops Standing Committee, 'Episcopal Ministry Act of Synod 1993: Guidelines for Good Practice Emanating from the Report of the Working Party of the House of Bishops Chaired by the Bishop of Blackburn ("The Blackburn Report"), GS1395' (7 March 2001), point 8).

participants on the same level. Although some were disappointed to lose the opportunity to renew their ministerial vows, and some clergy still preferred to attend the alternative Chrism Eucharist celebrated by the PEV, the change in tack appears to have gained widespread support. As one priest from a Resolution A and B parish reflected, it seemed pedantic to fuss over whether the oil of Chrism had been blessed by the right person – 'life's too short!! Besides, I find that whilst I do use oil of Chrism, my stocks tend to last me years ...' The last Chrism Eucharist attended by the speaker had been celebrated by the diocesan bishop, 'and I know full well that there were other priests there who share my view, and priests that were members of Forward in Faith'.[47] As this last comment suggests, attempts to offer traditionalist 'alternatives' to diocesan occasions could never be watertight, since a proportion of male clergy always participated sacramentally in both. The possibility that 'impaired communion' was not quite as impaired as some wished to maintain is explored further in Chapter 7.

6.4 Sector ministries

Although sometimes further removed from issues of communion and cooperation in parish, deanery and diocese, clergy working as chaplains in hospitals, prisons and educational establishments nevertheless found some of the same challenges as their colleagues in parish ministry. A key issue for female clergy working in hospital chaplaincy was how best to minister to patients who could not accept communion from an ordained woman. A majority were pragmatic about this, and though they did not agree with the patient's views, accepted that they should receive communion consecrated by a male priest:[48]

> *Every now and again, about once a year, you might have a patient who wants a male priest, and we just make provision – it's not an issue, really, because you could have a patient who, for other reasons, wants to see a woman ... [...] ...we do keep communion that's been consecrated by ...a male priest, so that if they particularly want it ... [...] Originally I wouldn't have thought like that, but now I think 'I don't want to take communion to someone who doesn't want to accept what I've consecrated' ...*[49]

Often, however, women expressed surprise and pleasure at having their priestly ministry accepted by patients who had come from parishes with resolutions in place. Some parish clergy made their parishioner's views known to the chaplain on admittance to hospital, whilst others encouraged hesitant individuals to avail themselves of the ministrations of the female hospital chaplain if they felt they could. In general, women working as hospital chaplains reported few instances where a patient asked for a male priest instead. For many, the problems came less with their hospital work itself and more in their interaction with the diocese: the female chaplain quoted above also recalled how she had offered her services as cover for interregna in her deanery of residence, but this offer had never been taken up.

---

[47] int. cs3:24:417.

[48] This was in accordance with recommendations made in the 1993 'Code of Practice' issued by the House of Bishops (Appendix D: 'The Ordination of Women to the Priesthood: Arrangements to Hospitals', para. 1).

[49] int. cs1:27:286.

6.5 Organized support for women clergy

Whilst most of the post-1992 developments in deanery and diocesan life discussed in this chapter came about through attempts to cater for the needs of clergy and laity who disagreed with women's priesting, new structures also emerged for ordained women themselves. In many dioceses, women clergy had begun to meet together long before the 1992 vote, for mutual support and sometimes as part of the wider campaign for women's ordination as priests. After November 1992, many groups had continued to meet, to help members prepare for priesthood and deal with the backlash from those angered by the result. However, after 1994, the purpose of such groups seemed less clear. In Diocese A, interviewees remembered how their group had lost momentum and many thought it of marginal importance now that the Measure was passed and women were entering priesthood. Gradually, the group stopped meeting, although a minority of women felt this was the wrong decision (given that the first years of their priestly ministry in a partly divided church were unlikely to be plain sailing).

At the time of researching, the value or otherwise of such groups was still under discussion. Few ordained women across the case studies believed these were a bad idea altogether (although some indicated they did not attend their local group because meetings tended to be negative in tone or merely provide a forum for discontentment over their diocese's policy towards women in priesthood). More commonly, female clergy simply felt that there was no need for a regular meeting – in Diocese B the Diocesan Adviser for Women's Ministry had invited all ordained women in the diocese to attend a conference on issues in women's ministry and only eleven had replied. Although disappointed at the response rate, the adviser was also reassured, since it might indicate that few women felt they were 'hiding behind the battlements'.[50] In Diocese E the Adviser for Women's Ministry had also surveyed female clergy in one part of the diocese, most of whom had indicated that whilst they would appreciate the opportunity of a twice-yearly catch-up with the Adviser to discuss their work, and a yearly group meeting to address major issues, they were less interested in regular group meetings – particularly for purely social purposes. A majority of ordained women simply wanted to get on with the business of being a priest, and saw this as the most important way of developing women's ordained ministry.[51] This was particularly true of many of the second generation of female clergy, who were often less likely to feel the same sense of strong group identity many of their more experienced colleagues felt as pioneers of women's priesthood.[52]

That said, some felt that occasional diocesan meetings for ordained women still had a role to play. In Diocese A, a group of female clergy had begun meeting again after a gap of some years, with several participants in the first event remembering a passionate meeting. Discussions centred around the 'glass ceiling' and a perception that the diocese was still asking women clergy to 'lie low' out of respect for the feelings of traditionalists, ten years on. And if the new generation of women clergy were less likely to feel the need for regular mutual support, they were often more likely to be brought together by a sense of

---

[50] int. cs2:1p.7.

[51] Helen Thorne's survey of the first generation of women ordained priest found 89.9% felt that 'the best way to change things was to get on with the job' (Thorne, *Journey to Priesthood*, p. 177). See also: Jean Cornell, 'Kairos Comes Too Soon: Are Women Priests in Retreat in the Church of England?', *Feminist Theology* 12 (1) September 2003, pp. 43–51.

[52] Thorne notes that this could leave the first generation of women to be priested feeling disappointed that the next generation seemed less interested in continuing the battle (Thorne, *Journey to Priesthood*, pp. 121–2). However, in the present study, those interviewed from the first wave of priestings in 1994 were generally extremely complementary about their less experienced colleagues, and glad they did not have to fight to fulfil their calling, as they had.

disappointment that some of the practical problems they faced as clergy were simply not being addressed (for example, as already noted in Chapter 5, many felt that the Church of England's appointments processes lagged well behind the best human resources practice they had encountered in their working life prior to ordination). Having not been schooled in the 'lie low' culture of the immediate post-1992 years, some were increasingly prepared to challenge unacceptable behaviour or policy when they saw it.

In many dioceses, the formal channel for raising matters relating to women's ordained ministry was through the Diocesan Adviser or Dean for Women's Ministry. It had originally been suggested that bishops should consider appointing an experienced female priest in an advisory capacity to provide a focus for support for ordained women and to offer them a means of raising any concerns they had with senior staff (at a time when bishops' staff meetings were overwhelmingly male – as many still are). In practice, as with most aspects of the current picture, the role was conceived somewhat differently in each diocese. In Diocese A the Adviser for Women's Ministry sat on the Bishop's extended staff meeting, whilst in Diocese B the role was more informal. In most dioceses, senior staff consulted with all ordained women before making the appointment, although there was some suggestion that care was taken to appoint 'moderate' candidates to the post.

Ten years on, the role of Adviser for Women's Ministry seems to have evolved: in Diocese C the current post-holder explained how her predecessor had primarily been an adviser *to* ordained women, but the current Adviser had developed the role further in the direction of offering advice to the bishop on issues affecting ordained women, in addition to encouraging the diocese's female clergy to take up development opportunities and apply for vacant posts.[53] However, there was also some discussion about how much longer such a post was needed. In several of the case studies, consultations had recently been carried out to establish a likely replacement for a retiring Adviser for Women's Ministry. In each case, female clergy suggested that a further appointment to the post would be welcomed, but that perhaps the role would not be needed indefinitely. Some suggested that the existence of an 'adviser for women's ministry' was anomalous when there was no corresponding post for male clergy. Others suggested that the post was tokenistic and no substitute for including women on bishop's staff meetings as archdeacons or deans. Indeed, the current post-holder from Case Study E had accepted the job with a view to putting herself out of business as soon as a woman was appointed an area dean or archdeacon.[54]

The emergence of groups and Adviser posts for women in ordained ministry raises several important questions about how women's priestly ministry is best developed in the future. The case studies revealed some tension over aims and methods: on one hand there was a growing conviction that specialist groups or advisers for ordained ministry are only a temporary measure with complete integration into diocesan structures the preferred course of action; on the other hand there was a growing sense of disappointment that dioceses have been slow to act on some of the issues facing ordained women, leading to a growing sense that ordained women may have to speak louder to ensure their voice is heard.

The research revealed a variety of different approaches to this, ranging from those increasingly prepared to campaign on unresolved issues, to those who preferred just to 'get on with the job' and bring about a gradual change in attitudes and policies. Some observers have been disappointed that women have not been more vocal in speaking out about injustice, feeling that it risks colluding with institutional sexism,[55] whilst others have felt

---

[53] int. cs3:12:4.

[54] int. cs5:6:190.

[55] For example, Cornell, 'Kairos Comes Too Soon', p. 46.

that campaigning might do more harm than good. Achieving a fine balance between the two continues to be difficult, particularly given the readiness of some to portray ordained women as self-serving or ambitious for raising problem issues. A preoccupation with one's own conditions of service is certainly to be avoided, but raising issues of relevance to ministry did not necessarily imply this. As Alan Aldridge has noted, the ideal of selfless service (whilst good in itself) has too often become a method of ignoring the legitimate concerns of the servants.[56]

Conclusion

This chapter has explored some of the main practical challenges at deanery and diocesan level faced by senior clergy in trying to implement the terms of the 1992–94 ordination of women settlement. Deanery clergy chapter meetings, providing cover for interregna, the existence of 'alternative' chapters for traditionalists, ordination services and Chrism eucharists all presented issues in trying to maintain unity, cooperation and a high degree of communion between those with differing views on women's priesting. In the years immediately following the 1992 vote, such occasions could often become the focus for disappointment and distrust, but as the decade wore on much of the palpable tension receded. In attempting to manage the settlement, dioceses worked their way towards a range of measures designed to maintain a sense of unity amongst diocesan clergy whilst sometimes remodelling the most contentious occasions, either to remove the source of disagreement or to allow alternative structures to emerge.

Whether these attempts to foster communion and cooperation were successful really depends on one's point of view. On one level, care should be taken not to overemphasize the importance of deanery and diocesan occasions such as these in the life of most clergy. The absorbing nature of parish or chaplaincy work afforded most clergy little time for wider diocesan activities. Nor was tension over the 1992–94 settlement the first or only issue to deter some clergy from engaging in wider deanery and diocesan life. In these respects, then, the extent of the problem should not be exaggerated. For those of a more pragmatic and participatory frame of mind, attempts to foster communion and cooperation at deanery and diocesan level had often proved a success: it was true that some of the clergy with the strongest objections to women's priesting had simply absented themselves from most aspects of deanery and diocesan life, but on the other hand the tense atmosphere of the early 1990s had largely dissipated and dioceses were becoming more experienced at balancing the sensitivities of the different constituencies. Of course, it was true that this had been achieved largely through the allowance of a measure of separation between these groups (for example, in 'alternative' chapters and ordinations), but if deanery chapter started with morning prayer rather than communion, this could be deemed an acceptable price to pay for the maintenance of good working relations.

For those who regarded the coexistence project as more theologically virtuous than pragmatic, the experiences of the first ten years were more ambiguous. Schism had been avoided, a high degree of communion had been maintained and some creative solutions to previous tensions had been developed. On the other hand, concern remained at the way cooperation had been achieved at the price of real communion (for example through shared ordination services or in eucharistic worship). Those committed to keeping the different constituencies on board together might also feel concern at the apparent loss of patience

[56] Alan Aldridge, 'Discourse on Women in the Clerical Profession: The Diaconate and Language-games in the Church of England', *Sociology* 26 (1), February 1992, pp. 45–57 (pp. 46–7).

with the current settlement in some quarters.[57] Meanwhile, for those who were already uneasy that the 1992–94 settlement was a compromise too far, attempts to balance the concerns of the different constituencies at deanery and diocesan level could look like further unwelcome concessions that only risked institutionalizing division. Nevertheless, whatever the philosophical or theological reservations about the settlement, it seems fair to conclude that in day to day terms, communion and cooperation amongst diocesan and deanery clergy were less problematic twelve years on from the vote than they had been in 1992.

---

[57] For example, the trend in Diocese A for male clergy in favour of women's priesting to become increasingly reluctant to cover resolution parishes during interregna, whilst their female colleagues were unable to do so.

Chapter 7

Opting out of women's priestly ministry: working the provisions

The third key area of continued contention from the 1992–94 settlement was the existence and operation of the provisions allowing parishes to opt out of the Church of England's decision to ordain women to the priesthood. Whereas many campaigners for women's priesting would ideally have wished for a simple, single-clause measure that permitted women's priesting, the main architects of the legislation had become convinced that certain exemptions should be available, in recognition of the strength of feeling against the proposals by a significant minority, and in an attempt to hold the different views together in the same church without greater schism. Many campaigners for women's priesting were disappointed at what they saw as a legitimation of discrimination, but reluctantly agreed to the inclusion of the 'safeguards' as the necessary price to pay for women's priesting. Of the several opt-out provisions that survived into the final version of the Measure, the ones that have proved most significant over the first ten years of women's priesting were those that permitted parishes to make legally binding declarations:

> 'That this parochial church council would not accept a woman as the minister who presides at or celebrates the Holy Communion or pronounces the Absolution in this parish' (Resolution A)

and/or

> 'That this parochial church council would not accept a woman as the incumbent or priest-in-charge of the benefice or as a team vicar for the benefice' (Resolution B)[1]

In 1993, the position of 'traditionalist' congregations was further bolstered by the formulation of the Episcopal Ministry Act of Synod, which gave parishes the additional option of petitioning to receive 'extended episcopal oversight' from a bishop who did not ordain women if they could not accept their diocesan bishop's decision to do so (popularly dubbed 'resolution C'[2]). This was ideally to be provided by a bishop in the diocese or region who did not ordain women, but where this was not possible, the Act in addition permitted the creation of 'up to two additional suffragan bishops ... to act as provincial episcopal visitors for the purposes of this Act ...'[3] (in fact three such appointments – popularly known as 'flying bishops' – were eventually made). These additional provisions undoubtedly helped many clergy with objections to women's priesting to remain within the Church of England, although as Chapter 1 suggested, many supporters of women's priesting have become increasingly concerned at the implications of the Act – both in theological and practical terms.

---

[1] *Priests (Ordination of Women) Measure 1993 (No. 2)*, Schedule 1, Section 3 (1).

[2] The phrase 'Resoluion C' wrongly implies that the petition for extended episcopal oversight has the same legal status as Resolutions A and B. The latter formed part of the Measure whilst the former appeared in the Act of Synod. This means that although its existence has the 'compelling moral authority' of the bishops and synod, it is not technically legally binding.

[3] *Episcopal Ministry Act of Synod 1993*, section 5.1.

Given the significant difference of opinion over the opt-out provisions at the time of the vote, how far have they since received wider acceptance across the Church of England, and what particular issues have surrounded their practical outworking? This chapter explores attitudes towards the package of opt-out clauses as a whole, considering first how far the provisions have been taken up, and then reflecting upon the extent of support for their existence amongst questionnaire respondents and interviewees. After outlining some of the main arguments offered for and against the provisions, the chapter turns to some of the key areas of continued difficulty clergy identified in their operation: the existence of competing understandings of the terms of the legislation, questions over the process involved in passing or rescinding a resolution, the unintended consequences that could arise from those occasions the safeguards did not cover, and the particular issues surrounding petitions for extended episcopal oversight. As with Chapters 5 and 6, the emphasis here is primarily on the practical outworking of this part of the settlement, rather than on the implied theology of the provisions or the culture of the organization that produced them, and that the provisions themselves help to create.[4] The chapter suggests that the resolutions remained one of the most controversial aspects of the 1992–94 settlement ten years on. And whilst the provisions had proved largely workable in practical terms, closer attention to their fair implementation (on all sides) might pay dividends in terms of greater trust between the different constituencies.

7.1 The uptake of the Resolutions: some general patterns

Late in 2000, a working party chaired by the then Bishop of Blackburn Alan Chesters published a report on the working of the Episcopal Ministry Act of Synod. Alongside its conclusions and recommendations, the report brought together the most detailed statistics yet produced on the numbers of parishes electing to pass Resolutions A and B, and petitioning for extended episcopal oversight. It found that roughly 7.3% of parishes had passed Resolution B (preventing a woman from acting as incumbent or priest-in-charge), whilst 6.21% of parishes had elected to adopt Resolution A (barring a woman from celebrating communion or pronouncing absolution in the parish).[5] In a majority of cases both resolutions had been passed together: a traditionalist Catholic parish with concerns about a woman celebrating communion would often pass Resolution B in addition to A, since inviting a female priest to become incumbent but forbidding her to celebrate communion was an almost wholly untenable prospect for both parties. Where Resolution B alone was passed, the parish in question was usually of a more conservative evangelical tradition. Here, the main concern was to preserve male congregational headship; often the celebration of communion by a woman was less problematic since for many churches in this tradition communion was primarily an act of remembrance that could potentially be led by any of the faithful, and did not imply headship.[6] In addition to the uptake of Resolutions A and B, the Blackburn Review suggested that 296 parishes (around 2.2% of the total number in the Church of England) had petitioned for extended episcopal oversight. These came almost exclusively from the Catholic tradition, although a very small number of conservative Evangelical parishes also petitioned.

[4] It is hoped to consider the wider question of organizational culture under the current settlement in a future publication.
[5] General Synod GS1395, *Episcopal Ministry Act of Synod: Report of a Working Party of the House of Bishops* (Church House, London, 2000), p. 39). Although the percentages are precise, the Blackburn report figures were probably not exactly correct, for reasons discussed below. Nevertheless, they remain a very good guide, and the most complete figures we have available.
[6] A very small minority of conservative evangelicals would disagree here, arguing that presidency at communion implied some kind of authority role. This was not a common view, however.

Table 7i: Percentage of parishes passing Resolutions A and B, and petitioning for extended episcopal oversight (EEO), by diocese, 1999[7]						
	Res. A	**Res. B**	**EEO**		**Res. A**	**Res. B**	**EEO**
Bath and Wells	3.12	3.33	1.25	London	16.67	16.67	6.06
Birmingham	9.09	9.09	4.24	Manchester	9.35	10.65	6.45
Blackburn	21.46	21.46	1.62	Newcastle	11.49	15.52	0
Bradford	6.77	9.77	1.50	Norwich	2.41	2.93	0.17
Bristol	5.39	5.39	1.80	Oxford	2.22	3.65	1.11
Canterbury	4.87	7.49	1.87	Peterborough	4.48	5.60	1.12
Carlisle	5.90	10.33	0.37	Portsmouth	9.42	10.87	3.62
Chelmsford	7.77	8.79	3.07	Ripon and Leeds	6.37	6.37	1.27
Chester	6.03	11.34	2.48	Rochester	6.94	7.87	4.63
Chichester	7.20	7.46	0.26	St Alban's	5.12	5.72	3.01
Coventry	5.13	5.64	2.56	St Ed. and Ips.	2.65	3.09	1.55
Derby	7.66	8.87	4.03	Salisbury	2.43	3.75	0.22
Durham	14.96	16.14	7.87	Sheffield	16.29	17.98	7.87
Ely	2.90	3.87	0.65	Sodor and Man	3.70	3.70	0
Exeter	3.17	5.36	6.15	Southwark	3.97	6.95	4.97
Gloucester	5.85	6.15	0.92	Southwell	2.34	5.86	1.95
Guildford	4.94	4.32	2.47	Truro	10.22	9.78	1.78
Hereford	1.42	1.13	0	Wakefield	8.99	8.99	4.23
Leicester	6.12	6.12	0.82	Winchester	4.61	5.59	1.64
Lichfield	9.20	9.91	2.59	Worcester	2.04	2.55	1.02
Lincoln	4.50	5.25	0.75	York	8.42	8.63	1.68
Liverpool	8.25	9.71	0.49	Europe	2.72	5.0	0

As can be seen from the figures presented in **Table 7i** and based on the Blackburn Review, the proportion of parishes passing resolutions in any particular diocese could vary markedly. Rural dioceses often contained amongst the lowest percentages of these: in Hereford, just 5 out of 353 parishes (1.4%) had passed Resolution A, with none petitioning for extended episcopal oversight. In neighbouring Worcester, the same figure was only a little higher at 2.2% passing Resolution A and only two parishes looking to the Provincial Episcopal Visitor. Meanwhile, in dioceses with a strong Catholic tradition, the percentage could be much higher: in nine dioceses, 10% or more of parishes had passed Resolution B, including London, Sheffield, and Manchester. In the Diocese of Blackburn, more than one in five parishes had passed either or both Resolutions A and B. In some cases, widespread adoption of the resolutions had resulted as much from parishes' expectations of their bishop as from any patterns related to 'churchmanship'. For instance, at the time of the vote, Bishop of Sheffield David Lunn made it clear he would not ordain women as priests, and so several parishes where a majority were against women's priesting did not pass any resolutions, feeling confident that they would not be forced to confront the question of accepting a female incumbent under his leadership. Bishop Lunn's retirement in 1997 raised the prospect of a new diocesan bishop who might be considerably more favourable to women's priesting, and a significant number of Catholic parishes passed the resolutions before his successor was announced, to ensure that their views were formally established.

In most cases, parishes passing resolutions seem to have done so as soon as the Measure came into force: information gathered from seven dioceses in 2001 suggest that 66% of parishes with resolutions still in force had voted to adopt these in 1994, compared to 22% passed between 1995 and 1997, and 12% from 1998 onwards. Since year-on-year records of

---

[7] Based on figures provided by the Blackburn Report (General Synod GS1395, *Episcopal Ministry Act of Synod: Report of a Working Party of the House of Bishops* (Church House, London, 2000), p. 39).

the numbers of parishes passing resolutions are not kept by either the dioceses themselves or centrally for the Church of England, it is very difficult to establish how far numbers of these have changed. A report in Forward in Faith's *New Directions* magazine of September 1996 suggested that 828 parishes had passed either Resolution A or B or both.[8] If this figure is taken as reliable, it suggests a net increase of 150 parishes over the following three years, based on the Blackburn Review figures (although there were variations between dioceses: Chichester had perhaps thirteen more resolution parishes in 1999 than in 1996, whilst York had perhaps twenty-two fewer).[9]

How might this increase be explained? An obvious possibility is that some parishes were changing their minds against women's priestly ministry. This could occasionally happen, such as in one parish in Diocese A where a parish with previous experience of women's priestly ministry opted to pass Resolution A (although how far this was due to the views of the new incumbent, or to the wishes of the congregation as a whole, it is not known). However, if it was right to suggest in Chapter 2 that the general tide of opinion is moving *in favour* of women's priestly ministry, and it was right to suggest in Chapter 5 that clergy with objections to women's priesting were finding it increasingly difficult to move to parishes without any resolutions in place, a widespread change of mind seems unlikely.

One possible explanation may be a different attitude towards the 'yes but not yet' parishes considered in Chapter 5. Evidence suggests that for most of the first decade, dioceses sought to discourage parishes from passing resolutions if they could possibly help it, often through reassurances that they would not be forced to accept a female candidate if they agreed not to adopt the resolutions. Since then, senior clergy have become more aware of the legal implications of that approach, and in some dioceses have begun to insist more clearly that any parish without the resolutions in place must be prepared to accept a woman's priestly ministry. This may have encouraged some 'wavering' parishes to opt for caution, and pass a resolution. On the other side, Forward in Faith have encouraged parishes to pass resolutions in order to make it more certain that a parish would not have to consider a female priest, and also to demonstrate the size of the 'traditionalist' constituency within the Church of England. This may explain the increase in resolution parishes even in dioceses such as Chichester, where a parish could be more confident than most that its bishops were not about to force them to accept an ordained woman.

Even so, precise figures for the number of resolution parishes remain difficult to ascertain. A number of dioceses did not appear to keep full records of voting on the resolutions, and in a few cases my request for information had clearly prompted a bishop's office to update its list. An additional problem came where there was a dispute between the parish and the diocese over whether procedure had been followed correctly. One bishop even reported that 'questions concerning validity have not been fully answered' in four parishes in his diocese.[10] Even where resolutions had clearly been passed, this was not necessarily a reliable guide to the views of the congregation since the resolutions only needed the support of the incumbent and a majority of the PCC (two-thirds of the PCC in the case of the petition for extended episcopal oversight). As the case of Church 3 illustrated in Chapter 4, Resolutions A and B could be in place whilst a majority of the congregation were apparently in agreement with women's priesting. Often only a hair's breadth could separate a parish whose resolution status was viewed ambivalently by a majority of the congregation and a parish with no resolutions that was clearly divided over whether to accept a female

---

[8] *New Directions* 1 (16) September 1996, p. 15.
[9] Although these figures offer only a rough guide, since the Blackburn figures and *New Directions* figures are not calculated according to the same criteria.
[10] Personal correspondence with the diocesan bishop.

priest. The decision to pass, or not to pass, the resolutions often owed at least as much to the views of the incumbent, or to the relationship between parish and senior diocesan clergy, as it did to the consensus of opinion within the congregation itself.

7.2 Clergy and lay attitudes to the opt-out provisions

How, then, did respondents view the existence of the resolutions and the Act of Synod as part of the 1992–94 settlement? Both the Clergy and Congregations Questionnaires featured questions on the 'safeguards'. This was felt to be important given that the post-1992 Church of England has been shaped by the existence of these exemptions as well as by the ordination of women as priests itself. Clergy were asked several questions, both about the justification for the resolutions and their perceived impact upon the church. Lay questionnaire respondents were asked a shorter and more straightforward set of questions about how far they approved of each of the resolutions, on the assumption that lay churchgoers were much less likely to know the terms of the resolutions in detail. So it proved: 21.5% of Congregations Questionnaire respondents overall ticked that 'I did not know these resolutions existed' and a further 22.5% did not know whether any of the resolutions were in force in their parish.[11] But once the terms of the resolutions were explained, how far did lay participants in the study agree with the possibility of opting out of women's priestly ministry? As **Table 7ii** suggests, agreement with the resolutions achieved majority support only in eight of the twenty-two case study congregations. Four of these (Churches 6, 8, 10 and 15) already had a resolution in place, and Church 21 was not legally able to pass the resolutions as it did not have parish status in its own right, although it would surely have done so given the opportunity. If these figures are at all representative of the case study congregations, one must conclude that a clear majority of laity surveyed were unconvinced that parishes should have the right to opt out of a woman's ministry as a priest.[12]

[11] This figure might have been even higher except that attenders at churches with female incumbents could establish by default that their parish did not have a resolution in place.
[12] One study of attitudes to women's priesting just after the vote also identified 'mixed feelings' about the resolutions amongst lay respondents (Hilary Wakeman, 'What Difference is Women's Priesthood Making in the Pews?' in Hilary Wakeman (ed.), *Women Priests: The First Years* (Darton, Longman and Todd, London, 1996), pp. 1–26 (p. 20).

147

Church	Resolution A		Resolution B		Petition for EEO	
(No. of cases)	Strongly agree/ agree (%)	Disagree/ strongly disagree (%)	Strongly agree/ agree (%)	Disagree/ strongly disagree (%)	Strongly agree/ agree (%)	Disagree/ strongly disagree (%)
1 (38)	24.3	64.8	29.7	62.1	22.9	51.4
2 (20)	26.3	52.7	26.3	52.6	25.0	40.0
3 (25)	38.5	46.2	36.0	52.0	57.1	38.1
4 (20)	10.5	73.6	5.6	77.7	5.6	72.2
5 (37)	17.6	53.0	23.5	58.8	11.8	55.9
6 (28)	66.7	20.9	70.0	20.0	75.0	5.0
7 (62)	13.6	67.8	15.5	60.4	15.5	67.3
8 (8)	62.5	25.0	62.5	25.0	62.5	25.0
9 (18)	17.6	70.5	17.6	70.6	18.8	66.8
10 (17)	53.4	33.3	50.0	21.4	42.9	21.4
11 (23)	23.8	61.9	23.8	61.9	14.3	61.9
12 (16)	42.9	35.7	35.7	42.8	21.4	42.8
13 (14)	18.2	45.5	20.0	40.0	20.0	40.0
15 (20)	79.0	10.5	79.0	10.5	73.7	10.5
16 (22)	50.0	45.5	54.6	36.4	45.4	45.5
17 (21)	61.1	27.8	61.1	27.8	66.6	16.7
18 (7)	57.1	14.3	57.2	14.3	14.3	28.6
19 (26)	24.0	48.0	28.0	44.0	20.8	45.8
20 (13)	16.7	66.6	16.7	66.6	16.7	66.6
21 (8)	57.1	14.3	57.1	0	42.9	0
22 (22)	15.0	75.0	5.6	83.3	5.6	66.6
23 (12)	33.3	11.1	37.5	25.0	25.0	25.0

Table 7ii: Percentage support for Resolutions A and B, and the petition for extended episcopal oversight, amongst respondents from the 22 case study congregations[13]

If these results are broken down by gender, there was a slight tendency for the resolutions to attract more support from men than women (for example, 36% of men agreed that parishes should be able to pass Resolution B, compared to 31.4% of women) – however, the difference here was not great. Church tradition was a more important indicator of opinion, as **Table 7iii** suggests. Here support for the resolutions seems most often to have come from Anglo-Catholics, with around 45% agreeing/strongly agreeing with Resolutions A and B, and 52% agreeing with the option of extended episcopal oversight. Amongst laity placing themselves along the 'liberal' or 'evangelical' spectrum, these figures were much lower – less than a third in favour in most categories.

A further feature of the results was that the resolutions attracted differing levels of support. Nor was it the case that those who were supportive of women's ministry were also in disagreement with the resolutions (and vice versa). The significant levels of disagreement with Resolution A may again suggest the extent to which Anglo-Catholic arguments from sacramental theology about the maleness of the priest at the altar cut little ice with the majority of active Anglicans. As Alyson Peberdy has indicated, the difference between priest and deacon seemed a small step for many congregations contemplating the future of women's ministry in the mid-1980s, and it may be that the inclusion of women in ministry but their exclusion from celebrating communion struck many observers as unnecessary and indeed unfair; as one man from Church 7 remarked, 'I don't see this being important – this

---

[13] The full question was: 'How far do you agree that it should be possible for a church to pass each of these resolutions if a majority of the PCC are unhappy about the ordination of women?'

is a person being ordained, a part of the body, who is facilitating this remembrance meal ... how can you stop a person being used in the body?'.[14]

Table 7iii: Percentage support for Resolutions A and B, and the petition for extended episcopal oversight, amongst lay questionnaire respondents
(total sample, by Church tradition, % strongly agree/ agree)

	Resolution A	Resolution B	Petition for EEO
Anglo-Catholic	45.1	45.7	43.3
Liberal-Catholic	28.2	31.3	35.5
Liberal	17.0	23.4	17.0
Liberal-Evangelical	28.6	28.6	21.4
Evangelical	28.5	27.8	19.7
Charismatic-Evang.	30.4	33.3	19.0
Catholic-Evangelical	42.9	42.9	42.9
Conservative-Evang.	34.0	32.7	24.5

For both Resolutions A and B, there was much discussion of the discriminatory effect of the resolutions, and the degree to which they seemed to present the Church as a bigoted institution: 'I think that must be very difficult for female ministers to handle, really', said one interviewee from Church 4; 'It seems almost double standards ... the signal it sends out I don't think is a very positive one'.[15] However, as Figure 7ii suggests, there was slightly more sympathy for the existence of Resolution B; even amongst some who were personally in favour of women's ordination as priests. One respondent suggested that 'It's mainly a concern for local democracy in the Church – it could even be unpleasant if people were getting a priest they didn't want. And I think local people ought to be able to choose for themselves. If they say no women, and that's the wish of the majority, that should be accepted'.[16] Concerns for congregational self-determination were also evident in some of the arguments offered *against* the existence of the resolutions: for several lay interviewees the primary reason for rejecting the resolutions was the fear that either the priest, or a small group within the congregation, could impose their will on the church against the wishes of the majority. In effect, then, attitudes to the resolutions depended almost as much on a concern for the wishes of the whole congregation to be respected as they depended on attitudes to women's priesting *per se*.

But whereas lay respondents often expressed strong opinions about the resolutions, there was much greater uncertainty over the Act of Synod: in sixteen of the twenty-two case study congregations, between ten and forty per cent of the congregation rated their view of the petition for extended oversight as 'neither agree nor disagree'. Nor was there any clear pattern amongst lay questionnaire respondents as to whether the petition for extended episcopal oversight was received more or less positively than the resolutions.[17] However, amongst interviewees, stronger opinions were in evidence: one churchgoer from Diocese E whose parish benefited from the Act of Synod's provisions argued that without it 'How can we stay? ... There are people out here who are perceived to be priests, who perceive themselves to be priests, who we cannot associate ourselves with as priests. The only way in

---

[14] int.cs3:27side2:306.

[15] int. cs2:22:340.

[16] int. cs4:11:377.

[17] Eleven of the twenty-two congregational samples were less favourable, three were more favourable and the remaining eight returned levels of support for the Act of Synod that were very similar to their attitudes to the resolutions.

which we can remain is if we have a separate arrangement'.[18] However, unlike the previous speaker, many lay defenders of the Act found it difficult to explain why its provisions were necessary. Some emphasized the need to maintain a 'true' church away from the 'heretical' actions of the Anglican mainstream; others saw the petition more as a protest action against a bishop they believed had committed a serious error; a few implied that they found within 'alternative'[19] episcopal oversight the kind of Anglicanism that otherwise seemed to have disappeared from the Church of England in recent decades. However, many lay interviewees seemed less positive: the Act of Synod was 'where it begins to get silly', replied one; 'I don't know how you draw the line, but it seemed fair, initially, to allow people to opt out – I think being out of communion with your bishop is ridiculous'.[20] Another argued, 'If the Church has decided ... that women should be allowed to be priests, you've got to make the best of it, really ... [the Church] should stand by that and not say "but we might be wrong so you can have your special bishop ..."'[21]

What of the views of the clergy? These were solicited through a more detailed set of questions about the principle of offering 'safeguards' and their practical outworking. First, respondents were questioned on the principles behind the resolutions and the justification for their inclusion in the legislation. When asked whether 'the safeguards provided by the 1992 Measure were an acceptable consequence of the decision to ordain women as priests', the overall balance of opinion was negative: just 28% of clergy from Diocese A either 'agreed' or 'strongly agreed' with the statement, compared to 39.5% in Diocese B and 44.6% in Diocese C. Only clergy in the selected deanery case study from Diocese E were in a slim majority in favour of the statement. As **Figures 7iv.a and b** suggest, men were significantly more likely to agree with the need for the safeguards than women. When this trend is analysed more closely, those most commonly in favour of the opt-out provisions were male clergy who disagreed/strongly disagreed with the 1992 decision. Male Anglo-Catholic clergy were most heavily in favour of the provisions. However, male clergy in favour of women's priesting were also more likely than their female colleagues to consider the possibility of opting out as an acceptable consequence of ordaining women as priests. One significant feature of attitudes to the 'safeguards' was a tendency for respondents to avoid statements of strong agreement or strong disagreement. Although a clear overall pattern of scepticism about the resolutions and petition for extended episcopal oversight emerged, clergy also felt to some extent that the case was not black and white.

---

[18] int. cs5:16:510. The speaker added that if the Church of England consecrated women as bishops, bringing an end to the Act of Synod, he would certainly feel obliged to join the Orthodox Church.
[19] Of course, the Act of Synod was intended to provide 'extended' episcopal oversight, but as will be seen further below, the flying bishop could sometimes become seen as an *alternative* to the diocesan.
[20] int. cs2:17side2:300.
[21] int. cs2:14:520.

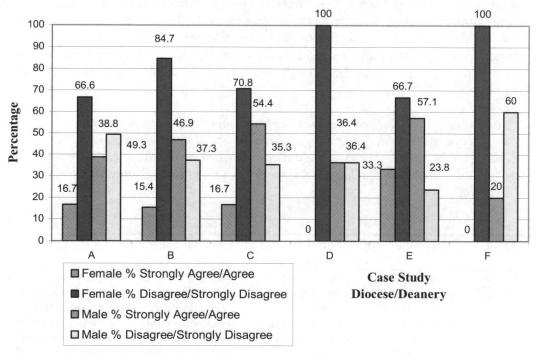

Figure 7iv.a: How far do you agree that the safeguards offered by the 1992 Priests (Ordination of Women) Measure were an acceptable consequence of the decision to ordain women as priests?

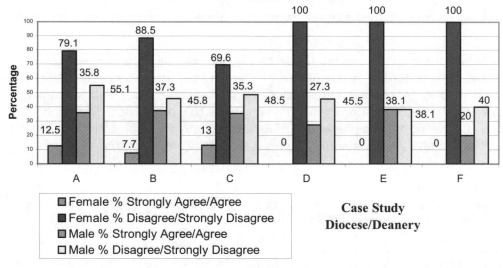

Figure 7iv.b: How far do you agree that the safeguards offered by the 1993 Episcopal Ministry Act of Synod were an acceptable consequence of the decision to ordain women as priests?

A similar pattern emerges from a set of questions on the possible discriminatory basis of the safeguards (a summary of the results is provided in **Table 7v**). A consistently large majority of clergy either 'agreed' or 'strongly agreed' that the safeguards in the Measure and the Act discriminated against women and against those who ordained them and supported them. As with Helen Thorne's research of 2000, criticisms of the principles behind the Act of Synod tended to fall into two categories: first, that the Act was divisive and corrosive of unity and trust; second (less common) that it was discriminatory towards women.[22] On the latter point, it was sometimes suggested that the Act's existence signified a lack of commitment to what had been decided in 1992: as one female priest from Diocese C argued, the bishops of the day 'should have [had] the guts to stand by their own decision'.[23] A second common theme was the negative impression of the Church that the Act seemed to give to others; as one female priest said:

> *It's like saying 'I know there's a thirty mile an hour limit here, but I'm allowed to do forty because ...' It's one thing to say we needed to have 'two integrities' to get through the period, but to perpetuate it in a world which is looking at equal opportunities and inclusive language in every other sphere ... I think that needs rethinking![24]*

Table 7v: Clergy views of discrimination in the 1993 Measure and the Act of Synod (% strongly agree or agree combined)				
Diocese (no. of cases[25])	**Safeguards in the 1993 Measure discriminate against women?[26]**	**Safeguards in the Act of Synod discriminate against women?**	**Safeguards in the Act of Synod discriminate against those who ordain women/support their ordination?**	**1993 Measure and Act discriminate against those who do not accept/are uncertain about women's priesting?**
Diocese A (90)	68.9	63.3	61.1	15.5
Diocese B (112)	63.4	65.7	63.6	16.7
Diocese C (91)	60.5	58.3	47.8	18.9
Diocese D (13)	61.6	61.6	46.2	15.4
Diocese E (24)	50.0	45.8	43.5	12.5
Diocese F (9)	66.6	77.7	77.7	55.5

However, whilst these concerns were shared by many clergy supportive of women's priesting, a curious feature of the results was that around half of respondents felt the opt-out provisions were also discriminatory towards those who supported or ordained women as priests as well as towards ordained women themselves. This may reflect Thorne's conclusion that the most damaging aspect of the exemptions was their effect on the Church of England as a whole. As one senior clergyman from Diocese B put it:

---

[22] Helen Thorne, *Journey to Priesthood: An In-depth Study of the Church of England's First Women Priests* (University of Bristol, Bristol, 2000), p. 123.

[23] int. cs3:3:507.

[24] int. cs3:1:582.

[25] The number of cases on which these figures are based varied slightly from question to question. To give a rough guide to the sample sizes, the number of responses to the first (left hand side) question are given.

[26] The percentage of respondents agreeing with this statement is roughly comparable to the 63% of women deacons in the survey by Francis and Robbins who agreed that 'The safeguards imposed by the Church of England in the Priests (Ordination of Women) Measure are discriminating against Women', perhaps suggesting a wider perception of discrimination in the current Clergy Questionnaire sample (Francis and Robbins, *The Long Diaconate*, p. 213).

> *What the Measure and the Act did was to enshrine in law something of the reality*
> *— I think probably regrettably — of the kind of church we are ... [you] tend to live*
> *in your camp, and only touch base through synodical processes and through*
> *your bishop — the rest of the time you talk to people who talk the same language*
> *... and I think the unfortunate thing about the Act of Synod was the way it made*
> *that very sharp ...* [27]

Indeed, many speakers regretted the way in which a historically broad church had found it necessary to institutionalize dissent rather than handle difference through informal means. However (as Chapter 9 will go on to suggest), whilst this view led some to call for the Act's rescinding, others were confirmed in the view that if legislation was needed, 'impaired communion' was at least better than schism, and no communion at all.

Arguably the central assumption of the provisions was that parishes should be permitted to establish a measure of distance between themselves and women's ministry as priests. However, many clergy seem to have harboured doubts about the acceptability of this: 27.8% of clergy in Diocese C agreed or strongly agreed with such a measure of distance, but this was the highest percentage amongst any of the diocesan or deanery samples. Clergy of a variety of different views on women in ministry regretted the way in which the resolutions made women's priesting a central tenet of orthodoxy in some parishes: 'the existence of Resolutions A and B has not helped the fact that the Church has polarized around the ordination of women to the priesthood as the defining issue — their existence means that people are allowed to ask you what you think on this issue', reflected one male priest from Diocese C.[28] The possible theological implications of the opt-out provisions also prompted the heaviest criticism of the Act of Synod. In allowing parishes to seek extended episcopal oversight if its bishop ordained women, the Act stood accused of encouraging dissenting clergy and congregations to regard their diocesan as 'tainted' by his association with women priests. This was arguably the most controversial and sensitive area of unresolved debate surrounding the 1992–94 settlement and is considered further in section 7.3d.

Meanwhile, what of some of the other justifications offered for the 'safeguards' in the Measure and the Act? Back in 1992, members of the House of Bishops had offered both pastoral and theological justifications for the inclusion of the opt-out provisions in the 1992–94 settlement: on one hand the 'safeguards' were necessary to avoid schism and offered a method of allowing dissenting clergy and congregations to receive sacramental ministry and pastoral care with which they could feel comfortable. Opting out also afforded breathing space to any minister or congregation wanting time to come to terms with the decision. On the other hand, leading architects of the Act also suggested more theological justifications: Archbishop John Habgood argued forcefully that — just like Gamaliel in Acts 5 — a prudent Church would allow space to see if the ordination of women would bear fruit. And if the Church of England was currently in a 'period of open discernment' over women's priesting, its structures had to reflect the existence of the different viewpoints on the matter that still existed. There was also considerable keenness amongst the bishops to avoid the recrimination and legal wrangling that had marred the US Episcopal Church's decision to ordain women to the priesthood and episcopate through a single-clause measure with no opt-out clauses. More positively, the provisions were said to offer a way of modelling continued coexistence and some measure of communion despite serious division; something that could almost be elevated to a theological virtue. As the second Eames Commission report put it, 'the pain of living together with sharp differences is itself a

---

[27] int. cs2:12:24.
[28] int. cs3:24:286.

profound experience with the God who suffers'.[29] But how far did the case study clergy samples consider the opt-out provisions justified in pastoral and theological terms? Caution must be exercised here, since it is impossible to know which pastoral and theological justifications respondents had in mind when answering their questionnaires. However, as **Table 7vi** suggests, there was considerable ambivalence towards the statements claiming 'good pastoral grounds' or 'good theological grounds' for the inclusion of the xemptions:

Table 7vi Clergy attitudes to the assertion that there were a) good pastoral grounds, b) good theological grounds for having provisions in the Measure and the Act for those who cannot accept the ordination of women as priests (% 'strongly agree'/'agree')						
	Good pastoral grounds			**Good theological grounds**		
	Women[30]	**Men in favour**	**Men against**	**Women**	**Men in favour**	**Men against**
Diocese A	25.0	35.5	100	4.2	16.7	64.3
Diocese B	25.0	47.8	90.9	3.6	20.3	81.9
Diocese C	20.8	48.9	93.4	0	12.8	53.3
Diocese D	50.0	42.9	100	0	0	0
Diocese E	33.3	47.1	100	33.3	35.3	100
Diocese F	0	40.0	n/a	0	20.0	n/a

(For nos. of cases, see footnote[31])

The possible pastoral justifications were more easily accepted; particularly by men. Male clergy who objected to women's priesting were almost unanimous in asserting a pastoral justification for the provisions. As one senior clergyman of that constituency reflected, 'that made a tremendous difference, having the Act of Synod, because it enabled us to have a valued position in the Church of England'.[32] Between a third and a half of male clergy in favour of women's priesting also saw some pastoral justification for the 'safeguards': as one male clergyman from Diocese A reflected, 'I think provision had to be made for all parties, and if you're a compassionate organization you couldn't just allow people to leave, no pension provision or anything like that – that would have been very wrong ... '[33] However, a majority were more sceptical, particularly amongst women clergy. Some, of course, had never been convinced of the need for exemptions, but probably a more representative view came from this female priest in Diocese C:

---

[29] *Report of the Archbishop of Canterbury's Commission on Communion and Women in the Episcopate*, Part II October 1989 and March 1990 (Anglican Consultative Council, London, 1990), p. 1.

[30] In this and successive tables, no separate columns were given for 'women in favour' and 'women against' since all the ordained women surveyed in this project turned out to be in favour of women's priesting. Across the Church of England as a whole there were, of course, ordained women who disagreed with the Church's decision of 1992, but none featured in any of the six case study samples – either because none returned their questionnaires or because none were to be found in any of the dioceses or deaneries surveyed.

[31] Space does not permit the provision of full details of the numbers of cases. However, by way of illustration, the question on 'good pastoral grounds' for the provisions was answered in Diocese A by 24 women, 48 'men in favour' and 15 'men against'. In the much smaller Deanery D sample, the same question was answered by 2 women, 7 'men in favour' and 2 'men against'. The results of Tables 7vii and 7viii were also derived from similar sized samples.

[32] int. 11:294. The speaker could still insist on this despite adding that his constituency had not always been treated well in practice.

[33] int. cs1:29:380.

At the moment we're in a situation where we're being dishonest because we're trying to pretend there's a way through this which doesn't involve people breaking away. I don't like the idea of people breaking away, but I think we're at the moment [where] we're just reinforcing the barriers because of the legislation [...] You just can't go on forever like that ... I don't think it was wrong to have been there ... we've held things together long enough for people who needed time 'for the paint to dry' to let it dry ...[34]

However, whilst comments such as this showed a willingness to engage (if not agree) with the pastoral justifications for the opt-out provisions, there was much less sympathy with the idea that the 'safeguards' were theologically justified. Again, male clergy who objected to the 1992 decision were most likely to see a theological underpinning for the provisions, although many acknowledged that the Act was in some sense anomalous. One priest who spoke at length of his relief at being able to petition for extended episcopal oversight nevertheless reflected 'if you were creating a church based on ecclesiology derived from scripture and apostolic tradition you wouldn't throw up flying bishops ... you can justify it pastorally and out of the arrangement you can bring certain theological bricks into place to give it some sort of foundation'.[35] Nevertheless, for a majority of male clergy, and for all but three female priests surveyed, the Act had no theological justification. This marked ambivalence to the Act of Synod also became an important theme when respondents turned to consider the future shape of the Church of England and its ministry – as Chapters 8 and 9 go on to suggest.

Figure 7vii: Clergy attitudes to the statement that 'overall, on balance, the provisions are working well' (% 'strongly agree'/'agree')			
	Women	**Men in favour**	**Men against**
Diocese A	13.0	31.3	53.4
Diocese B	20.8	19.4	70.0
Diocese C	20.0	42.5	56.3
Deanery D	0	85.7	0
Deanery E	66.7	47.4	50.0
Deanery F	0	33.3	n/a

A similar ambivalence was evident when clergy were asked to comment on their experience of the resolutions in practice. For example, when asked whether 'overall, on balance, the provisions are working well', 31% of clergy in Diocese A agreed or strongly agreed, 48% disagreed or strongly disagreed, and 21% felt uncertain (results from each of the case studies, broken down by gender and attitude to women's priesting, are summarized in **Table 7vii**). Such a high percentage of respondents neither agreeing nor disagreeing was a common feature of the responses to statements on the practical outworking of the resolutions. Interviews suggested this was partly because many clergy felt ill-placed to comment on the overall picture. (Most encountered issues relating to the resolutions through their own personal experience or through hearsay.) There was little evidence that clergy regarded the 1992–94 settlement as practically unworkable, but some problems were also identified: participants were asked to consider how far the existence of the 'safeguards' was affecting the position of ordained women, and of those who could not accept women's priesting. A majority felt that they were restricting women's ability to function fully as priests, whilst only a minority felt that the safeguards were vital to allowing those who

---

[34] int. cs3:8:83.
[35] int. cs2:5:588.

objected to remain within the Church of England. This last finding was surprising, given the widespread expectation that more clergy would have left if the 1992 vote had turned around a single-clause measure to ordain women as priests. Interviewees who rejected the need for the provisions seemed to suggest the number of clergy who would have left had the 'safeguards' not been in place would have been small, and that most of the discontented would have been able to work out some mode of survival even without the safeguards. Here, however, we are in the realm of speculation, and the research is unable to offer any answers to what might have happened if the 1992 legislation had taken the form of a single-clause measure.

	% Perceiving occasional abuse of provisions			% Perceiving regular abuse of provisions		
	Women	Men in favour	Men against	Women	Men in favour	Men against
Diocese A	82.6	58.7	53.3	47.8	23.9	13.3
Diocese B	68.0	56.7	60.0	22.7	16.7	30.0
Diocese C	58.3	57.5	68.8	21.7	23.9	31.3
Deanery D	100	42.9	50.0	100	25.0	50.0
Deanery E	66.7	47.4	25.0	0	0	25.0
Deanery F	70.0	66.6	n/a	50.0	33.3	n/a

Table 7viii: Clergy attitudes to the statements that the provisions are a) occasionally, b) regularly being abused to extend the power of one constituency over another (% 'strongly agree'/'agree')

The final set of questions on the resolutions and petition for extended episcopal oversight asked clergy about the manner of their implementation. Those who supported the principle of providing 'safeguards' insisted that they must nevertheless be applied sensitively if the project of coexistence was to work. But how far had this proved to be the case? Generally, clergy seemed quite evenly divided over whether 'the resolutions do not produce disharmony if they are implemented with goodwill on all sides': between 44 and 49% of clergy in the three main diocesan case studies agreed or strongly agreed with this statement, whilst less than a third disagreed or strongly disagreed. Nevertheless, a majority of clergy seem to have believed that in places goodwill was sometimes lacking, and occasional abuses of the safeguards were taking place: as **Table 7viii** suggests, around two thirds of female clergy and over half of their male colleagues felt concerns over this issue. Even one of the original architects of the legislation, who remained a passionate defender of it, conceded that 'a lot of it was dependent on the way in which the Act of Synod was implemented ... now in this level it's been disappointing – there's been a tendency to use it to a bit more division [*sic*] than is absolutely necessary'.[36] Even so, care should be taken not to over-exaggerate the scale of the problem. Whilst many clergy could cite occasions when the resolutions had caused problems, only a minority believed that the legislation was frequently being manipulated to extend the power of one constituency over another. As with clergy attitudes to other 'unresolved issues', interviewees suggested that a comparatively small number of actual cases of malpractice could easily create a much wider climate of suspicion.

In the eyes of the majority of clergy surveyed, then, the existence of the opt-out provisions was regarded as an unacceptable consequence of the decision to ordain women and discriminatory towards women and those who ordained or supported them. There was some

---

[36] int. 12:67.

acceptance of the pastoral value of the resolutions but a majority of clergy remained deeply sceptical of any attempts to make a theological virtue out of their existence. Whilst few believed the safeguards were regularly being manipulated, there was nevertheless concern that goodwill was too often absent and occasional abuse of the provisions was taking place. It should be added that this comparatively negative assessment did not necessarily imply a general desire to remove the safeguards immediately (as Chapters 8 and 9 will suggest). However, for the moment, the remainder of this chapter turns to consider the challenges that clergy identified in the implementation of the resolutions and petition for extended episcopal oversight.

7.3 Unresolved issues

a) Interpreting the legislation

One important cluster of issues related to suggestions that the precise terms of the legislation were sometimes improperly understood. This was not simply an issue relating to the 1992–94 settlement, but appeared to be a wider source of concern amongst clergy on a variety of other issues: one 2002 study by Neil Burgess suggested that ignorance of the Church's legal obligations to its workers was one of main sources of job dissatisfaction amongst diocesan officers.[37] With regard to the opt-out provisions in the 1993 Measure, one key issue was the wording of the resolutions themselves, which allowed parishes to say that they 'would not accept' aspects of a woman's ministry as priest or presbyter. The negative wording of the statements was with good reason, since the main point of the Measure was to enable women's priesting and the 'safeguards' were to be understood as exemptions from the default position (although some leading advocates of an all-male priesthood insisted that the resolutions were an official acknowledgement that belief in women's priesting was optional). Beyond this more theoretical debate, however, the phrasing of the resolutions seems to have led to occasional confusion at parish level. As the bishop of Diocese D remarked, 'the questions are so worded that ordinary people misunderstand them ... now, you do get cases where we're referred [a decision on the resolutions] back because they've misunderstood the question; they've voted 'no' when they meant 'yes' – and that's in their interest, not ours ... '[38] In none of the case studies did this seem to have caused major problems. However, both the Clergy and Congregations Questionnaires revealed occasional cases where laity (and even clergy!) mistakenly ticked that their parish had a resolution in force when it did not, and vice versa. Given this, extra vigilance is needed on the part of both parish officials and senior diocesan clergy to ensure that the meaning of the resolutions is properly understood. The case also highlights the value of clear guidelines to parishes on procedures for passing and rescinding resolutions – particularly (as will be seen in section b) during an interregnum.

A more serious issue arose where there was disagreement over what the resolutions did (not) permit. In one of the most sensitive cases encountered, priests from resolution parishes and senior diocesan clergy seem to have held differing interpretations of how long a resolution remained in force once it had been passed. In the experience of one priest:

---

[37] Neil Burgess, 'Not all is well in the Church's Daily Office', *Church Times*, 23.02.02, pp. 15–16. The survey was based upon the views of Diocesan Adult Education and Social Responsibility Officers.
[38] int. cs4:9:341. There was no suggestion that the Diocese was deliberately muddying the waters here; the speaker did not ordain women, and if he had wished to be partisan would surely have preferred parishes to pass the resolutions rather than not to do so.

> *it came to my attention that [senior clergy] were appointing a woman priest to*
> *parishes that had passed the resolutions, and I pointed this out, and they said*
> *'oh, but the resolutions have to lapse after five years' and I said 'no they don't!'*
> *... I had to send a copy of the resolutions ... to show they were breaking the law.*[39]

Indeed, upon further investigation it did seem that some senior clergy had been working on the assumption that Resolutions A and B were time-limited. As one told me: 'I think if you look at the legislation carefully you're supposed to review it after five years. Now, virtually none of our parishes have done that'. The speaker in question did not consider it his business to go around reminding parishes that the resolutions needed revisiting.[40] Extreme caution is needed in interpreting this case: this was the only instance of this problem I encountered in any of the six case studies, suggesting that misinterpretation of the resolutions in this way is not a common occurrence. Neither does it necessarily suggest wilful or systematic abuse of the terms: I gained no sense that the speaker in question was deliberately misapplying the legislation, but clearly no one had properly checked what the 1993 Measure actually said. In addition, if blame is to be apportioned it must also lie with the officials of the parishes in question, since they had apparently changed their minds and accepted a female incumbent quite readily without rescinding their resolutions – or perhaps without even remembering they were in force. Nevertheless, the case suggests that care should be taken to understand the terms of the legislation – particularly on such a sensitive subject as this.

b) Voting on the Resolutions

A second cluster of issues surrounded the actual procedure for passing or rescinding a resolution, or petitioning for extended episcopal oversight. On one hand, views differed on the most appropriate timing of any debate on the resolutions:[41] one senior clergyman from Diocese A explained how 'I think where there's a vacancy we try not to change the situation in the parish ...'[42] whilst the incumbent of a resolution parish in the same diocese concurred that he usually told his parishes to leave any decision about rescinding the resolutions until the arrival of the new incumbent.[43] However, conversations around the case study dioceses suggested an increasing tendency for parishes to revisit the resolutions *during* an interregnum rather than *after* the appointment of a new vicar. This gave those who were more tenacious about defending the resolution status of parishes an additional reason for encouraging stability during an interregnum: the fear that senior diocesan clergy would attempt to take advantage of the absence of the priest and pressure the parish to rescind the resolutions. Some senior clergy acknowledged that they did encourage parishes to rescind where possible: in the experience of one senior clergyman in Diocese B:

---

[39] Not referenced in order to preserve the anonymity of the diocese and clergy involved in this sensitive case.

[40] Here, there seems to have been some confusion between the terms of the resolutions in the 1993 Measure that 'shall continue in force until rescinded' (*Priests (Ordination of Women) Measure 1993 (no. 2)*, Part 2, 3 (2)) and the conditions for petitioning for extended episcopal oversight in the Act of Synod that must be reviewed at least once in every five year period (*Episcopal Ministry Act of Synod 1993*, section 9.2). Not referenced in order to preserve the anonymity of the diocese and clergy involved.

[41] For the position of the 'Priests (Ordination of Women) Measure 1993: Code of Practice', and the possible ambiguity of the guidance, see footnote 26 in Chapter 6.

[42] int. cs1:5:425.

[43] int cs1:6:p.3.

we have to say [to the parish] 'now what are your views about women?' we say to them 'you've passed A and B; they're kind of on the record book, is that what you want to say, where are you?' and of course once the vicar's gone, certainly in most cases people say 'well, actually that was because the vicar was keen – we're not that bothered.'[44]

There was considerable evidence (as Chapter 5 suggested) that senior clergy were sometimes prepared to go along with a parish's wishes not to have a female incumbent, if this meant that the parish did not need to pass a resolution.

Amongst clergy with objections to women's priesting, it was commonly suggested that 'the diocese' was unsympathetic to their opted-out status and tried by a variety of methods to reverse it. One alleged approach was to take the chair in section 11 and 12 meetings[45] during interregna and pressurize the congregation to justify their decision to pass the resolution or make the petition. If this took place, it was certainly outside the spirit of the provisions: the draft Code of Practice accompanying the *Guidelines for Good Practice* following the Blackburn report stated that 'neither the archdeacon nor rural dean nor any other person who is not a member of the Council has the right to chair the Council'.[46] Second, it was sometimes suggested that parishes were warned they would struggle to get another priest if they confined themselves to searching only for a 'traditionalist'. It was not possible to establish within the limitations of the project whether vacancies in resolution parishes were harder to fill than other parishes, although much of the anecdotal evidence pointed in this direction. Third, it was even occasionally suggested that churches were threatened with closure or reorganization if they continued to resist the appointment of a female priest (such was the case in Church 21, which was in the midst of a long interregnum when I visited. On one occasion I had to reassure a nervous parishioner that I was not a spy sent by the diocese to gather information on the church in preparation for its closure).

On the other hand, across the diocesan case studies, senior clergy denied any concerted attempt to pressurize resolution parishes, whilst admitting that occasionally mistakes were made and insensitivities sometimes committed. Certainly some were keen to discover a parish's reasons for passing a resolution or submitting a petition, but suggested that this was to test out whether the provisions were adopted for the reasons for which they were intended (see section c). Of course, most parishes that opted out did so primarily because a majority of their PCC had reservations or objections over women's priesting (this was clearly the case in Church 8, for example). But some traditionalist clergy also seemed to feel that a congregation that supported women's priesting displayed a lack of education on the theological issues, and sought to 're-educate' them. This should not be taken to imply that clergy who were against women's priesting regularly manipulated their PCC's in order to get the resolutions or a petition for extended oversight passed (although several members of Church 3 believed that their previous incumbent had placed unacceptable pressure on the PCC to do so[47]). However, in the immediate aftermath of the vote, it seems not to have been

---

[44] int. cs2:3side3:343.

[45] A 'Section 11' meeting is the first meeting of the PCC after the departure of an incumbent, at which a parish profile is drawn up stating the parish's wishes for its next incumbent. At the 'Section 12' meeting, which follows some time after this, the parish representatives meet with the patron and the bishop/archdeacon to discuss the parish profile.

[46] House of Bishops Standing Committee, 'Draft Guidelines for the Review of a PCC Petition' Appendix 1 of *Episcopal Ministry Act of Synod 1993: Guidelines for Good Practice Emanating from the Report of the Working Party of the House of Bishops Chaired by the Bishop of Blackburn ('The Blackburn Report', GS1395)* (2001), point 97.

[47] See Chapter 4.

unknown for clergy with objections to women's priesting to suggest that they would have to resign if the resolutions were not in place.

Many of the observations offered in this section have necessarily been based on anecdotal evidence, given the difficulty of establishing a case through questionnaires and interviews alone. As a result it is difficult to offer precise conclusions as to how the procedure for voting on the resolutions could be conducted better. Nevertheless, some conclusions are possible.

- First, to ensure that a resolution or petition is passed or rescinded in a harmonious manner, wide consultation seems important. Members of congregations felt marginalized when an incumbent and/or PCC pushed the resolutions through against majority opinion, or alternatively when a senior representative from the diocese seemed not to take seriously their wish to receive the ministry of only male priests. Of course in official terms, decisions on the 'safeguards' did reside solely with the incumbent and PCC,[48] but full and open consultation with the wider congregation could help to defuse suspicion and ensure a decision that accurately reflects the wishes of a majority of churchgoers. In this respect, the findings of this research project support the recommendation made by the Blackburn Review that all members of the electoral roll should be consulted in the case of a petition for extended Episcopal oversight.[49]
- Second, many of the problems arising from votes on the opt-out provisions seemed to derive from a fundamental lack of familiarity with the terms of the Measure and the Act. It is not suggested that every church member needs to become an expert on ecclesiastical law and inevitably the terms of the 1992–94 settlement form only a small part of the larger body of ecclesiastical legislation and procedure which senior and parish clergy encounter. However, an occasional refreshment of the memory might help avoid unnecessary problems, and would receive support from across the different positions on the question of women's priesting.[50]

c) Unforeseen circumstances

A third area of concern was that whilst the 'safeguards' were developed to allow parishes to opt out of women's priestly ministry their existence could have consequences quite unintended by the architects of the legislation. For one thing, it was occasionally suggested that some parishes were passing or renewing their opt-out provisions partly for reasons not connected with women's priesting; for example, to seek to prevent pastoral reorganization. The resolutions and petition for extended episcopal oversight also seemed to offer refuge for clergy and congregations discontented with the wider direction of the Church of England: the incumbent of Church 15 was certain that many of his PCC had originally voted to come under their Episcopal Visitor primarily because they found their previous bishop abrasive and unsympathetic to Anglo-Catholicism.[51] Others appeared to fear the changes that a female incumbent might bring (for example, that the Prayer Book might be abandoned, or prayers would henceforth be to 'God our Mother'). Without extensive participant observation in a large number of parish situations, evidence for many of these suggestions must necessarily remain anecdotal. It is possible that alternative explanations

---

[48] And in the bishop's power to grant the petition for extended episcopal oversight, in the case of the (quasi-legal) Act of Synod.

[49] *Guidelines for Good Practice*, point 4.

[50] The 1998 Windsor Consultation on women's ordained ministry recommended, amongst other things 'widespread education and communication' on the provisions of the Act of Synod, something echoed by Forward in Faith's document 'The Case for a Free Province of the Church of England' (December 1998, p. 4).

[51] int. cs5:12:490.

for a parish's decision to pass the resolutions were sometimes sought by some senior clergy who were genuinely perplexed that conscientious opposition to women's priestly ministry could still exist. Nevertheless, given what has already been suggested in this chapter, it is difficult to deny that on occasion, the resolutions could acquire a highly political significance beyond their original intention, and it would not therefore be surprising if resolutions were sometimes passed or rescinded for a whole variety of different reasons. If so, it is incumbent on parishes and their clergy to ensure that the resolutions themselves do not become a justification for greater isolation from the rest of the diocese, or a way of demonstrating opposition to the bishop.

Passing a resolution could also have unintended consequences for women's own ministry. This was well illustrated in one case that came to the attention of *Church Times* readers in early 2002. The Revd Alison Hardy, vicar of St John's Irlam, Salford, had regularly presided at the Eucharist in a nearby high school as part of a rota of local clergy. However, she was asked to cease her contribution to school worship by the Diocese of Manchester early in 2002 when churchwardens from the parish of St Michael and All Angels, Peel Green (in which the school was situated) and individuals from a neighbouring resolution parish alerted the diocese to the fact that the parish had Resolution A in place under the women priests legislation. Technically it seemed, the Revd Hardy was prohibited from celebrating communion in the school. However, in response to the decision, the school's head teacher Neil Whitehead suspended all eucharistic services whilst the dispute was solved. The Diocese of Manchester sought national legal advice on the matter, which was eventually solved by designating the school an 'extra-parochial place' with the Revd Hardy continuing to exercise her ministry at the school.[52] However, this was not before the case had made national Church news. Whilst the dispute presented immediate problems for the parish and diocese, it also raised much larger questions about who the resolutions were really designed to serve. Formally, of course, the opt-out provisions applied to the parish, although in practice they generally owed their existence to the views of the incumbent and PCC, and perhaps the regular congregation. Potentially, a PCC's decision could therefore bar a parish from experiencing a woman's priestly ministry even if it was accepted by the wider community. The resolutions had been put in place to satisfy the concerns of members of the congregation, but resulted in much wider implications for the whole parish (when no similar reservations about the Revd Hardy's ministry had been raised in the school or wider community). Nor did it require a high profile case such as this to make this anomaly plain; one female priest in Diocese C expressed her frustration at being (at least officially) unable to take home communion to a woman on the electoral roll of her own church because the neighbouring parish in which she lived in had resolution status.

The resolutions also seem to have presented wider issues for the community in rural areas, where parishioners were often more likely to identify with their church – even if they did not attend regularly. One priest in Diocese B remembered how when his PCC had voted for Resolutions A and B and petitioned for extended episcopal oversight, the meeting was attended by an unusually large number of villagers who were angry at what the church was about to do.[53] Of course, in legal terms, the PCC was the representative church body for the parish and not just the congregation, and so in one sense perfectly entitled to pass a resolution on behalf of the whole community. On the other hand, most clergy and laity generally understood the resolutions as primarily intended for the benefit of the congregation. Indeed, where members of the wider parish community sought to try to prevent a parish 'opting out', clergy with strong objections to women's priesting sometimes seemed to resent what they regarded as outside interference by people who knew little of

---

[52] *Church Times*, 22.02.02 and conversations with individuals from the diocese concerned.
[53] int. cs2:5:385.

the theological issues. The cases cited here amply demonstrate the degree to which safeguards originally designed to maintain the comprehensiveness and catholicity of the Church of England had in some respects strengthened the congregationalist element that was already a feature of some aspects of Anglican culture and legislation. Given the variety of cases discussed here, it is difficult to suggest straightforward recommendations that might address the problem of churches passing resolutions for 'invalid' reasons. To a large extent it must be taken on trust that parish decision-makers should act only according to conscience and resist the temptation to wield the provisions for other purposes. But is this enough?

d) Petitioning for extended episcopal oversight

It was quite widely recognized that the process and experience of petitioning for extended episcopal oversight raised a number of challenges of its own, with the practical aspects of these also raising important theological/ecclesiological questions. The working of the Act has already been the subject of extensive scrutiny by the former Bishop of Blackburn's working party on the Act of Synod and so it is not proposed to cover the same ground at length again. However, it is worth highlighting briefly some of the key unresolved issues clergy identified about the working of the Act, given that it was a regular feature of the interview conversations.

On a purely practical level, the diversity of views possible in teams, groups and united benefices posed questions about how 'appropriate' Episcopal care should be provided to each constituency. The Blackburn Review of the Act of Synod suggested that here, informal arrangements could resolve the problems where the legislation could not. By mutual agreement of the benefice, diocesan bishop and PEV, a parish could agree to the appointment of a woman for those centres within the group that could accept her ministry, whilst explicitly agreeing (perhaps through a 'letter of comfort') that the congregation that could not accept women's priesting could call in the relevant Episcopal Visitor.[54] This greatly depended on the willingness of all parties concerned to work together. Several interviewees cited cases where this had worked well and the different positions were enabled to cooperate whilst respecting each others' views. Elsewhere however, this had not been achieved: one male clergyman in Diocese B recalled how one church in his care had misread his intentions and assumed that he was planning to force them to accept a female priest for communion. The resultant wrangling had caused much bitterness and was only solved with the arrival of a priest who was acceptable to the 'traditionalist' constituency and willing to work in a team with clergy supportive of women's priesting.[55]

Practical issues such as this also demanded good working relationships between diocesan clergy and the Episcopal Visitors. Again, wide variations were possible: first, on all sides there was extensive agreement that where a diocese made its own arrangements for extended episcopal oversight, cooperation was generally achieved more easily. Second, it was frequently suggested that relations between Episcopal visitors and diocesan bishops were generally more harmonious in the Province of York than in Canterbury. Third, that the 'second generation' of PEVs had been more conciliatory than the first. This certainly reflected the PEVs' own conceptions of their task: one of the first to be consecrated recalled how he had 'got out there, met the people ... encouraged them to pass the resolutions, take advantage of our services – I think it had just been assumed that we'd do the odd confirmation, but there would not be this gathering together of the troops, if you like'.[56] In

---

[54] House of Bishops, *Episcopal Ministry Act of Synod: Report of a Working Party*, section 7.9 (p. 27).
[55] int. cs2:13:480. See also: Lesley Bentley, 'At the Grass Roots: The Act in the Parishes' in Monica Furlong (ed.), *Act of Synod: Act of Folly?* (SCM Press, London, 1998), pp. 101–114 (p. 105).
[56] int. 17:62.

contrast, one second-generation PEV spoke of how he saw his task as 'to discover how to be the church – sounds pious, but we have to move on from being a protest movement, which is about arranging meetings ... to get on with being authentically the church'.[57] Fourth, working relationships were also dependent on the personalities of the Episcopal visitors and senior diocesan clergy themselves, and their willingness to consult with each other. Some diocesan bishops were said to be reluctant to consult the PEV, whilst some PEVs were said to show little interest in the dioceses beyond encouraging more parishes to petition for extended episcopal oversight. The growing volume of guidance on the operation of the Act of Synod recommended a proper working relationship between PEV and diocesan bishops, and mutual agreement on the PEV's role within the diocese.[58] However, the evidence of this research was that – despite the recommendations of the Blackburn report – a greater exercise of mutual cooperation was still needed in some parts of the Church of England.

Of most concern to clergy supportive of women's priesting was the way in which some parishes receiving extended episcopal oversight appeared increasingly detached from their diocese. (As an illustration, several interviewees spoke of how 'C' parishes they knew of prayed for their PEV but not for their diocesan bishop.) Of course, 'C' parishes were not always detached or isolated: all but one of the parishes coming under the PEV in Diocese B seemed reasonably well integrated into the rest of diocesan life, and in Diocese C, the story of Church 8 showed how a parish previously isolated from the diocesan bishop had once again begun to play more of a wider role, through a careful process of building trust between bishop, incumbent and congregation. Church 15 in Diocese E likewise seemed to participate equally in diocesan and 'alternative' events. The relevant Episcopal Visitor was a regular visitor to the parish, whilst members of the congregation also spoke in glowing terms about their local suffragan bishop, who ordained women and who came to preach at the parish on several occasions. Nevertheless, on some occasions a 'C' parish seemed to become much more isolated: around 12.5% of the parishes petitioning for extended episcopal oversight did so despite the fact that their diocesan bishop did not even ordain women to the priesthood.[59] The Bishop of Diocese D was one who expressed exasperation not only that some of his parishes opted for extended episcopal oversight even though he ordained women, but also that some of these parishes still assumed they could call on him for sacramental care – why petition if the diocesan bishop's sacramental actions are sufficient, he wondered.

What was the appeal of extended episcopal oversight to parishes? Normally, clergy and congregations making the petition did so because in some sense they believed their diocesan bishop had acted wrongly in ordaining women to the priesthood (although as will be discussed further below, the precise nature of his 'offence' was subject to a variety of interpretations). However, given that some parishes petitioned even when the diocesan bishop's actions were not 'in doubt', other factors must also sometimes have come into play. It was frequently suggested that both 'push' and 'pull' factors could offer additional motivation for seeking extended episcopal oversight. As already suggested, a petition might occasionally be partly motivated by a desire to stave off pastoral reorganization with parishes that might be supportive of women's priesting, or to distance oneself from a bishop with sharply differing views on other matters. It should be added that there were regular calls from members of Forward in Faith (and occasionally members of Reform) for more parishes to pass 'Resolution C' as a way of protecting their identity and independence from

---

[57] int. 15:422.

[58] House of Bishops, *Episcopal Ministry Act of Synod: Report of a Working Party*, section 3.7 (p. 12).

[59] This point was also brought to the attention of the Blackburn Review of the Act of Synod by the group Women and the Church (WATCH) (ts. 'WATCH response to the Blackburn Review').

senior clergy who might wish them to rescind the resolutions and accept a female incumbent.[60] On the other hand, extended episcopal care also contained some positive attractions for some parishes: one clergyman from Diocese B explained how 'we've had far better episcopal care than we've ever had from the diocese – though he lives in [***], I could be on the phone to him and he'd be here tomorrow'.[61] Likewise one PCC member from Church 8 in Diocese C observed, 'I've never seen a bishop so often as when we had our provincial visitor – whether it's because he had fewer churches I don't know, but he took more interest in St [Y]'s, than it would appear the Bishop of [X] does ... it wasn't a problem for him to come and talk to us, give us any advice or information... he was a smashing guy ... it sounds terrible but we just didn't get that quality of care from the Bishop of [X]'.[62] Indeed, as the speaker suggested, in many cases the PEV was freer to provide such a level of care because he was not encumbered with some of the usual responsibilities of a diocesan or suffragan bishop.[63] For some PEVs themselves, this was a positive virtue:

> *many parishes that have said in a rather flattering way that the PEV has shown us what a bishop ought to be – it's a new way of being a bishop. It isn't a new way at all; it's an old way, it's the way, I think... relating to the parishes directly and caring for them as best you can pastorally. Some of the diocesan bishops ... say 'we have to be in the House of Lords, we have to chair the diocesan synod, we have to do so many other things, so it's all very well for you, you don't have these burdens ...' but it's a matter of priorities, really ...*[64]

The freedom of PEVs to focus directly on individual parishes also perhaps offers a partial explanation of the increased trend towards preferring provincial rather than diocesan or regional solutions to extended episcopal oversight – despite the original intention being to work through the diocesan and regional arrangements where possible. As the Blackburn Review of the Act of Synod noted, 25 dioceses had opted for wholly provincial arrangements, with only 5 choosing a mixture of diocesan and provincial oversight, 6 for wholly diocesan arrangements and 7 for a regional arrangement.[65] However, whilst parish preference was not inconsequential, this trend owed most to the fact that few dioceses had made Episcopal appointments from amongst those who opposed women's priesting. As already suggested in Chapter 5, there was a widespread conviction that appointing a 'traditionalist' suffragan primarily out of consideration for a small minority of parishes seeking extended episcopal oversight would be (in the words of one speaker) 'a very large sledgehammer to crack a very small nut'.

Aside from the more practical issues raised by the Act, there also seemed growing unease at its possible theological implications. Most seriously, it was suggested that the Act of Synod's allowance of a measure of distance between dissenting clergy and bishops who ordained women perpetuated a belief that one could be 'tainted' by contact with women. At

---

[60] Robbie Low, 'Alphabetical Alliances', *New Directions* 2 (29) October 1997, p. 4; Jonathan Redvers-Harris, 'Back to ABC', *New Directions* 2 (38) July 1998, pp. 12–13; Michael Fisher, 'Simple as ABC', *New Directions* 3 (56) Jan 2000, p. 12; Wallace Benn, 'Lessons to be Learned', *Reform Newspaper*, No. 3 Pentecost 1999, p. 3.

[61] int. cs2:7:502.

[62] int. cs3:15:455.

[63] Of course, whilst this may well raise questions about the level of bureaucracy facing diocesan bishops and their senior colleagues, preferring a different 'style' of episcopate did not in itself justify the existence of the PEV; something on which there was considerable agreement across the board.

[64] int. 2:340. However, it should be added that this reflects a more historic tendency for laity to expect their clergy not to spend too long on administration and organization (Stuart Ransom, Alan Bryman and C. Robin Hinings, *Clergy, Ministers and Priests* (Routledge and Kegan Paul, London, 1977), p. 13).

[65] House of Bishops, *Episcopal Ministry Act of Synod: Report of a Working Party*, section 4.2 (p. 15).

very least, critics claimed, the Act of Synod's introduction of additional bishops for dissenters contained strong echoes of the fourth century Donatist heresy, which held that any unworthiness on the part of the minister could affect the validity of his sacramental actions, in which case a believer could call upon the ministry of one who had remained 'pure'. In the case of the Act of Synod, however, the 'impurity' was not those who had betrayed the faith under persecution (as in the fourth century North Africa[66]), but complicity with the ordination of women as priests. The most powerful criticism of the apparent theological implications of the Act has come from Judith Maltby:

> *Your bishops can deny the resurrection, the Trinity, and the incarnation; he may be a racist, liar, or thief – but no one will offer you a PEV. But if he ordains a woman to the priesthood, you can call in a 'safe pair of hands'.*[67]

Against such criticisms the Act has been defended by its original architects, with former Archbishop of York John Habgood arguing that the legislation was necessary because, simply, 'we do not unchurch those who disagree with us'.[68] Those who took advantage of the Act's provisions were also keen to defend its theological integrity, insisting that their decision to opt out of receiving sacramental ministry from their diocesan bishop was nothing to do with his actual contact with women and more to do with his action on ordaining women, which they regarded as schismatic. As one contributor to *New Directions* wrote in 1995, those petitioning for extended episcopal oversight wished to avoid 'doubt about the acceptability of women priests ... which destroys the collegial nature of the presbyterate and breaks the relationship with the bishop. How can a priest act on behalf of a bishop who ordains women and acts collegially with them?'[69]

Unfortunately this report can only report differing views of what 'impaired communion' actually meant. A full, theological exploration of the subject is left to other authors to provide. But how far did the interview testimony point towards the *practice* of a theology of 'taint' in the Church of England in reality? Clearly no one would be prepared to admit to a researcher that they believed their bishop to have been 'tainted' through his contact with women. Without extensive participant observation it is therefore impossible to chart the different ways in which 'sacramental distance' was practised, so only very tentative conclusions can be offered here. First, it seems fair to say that 'opposed' clergy and laity gave a variety of reasons for distancing themselves from their diocesan bishop. At Church 8, some interviewees seemed to imply that they came under the PEV because the diocesan bishop had acted heretically in ordaining women. As one explained:

> *I think some people view it as a watered down faith... but they're far happier receiving communion and being confirmed by [the PEV] because as they see it, he's stuck to his vows, and has not been swayed by any arguments.*[70]

---

[66] Although in an important sense some of those who disagreed with women's priesting *did* regard the Church of England's decision as a betrayal of Christian orthodoxy in the face of secular pressure.

[67] Judith Maltby, 'One Lord, One Faith, One Baptism, but Two Integrities?' in Furlong (ed.), *Act of Synod: Act of Folly?*, pp. 42–58 (p. 57).

[68] The Most Revd Dr John Habgood, quoted in General Synod, November Group of Sessions, 1989, *Report of Proceedings* 20 (3) (General Synod, London, 1989), pp. 1009–11.

[69] Based on the Forward in Faith Statement on Impaired Communion, introduction in *New Directions* 1 (4) September 1995, p. 22.

[70] int. cs3:19:420.

Here, there was no sense that the Bishop had been somehow 'polluted' by his ordaining women, or that his sacramental actions were thereby invalidated. The view that receiving extended episcopal oversight was primarily an abstention from involvement with a bishop who ordained women was also found amongst clergy with a higher level of theological education. As this senior clergyman from Diocese D explained:

> *...this is caused by [the bishop's] action of fracturing the traditional teaching and practice of the Church – in the same way as, for example, we had a bishop who denied the Nicene Creed ... Although such a bishop would have been ordained, consecrated by the Church, and* would be a bishop, *we might want to say that this is not where the Church is, and therefore action needs to be taken by the faithful of the Church, of disapproval of that action ...*[71]

Others suggested that establishing a 'measure of distance' between themselves and bishops who ordained women was not about gender but authority, as this male priest from Diocese E explained:

> *I'm just saying that [the bishop has] cut himself off from me, because he's gone against what the Church has taught for 2000 years [...] he and I don't have full Eucharistic communion ... that means effectively that when he celebrates, he's doing so in a state in which he and I cannot fully participate. It's very difficult, in theological terms, to say precisely where that comes. But that is the problem. It is still a valid mass, but he has acted in such a way, that he is doing something for which there is doubtful authority, so I have to say sorry this has put a question mark over our communion together in that mass which we are celebrating.*[72]

If establishing 'sacramental distance' should primarily be understood as a protest action or statement of belief that the bishop had acted beyond his authority, one would expect to find similar protests at communion over other issues – for example, a refusal to share communion with a bishop whose views on core Christian doctrines were considered suspect. However, there was very little evidence of this taking place either before or since the ordination of women as priests.[73] Furthermore, a small number of cases were reported anecdotally that cannot be explained except with reference to the existence of belief in a concept of 'taint' or something very like it. For example, one senior clergyman reported an instance where one priest with objections to women's ordination had chosen not to accept a parish where a woman had previously celebrated during the interregnum 'because the altar had been contaminated'.[74] In addition, at least two senior figures with objections to women's priesting acknowledged that a small minority of individuals in their constituency with very extreme views did hold to something very like a 'theology of taint', although the two speakers themselves did not subscribe to it.

---

[71] int. cs4:10:430.

[72] int. cs5:12side2:172.

[73] Although one interviewee alleged that in the 1980s, some 'traditionalist' parishes in a diocese with a liberal bishop did quietly take their confirmation candidates over the border into the neighbouring diocese, to ensure they were confirmed by a bishop of more 'orthodox' theological views.

[74] Because the priest in question was not identified, it was not possible to hear a first-hand explanation of his actions. However, these words were reported to me as verbatim by several sources (including one priest with his own reservations about women's ordination as priests) and so there seems no reason to doubt the authenticity of the story.

It is impossible to build any firm conclusions on such anecdotal evidence, but it is probably safe to conclude that individuals could hold very different reasons (some of them conflicting) for opting for extended episcopal oversight and out of full communion with their bishop, and that some of these reasons were closer to the official justifications for the Act of Synod than others. Given this, it would seem unwise either to suggest that a theology of 'taint' was widely practised, or equally that it was non-existent. What *was* clear was that many of those taking advantage of the provisions of the Act of Synod found it very difficult to elucidate a sustained theological justification for why the sacramental actions of their bishop were unacceptable, or to be avoided. Moreover, despite the best attempts of some to establish a 'measure of sacramental distance', it was clear that the boundary separating those receiving extended episcopal oversight and those who supported and ordained women as priests were by no means hermetically sealed.

The priest from Diocese E quoted above himself acknowledged that he had concelebrated communion with another male priest who had concelebrated with a female priest. One bishop who supported women's priesting reported holding a separate ordination service for a 'traditionalist' ordinand and being surprised to find clergy from 'C' parishes receiving communion from him and joining him to lay hands on the candidate.[75] A further anomaly existed in the fact that even Provincial Episcopal Visitors were ordained by the Archbishop of Canterbury, and yet those receiving extended episcopal oversight would on occasion decline to receive communion from the Archbishop. Clearly 'impaired communion' was not quite so impaired as some might have wished.

Conclusion

This ambiguity marks attitudes to the opt-out provisions and experiences of their implementation as a whole. Whilst for some the resolutions offered the only way of staying within the Church of England with integrity, others regarded them as discriminating towards women and towards those who supported and/or ordained them. In practical terms, most clergy and congregations had worked out ways of living and working with the provisions and their consequences, often acknowledged some pastoral justification for their existence and rarely believed they were regularly misapplied. Nevertheless, the research did identify occasional problems with the 'safeguards': parishes and senior diocesan figures could sometimes be insufficiently aware of the precise terms of the resolutions and this could foster a climate of suspicion between the different constituencies. The most serious contention arose from suggestions that the correct procedure for voting on the resolutions had not been followed, and from accusations that parishes had sometimes been unfairly pressured into passing or rescinding them. On an ecclesiological level, the terms of the resolutions prompted serious questions about who the opt-out provisions were actually intended to benefit, and particularly about the relationship between a congregation and its wider parish community (although this was only one part of a much wider debate about the identity, status and responsibilities of the Church of England as a national-cum-established church that was nevertheless frequently highly differentiated from wider social values).

Where there was common agreement on the interpretation of the resolutions, their procedure for implementation and a spirit of cooperation, the resolutions rarely proved problematic. However, it was clear that all sides needed to do much more to dispel the climate of suspicion that could surround the 'safeguards' and their implementation. But whilst serious disagreements over the resolutions were comparatively few and their existence did not prove a daily stumbling block even for those who resented their existence, a nagging suspicion remained amongst a majority of clergy that the safeguards were an

---

[75] int. cs5:1:512.

unacceptable consequence of the decision to ordain women to the priesthood. However, this was not to say that most clergy wanted to see the terms of the legislation rewritten with immediate effect. As shall be suggested in the final part of the report, timing was seen to be of the essence when the future of women's ministry and the current settlement was considered.

Part III

Looking to the Future

Chapter 8

Coexistence and the future

At several points this report has suggested that for many churchgoers, the debate on women's ordination as priests was now part of history: the vote had been taken in 1992, the first female candidates had been priested in 1994, and after an initial period of settling down, female clergy had been largely accepted as a normal part of life in the Church of England, even though sometimes not quite on exactly the same terms as men. From the viewpoint of the active churchgoer whose sights were focused primarily on local church and community life, and whose friends, clergy or reading habits did not tell them otherwise, this was a reasonable conclusion to reach. However, for those whose interests encompassed something of the wider affairs of the Church of England, or whose parish had been touched directly by the 1992–94 settlement, it was clear that the story did not stop there. For clergy in particular, women's priesting brought major changes and had also left several important pieces of unfinished business. Part II explored some key issues arising out of the settlement, and the practical implementation of the 1993 Measure and Act of Synod. However, there was also a sense in which the present settlement *itself* had an air of provisionality about it.

Of course, as suggested in Chapter 1, only the Ordination of Women (Financial Provisions) Measure came with any specific time limit attached (in this case a ten year window in which clergy and church workers could claim financial assistance if they resigned over the ordination of women). The theological papers accompanying the Measures and the Act implied that the wider 'process of discernment' over women's priesting might take considerable time. Nevertheless, many observers recognized from the beginning that the Measure's explicit exclusion of women from the episcopate would at some point be challenged again (whether in five years or fifty). It was also widely acknowledged that any move to allow women to become bishops would also spell an end to the Act of Synod (and probably some aspects of the 1993 Measure) in its current form. Misgivings about the settlement had been expressed from the beginning – both by those who felt it did not deliver the full measure of women's ordination and by those who felt it did not go far enough in protecting advocates of an all-male priesthood/presbyterate. But by the late 1990s, calls for an end to the current settlement were beginning to take on organized expression, with the foundation of GRAS (the Group for Rescinding the Act of Synod) in 2000 and – from a different end of the spectrum – the Third Province Movement in 2002. The controversy over the ordination of 'practising' homosexuals that boiled over across the Anglican Communion in 2003 also served to place increasing strain on commitments to coexistence, and raised significant questions about the acceptable limits of diversity within the same church. On the other hand, equally determined attempts were made to keep the different positions together.

Against this background, Chapter 8 explores the views of grass roots clergy and laity towards the future of this 'coexistence project'. How was the Church's current position on women's priesting to be understood? How viable was the 1992–94 settlement felt to be? At what pace, and at what price, should change come? Here, care must be taken in interpreting the source material, since attitudes to the future are necessarily speculative and impressionistic. Even so, a survey of attitudes to women and priesthood 'ten years on' remains incomplete without some consideration of these questions, given the extent to which expectations of the future can exert great influence on present action. Chapter 9 will give in-depth consideration to questions of women's ordination to the episcopate and the future of the Act of Synod, but first this current chapter explores attitudes to life under the

1992–94 settlement and its immediate viability. It concludes by drawing on the work of anthropologist Mary Douglas and sociologist Alan Aldridge to argue that respondents' views of the future of the 'coexistence project' differed in ways quite different to the usual division made between 'supporters' and 'opponents' – a point further developed in Chapter 9.

8.1 The 'reception' of women's priestly ordination

First though, how was the settlement framed and presented to the Church of England by some of the most influential architects of the legislation? Key to the aim of keeping the whole Church of England on board despite serious differences was the idea that important developments of doctrine and order were (and should be) subject to a 'process of reception' by the Church. The theological idea of 'reception' is to some extent implicit in the Christian faith: for the Christian, beliefs are not arrived at through reason alone, but by 'receiving' them – ultimately from God, but via scripture, experience, reason and tradition (this last word denoting that which is 'handed on' to us).[1] Although truths about God are unchanging, the flux of history means that these statements of faith and belief require amplification, clarification and explication in each generation. But these restatements also have to be *received*; i.e., accepted as authentic developments consonant with foundational Christian beliefs. As one scholar has written, 'reception' may therefore be said to be 'the process through which an ecclesial community incorporates into its own life a particular decision, teaching or practice'.[2] At times of apparently rapid social and religious change, such as the past fifty years, finding a proper balance between continuity and change in doctrine and order becomes particularly challenging, and with it the question of how changes are accepted becomes more important. The late twentieth century has seen an unprecedented interest in the idea and 'reception' has become common currency in ecumenical circles,[3] as ecclesial communities seeking to journey together 'receive' the insights and practices of the other. This is an active process of discernment.

The idea that women's ordination might be subject to such a 'process of reception' formed part of the debate from at least the 1980s. Faced with the prospect that some Anglican provinces might move towards ordaining a female bishop whilst other provinces maintained the idea of a male-only priesthood, the 1988 Lambeth Conference commissioned further study into how 'the highest possible degree of Communion' could be maintained despite differences.[4] Central to the resulting series of reports was the idea of an 'open process of discernment' over the rightness of women's priesting 'until consensus one way or the other has been achieved'.[5] When the Church of England's turn came to debate women's ordination as priests, the idea of 'reception' again played a key part in the thinking of the House of Bishops: a vote on women's priesting was to be seen as part of a much larger process of 'receiving' women's ordination within the worldwide Church as a whole.

---

[1] G.R. Evans, *The Reception of the Faith: Reinterpreting the Gospel for Today* (SPCK, London, 1997), pp. viii–ix. For an alternative, shorter introduction to the concept, see: William G. Rusch, 'The Landscape of Reception' in Paul Avis (ed.), *Seeking the Truth of Change in the Church: Reception, Communion and the Ordination of Women* (T & T Clark, London, 2004), pp. 1–18.

[2] Thomas Rausch, quoted in Martyn Percy, 'The Doctrine of Reception and Division in the Church' (unpublished paper, n.d.), p. 1.

[3] Günther Gassmann, 'From Reception to Unity: The Historical and Ecumenical Significance of the Concept of Reception' in Colin Podmore (ed.), *Community – Unity – Communion: Essays in Honour of Mary Tanner* (Church House Publishing, London, 1998), pp. 117–129.

[4] Quoted in: General Synod GS Misc 418, *Being in Communion* (Church House, London, 1993), para. 18.

[5] *Eames Monitoring Group Report, August 1997*, pp. 1–13.
[http://www.anglicancommunion.org/lambeth/reports/report10.html, downloaded 2 October 2003]

Moreover, the need to allow space for this 'open process of discernment' became an important underpinning for the Act of Synod.[6]

However, the elucidation of 'reception' given in official Anglican reports did not mean that all were agreed (or happy) with what reception meant in theory or in practice. These differences of opinion were amply demonstrated when, in November 1989, the General Synod came to debate the draft legislation. Was reception in fact a way of justifying any new thing that came along? Debate participant Fr Richard Oakley voiced the concerns of many traditionalists in warning against 'this strange and novel doctrine that is now in vogue, that a small group can make an isolated change that the rest of the Church will later catch up and agree to what has been done unilaterally'.[7] In contrast, Archbishop John Habgood, one of the main architects of the legislation, responded that this 'period of discernment'[8] meant 'no more than the traditional recognition that councils of the Church can and do err'. However, whilst acknowledging the room for error, he nevertheless insisted that a 'process of reception' did not make women's orders provisional. Instead, it was important to allow women's ordination to be received by the whole Church because 'we do not claim freedom from error; we do not unchurch those who disagree with us'.[9]

But did this mean that the 'period of discernment' was taking place before the vote, or that women's priesthood could only be received once it had become an ecclesial reality? Timothy Bavin, then Bishop of Portsmouth, insisted 'It will not do to speak of reception after ordinations have taken place …its sacramental nature means that it cannot be undone if it does not work […] I do not believe that it is unreasonable to ask for longer for the process of reception, and to see whether or not this be of God'.[10] However, for George Austin, then Archdeacon of York, 'reception' was best understood as 'a pious belief that gradually gained ground, and when there was fairly full and comprehensive acceptance… it became a dogma […]'. For him 'reception' merely seemed to mean 'not making the decision and then gradually hoping that everyone comes into agreement'.[11]

A further question related to whether 'reception' could be time-limited. The draft measure had originally contained a twenty-year expiry date[12] on the opt-out 'safeguards' for those who opposed it, but for the Revd John Broadhurst, now Bishop of Fulham, 'to be provisional has to be to enter into an open-ended process. When we look at this legislation, what is provisional in it? Not the process, not the issue of women priests, which is written in like tablets of stone, never to be changed'.[13] Eventually, the steering committee invited Synod to reject the twenty-year time limit, though adding that 'this does not mean that we envisage the safeguards as existing for ever; they remain, in our view, temporary and interim arrangements'.[14] Did this mean reception created space to move towards consensus over women's priesting? Or did it simply give doubters a chance to catch up with what had been decided, leaving traditionalists feeling (as one speaker in the 1989 debate suggested)

---

[6] See: *Being in Communion* and also: General Synod GS1074, 'Bonds of Peace' in *Ordination of Women to the Priesthood: Pastoral Arrangements* (Church House, London, 1993).

[7] General Synod, November Group of Sessions, 1989, *Report of Proceedings* 20 (3) (General Synod, London, 1989), p. 988.

[8] His preferred phrase.

[9] November Group of Sessions, 1989, pp. 1009–11.

[10] November Group of Sessions 1989, p. 1008.

[11] November Group of Sessions 1989, p. 1238.

[12] Although it was also proposed that this could be extended by a simple vote of Synod.

[13] November Group of Sessions, 1989, pp. 1136–7.

[14] Peter Forster, November Group of Sessions, 1989, pp. 1236. Although this was the opinion of the steering group, the Measure remains law until such time as it is repealed.

like '…a carbuncle on the Church of England and that reception means that you can tie a piece of string round the carbuncle and slowly tighten it until we pop off'?[15]

Table 8i: Clergy's levels of agreement with nine statements on the theological idea of 'reception' (overall figure for clergy samples[16])			
Reception is…	**SA/A**	**NAND**	**D/DS**
Sufficient time and space in which those who have misgivings about the Church's decision to ordain women to the priesthood can be reconciled to what was decided in 1992	64.2	13.0	22.8
An acknowledgement that we cannot yet be sure that ordaining women to the priesthood is definitely the will of God for the Church	20.5	6.9	72.6
A concept created by theologians to justify the currently divided nature of the Church of England	44.7	22.9	32.4
A period in which we wait to see whether the Roman Catholic and Orthodox Churches also move towards ordaining women to the priesthood	19.6	18.7	61.7
A theological/theoretical framework to allow people of different positions on the ordination of women to remain within the same church	59.4	20.7	19.9
An acknowledgement that the final decision over the ordination of women to the priesthood can only be made as part of a wider process of discernment by the whole Church; not just Anglicans	21.8	12.6	65.7
An acknowledgement that the ordination of women to the priesthood may well be reversible	15.3	5.0	79.8
An acknowledgement that ideas on faith and order that begin life as minority opinions may gradually come to be recognized as the will of God for the Church	50.4	19.8	22.4
A concept with no useful meaning whatsoever	37.2	22.7	40

'Reception' has regularly been discussed amongst church leaders and campaigners on all sides of the debate ever since – notably in debates over the Act of Synod, which extended the opt-out provisions available to clergy and their congregations. But was 'reception' a powerful concept for enabling a greater degree of communion across difference, or a way of avoiding making a final decision that would risk alienating one group or another? And how widespread was support for the concept, across the Church of England? In an attempt to gauge the wider response to the idea of a period of reception for women's priesting, the Clergy Questionnaire included two questions on the subject, one open-ended and the other requiring clergy to indicate their level of agreement with nine possible statements on the subject. **Table 8i** summarizes the closed-answer responses.

The most striking feature of the results is that only three of the nine statements receive support from a majority of respondents, suggesting little common agreement amongst clergy over what 'reception' might actually mean in this context. Whether this is encouraging or not depends on one's standpoint: the fact that only 15% of the sample believed reception meant women's priesting might be reversible may (on one hand) suggest a significant minority of clergy who think the move is provisional, or (on the other hand) that even some of those who disagreed with the 1992 decision accept that women are here to stay as Church of England priests/presbyters. Likewise, that 37% of the sample thought reception had 'no useful meaning whatsoever' might give encouragement to those who

---

[15] November Group of Sessions, 1989, p. 1264.

[16] Each statement was considered by between 352 and 362 respondents, varying from one to another.

think the concept has been unhelpful (more than one in three is a substantial number), or might alternatively afford proponents of the concept some reassurance (a clear majority believe the idea is not irrelevant to the acceptance of women's priestly orders).

What happens if the responses of different groups of clergy are compared? Amongst both men and women, 'reception' was most likely to suggest time and space to become reconciled to the decision, a framework to allow the different views to coexist and an acknowledgement that sometimes new or minority beliefs come to be recognized as God's will for the Church. Ordained women (being more uniformly in favour of women's priesting) particularly tended to see reception as a time of adjustment, or as a meaningless concept, and were much less favourable towards those statements that suggested that women's orders were provisional, or that their final acceptance depended on some new revelation from God or greater consensus throughout the worldwide Church. However, generally, the difference of opinion between female clergy and male colleagues who were supportive of their ministry was slight, the latter being only slightly more likely to agree with most of the statements. However, if the results are broken down according to respondents' *current* views on the 1992 decision, the value of the statements becomes more hotly contested. Those in agreement with women's priesting are more likely to be more sceptical about most of the statements, whilst those who are uncertain about the decision, or disagreed/strongly disagreed with it, are more likely to agree with more of the statements. As **Table 8ii** suggests, there are particular differences over the statement that reception provides a time of adjustment, and over the idea that it acknowledges that God's will is not yet known on the question. Even so, the fact that clergy were quite evenly divided over most of the statements[17] strongly suggests a high degree of ambivalence or difference amongst clergy over the concept as a whole.

---

[17] Most of the statements attracted between 33% and 66% support from the total clergy sample.

Table 8ii: Clergy attitudes to the use of the concept of 'reception' in the ordination of women debate, comparing support for the terminology amongst those of differing views on women's ordination as priests (amongst total clergy sample[18])
[Column SA/A = agreement with the statement amongst clergy agreeing/strongly agreeing with women as priests]
[Column NAND = agreement with the statement amongst clergy who neither agree nor disagree with women as priests]
[Column D/DS = agreement with the statement amongst clergy who disagree/strongly disagree with women as priests]

Reception is...	SA/A	NAND	D/DS
Sufficient time and space in which those who have misgivings about the Church's decision to ordain women to the priesthood can be reconciled to what was decided in 1992	73.4	50.0	14.3
An acknowledgement that we cannot yet be sure that ordaining women to the priesthood is definitely the will of God for the Church	10.0	80.0	71.4
A concept created by theologians to justify the currently divided nature of the Church of England	41.2	80.0	63.6
A period in which we wait to see whether the Roman Catholic and Orthodox Churches also move towards ordaining women to the priesthood	14.6	50.0	42.0
A theological/theoretical framework to allow people of different positions on the ordination of women to remain within the same church	60.7	80.0	49.0
An acknowledgement that the final decision over the ordination of women to the priesthood can only be made as part of a wider process of discernment by the whole Church; not just Anglicans	12.5	70.0	66.0
An acknowledgement that the ordination of women to the priesthood may well be reversible	7.4	30.0	61.2
An acknowledgement that ideas on faith and order that begin life as minority opinions may gradually come to be recognized as the will of God for the Church	56.5	40.0	46.3
A concept with no useful meaning whatsoever	35.9	50.0	40.8

This plurality of views on 'reception' was also evident from the open-ended answers. For one thing, it was commonly suggested that whilst the concept contained a kernel of valid theological thinking, 'reception' often meant something quite different in practice: 'Parishes are experiencing women as priests, and that period of reception is a period of acceptance. However, it is also a classic Anglican "fudge"',[19] wrote one male curate from Diocese C. A male incumbent from the same diocese suggested that reception 'should mean being open to the possibility of reversing the decision; it seems to mean the time it takes to eliminate the opposition'.[20] As these two views suggest, the idea of a 'period of reception' had political implications as well as theological[21] implications (for example, those with objections to women's priesting could complain that on one hand 'reception' had been a useful tool for bishops wanting to encourage traditionalists to stay on board after 1992. On the other hand, objectors to women's priesting could also enlist the concept of 'reception' in defence of extended episcopal oversight). This ambivalence towards the concept *within* each

---

[18] The total sample size varied between 334 and 353 respondents to each statement. The SA/A column is derived from between 279 and 294 respondents; the NAND column is based on the replies of 10 respondents; the D/DS column is derived from between 45 and 49 respondents (sometimes participants omitted to respond to particular statements).
[19] CQ398, male curate 30–39, Diocese C.
[20] CQ315, male incumbent 40–49, Diocese C.
[21] Insofar as 'political' and 'theological' were separate spheres at all.

constituency should also remind us that differences of opinion over the 'period of reception' do not neatly reflect the dividing lines over the question of women as priests.

In the open-ended responses, the most common suggestion by far was that a period of discernment allowed time to reflect, take stock of the decision that had been taken, and become reconciled to it: 'some people still hold entrenched positions on both sides', wrote one female vicar; 'we are living in a period of adjustment for those who feel able to move forward'.[22] One male vicar agreed that 'it has given me time to adjust to the Synod vote'.[23] However, those with objections to women's priesting usually rejected this interpretation and its implication that doubters simply needed to catch up with the correct step the Church had already taken. For many of these, it was far from clear that this was the case: 'I'm not sure the Church of England *has* said that [women] are priests. The Church of England, it has said well, we're not sure ... until it's been *received*'.[24] Several interviewees who were closely involved in the process of drafting the legislation refuted this interpretation, insisting that reception in no sense made women's orders provisional. As one remarked:

> *I would say a legitimate place is provided for those who dissent from a decision made by the Church of England, but that the mind of the Church of England, as expressed in law, is that we ordain women, full stop. [...]*

> [IJ: Does that, then, make women's priesting an optional extra?]

> *No it doesn't; it's the other way round because the majority of parishes in the dioceses accept women as priests, every bishop accepts women as priests, the law accepts women as priests, but there is a possibility of opting out of this on conscientious grounds.*[25]

Certainly ordained women themselves were particularly keen to counter the suggestion that the validity of their priesthood was in any way dependent upon a process of reception. Several expressed their suspicions that reception had become a gendered concept:

> *this isn't the first change the Church has undergone, and that the Church already has a theology of change – or certainly ought to have – the break with the Church of Rome, or whatever – that's a change, and that was handled without 'reception' ... You don't say, 'oh, let's have a period of reception for Common Worship'...*[26]

To many clergy who were supportive of women's priesting, talk about reception seemed to indicate a lack of official or institutional confidence in the step the Church of England had taken. Some even suggested that it represented indecisive or cowardly leadership. However, amongst those who defended the pluralistic nature of the 1992–94 settlement, a period of discernment or reception was vital to avoiding the schism and legal wrangling that had taken place in the Episcopal Church of the USA over women's ordination. John Habgood's comments on p. 178 also convey the strong conviction amongst many of the bishops of the day that a time of discernment and reflection was important not just for pastoral reasons but also because this was an authentically Anglican, and more civilized, way of working than simply 'unchurching those who disagree with us'. But amongst the current clergy sample, a

---

[22] CQ83, female vicar 50–59, Diocese A.
[23] CQ309, male incumbent 40–49, Diocese C.
[24] int. 3:p.3.
[25] int. 12side2:425.
[26] int. cs4:7:317.

large measure of disagreement and confusion remained as to what 'reception' really meant. If nothing else, there was widespread uncertainty across the different constituencies as to how 'reception' would actually be measured. Indeed here, differences between those 'for' and 'against' women's priesting were often less important than a division between those who found the idea of a 'period of reception' problematic and wanted a new kind of settlement in place, and those who found it more useful and wished to see the settlement remain in place for the foreseeable future. The following two views (first from a leading member of Reform, the second from a leading member of Watch), both express doubt about the measurability of the concept whilst the third view (from a diocesan bishop) seeks to answer those criticisms:

> *Who is going to decide that [women's ordination as presbyters] is received? Is it going to be some bigwigs up in Canterbury or York? I mean, who's going to decide this?*[27]

> *The dangerous thing about it is that it's not defined – we've provided no criteria saying 'OK, it's not received now'.... [Reception] is not studied ambiguity; it's sloppiness.*[28]

> *I don't see the process of reception as a reduction of objections, but as a growth of conviction [...] What I sense here in this diocese is that people have moved from saying they'll accept women's ministry, to having a conviction that it's right and true and good and reflects something about the way God includes all in his ministry...*[29]

Indeed, if this last definition of 'reception' is to be taken, then Chapters 2 and 3 strongly suggest that this 'growth of conviction' is already well under way. Several observers found John Habgood's advocacy of the 'Gamaliel Principle'[30] very useful, and suggesting that if women's priesting really was of God, it would bear fruit. In the view of the majority of participants in the current research – and despite the division that the debate had caused – women's ministry as priests was certainly bearing fruit.

8.2 The short-term future

The concept of 'reception' was important in giving a theological underpinning to the 1992–94 settlement[31] and the bishops' commitment to 'maintain the integrity of both positions'.[32] Somewhat misleadingly, this bequeathed the idea to popular Anglican phraseology that the Church was henceforth divided into 'the two integrities'.[33] But whilst the use of this term is both linguistically and philosophically problematic, it remains important to consider how far the different views and constituencies (however defined) have been able to coexist over the first ten years of the present arrangement. The partial confusion over the terms of the

---

[27] int. 3:p.7.

[28] int. 9side2:421fwd.

[29] int. 13:460.

[30] cf. Acts 5:34–40.

[31] Although it also made an appeal to 'comprehensiveness' as a key part of an authentically Anglican methodology.

[32] *Being in Communion*, para. 23.

[33] Interestingly, Mary Tanner notes that the original Manchester Statement by the House of Bishops contained more nuanced language, expressing the belief that 'differing views about the ordination of women to the priesthood can continue to be held with integrity' (House of Bishops, 'Statement by the House following its Meeting in Manchester' 11–14 January 1993, p. 2). See: Mary Tanner, 'The Episcopal Ministry Act of Synod in Context' in Avis (ed.), *Seeking the Truth of Change in the Church'*, pp. 58–74 (p. 70).

'period of reception' might be taken to imply that the current settlement was in danger of becoming increasingly unviable. But was this the case? First of all, it is important to recognize the strength of forces working for the maintenance of the status quo. As Chapter 4 (on the parish experience) and Chapter 6 (on cooperation amongst clergy) suggested, much of the tension and ill-feeling that surrounded the immediate aftermath of the vote had dissipated as the 1990s wore on. 86% of those resigning under the 1993 Financial Provisions Measure after the vote had left by the end of 1996.[34] Many senior diocesan clergy and campaign networks from the different constituencies invested considerable effort into enabling individuals to move beyond the vote and turn their attention to the everyday business of ministry. As has already been suggested, many lay people, and even some clergy, remained largely unaware of the unresolved issues considered in Part II of this report. Even many clergy reported that life was now very much 'business as usual': one curate from Diocese D observed that 'the issue just hasn't come up, which of course the Church of England's brilliant at – you just drift along with your "two integrities" – and I guess to a large extent that's how it's worked so far'.[35] This speaker's diocesan bishop also remarked on how seldom issues surrounding the 1992–94 settlement called for his adjudication. Indeed, he often found it difficult to tell whether the real source of the disagreement was a tension over women's ministry or over the opt-out 'safeguards', or over some other issue.[36] Differences over the women priests settlement often simply overlay existing divisions.

Here, it is possible that something of the historic character of the Church of England contributed to the lessening of tension. Some saw the Church's strength as lying in its breadth; as one interviewee from Diocese A remarked, 'the Church of England should be used to working with people and disagreeing'.[37] The viability of the coexistence project perhaps also benefited from the parochial focus to Anglican life that (as Alan Aldridge has noted[38]) tended to keep clergy and active laity occupied with local church activities rather than national structures, but also allowed parish clergy to avoid other clergy with different views if they so chose. Parish life was also already full: 'we're very parochial here, really because we're so busy looking after our own affairs', reflected one member of Church 3; 'we don't take a lot of time to notice what's going on elsewhere. Its had very little impact up here'.[39] Some clergy also said that whilst they were unhappy with the settlement as it currently stood, there was a certain amount of peer pressure (particularly from senior diocesan colleagues) that discouraged protest. Several ordained women in particular remembered being encouraged 'to hold this together, not to be radical, not to speak up, not to rock the boat, two integrities, we've all got to bind ourselves into each other ...'[40] For more experienced female clergy, however, this brought back memories of the 1980s, and the way in which exhortations to wait patiently for ordination as deacons and priests seemed sometimes to function as a delaying tactic.[41] Even so, many ordained women and their supporters continued to wait patiently (as suggested below, the immediate viability of the 1992–94 settlement may have been bolstered by the fact that only a proportion of clergy seemed to be calling for immediate change). In many places, a studied discretion also played its part in maintaining stability. One priest from Diocese D remarked that:

---

[34] Based on figures provided in: Archbishop's Council Ministry Division GS Misc 721, *Statistics of Licensed Ministers 2002* (Church House, London, 2003), p. 32.
[35] int. cs4:1side2:387.
[36] int. cs4:9:8.
[37] int. cs1:12:415.
[38] Alan Aldridge, 'Discourse on Women in the Clerical Profession: The Diaconate and Language-games in the Church of England', *Sociology* 26 (1), February 1992, pp. 45–57 (pp. 54–5).
[39] int. cs1:7:221.
[40] int. cs3:8:300.
[41] Aldridge, 'Discourse on Women in the Clerical Profession', p. 52.

> *the question's never raised, that's my perception; you know that it sort of simmers away underneath somewhere, but you don't know what anybody else thinks, it's never raised, so you don't talk about it, so you just do everything else. You might call it a classic Anglican fudge, I suppose – I don't know what it is, but it seems to work rather well.*[42]

There was particular awareness that the Act of Synod had contributed to the ease with which day-to-day tension could be avoided, although here, many supporters of women's priesting disappointedly expressed the conviction that this had been achieved not by encouraging reconciliation but by formalizing a gulf between constituencies:

> *the two integrities were put up so that the sides could work together, and what has actually happened is that it's driven the wedge further in ... because we're not working together and not making an attempt to understand what's going on.*[43]

In this sense, many believed that whilst the settlement allowed a definite measure of coexistence, the active and positive engagement required for true process of reception to take place was often absent. As one bishop who did not ordain women observed, 'people have got into a kind of laager mentality and are not talking about the issue; so reception has not resulted in continuing dialogue – which has actually resulted in people staying where they were, really – on either side, for that matter'.[44]

However, if a sense of 'business as usual' and a lack of communication or engagement provided a 'negative' pressure towards the maintenance of the current settlement, there was also much evidence of active cooperation, as Chapters 4 and 6 have suggested. This contributed to a widespread acknowledgement that some positive steps were being taken to make the present arrangements work. 'I was ordained and eventually "priested" while in one of the most "traditional" deaneries in a "traditional" diocese', wrote one female priest from Diocese A; 'We all survived and remained almost entirely on friendly terms. I have not yet found a serious problem coexisting'.[45] One female curate (who confessed she would once have 'raised merry hell' over any concession to traditionalists) explained how in her current parish, she had met parishioners struggling to accept women's priesting in conscience but 'I would never have known, the way they behaved'. Whilst she felt angry at the rudeness she had encountered in some quarters at theological college, she felt that one's view on women's priesting was ultimately irrelevant if disagreement was handled with respect.[46] Several interviewees offered examples from their own experience of how a colleague or fellow churchgoer they had expected to find difficult turned out to be friendly and cooperative. In one sense we should expect nothing less, but in the light of some of the difficulties of the early 1990s, this was certainly progress. Indeed, part of the problem seems to have been the expectation that relationships across the different constituencies *would* be problematic. Correspondingly, some suggested that at least to some extent, division between the different constituencies was more real than imagined: 'there is perceived to be a greater degree of polarization than there actually is', wrote Church 8's male priest; 'the biggest problem in the whole thing is that it breeds a sense of suspicion'.[47] A number of senior clergy were also quite firm in their view that maintaining the present

---

[42] int. cs2:4side2:287.
[43] int. cs1:25:283.
[44] int. cs4:9side2:585.
[45] CQ8, female priest-in-charge, 40–49.
[46] int. cs4:7side2:490.
[47] int. cs3:11:319.

settlement was the best way forward for the Church of England. The evidence offered here thus suggests that the 1992–94 settlement was far from being in imminent danger of collapse.

That said, if the present arrangements were not generally seen as immediately unviable, they were perhaps seen as increasingly anomalous. Some argued that the 'safeguards' were now superfluous because the process of reception over the first decade had been so successful. For the majority however, change was needed because of certain shortcomings in the current framework. For some, this anomaly was habitable provided the Church was moving forward. As one bishop explained:

> *the Orthodox use the notion of 'economy', for arrangements which are ... alright, as long as we know the direction in which we're going. But really if you start looking at them as a stable state, they're not very satisfactory or very tidy, so this is not envisaged as a stable state; this has been a process ...*[48]

However, many interviewees also perceived some hardening of attitudes in recent years, which seemed to threaten continued coexistence. Some thought that over-familiarity with the arrangements had perhaps led to some loss of sensitivity when dealing with those of differing views. Others expressed a loss of patience with the other 'constituency': one respondent wrote that 'we were asked by our then bishop to ... "lie low". We have done this – but I'm now feeling increasingly angry [about] ... the treatment of women by those against, esp. by members of FiF'.[49] Indeed, 30.7% of respondents in Thorne's survey of the first generation of women to be priested reported feeling a similar pressure to stay silent.[50] Several interviewees (on all sides) expressed frustration that they had 'bent over backwards' (a common phrase) to accommodate others of different views and found their efforts apparently rebuffed. For others, the 1992–94 settlement seemed increasingly anomalous not so much because of negative personal experiences, but because of a more general conviction that it was not, ultimately, going to solve anything. 'In my view, how long can you go on holding this?' asked one experienced observer of Anglicanism from Church 1; 'it seems to me as though you're only putting off the 'evil day' – it may be a kindness to a lot of people, but you're not solving anything'.[51]

8.3 Four responses to 'anomaly'

An important underlying theme of this report has been that differences of opinion between 'supporters' and 'opponents' of women's priesting were not always hard and fast divisions, and quite frequently not the most important lines of response either. As this chapter has already hinted, this was also true of respondents' views of the future shape of the coexistence project. Supporters of women's priesting and those who could not accept it could often be heard calling for an end to the present arrangements (albeit for very different reasons and often with different ends in mind) whilst defenders of the legislation included both those who voted for women's ordination as priests, and those who voted against it. If the crude categories of 'supporters' and 'opponents' are therefore too simplistic to understand the range of response to the future, what other, more appropriate, framework can be found? One possible approach begins with the common description of the 1992–94 settlement as 'anomalous'. This is not intended as a pejorative term, but is simply meant to convey the point that the settlement introduced an element of the unfamiliar and the

---

[48] int. cs5:15:118.
[49] CQ36, female incumbent, 50–59.
[50] Helen Thorne, *Journey to Priesthood: An In-depth Study of the First Women Priests in the Church of England* (University of Bristol, Bristol, 2000), p. 130.
[51] int. cs1:21:480.

unresolved into Anglican life and ecclesiology.[52] This sense of anomaly was implicitly or explicitly common to many views of the debate on women as priests. Many implied that in an ideal world, the Church would either reach a consensus that it was right to ordain women as priests and would do so, or that the consensus would be against, and it would not. The arrangement bequeathed by the 1993 Measure and Act of Synod fell somewhere in the middle: the Church had made a decision but consensus had not yet been reached and some questions remained unresolved.[53] Different groups tended to identify the source of the anomaly in different places: for the 'traditionalist' constituency, the anomaly was women's ordination as priests; amongst many campaigners for ordained women, the chief anomaly was the Act of Synod. But in a very important sense, the whole settlement itself could be regarded as 'anomalous': it was not a settled part of Anglican order but something provisional, and certainly something unfamiliar that required 'reception' by the Church of England. But how should this anomaly be resolved?

Here, the work of anthropologist Mary Douglas and subsequent work by sociologist Alan Aldridge offer one useful way of reading respondents' views of the future. In her 1966 work *Purity and Danger*,[54] Douglas proposes that responses to the unfamiliar, the unresolved or the anomalous are too complex to be understood simply in terms of acceptance or rejection. (To offer a contemporary illustration, it would be wrong to suggest that some churches 'embrace the modern world' whilst others are entirely anti-cultural. All religious cultures blend both acceptance and rejection of certain elements of contemporary culture, with church life a blend of both the 'traditional' and the 'modern'. For example, churches that reject many contemporary moral and ethical standards are nevertheless amongst the most likely to employ modern styles of worship or aspects of technology in their services. Many congregations where modern science or morality are accepted with little questioning are also amongst the most resistant to 'updating' their worship.) Douglas suggests that instead of a simple bipolar model of acceptance or rejection, social tension over an anomaly may be resolved in several different ways. She lists five: either by a) incorporating the anomaly as a new category into an existing system of thought, b) eliminating the anomaly so that it no longer poses a threat, c) avoiding the anomaly, thus reinforcing the existing system, d) labelling the anomaly as dangerous so as to negate the need to engage with it, or e) regarding the anomaly as a pointer towards something sacred.[55] Adopting David Bloor's synthesis of these responses to anomaly and the 'grid and group' approach to social analysis pioneered by Douglas in her subsequent book *Natural Symbols*,[56] Alan Aldridge has developed a four-fold framework of response to anomaly that allows for more subtle analysis of responses than a crude two-fold typology that expects individuals and groups either to 'accept' or 'reject' the new phenomenon.[57] This is reproduced in **Figure 8iii**.

---

[52] The relevance of this concept (discussed at the 1998 Lambeth Conference) has also recently been noted in: Paul Avis, 'The Episcopal Ministry Act of Synod 1993: A "Bearable Anomaly"?' in Avis (ed.), *Seeking the Truth of Change in the Church*, pp. 152–69.

[53] This tallies with Paul Avis' recent suggestion that the key question for the Anglican debate on reception is what it means to have 'a formal decision within an open process' (Paul Avis, 'Reception: Towards an Anglican Understanding' in Avis (ed., *Seeking the Truth of Change in the Church*, pp. 19-39 (p. 25).).

[54] Mary Douglas, *Purity and Danger; An Analysis of the Concepts of Pollution and Taboo* (Routledge and Kegan Paul, London, 1966).

[55] Douglas, *Purity and Danger*, pp. 37–40.

[56] Mary Douglas, *Natural Symbols* (Barrie and Rockliff/The Cresset, London, 1970), pp. 59–60.

[57] Aldridge, 'Discourse on Women in the Clerical Profession', pp. 45–57; David Bloor, *Wittgenstein; A Social Theory of Knowledge* (Macmillan, London and Basingstoke, 1983), pp. 140–45.

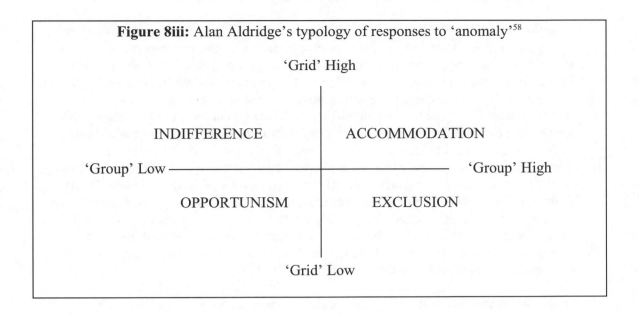

Figure 8iii: Alan Aldridge's typology of responses to 'anomaly'[58]

'Grid' High

INDIFFERENCE   ACCOMMODATION

'Group' Low ————————————————— 'Group' High

OPPORTUNISM   EXCLUSION

'Grid' Low

According to this framework of understanding, the two key variables in a response to any 'anomalous' situation are 1) the boundaries within a group, its internal cohesion, and the need for/willingness of members to be allotted specific roles (the 'grid') and 2) the boundaries between the group and the outside (the 'group' dimension). Where 'grid' is 'high', this implies a strong impulse towards the incorporation of new elements or individuals into a strong internal framework. Where 'grid' is 'low', this dimension is not of primary importance. Where 'group' is 'high', collective identity is important and where it is 'low' the boundaries of the group are more porous. If Aldridge's resulting four categories are outlined briefly:

- **'Exclusion'** sees the boundary between 'insiders' and 'outsiders' as of primary importance. The 'anomaly' is perceived as a serious threat to the purity of the group.
- **'Accommodation'** also treats the boundary between 'group' and 'not group' as important, but is more open to accommodating the anomalous, and can often positively incorporate and celebrate difference within the group.
- **'Opportunism'**, in Aldridge's words, 'implies a selective welcome to any anomalies that are calculated to be advantageous'.[59] As such, neither internal nor external roles and boundaries require strict maintenance.
- **'Indifference'** demands no active response to the anomalous, which is not seen to require either integration or expulsion. The existing order of things can continue seemingly unaffected by the presence of the anomalous and unthreatened by it.

These four categories must be handled carefully: they do not constitute labels for particular groups ('the exclusivists', 'the indifferent', etc.); nor do individuals' views fall exclusively into one category or another, or remain static over time. Instead, the four types represent the 'poles' of the debate, with individual attitudes triangulated and renegotiated between them. In Aldridge's original article, the 'anomaly' in question was the growing body of pressure for women's ordination as deacons. But what happens if this typology of response to anomaly is applied not to women's priesting, but to the 1992–94 settlement as a whole?

---

[58] Aldridge, 'Discourse on Women in the Clerical Profession', p. 54.
[59] Aldridge, 'Discourse on Women in the Clerical Profession', p. 55.

To begin from the most fully developed manifestation of each response:

I   '**Exclusionism**' may denote the view that, whatever one's position on the rights and wrongs of women's ordination, the Church can only admit to one version of the truth of the matter. If it is right that women should be ordained as priests, they should also become bishops and the safeguards afforded to opponents should be removed to tackle the final vestiges of discrimination. If women's priesting is not right, women should not be ordained, and the Church should either reverse its decision or provide a 'safe space' for advocates of an all-male priesthood away from the heretical mainstream. Either way, a 'pure' exclusionist response regards the 1992–94 settlement as anomalous because it appears to prize a hollow unity at the expense of truth. Although they have very different agendas, the official views of both GRAS and Forward in Faith could be said to tend towards the 'exclusionist' pole. Neither group would wish deliberately to unchurch those that disagree with the position, but both were formed on the premise that the current settlement is ultimately unsustainable, and the logical conclusion of both positions is that the opposing view should either change their minds, outwardly conform, or leave the Church of England.

II In the '**accommodationist**' view, the settlement is regarded not as a threat but an opportunity, and holding together the different positions on women's priesting within the same church is regarded as a positive virtue. Here, an 'accommodationist' argument might enlist the tradition of Anglican comprehensiveness in support of its position. An 'accommodationist' response would regard any attempt to push for women in the episcopate or a third 'traditionalist' province as a dangerous threat to that balance, and would lead to an impoverished Church. (In this sense, 'accommodationism' may become 'exclusionist' towards anything that would upset the equilibrium). 'Accommodation' is perhaps most clearly shown by the official reports of the House of Bishops and their collective actions. A number of its leading thinkers have, over the past ten years, insisted that the Act of Synod has not only been a necessary response to the Church's divisions over women's priesting, but also a theologically sustainable example of how those who disagree can nevertheless continue to live in communion together. Within the Bishops' Meeting, individuals hold a range of different opinions on the fundamental issue of women as priests and bishops, but as a group it has nevertheless decided to set those differences aside in an attempt to hold the Church together.[60]

III '**Opportunism**' frequently has negative connotations in the English language but here should not be taken to mean a lack of principle or belief. Many people have strong views on women's priesting but reject the idea that these principles must be implemented immediately (or alternatively, reject the suggestion that action should only be taken when the group reaches a complete consensus). In the 'opportunist' view, the 1992–94 settlement is clearly felt to be anomalous, but may be the 'least worst' option whilst the Church recovers from a damaging split. However such a settlement is regarded as having only pragmatic, rather than intrinsic, virtue. Whilst an attempt to move the debate on in one's preferred direction (either 'for' or 'against' women in the episcopate) is in the long-term desirable, an 'opportunist' response waits for the right moment. This position might be reflected in those (on all sides of the debate) who have accepted the coexistence project and the idea of 'reception' as a pastoral necessity but wish to see the Church move towards women in the episcopate (or, alternatively, towards a more distinct ecclesial community for 'traditionalists') when conditions are propitious.

---

[60] Bishops do not universally agree on this either, but this has been the dominant collective approach.

IV   Finally, '**indifference**' might be to regard the settlement (and any attempt to modify or rescind it) as an irrelevance to the current business of ministry and mission. An individual whose response is characterized primarily by indifference may well have an opinion on the matter of women in the episcopate, the future of the Act of Synod, or the creation of a third province, but does not regard any of these as sufficiently important to be personally and actively engaging prospects. The anomaly of the Church's current position can safely be ignored. 'Indifference' does not figure as the official response of any particular church group but is to be found in various places across the Church of England – particularly in the attitudes of some individuals.

Conclusion

Each of the above tendencies were evident amongst the clergy and laity samples featured in the current research, but what groups and individuals tended towards which pole(s), and what could be said to be the *dominant* response to the 1992–94 settlement? Did a majority wish to see an end to the coexistence project as currently constituted, and a one-clause measure on women as priests and bishops? Did a commitment to fairness, comprehensiveness and ecclesiological pluralism mean widespread support for the continuation of the present legislation and the delay of any change until consensus had been reached? Were the majority of clergy and laity biding their time until the right moment occurred to campaign for change? Or did most simply remain indifferent to the respective claims of the different groups seeking to lead the debate? To address these questions, the final chapter turns to consider attitudes towards the Episcopal Ministry Act of Synod itself, and the prospect of women in the episcopate of the Church of England.

Before doing so however, it is worth returning to the question posed at the beginning of the chapter: if the settlement currently in place is in some senses a temporary solution, how is the Church of England to tackle the business of change? This question has an important practical dimension to it, but also deep theological roots: the Christian faith is strongly eschatological – it accepts the reality of historical change and indeed sees divine direction in history. The Bible emphasizes the fleeting nature of earthly things but holds out hope of a sure direction to history and a moment when God will 'make all things new'. But how then should Christians engage with the reality of intellectual and cultural change, whilst seeking to remain faithful to the foundations laid down by Jesus and his earliest followers? How are new developments to be incorporated into an ancient faith, and situated theologically with the much longer story of God? One answer to this question has been the concept of 'reception', which has sought to emphasize the need for a critical incorporation of new theological insights. But when applied to the question of women's priesting, clergy expressed some ambivalence about the relevance of the concept, and thereby questioned one of the key theological foundations of the 1992–94 settlement. If 'reception' is to be regarded as relevant and important to the contemporary situation, much harder work is required to explain the Christian credentials of the concept. However, if 'reception' is to be discarded, how can the Church develop a better theological understanding of change, and of the continued revelation of unchanging truths in times of constant flux?

Chapter 9

Women bishops, the Act of Synod and the future

The current situation is not logical. If there is a case for women to become priests, then it must allow them to progress as their skills merit.
(LQ443, male, 70-79, Church 22)

If women have the right to become priests, they should also have the right to become bishops, although I can see that this could cause further problems in the Church.
(LQ482, female, 50-59, Church 19)

This will be even more divisive and the validity of ordination will become more obscure.
(LQ366, female, 70-79, 17)

I think you can see the Act of Synod as the most wonderful thing the Church of England ever did, in order to keep people together, or the biggest mistake the Church of England ever made, and should expel people by the bucketful.
(Bishop of Deanery D)

By the last years of the twentieth century, an organized campaign for the ordination of women as bishops had begun to coalesce. Hot on its heels came calls from Church of England 'traditionalists' who could not accept women's priesting for a third, non-geographical province that admitted only men to the priesthood. Neither argument was new (indeed, both pre-dated the 1992 vote), but both became more prominent and the subject of organized campaigns. But how far did the mass of clergy and laity themselves demand or expect an episcopate open to both men and women? How widespread were calls for a more autonomous jurisdiction for those who wished to retain a male-only priesthood? What were the acceptable limits of diversity within the Church of England felt to be? And at what price to the provisions of the Measure and Act of Synod were these to be maintained?

This final chapter explores interviewees' responses to these questions about the future. As with Chapter 8, the raw material for this task is necessarily speculative, and should be read in the context of its time: most of the research for this report was conducted before the announcement of Rowan Williams as the new Archbishop of Canterbury, before the issue of ordaining 'practising' homosexuals was blown into the national and international spotlight, and whilst the Bishop of Rochester's working party on women and episcopate was embarking on its work. Clergy and lay attitudes to women as bishops and the Act of Synod were clearly shaped by the uncertainty of this period, and views may well be different again now. This chapter does not attempt to second-guess the future. Nor, most importantly, does it attempt to prejudge the work of the Rochester working party. For one thing, the focus of the working party is primarily theological, while this report is written from the standpoint of contemporary history and social research. Therefore rather than providing a theological evaluation of the arguments for women as bishops, the chapter seeks to investigate the actual climate of opinion amongst grass roots clergy and laity and explore some of the key considerations shaping their views of what the next step should be.

9.1 Women in the episcopate

At the beginning of the twentieth century, the debate on women's ministry focused on the role of lay women as pastoral workers and leaders of public worship. As the century wore on, the debate shifted to consider women's eligibility for the diaconate and the priesthood. Now, the final decade of the twentieth century saw the question of women in the episcopate take centre stage. Beginning with the election of Barbara Harris as Suffragan Bishop of Boston in 1989, a string of denominations and communions have since admitted women to all levels of ordained ministry: further Anglican communion 'firsts' included the appointments of Penny Jamieson to Dunedin, NZ (1990) and Victoria Matthews as Suffragan Bishop of Toronto in 1994. Across Europe the evangelical Lutheran Churches appointed their first female bishops in Hanover, Germany (1992), Hammar, Norway (1993), Helsingør, Denmark (1995) and Lund, Sweden (1996). In June 2003, draft legislation permitting women's entry to the episcopate was passed overwhelmingly in the Scottish Episcopal Church,[1] and at time of writing the Anglican Church in Australia was debating a similar move. But what did participants from the case study dioceses make of the prospect of ordaining women to the episcopate in the Church of England?

At the time of researching, the question of women in the episcopate had not acquired the status of a pressing issue for most of those surveyed. Indeed amongst laity in particular, it was not uncommon to hear expressions of surprise from interviewees that women were still barred from becoming bishops – many had assumed it was simply a matter of time before the first female bishop was consecrated. Any campaign for or against women in the episcopate therefore had to contend with the fact that a significant part of the Church of England was unaware that there was even an issue to resolve. Nevertheless, this is not to suggest an absence of strong views on the question. **Figure 9i** and **Table 9ii** summarize the percentages of agreement/disagreement with the idea of the Church of England ordaining women as bishops amongst case study clergy and laity respectively.

---

[1] 'Woman Bishop Motion receives overwhelming support';
http://www.scotland.anglican.org/news_headlines_78.html, 10 October 2003.

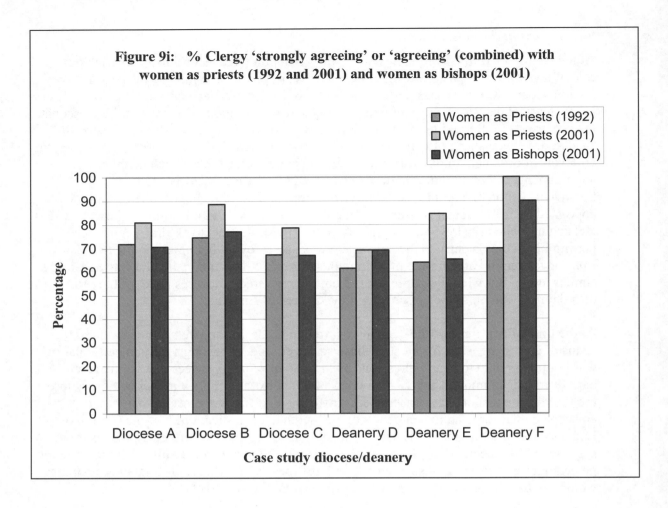

Figure 9i: % Clergy 'strongly agreeing' or 'agreeing' (combined) with women as priests (1992 and 2001) and women as bishops (2001)

Taking clergy responses first, the results suggest a clear majority supporting women's entry into the episcopate in each of the diocesan case studies, with the overall level of agreement/strong agreement around 72%. This figure is considerably higher than that suggested by the 2002 Christian Research survey commissioned by Cost of Conscience, 'The Mind of Anglicans', which suggested Church of England clergy were split almost 50:50 over the question.[2] Given that the full details of this survey have not yet been published, it is difficult to speculate on the reasons for this quite significant difference. One factor may be the different sampling methods used: research for 'The Mind of Anglicans' sought to achieve a representative sample based on the strength of different groups and constituencies, whilst the current survey employs a diocese/deanery-based case study approach. Whatever the reason, seeking to understand the difference between the two figures may provide a fruitful subject for discussion in the future. One significant feature of **Figure 9i** is that current levels of support for women in the episcopate were strikingly similar to support for women's priesting amongst the same sample in 1992, but slightly lower than for current attitudes to women's priesting. This may partly reflect a greater hesitancy to support something that has not yet been experienced first-hand.[3]

To a large degree, the lower levels of support for women in the episcopate amongst case study clergy owe a considerable amount to the attitudes of male clergy. Ordained women were almost unanimously in agreement/strong agreement with ordaining women to the

---

[2] Robbie Low, 'The Mind of Anglicans', *New Directions* 5 (86), July 2002, pp. 17–19 (p. 18).
[3] At least by the vast majority of clergy. A very small number may already have met bishops who are women through international church gatherings.

episcopate, with only a few declaring themselves uncertain (none said they disagreed/strongly disagreed[4]). However, support was much lower amongst male clergy, with almost a quarter of male clergy respondents disagreeing or strongly disagreeing. Serious differences of opinion clearly still exist amongst the clergy, although the actual figures presented here may slightly underestimate the degree of support within the Church of England as a whole. As suggested in the Introduction, the case study samples slightly over-represent size of the 'traditionalist' constituency, by virtue of the dioceses selected.

As with the question of women's priesting in Chapter 2, levels of support for women's priesting differed significantly between clergy of different church traditions. 95% of clergy who described themselves as 'liberal' agreed or strongly agreed with women as bishops,[5] compared with just 24% of 'Anglo-Catholics' (support falls to just 17.6% if only male Anglo-Catholic clergy are considered). In the light of the results presented in Chapter 3, none of these figures will be surprising. Of more interest (and of potentially greater significance in the event of a vote on the question) are the views of evangelical respondents. The survey revealed considerable differences in levels of support between the different traditions within evangelicalism: whilst all of those describing themselves as 'liberal-evangelical' supported women as bishops, this was true of only 57.1% of those ticking 'evangelical'.[6] (The other figures were: 'charismatic evangelical' = 64%; 'Catholic evangelical' = 72% and 'conservative evangelical' = 63.7%). Of most interest here is the 'conservative evangelical' figure, given the frequent predictions that this constituency would present more trenchant opposition to women in the episcopate than over women as presbyters. In fact conservative evangelicals appear no less likely to oppose women as bishops than any other evangelical, although the number of cases considered here is small, so it would be wrong to read too much significance into the figure. However, with liberal clergy overwhelmingly in favour of women as bishops, and Anglo-Catholic clergy strongly against, it seems likely that – just as in 1992 – any vote on women in the episcopate could be greatly influenced by the views of evangelicals.

How do the clergy figures compare to levels of support for women as bishops amongst lay questionnaire respondents? As **Table 9ii** suggests, most of the case study congregation samples returned majority support for women's entry into the episcopate, although just as with the clergy, levels of agreement are lower than for women's priesting. One marked feature of the responses was the large number of churchgoers indicating that they 'neither agreed or disagreed' with women as bishops (in Church 5, for example, where 63.2% of respondents were supportive of the idea, 23.7% were uncertain, and only 13.2% disagreed or strongly disagreed. In Church 16, which had no experience of women's priestly ministry at all, 36.4% ticked 'neither agree nor disagree'). There were also strong variations in support between the different church traditions: 85.7% of 'liberal evangelicals' agreed or strongly agreed with women in the episcopate, but only 42.2% of 'Anglo-Catholics'.[7] Again, evangelicals were amongst the most likely to be undecided. However, whilst church tradition seemed a significant variable, gender-related differences were less clear: across the whole lay sample, agreement/strong agreement with the idea of women as bishops reached

---

[4] This very slightly overstates the strength of opinion amongst female clergy, since anecdotal evidence suggests a small number of permanent deacons do not believe women should exercise headship over men, and some members of religious communities also hold reservations over women in the episcopate. However, the numbers in each case are very small compared to the overwhelming vote of support amongst current female diocesan clergy.

[5] The remaining 5% ticked 'neither agree nor disagree'; none declared themselves against.

[6] Although only 24% of the 'evangelical' sample came out in favour of retaining an all-male episcopate; the other 12% ticked 'neither agree nor disagree'.

[7] This was the only 'church tradition' group showing less than 50% support.

60.3% amongst women and 58.4% amongst men.[8] The main significant differences emerged when men's and women's responses were compared on a congregation by congregation basis: in eleven out of fourteen parishes that had experienced a woman's priestly ministry, men were slightly more likely to support the ordination of women as bishops than women. Conversely, in evangelical parishes, or parishes where the resolutions were in force, women were more supportive than men in ten out of fourteen cases. This offers further evidence for the suggestion made in Chapter 3 that where a congregation has made a strong theological stance in favour of male-only priestly/presbyteral ministry, male members of the congregation are far less likely to support women's ordination. In a separate question, male respondents were also somewhat less likely than women to feel comfortable with the idea of their new vicar being ordained by a female bishop.

Table 9ii: Percentage of laity 'strongly agreeing' or 'agreeing' (combined) with the Church of England's decision to ordain women as priests (**P**) and with the idea of the Church of England ordaining women as bishops (**B**)

Case study sample (characteristic) [no. of cases[9]]		P	B	Case study sample (characteristic) [no. of cases]		P	B
Church 1 (WP[10])	[39]	92.4	79.5	Church 12	[17]	52.9	29.4
Church 2	[21]	80.9	57.1	Church 13	[14]	93.3	78.6
Church 3 (AB[11])	[26]	61.5	46.2	Church 15 (AB'C')	[20]	10	15
Church 4	[20]	90	75	Church 16	[23]	82.6	56.5
Church 5 (WP)	[38]	92.1	63.2	Church 17	[22]	45.5	22.7
Church 6 (AB)	[28]	25	21.4	Church 18 (WP)	[7]	57.2	28.6
Church 7 (WP)	[62]	90.2	77.4	Church 19 (WP)	[26]	88.4	80.8
Church 8 (AB'C')	[7]	12.5	14.3	Church 20 (WP)	[14]	85.7	71.4
Church 9	[19]	94.7	89.5	Church 21 (AB'C')	[8]	37.5	12.5
Church 10 (B, WP)	[18]	88.9	50	Church 22	[22]	100	86.3
Church 11	[23]	82.6	73.9	Church 23	[12]	75	50

No doubt the patterns outlined above will seem more or less reassuring depending on the reader's point of view. On one hand, those committed to an all-male priesthood and episcopate may be disappointed at the majority support for women as bishops in most of the non-resolution parishes (which account for over 90% of the Church of England as a whole), but may be encouraged that the proportion in favour is by no means unanimous. Supporters of the ordination of women as bishops may be disappointed that a large minority seem yet to be convinced on the issue, but take heart from the possibility that if the experience of 1992 was repeated, many of those harbouring reservations before a vote might nevertheless decide to accept the result and embrace the change after the matter had been decided in Synod.[12]

---

[8] No generalization about support for women as bishops should be made on the basis of these totals, since they are derived from a diverse selection of case study churches rather than an accurate cross section of churchgoing Anglicans. The figures are only provided to illustrate the point that amongst the random sample of respondents, levels of support amongst men and women were little different.

[9] The two questions were answered by slightly different numbers of people in most cases. As a rough guide to the sample size, the numbers responding to the question on women as bishops are given in square brackets.

[10] WP = parishes with current experience of women's ministry as priests.

[11] AB (C) = Indicates which (if any) resolutions a parish has passed.

[12] See Chapter 4. The same phenomenon can also be seen with regard to Anglicans' first experiences of women in deaconess ministry, where a similar initial tendency towards hostility, curiosity or caution amongst congregations receiving a female deacon for the first time was often quickly replaced by more positive acceptance (Alyson Peberdy, *A Part of Life: A Study of Lay People's Response to Women's*

What reasons did interviewees and questionnaire respondents give for their views on women in the episcopate? Here, several definite points of continuity with attitudes to women's priesting may be found. For one thing there remained a substantial number of respondents who simply could not see any compelling theological argument to refuse. One of the most popular responses was that women bishops were the logical next step, just as women's ordination to the diaconate had led to growing calls for their priesting. 'I see no reason why they should not if they can become priests – surely it is a natural progression', wrote one woman from Church 1.[13] (The strength of expectation that the episcopacy would one day include women was demonstrated as early as the early 1990s, Leslie Francis and Mandy Robbins' survey of the 'waiting' women deacons. Of these, 45% expected that women would be consecrated as bishops 'within the next decade', with only 17% disagreeing.[14]) Issues of biblical or natural justice were once again commonly raised, along with a belief in the parity of women and men both in the eyes of God and in the new creation. Most common was the conviction that women displayed discernible gifts for the job; not least in leadership, as the following short responses from the questionnaires suggest:

> *The hurch is currently missing out on leadership gifts which women can offer.*[15]
> *The breadth of 'gifting' to be found among priests, both men and women, is also needed among bishops.*[16]
>
> *Demonstrable evidence of God gifting women with leadership capacity – in both church and 'secular' settings.*[17]

As with the discussion of women in priesthood, there was widespread difference of opinion over whether women would bring something different to the episcopate *as women*, or whether the move would simply widen the pool of available gifts for the office. Whilst only a few thought certain gifts were given only to one sex, there was more support for the idea that a more feminine approach to leadership might begin to enrich an episcopate currently beholden to a more masculine approach. Several spoke of the need to 'transform the style and substance of leadership that has the hallmarks of an old boys club'[18] – an attitude particularly common amongst female clergy but also to be found (as with the speaker quoted here) amongst their male colleagues. Again, as with discussion of attitudes to women's priesting in Chapter 3, respondents generally found it extremely difficult to be precise about what constituted a 'feminine style of leadership' (and indeed, many were deliberately cautious of generalizing), but were often adamant that a distinctive approach could be discerned. Many comments implied that women would model a less confrontational style of leadership, whilst others thought female bishops would be less likely to revel in status for its own sake. As one couple from Church 10 suggested, 'having met one or two bishops we found to be pompous and insincere, we think it would be refreshing to have a few women in charge'.[19]

Ministry in the Church of England (Movement for the Ordination of Women, London, 1985), p. 12).

[13] LQ22, female 40–49, Church 1.

[14] Leslie J. Francis and Mandy Robbins, *The Long Diaconate, 1987–1994; Women Deacons and the Delayed Journey to Priesthood* (Gracewing, Leominster, 1999), p. 222.

[15] CQ77, female 30–39, Diocese A.

[16] CQ140, male diocesan development officer, 50–59.

[17] CQ320, male NSM curate, 50–59.

[18] CQ75, male priest-in-charge, 50–59.

[19] LQ252, husband and wife answering questionnaire together, 70–79, Church 10.

What is notable about much of the argument here is the pragmatic tone of the reasoning. Many clergy and lay respondents offered arguments based in the Bible, theology and tradition for their views, but few appeared to believe there was any *new* theological dimension to bring to the question of women bishops that was not already present (and, for most, satisfactorily resolved) in the debate on women as priests. Similarly, most of the matters of theological principle raised *against* women in the episcopate also frequently returned to the same theological ground. The most common of these was the argument put forward by some conservative evangelical respondents that the Bible seemed to require the leader of the Christian congregation to be male (although there was some disagreement over how far this command stretched; one curate in Deanery D even wondered whether a classical reformed doctrine of male headship might even prohibit female churchwardens, chief police officers or prime ministers[20]). However, this was an unusually rare argument, and where the scriptural witness was raised against women as bishops, respondents more typically argued that the commands applied to ordained ministry only. Amongst Catholic clergy, one of the most frequent objections to women in the episcopate was that the diocesan bishop should act as a focus for unity, and a female bishop could not do this whilst a significant number doubted the validity of her orders. Others maintained that as with the 1992 debate, General Synod did not have the authority to take this step in isolation from the worldwide church. Several suggested that if they could not support women's priesting, they certainly could not agree with women as bishops. For some members of parishes receiving extended episcopal care, this created an additional problem of lineage; in order to ensure the 'validity' of the sacraments consecrated by any male priest, one would have to know whether they were ordained by a male or female bishop. As one lay respondent wrote, 'if [women's] priestly orders are not valid (other than in an expedient, legal sense) then they cannot be allowed to advance themselves'.[21]

However, whilst theological/ecclesiological objections were common, those who did not support women's ordination as bishops were no less likely to give pragmatic arguments for their views than those who were supportive of it. As the previous quote suggests, some suspicion remained (just as there had been in 1992) that women were primarily pushing at the doors of episcopacy to 'advance themselves' (although this implied that women were uninterested in serving the church – an accusation strongly denied by ordained women themselves – and ignored the fact that men were also strongly represented in the campaign for women as bishops). A minority of lay respondents acknowledged their views were partly based on a gut feeling that leadership roles were best fulfilled by men, and there was some concern that women might react badly to receiving such a level of power and responsibility: 'It could be a little bit over the top as some could be a bit domineering', wrote one woman from Church 5.[22] Women's entry into the episcopate was also opposed on the grounds that the weight of evidence or opinion from other parts of the Anglican communion was unsatisfactory. Some also suggested that it would be particularly difficult for a lay person to travel to another diocese if they disagreed with women as bishops. More commonly, the potential divisiveness of any decision on women in the episcopate was also frequently noted: one respondent from Church 15 argued that 'I do not think that the C of E is ready for this and I think it would divide us further from other Xian religions – [e.g.] Roman Catholic'.[23] However, the most common reason for expressing uncertainty or disagreement over women as bishops was that of timing: some suggested that timing was

---

[20] int. cs4:1side2:340. Indeed, several lay respondents cited Margaret Thatcher's premiership as ample justification for not entrusting major leadership roles to women: 'we had a lady Prime Minister who I believe divided this nation' (LQ18, female 80+, Church 6).
[21] LQ325, male 80+, Church 15.
[22] LQ138, female [age not given], Church 5.
[23] LQ317, female 30–39, Church 15.

crucial because the Church needed to settle into women's priestly ministry before making any further changes, or because a debate on women in the episcopate would be divisive at this stage. Others suggested that women did not yet have sufficient experience as priests to be considered for preferment. This was strongly denied by several ordained women, who suggested that this argument sometimes constituted a 'stalling tactic' by those who privately held more fundamental objections but did not want to be seen as unreasonable. Women ordained before 1994 also complained that too often their level of experience was assessed without reference to their years in diaconal ministry.

Significantly, concerns over the timing of a move towards women in the episcopate were raised by some who supported women as bishops as well as some who did not, as these two representative comments suggest:

> *I can accept the ordination of women though I am not totally comfortable with it, but I would have a problem with women bishops for I think their advent could prove to be divisive for the Church.*[24]

> *We need another 20 years, then it should be acceptable. I believe it will be totally divisive if done too early.*[25]

Conversely, those who believed it was a nonsense to ordain women as priests and not bishops were drawn from amongst 'supporters' and 'opponents' of women in the episcopate. As one leading member of Reform asked:

> *How can you say to a female presbyter, 'here you are – [we're going to] give you the highest spiritual authority in the church but oh, by the way we're not going to allow you to be an incumbent' ... How can you then go and say 'we're not going to allow you to be a bishop either' – I mean, that's nonsense as well. [...] You can't ordain them and then disable them.*[26]

Here we return to the fourfold typology of responses to 'anomaly', based on the work of Mary Douglas and Alan Aldridge introduced at the end of Chapter 8. In seeking to set the right course for the future, respondents agreed or differed on questions of timing or the acceptable limits of diversity in ways which cut across the traditional dividing lines of 'supporters' and 'opponents'. Indeed, in the years after the 1992 vote, one of the first Synod motions calling for legislation on women in the episcopate was brought forward by one of the leading campaigners against women's priesting. Fr Geoffrey Kirk's motion of 1997 had proposed that the Church should move towards opening the episcopate to women immediately since maintaining the current position was both discriminatory and contrary to Catholic ecclesiology. The motion was defeated (partly because it was assumed to be less an attempt to assist ordained women and more a move to force discussion of a third, non-geographical province for 'traditionalists'). However, Fr Kirk's premise that the current settlement was both theologically and socially intolerable was also shared by many who actively supported the cause of women in the episcopate. Just as questions of timing and the acceptable limits of diversity were of secondary importance to 'impossibilists', so some supporters of women's priesting also felt there was no valid excuse for delaying legislation on women in the episcopate – including some members of organizations such as the Group for Rescinding the Act of Synod (GRAS). Acting quickly to establish (once and for all) whether the Church of England should ordain women as bishops, regardless of the further

---

[24] LQ416, male 60–69, Church 21.
[25] LQ183, female 60–69, Church 10.
[26] int. 5:85.

(regrettable) division in may cause, strongly echoed the 'exclusionist' type of response to anomaly. The purity and integrity of the Church of England was of paramount concern, making it an unacceptable anomaly for the Church to ordain women as priests but not bishops. Whether this meant a 'safe' province for traditionalists (as some supporters of a male-only priesthood wished to see) or an end to the opt-out provisions for opponents (as some supporters of women's ordination to the episcopate wanted), this position found it difficult to accept coexistence with the opposing view within the same church.

By contrast, the 'indifferent' response on the four-fold typology was evident in those who shared a disregard for timing, but seemed unconcerned about the plurality of views on women in the episcopate. Here, some 'supporters' and some 'opponents' of women bishops shared a conviction that a debate on women in the episcopate would be largely irrelevant to them, or make little difference to their continued presence in the Anglican Church. This could manifest itself in a complete apathy to the subject, or in a conviction that the best solution would be either to push the question into an indeterminate future or to address it straight away and resolve it once and for all, but with little strong idea of what the subsequent settlement would look like. 'We just need to get it out of our system, and get on with our life', suggested one male priest from Deanery D; 'trust, in the view of the way things have been in the last ten years, that life can still go on'.[27]

On the other hand, timing was crucial to those who saw merit in trying to continue the coexistence project, or who believed that further division could be avoided if the Church was willing to find the right moment to revisit the 1992–94 settlement. These considerations could override even strong views on the rightness or otherwise of opening up the episcopate to women. One male curate from Diocese B, who believed that the 1992–94 settlement had somewhat fudged the issue, nevertheless reflected:

> *My personal feeling is that I'm not quite sure that we are ready, in terms of maturity, to deal with women bishops as a church ... [...] When it comes down to it, personally, I think we should just try and stall it slightly; not too long, just to try and bring people on board ... I think there should be a lengthy ... not consultation process, but process of bringing people round.*[28]

However, the 'opportunist' response was also evident amongst many who held objections to women's priesting. Both the 1992–94 settlement and the prospect of women in the episcopate were regarded as undesirable, but also as ultimately habitable on the understanding that provisions for those seeking an all-male priesthood would continue to exist in some form. Others were more optimistic about the viability of the settlement, leading them to hope that women's ordination as bishops could be postponed into an indefinite future for the sake of the greater prize of unity across the episcopally-ordered churches of Christendom. As one senior clergyman with extensive experience of ecumenical dialogue suggested:

> *both theologians and people in the Vatican ... actually say to me that they think the episcopate is a distinctively different issue [from priesthood], and it might be possible that someone in the future could envisage a situation where the unity of the episcopate is maintained by an all-male episcopate, and there's a degree of freedom for local churches as to whom the bishop may delegate those aspects of the episcopate that are represented by presbyteral order'.*[29]

---

[27] int. cs4:2:511.
[28] int. cs2:15:513.
[29] int. 18:262. Similar views were also expressed by proponents of women's priesting. One interviewee

The idea that it might be theologically or ecclesiologically sustainable to proceed with women as priests whilst continuing with an all-male episcopate (a more 'accommodationist' type position) was also occasionally expressed by proponents of women's priesting, although this was comparatively rare. The question of which one of these four types of response was most common amongst participating clergy and laity is left to the end of the chapter. Meanwhile, it was clear to informed observers on all sides of the debate that future prospects for women's entry into the episcopate were intimately bound up with the fate of the 1992–94 settlement as a whole. If women were made bishops, the shape of the coexistence project would have to be redrawn. In particular, it was widely acknowledged that the Act of Synod would be rendered unworkable in its present form if both women and men were included in the episcopate, since the Act hung crucially on a mutual recognition of orders amongst the bishops as the guarantee of continued communion. But how far were respondents prepared to see this arrangement rescinded in order to allow women to enter the episcopate? And if this took place, what (if any) alternative arrangements would be made for those who dissented from it?

9.2 The Act of Synod, a third province and the limits of diversity

In the first ten years after 1994, the component of the coexistence settlement that arguably received more scrutiny than any other was the Episcopal Ministry Act of Synod of 1993. Chapter 7 has already explored clergy and lay attitudes to the justifications for the Act and experiences of its practical outworking. But how far did support exist for retaining the Act of Synod or a successor into the future? The official position of the Church of England remains most strongly characterized by an 'accommodationist' response, with an added dose of pragmatism. Official reports from the House of Bishops have continued to emphasize the value of maintaining unity in diversity through ecclesial structures and the collegiality of the episcopate, as outlined in the Eames Commission documents.[30] Individual ecclesiologists have also made extensive use of this approach.[31] In this view, continuing the coexistence project for the medium- to long-term was crucial, even at the expense of delaying resolution of questions about women as bishops and the future of the Act of Synod. Some support for this position could be found amongst both those 'supportive' of women as priests and bishops, and those opposed to such a move. One retired bishop who did not ordain women argued that the Act of Synod was justified by the existence of a 'period of reception' on women's priesting – to promise space for reflection and then renege on it was for him to undermine everything that had been said about the discernment process.[32]

Even if it was widely accepted that the advent of women bishops would spell the end for the Act of Synod in its present form, there was some optimism that continued accommodation might be possible by allowing the different positions a greater degree of autonomy within the Anglican Communion as a whole. In 2002, those seeking such an arrangement were encouraged by remarks from the new Archbishop of Canterbury Rowan Williams, who

who had been involved in drafting the Act of Synod felt that 'there's no actual necessity for women to be bishops... there's no right to be a bishop; there's nothing fair about it!' 'You're chosen to do a job, and one of those jobs is to represent the unity of the Church, and if you're going to exacerbate the disunity of the Church, I don't see that anyone can complain if you're not chosen (int. 12side2:end).

[30] See Chapter 8.

[31] See for example: Stephen Sykes, *The Integrity of Anglicanism* (Mowbray, London, 1978); Stephen W. Sykes (ed.), *Authority in the Anglican Communion; Essays Presented to Bishop John Howe* (Anglican Book Centre, Toronto, 1987); Paul Avis (ed.), *Seeking the Truth of Change in the Church: Reception, Communion and the Ordination of Women* (T & T Clark, London, 2004).

[32] int. 17side2:555.

indicated he looked 'with some sympathy' on the idea of a third, non-geographical province, acknowledging that 'You can't indefinitely perpetuate a situation in which, in one body, the ministry of some is regarded wholly negatively'.[33] Did this mean that an 'accommodationist' response to differences over women as priests and bishops was still a workable option? The answer here seemed a potential 'yes', but only with some modifications: in the language of Mary Douglas, moving discussion of coexistence from Church of England to Anglican Communion level meant pushing the boundaries of the 'group' wider to relieve pressure on the existing 'grid' and incorporate into it a greater degree of diversity. Effectively, if an 'accommodationist' response was still a possibility on the worldwide Anglican stage, it may have appeared less viable as an internal solution for the Church of England. Certainly only a few interviewees in the current research believed so. Even those who were most committed to the Act of Synod as the practical underpinning of the coexistence project acknowledged the growing critique of the Act.

Amongst the loudest voices calling for the removal of the Act of Synod were those who felt it represented an intolerable anomaly that required swift resolution. At national level, the foundation of GRAS (the Group for Rescinding the Act of Synod) in 2000 represented the first organized expression of this position amongst those supporting women's ordination as priests and bishops. Although views on the right time to rescind were a matter of individual opinion, the organization's first newsletter warned against being distracted from a speedy resolution by those who insisted 'don't worry about the Act of Synod; concentrate on getting women made bishops!'. 'And what kind of time are women going to have with the Act dogging them like a ball and chain at every step?', responded one contributor.[34] At the other end of the spectrum, some of those who maintained objections to women as priests and bishops were similarly convinced that the 1992–94 settlement was increasingly unsustainable, and advocated a free (or third, non-geographical) province as the solution. Although it had long been acknowledged that the Act of Synod would become unworkable once women were consecrated bishops, the question of a third province for 'traditionalists' had only moved onto the official agenda of Forward in Faith in 1998.[35] Nevertheless, by early 2003 a dedicated campaign organization – the Third Province Movement – had been founded, with a mixture of Conservative Evangelical and Anglo-Catholic patrons. Of the current coexistence project, Fr Geoffrey Kirk told a Pusey House conference in 2003 that 'that battle was lost some while ago, and that apart from a few trifling but necessary rearguard actions we should now be calling it to its close'.[36] Already by this stage, an audit of parishes affiliated to Forward in Faith had found the constituency 'could be self-sufficient and self-financing, should the need arise'.[37]

Amongst the grass roots clergy and laity interviewed here, calls for the swift rescinding of the Act from supporters of women as priests and bishops most often focused upon the status of women under the settlement. As one female curate in Diocese A remarked:

[33] *Church Times*, 29.11.2002.
[34] Group for Rescinding the Act of Synod, *GRAS Newsletter* (GRAS, London, December 2000), p. 4.
[35] Council of Forward in Faith, 'The Case for a Free Province of the Church of England' (Forward in Faith, London, December 1998). Indeed, the paper suggested that traditionalists should see the arrival of women bishops in the Church of England as a positive choice, in that total schism would be avoided whilst leaving each side of the debate freer to pursue the kind of church they wanted.
[36] Geoffrey Kirk, 'A New Province for the Anglican Communion' (paper presented to the Conference 'A Free Province? A Third Province?', Pusey House, Oxford, 22–3 September 2003) [available online at: http://www.forwardinfaith.com/artman/publish/03-09-26-kirk.shtml, downloaded 15 October 2003].
[37] 'Editorial' in *New Directions* 5 (90), November 2002, p. 3.

> *I think probably it'll be necessary to campaign for rescinding of those measures, because it's a justice issue. Although there'll be people who'll be hurt by it ... we can't allow it to stay in place because it appears to make the ordination of women provisional ...* [38]

In complete contrast, others suggested that the Act could now be rescinded because it had accomplished its aim of allowing a period of 'breathing space' for those who could not accept women's priesting. If women's priesthood had very largely been accepted across the Church, it was thought, this 'safe space' for dissenters could now be removed. Others felt that legislation was simply the wrong method of dealing with the continued differences of opinion. Speaking at the launch of the Group for Rescinding the Act of Synod in October 2000, Canon Martyn Percy spoke of how 'the Act of Synod is divisive because, in effect, it keeps us apart and constructs an ecclesial ghetto within a wider Church'.[39] Other clergy also believed the Act should be rescinded in favour of a more flexible arrangement; as one interviewee from Diocese E remarked, 'the problem is that it institutionalizes [difference] ... it's going to be a lot harder to break up, and resolve [...] if you don't like your bishop, go and find someone you do like; you shouldn't be able to pull out of diocesan jurisdiction ...'[40] Others simply felt that the current arrangement was quickly becoming morally, theologically and practically intolerable, and the best solution would be to rescind the Act as soon as possible, even if this meant that some would create further division. As one lay woman from Church 4 remarked:

> *If the Church is going to have women priests, it seems silly that you're going to have all these other churches that are having a bit of a cop-out, and a get-out clause. I think you've got to grasp it, and this is why you've got this weak, wishy-washy appearance outside – 'oh no, we might offend somebody' – please! Let's start offending a few people!*[41]

The insufficiency of the Act was also occasionally highlighted by clergy with objections to women's ordination as priests and bishops: the only realistic way forward for one priest from Diocese B was for 'a clear apostolic area with a clear hierarchy'. The Act was insufficient, he argued, because the credibility gap between the two constituencies 'goes down to the roots'.[42] In this view, if women became bishops, nothing but a greater degree of separation would suffice.

In all of these cases, speakers insisted in different ways that 'accommodation' within the Church of England was no longer a viable option and a further measure of separation between the different constituencies had to take place. As a result, each constituency hoped it would be enabled to exist in a way that was true to its core values, without the troubling anomaly of either women in priesthood/episcopacy or the presence of the Act of Synod to bind them together in a 'compromise' measure. In a significant sense, then, these views tended towards the 'exclusionist' response outlined in the work of Mary Douglas and Alan Aldridge. Such voices were undoubtedly amongst the loudest on the national stage at the beginning of the twenty-first century, but did they also attract widespread support?

'Exclusionist' type responses were certainly to be heard much more widely in the church than the comparatively small memberships of GRAS and the Third Province Movement

---

[38] int. cs1:11side2:336.
[39] Quoted in *GRAS Newsletter*, December 2000, p. 1.
[40] int. cs5:5:223.
[41] int. cs2:23:247.
[42] int. c2:5side2:323.

would suggest. However, as Chapter 7 suggested, few lay respondents had even heard of the Act of Synod, and few who had found its nature and purpose comprehensible.[43] Acts of Synod, in addition, sounded more like a matter for the Anglican hierarchy than for grass roots churchgoers. Thus, one significant force working for the maintenance of the present arrangement was that of 'indifference'. However, this should not be taken to mean 'apathy'. As one of the four cultural categories of response to anomaly suggested by Mary Douglas/Alan Aldridge, 'indifference' here means that the anomalous was regarded as irrelevant to more important matters or sufficiently unthreatening as to be ignorable. In addition, few at the time had considered the possibility that some kind of 'third province' might be needed. Even amongst supporters of a male-only priesthood, the idea seems to have attracted 'quite a lot [of support] amongst clergy, not much care or understanding amongst lay people yet', according to one retired PEV.[44]

'Indifference' was also strengthened by a disinclination to spend yet more time revising the 1992–94 settlement, since this was yet another distraction from the most important business of ministry and mission. In this view, the Church of England again seemed to be more interested in its own internal management than with spreading the Gospel.[45] (This was most commonly suggested by evangelical interviewees – although by no means always.) Others reckoned the future of the Act an irrelevance to their parish situation. As Alan Aldridge suggested in relation to the debate on women in the diaconate, the ease with which clergy and congregations could 'disappear' into their own parish and ignore anything that was adjudged to be a matter for 'the hierarchy' could have a powerful braking force on any attempt at change.[46] This continued to apply with regard to women's ordination as bishops and the future of the Act of Synod. Overall, then, 'indifferent' responses to the present arrangements undoubtedly ensured that 'exclusionist' responses could not predominate, and more generally acted as a conservative force against any impulses to rescind the Act.

Moreover, even those who tended towards an 'exclusivistic' solution were frequently forced to accept some measure of compromise in practice.[47] Even where interviewees expressed strong dislike for the Act of Synod, this was often tempered with an acceptance of the difficulties of rescinding it. As one ordained woman in Diocese C remarked, 'Being a bit radical, I would say get rid of [the Act]! Don't allow a third province, and those who don't like it go elsewhere. But you can't do things like that, unfortunately…'[48] A measure of pragmatism also characterized the responses of many of those who continued to disagree with women's ordination as priests and seek an alternative future in a third province – in the view of one bishop who did not ordain women, 'no one should get into the lifeboat until the ship is actually under water'.[49] Others with objections to women's priesting explicitly rejected calls for a third province, arguing that it represented the defeat of any attempt to

---

[43] Except where the respondent's congregation benefited directly from its terms.

[44] 2side2:580 (although since this interview was conducted in late 2000, the idea has become more widely known, not least because the debate over the ordination of homosexuals has raised the prospect of parallel jurisdictions).

[45] Although this concern could equally lead to a more 'exclusionist' response; one speaker from Diocese C felt that the Act 'had gotta go' immediately, so that the Church could get on with endorsing what had been decided in 1992, and return to 'kingdom issues': 'we only have a limited amount of time... to really sort out who we are, and how we're going to fulfil our great commission' (int. cs3:10:526).

[46] Alan Aldridge, 'Discourse on Women in the Clerical Profession: The Diaconate and Language-games in the Church of England', *Sociology* 26 (1) February 1992, pp. 45–57 (p. 55).

[47] Indeed, a pure 'exclusionist' response to the Act of Synod would have entailed leaving the Church of England upon its introduction – anecdotal evidence suggests a small number of (mainly) clergy did so.

[48] int. cs3:3:419.

[49] int. 5:p.16.

return the Church of England to what they regarded as an 'orthodox' position.[50] Others asked why they should be jettisoned from the mainstream of the Church of England when they considered themselves to be representing the authentic Anglican mainstream.[51]

Indeed, out of the four responses to 'anomaly' proposed by the 'grid and group' model of cultural analysis, responses to the Act of Synod and the future shape of the settlement were most strongly characterized by an 'opportunistic' approach. As already suggested, this should not be taken to denote a lack of principle; merely an acceptance that in the concrete world of church life, compromise was inevitable even whilst working to put one's beliefs and principles into practice. Of course, there was no single 'opportunistic' view of the settlement's future, but many shades. At one end of the spectrum stood the female speaker above, who felt strongly that the Church of England should remove the Act of Synod immediately and introduce women bishops, yet conceded that this might not be realistic at this stage. Others stated themselves in favour of a swift settlement but highlighted the possible consequences of doing so. As one bishop remarked, 'if there was real disruption here, then it would be significant for everybody. If, for instance, we lost the confidence of large numbers of priests, there would be real fuel behind the Third Province Movement'.[52]

Many of the bishops interviewed here shared this speaker's reluctance to contemplate any kind of additional province or parallel jurisdiction, and although they were not natural supporters of the Act of Synod, they felt that to remove it immediately might cause more trouble than it was worth.[53] In particular, those with experience of Church law and the drafting of synodical legislation emphasized the practical obstacles to replacing the Act with a third, non-geographical province: 'One of the things we examined was the possibility of extraterritorial dioceses and provinces – I mean, that simply would not work; you could not run a church sensibly on that basis...', said one experienced Synod lay man.[54] Others were more positive, suggesting that although the Act was not ideal, it clearly had its uses; particularly for helping the Church of England through a period of division and for showing pastoral sensitivity to those disappointed with the 1992 decision.

Suggestions of the right time to rescind the Act of Synod also varied widely. For some, the best moment was in the near future, especially given the probable advent of women to the episcopate; for others, the time frame seemed much longer. As one lay member of Synod from Diocese D remarked, 'I think it's just got to be left as it is, and let it die, because I think anything else will be dishonourable. [...] We've got to wait until that generation dies...'[55] The theological problems inherent in rescinding the Act were also occasionally highlighted: if there was no possibility of opting out from women as priests and bishops, would this imply that women's priesthood was a defining doctrine for the Church of England? More practically, both 'supporters' and 'opponents' of women's priesting acknowledged that their own constituency might be enabled to grow in size and confidence if the Act was left in place for the short-term. A common theme to the testimony gathered from (present and former) PEVs was that the Act had given breathing space to

---

[50] Rodney Schofield, 'Too Soon for Women Bishops', *New Directions* 2 (42) November 1998, p. 4.

[51] As one conservative evangelical vicar argued, 'I'm not interested in just carving out a niche for myself so that I can survive the next thirty years – I want a Church in which my sons... can become priests... and daughters... *they* can become deacons' (int. 3side2:c.450).

[52] int. cs5:15:118.

[53] A similar picture is apparent from replies received to a letter on the Act of Synod sent by GRAS in 2000 to forty-six Church of England bishops. Of the six who replied, three were sympathetic to removing the Act but felt unable to call for this officially in their current post, whilst three felt that the Act should be kept in place for the time being (*GRAS Newsletter*, December 2000, p. 4).

[54] int. 4:p.10.

[55] int. cs4:8side2:319.

'traditionalists', and its continued presence was allowing those unhappy with women as bishops to make preparations for that eventuality. Amongst ordained women themselves, it was commonly suggested that rescinding the Act immediately might be counterproductive. As one female curate from Diocese A remarked:

> *I think the Act should stay as it is, because I suppose if you persecute groups,*
> *they tend to draw their boundaries even more stringently, and my instinct is...*
> *removing flying bishops would do more harm than good.*[56]

Another added that rescinding the Act would not necessarily stop discrimination against women who are priests:

> *I think the impression would be given that you could go anywhere, but that*
> *wouldn't in reality be true – a parish could potentially make life quite*
> *unbearable, if they felt they'd been pushed into a corner in having a woman.*[57]

Only a minority of ordained women saw some practical value to the Act of Synod in this way, but even amongst some leading campaigners for women in the episcopate, there seemed to be a growing conviction that it was better to delay rescinding the Act of Synod if this improved chances of obtaining a one-clause measure on women bishops a few years further down the line. A rush to vote on women bishops might correspondingly be counterproductive if this meant having to accept an enhanced package of opt-out provisions. At the far end of the 'opportunist' spectrum, a small number of interviewees admitted that whilst they would ideally like to see the Act of Synod rescinded and women bishops in place, they were just too tired of campaigning to become active in bringing this about: 'leave this to the next generation', said one.[58]

In conclusion, speculation on the future of the Act of Synod prompted a complex mixture of views amongst those who were aware of its existence. Emerging most strongly from the interview testimony was a sense that any current 'anomaly' was most likely to be solved pragmatically: an immediate rescinding of the Act was widely thought to be counterproductive and along the whole spectrum of clergy views there was some consensus that if a change in the current arrangements could be made consensually, this was the most preferred option. Of course, within this, respondents held very different conceptions of what the right time and the right outcome might be, and one should certainly not underestimate the divergence of opinion over the future shape of the Church of England. Nevertheless, the fact that a majority seemed to take an essentially pragmatic approach to the future of the settlement, and the fact that differences of opinion did not straightforwardly reflect a traditional division between 'supporters' and 'opponents', may give some cause for optimism that a multilateral resolution may yet be found. However, this prospect remains far from certain.

Whilst the majority of respondents seemed to accept (however reluctantly) the need for a pragmatic approach, any attempt to 'play it long' may yet be overtaken by events: in June 2002, the Guildford diocesan synod became the first to pass a resolution calling for the House of Bishops to bring forward legislation to permit the ordination of women to the episcopate 'without delay'.[59] A year later Worcester Diocesan Synod passed an even more radical motion (unanimously save for two votes against in the House of Laity) calling on

---

[56] int. cs1:14:225.
[57] int. cs4:7side2:267.
[58] int. cs2:1:p. 3b.
[59] *Church Times*, 02.08.02.

General Synod to debate a motion that gender would cease to be a relevant qualification for consideration for the episcopate, with effect from 2005.[60] Neither motion has found its way into General Synod business to date, but the very emergence of such resolutions reminds us that any reassessment of the 1992–94 settlement is just as likely to move on by sudden leaps and bounds as by a gradual formulation of consensus. If so, many of those who would otherwise have settled for pragmatic compromise in the short to medium term may instead feel compelled to revert to their more natural allegiance. If this happens, the appeal of the 'exclusionist' response to the settlement may broaden. If as already suggested a majority of respondents naturally favoured women in the episcopate, a proposal to allow women to become bishops might be difficult to refuse, no matter what the concessions accompanying it, and despite widespread ambivalence to the existing opt-out provisions. This support would certainly be grounded in a conviction that there was no theological justification for refusing (and a good many reasons for proceeding) but may also rest on a feeling that it would be unfair (and certainly incomprehensible to the general public) to refuse – just as had arguably been the case with the ordination of women to the priesthood. If so, the historic Anglican attachment to politeness, breadth and consensus may once again meet its match in a (no less Anglican) concern for natural justice and regard for the values of the society it was given established status to minister amongst.

Conclusion

Of course at this stage, any statement on women's ordination to the episcopate and the future of the Act of Synod as part of a wider coexistence settlement remains a matter of pure speculation. As the experience of 1992 demonstrated, predicting the outcome of Synod votes is a notoriously difficult business and it is not the remit of this report to try. In particular, it would be wrong to prejudge the findings of the Bishop of Rochester's working party on the theological issues surrounding women in the episcopate. However, it is fair to suggest some possible issues over which the popular support for women as bishops may be won and lost:

- The first concerns our understanding of the Bible. Whilst 'fundamentalist' readings of the Bible were rare, many seemed to take seriously the scriptural evidence on the teaching of Jesus and women's ministry in the early Church. Does the maleness of the apostles or the apparent prohibition of women teaching in church in the Epistles constitute a compelling barrier to women undertaking a ministry of oversight in the Church today, or does the Gospel preached by Jesus and the early Church actually encourage and celebrate women's participation in the Church's ministry at all levels? Given what has already been suggested about the possibly decisive patterns of support/opposition to women as bishops within the Church of England's evangelical constituency, the biblical witness may turn out to be a crucial theme in the debate.

- The second key node of discussion is the nature of ministerial order.[61] Few respondents and interviewees could understand why, at present, women could be ordained priest but not bishop. If there is no good theological reason for maintaining this distinction, it will be difficult to resist the calls for the episcopate to be opened to women. If a good theological reason for continuing the distinction exists, this has yet to make an impact on popular belief.

---

[60] Details gained from personal conversation with a member of General Synod who is also active in campaigning for women as priests and bishops.

[61] Indeed, the Rochester Working Party has already identified this as a central issue (House of Bishops, *Working Party on Women in the Episcopate: A Progress Report from the House of Bishops* (General Synod GS1457, London, 2002), p. 5).

- A third set of issues surrounds the question of gender. What many respondents seemed to find so unconvincing about arguments for an all-male priesthood and episcopate was the suggestion that gender was somehow a relevant qualification for these two orders of ministry. This was partly because of much wider reservations about *a priori* role categorizations *per se*. It is incumbent upon those who retain an attachment to such categorizations to explain in a more widely comprehensible way why femaleness might function as an automatic disqualification from priesthood. Having said that, a significant minority of respondents clearly perceived a difference between men's and women's leadership style, and some retained a feeling that men were more naturally suited to leadership, whilst women could occasionally be 'domineering' or 'controlling'. Clearly these kinds of assumptions need a great deal more critical scrutiny. Equally, more reflection and empirical work is needed around the question of whether women and men would bring a different *style* or approach to the episcopacy.

- Fourth, timing was widely regarded as critical in any attempt to modify the 1992–94 settlement. Here opinions by no means divided along familiar lines of 'supporters' and 'opponents'. Most interviewees favoured the avoidance of conflict and schism if at all possible, but a majority also felt that the settlement was increasingly anomalous. Events may of course overtake the best attempts at measured development, but insofar as the Church of England, collectively, is able to manage the debates and discussions, how best should it approach the future of women's ministry and the Act of Synod, to ensure a maximum of consensus and a minimum of theological compromise and ill-feeling? This must address not just current issues themselves but also trace back to the roots of divergence between the different traditions, and seek to find common ground. Moreover, timing remains not merely a pragmatic matter but a theological one: if history is subject to God, and it is finally agreed that God is calling both men and women to serve at all levels of ordained ministry, this must be enacted at the right time; the *kairos*[62] moment: 'for someone whose meat and drink is to do the will of God the decision is not their own to make; they must wait for God's moment'.[63]

- Fifth, an important question mark hung over the current structure of the ministry more generally. The grass roots of the Church of England has long been characterized by an ambiguous attitude towards its episcopate; at once expecting strong leadership and admirable personal qualities from its bishops, whilst also harbouring a suspicion of the Anglican hierarchy more generally. In recent years Anglican ecclesiology has placed considerable emphasis on the uniting role of the bishop within his own diocese and the achievement of unity through mutual recognition as part of an episcopal college. But this idea remains extremely marginal to the experience of most clergy and congregations. Furthermore, some suggested that the Church of England was 'obsessed with ministry' to the detriment of mission and pastoral care, and others felt that in the current climate, bishops in general seemed a financial burden the Church could easily do without. This is quite an extreme view, of course, but it begs an important question about how central questions about ministerial orders actually were to many lay people in particular. In

---

[62] i.e., the 'right' or 'critical' time. This idea has not received universal acceptance: radical feminist theologians have objected that citing the kairos moment in the near future effectively excuses previous societies from their patriarchalism, whilst traditionalists have objected that it simply offers a convenient justification for the abandonment of tradition.

[63] John Austin Baker, *The Right Time; A Lecture Delivered at the First Annual Conference of the Movement for the Ordination of Women* (MOW, London, 1981), p. 3. This idea has not received universal acceptance: radical feminist theologians have objected that to situating the *kairos* moment in the near future effectively excuses previous societies from their patriarchalism, whilst traditionalists have objected that it simply offers a convenient justification for the abandonment of tradition (Geoffrey Kirk, 'Church Dogmatics', *New Directions* 1 (8) January 1996, pp. 9–10).

putting their case in the debate over women as bishops, all sides of the argument must also explain the importance of episcopacy *per se*, in addition to arguing for a particular sexual configuration of the episcopate.

- Finally, the whole debate about women bishops and the Act of Synod throws up a number of wider issues about the nature of the Church of England itself. Differences of opinion on these central questions often rested upon fundamentally divergent views of the locus of authority within the Anglican church and the most appropriate method of decision-making. Differences over the extent to which 'anomaly' could be incorporated within the current structures raised important questions over the acceptable limits of diversity, and prompted the question of how far Christian faith and practice was a totalizing system into which every development must be integrated, whether an element of provisionality could be permitted in the many matters that surrounded the core doctrines of faith, or whether unity was maintained chiefly by process and management. A continued dialogue on these questions and others will encourage greater understanding between the different views and constituencies, and may also have implications for future unity.

Summary and conclusion

The elapse of a decade since the Church of England took the historic step to admit women to the priesthood presents a valuable opportunity to reflect upon the story so far, the extent of continuing theological debate over gender and ordained ministry, the practical outworking of the legislation, and the 'unfinished business' arising from it. The picture is changing fast: as the Church of England moves closer to a potentially decisive discussion on women in the episcopate, the state of play is already being altered by wider debates about the ordination of practising homosexuals, the limits of diversity in the Anglican Communion, new employment and human rights legislation from the European and Westminster Parliaments, pronouncements on ordination from the Roman Catholic and Orthodox churches, the recently signed Covenant between the Church of England and the Methodist Church of Great Britain, and the need to combat numerical decline and a scarcity of resources. However, as clergy and churchgoers reflected on the first ten years of women's priesting in the Church of England during 2000-3,[1] the following main features emerged:

Summary

1. The case study research suggests a high degree of acceptance of women's ministry as priests amongst both clergy and congregations, with 'churchmanship' a more significant variable than age or gender.

2. Acceptance of women's priestly ministry appears to have increased over the first ten years, with particular growth in the ranks of those who 'strongly agree' with the 1992 decision (although most of those who were strongly opposed to the move in 1992 remain so today).

3. It was widely assumed that personal experience of the ministry of ordained women led to a more positive attitude towards women's priesting, meaning clergy deployment issues were closely monitored on all sides. In line with previous studies, this report suggests some evidence that personal experience of a priest who was a woman led to a greater degree of acceptance, but in many respects, the priesthood of women and the priesthood of men were not necessarily accepted on the same basis.

4. The main reasons respondents gave for supporting the decision to ordain women as priests were: women's sense of personal calling to priesthood, the Bible's endorsement of inclusivity and equality between women and men, the belief that gender should be no bar to ordained ministry, and an awareness of what women's ordination as priests might bring the Church, society and priesthood.

5. The key factors working against acceptance of women's priesting (in the views of participants) were: concern over the divisive impact of the debate (and its ecumenical implications) and a more intuitive/aesthetic sense that priesthood was a male role. The Bible and tradition were also important, but arguments on male symbolism derived from sacramental theology only attracted significant support from male Anglo-Catholic clergy.

---

[1] The period over which this study was conducted.

6. Against an overly neat division of opinion between opposing intellectual arguments, the role of 'gut feeling' was also evident, as was the fact that respondents 'for' and 'against' women's priesting often shared similar hopes and fears for women's priesting despite disagreeing on whether it was right or not.

7. Parish case studies suggested that ten years on, women's priesting had become largely accepted on a day-to-day basis, with women's gifts in ministry greatly appreciated, to the extent that the ordination of women had become a 'non-issue' for most respondents.

8. Women's ministry as priests was widely felt to have enriched the Church, particularly through the particular life experiences that women had to offer. However, there was some acknowledgement that the changes brought about by women's priesting did not yet seem to be as revolutionary as some had hoped, and others had feared.

9. Nevertheless, one important reason for the large-scale acceptance of women's priestly ministry in practice was that it seemed entirely consonant with some quite traditional expectations about the nature of ordained ministry and what made a good priest/vicar. As one clergy respondent wrote: 'the iconoclasm has not happened!'.

10. In a majority of congregations a diversity of opinion on women's ordination as priests remained and in a minority of cases it was still an issue of concern, disappointment or conflict. However, parish decisions over the resolutions could prove at least as contentious as women's priesting itself.

11. Debates on women as priests and the resolutions allowing parishes to opt out of it have both resulted in a certain amount of two-way traffic between congregations, although this became less common as the decade wore on. However, in many cases the 1992 decision did not single-handedly create conflict but added a further dimension to existing sources of difference.

12. If women's priesting had become largely accepted (particularly amongst the laity), it was nevertheless recognized that the 1992–94 settlement and its practical outworking continued to pose challenges (particularly for the clergy).

13. Appointments and deployment proved an issue of particular concern for women clergy; in particular the disproportionate number of women in non-stipendiary ministry and a corresponding lack of women in senior appointments. The appointments process itself was considered to be insufficiently open and regulated, and there was concern over the ease with which parishes could say 'no' to appointing a female priest even when it had not passed the resolutions.

14. Clergy with objections to women's priesting were most likely to feel ignored for jobs by senior clergy because of their views.

15. Dioceses have begun to explore a range of responses to feelings of marginalization on all sides (e.g., training to interviewers, feedback for unsuccessful candidates, greater flexibility over patterns of ministry). Whilst such approaches seem likely to benefit all clergy, more still needs to be done to defuse the climate of suspicion over appointments.

16. Second, clergy's experience of deanery and diocesan occasions suggests a discernible defusion of tension over the past decade – though probably as much because the 1992-94 settlement (and the nature of Anglican life in general) enabled the different constituencies to avoid occasions of real difficulty, as much as for positive attempts at bridge-building.

17. Working relationships with laity and other clergy with different views on women's priesting are generally considered good by a majority of clergy respondents, although occasional problems are still reported.

18. Deanery clergy meetings and diocesan occasions involving a sacramental element could still prove particularly contentious. The parallel structures that have grown up to allow those with objections to women's priesting a 'measure of distance' from women clergy and those who ordain them are greatly valued by those who participate in them but are viewed with considerable disappointment by many supporters of women's priestly ministry.

19. Some creative solutions to the current divisions have been explored (e.g., reconfiguring the Chrism service, rethinking the purpose of the deanery clergy chapter) and many of these have proved quite successful in practical terms, although regret still remains over the loss of full communion.

20. A third key cluster of 'unresolved issues' from the 1992–94 settlement surrounds the existence of the resolution allowing parishes to opt out of accepting a woman's ministry as a priest, and the petition for extended episcopal oversight that allows a parish to receive 'extended episcopal oversight' from a bishop who ordains only men, if their diocesan bishop ordains women.

21. Although there was some acknowledgement that the resolutions and Act of Synod had been useful in enabling some to remain within the Church of England, few could see a pastoral justification (still less a theological justification) for keeping them in place in the long term.

22. A significant percentage of clergy believed they identified 'occasional abuse' of the provisions (sometimes by parishes and their clergy, sometimes by senior diocesan clergy) to extend the power of one constituency over another.

23. The opt-out provisions were also regarded as problematic because of: ignorance or differences of opinion over the terms of the legislation and the process by which they were implemented; unforeseen problems in their operation – notably in bringing the wishes of the congregation (or a part of it) into conflict with the views of the wider community; the tendency for 'extended episcopal oversight' to become 'alternative episcopal oversight', leading to a greater isolation from the diocese amongst some 'Resolution C' parishes.

24. In all three clusters of 'unfinished business' the interregnum was surrounded by particular sensitivities. This was because it was assumed (often correctly) that an incumbent (and, by extension, those who appointed them) could exert great influence over a congregation's view of women's priesting.

25. In a similar way, many of the unresolved issues from the 1992–94 settlement also focused attention on communion as a site of potential reconciliation, but also of separation.

26. There was considerable variation of experience across the dioceses, with some issues proving controversial in one diocese which were almost entirely unproblematic in another. There was some debate as to whether these were best addressed through national policy or local solutions.

27. Although much of the report focuses on the challenges arising from the 1992–94 settlement, it is also important to acknowledge the way in which good relations have been built up between those of different views and coexistence has been viable. Divisions over women's priesting have not resulted in the division that some expected in 1992 and in many respects play little part in the day to day life of the Church of England.

28. The current position of the Church of England has sometimes been framed as a 'period of reception' of women's ordination as priests. However, many respondents were ambivalent about attempts to justify the present arrangements theologically.

29. Although a majority of participants in the study believed the current settlement was practically habitable, few believed that the present arrangements should continue indefinitely.

30. A majority of clergy and laity surveyed are in favour of opening the episcopate to women, feeling that it presented few new theological questions not already considered in the debate on women as priests. One of the most common views amongst respondents was that women bishops was a logical extension of what was decided in 1992.

31. However, there was considerable difference over how quickly, and at what price, any change to the current settlement should be made. The division over this question cut across familiar distinctions between 'supporters' and 'opponents' of women's priesting. A key difference seems to come between those favouring a 'pragmatic' approach to the future, those seeking an immediate and 'exclusionist' settlement and those wishing to continue with an 'accommodationist' approach to all sides.

Conclusion

The points above represent some of the main features of the Church of England's experience over the first ten years of ordaining women as priests, with particular focus on the beliefs, attitudes and perspectives of clergy and laity, and the practical outworking of the 1992–94 settlement. However, the experience of the past decade also raises some much wider (and potentially central) underlying questions that the remit of this report (and the space available) have not allowed us to consider in depth so far.[2] Some of these are cultural and historical in nature, others theological and ecclesiological, and they are explored briefly here by way of an extended conclusion to the report.

First come questions about the Church of England as an organization. The smooth running of any large and complex organization can be a delicate balancing act at the best of times, but large-scale change can place particularly heavy pressure on the vertical processes of decision-making and raise questions about the boundaries of the organization and the locus of authority within it. The Church of England's experience of ordaining women provided a key focus for three much wider ongoing dilemmas of identity and organization for organized religious institutions in the contemporary world. Firstly, it provided evidence of

---

[2] It is hoped to explore these further in a subsequent publication.

continuing tension between democratic and monarchical forms of decision-making: on one hand this was evident amongst those objectors to the 1992 decision who felt that General Synod was an inappropriate body to have final authority on the matter. On the other hand some campaigners for women's priesting expressed frustration that a significant component of the 1992–94 settlement – the Act of Synod – could be developed by the Bishops and passed by Synod without being referred to the dioceses as the Measure itself had been. While these complaints to some extent reflected the wider division between 'supporters' and 'opponents' of women's priesting, tensions over monarchical *versus* democratic styles of leadership also cut across these divisions (for example, whether a diocesan bishop was said to be showing 'strong leadership' or 'dictatorial tendencies' seemed to depend more on whether a group or individual was on the receiving end of a favourable or unfavourable decision from their bishop than anything else). Across the 1980s and 1990s there have been numerous attempts to delineate more clearly the relationship between democratic and episcopal modes of authority, but this research suggests that concern still exists at the current trend towards placing more theological and moral authority in the hands of the episcopate.

The enhanced role of the episcopate was part of a second, much wider set of questions concerning the relationship between local autonomy and national direction. The report has already noted the irritation expressed by many at the apparent 'postcode lottery' of solutions to problems raised by the legislative settlement (for example, why some dioceses seemed more willing to appoint women to senior positions than others, why some dioceses preferred to use the PEV rather than a diocesan or regional arrangement). But 'national' solutions were also viewed ambivalently, as suggested by the cool reception given to the 2001 guidelines for the implementation issued by the House of Bishops, and a more general suspicion of 'ecclesiastical quasi-legislation'.[3] (Again, such criticisms have not been confined only to 'supporters' or 'opponents' of women's priesting. Instead, 'supporters' and 'opponents' who seek a primarily 'exclusivist' solution to current unresolved issues have sometimes found themselves lining up alongside each other to criticize the present arrangements whilst 'supporters' and 'opponents' who seek a more 'accommodationist' or 'pragmatic' solution have also found themselves on the same side in some matters.) A strong vein of parochial self-determination amongst many grass roots churchgoers also militates against too strong a national settlement to any major issue, and neither a highly centralized nor highly congregationalist approach are particularly characteristic of the historic Anglican mainstream. Nevertheless, it may be important that more is done to share good practice on women's ministry (and related matters) across the dioceses than is currently being done. Most systematic sharing of information was being carried out by specific interest groups (for example, NADAWM[4]) rather than by senior diocesan clergy as a matter of course. This report has attempted to present some of the solutions and good practice procedures that emerged from the diocesan case studies, but also to highlight cases of bad practice, and it is hoped that this may stimulate further discussion and exchange of information. The experience of division should not be taken as an excuse to do nothing.

Third, at a much more fundamental level, the Church of England's experience of ordaining women as priests and the practical outworking of the relevant legislation raised important issues about the relationship of the individual to the wider body of the Church. Little of this discourse was explicitly articulated, but was often implied when a group or individual came to defend the legitimacy of their views on women's priesting within the Church of England.

---

[3] For a discussion of the problem, see: Norman Doe, 'Ecclesiastical Quasi-legislation', in Norman Doe, Mark Hill and Robert Ombres (eds.), *English Canon Law; Essays in Honour of Bishop Eric Kemp* (University of Wales Press, Cardiff, 1998), pp. 93–103.

[4] The National Association of Diocesan Advisers for Women's Ministry.

We have noted how a variety of groups felt themselves to be misunderstood or marginalized within the history of the debate or the subsequent settlement. The question of how far the integrity of marginalized groups should be protected also reflected considerable ambivalence towards the use of 'rights' language: amongst supporters of women's priesthood, some argued that it was a person's right to be ordained priest if their gifts and calling were clear, whereas there was some distancing from the suggestion that women's ordination was a 'women's rights' issue. Likewise, objectors to the 1992 decision were scornful of any attempt to base women's priesting on rights language, yet frequently resorted to classically liberal rights language (of self-determination, freedom and tolerance) to defend themselves and the opt-out provisions in a church that had now decided to ordain women. Against this, the language of role or duty was treated in a similarly complex manner: for some with more conservative values, women had a duty to remain within their ascribed roles and not clamour for priesthood. For others, the burden of duty fell on objectors to women's priesthood to fall into line now that the vote had been taken so decisively in favour. The language of 'catholicity' was at each stage particularly subject to use by those in the ascendancy: before the vote, advocates of a male-only priesthood appealed to women to accept the status quo in the name of Catholic order. Since 1992, the Act of Synod has frequently been criticized as 'unCatholic' by campaigners on behalf of women as priests and bishops. This lack of agreement over what 'catholicity' actually means, and how the term should be deployed, suggests there is much scope for further theological work here; both to explore the relationship between the individual and the whole body of Christ, and to unmask the discourses of power that can be hidden behind these common theological terms of reference.

The experience of the first ten years also raises a potentially important set of cultural and historical questions over the identity of the Church of England itself. Whilst the report has offered some conclusions about respondents' views of women's priesting, and addressed some specific practical issues arising from the settlement, it has said little about the Church of England as a cultural entity. What does the kind of settlement reached say about the kind of organization that created it? What kinds of linguistic and symbolic changes have taken place in the Church as a result of the decision to include women in the priesthood? If increasingly distinct constituencies have emerged over the past ten years, in what ways do they construct their identity, and what kinds of 'markers' help to define their identity? What kinds of long-term expectations did respondents express about what the ordination of women as priests would entail? And what kinds of stories were told about how the Church had arrived at this point?

When any group or community undergoes an experience of profound change, this almost always prompts a general re-examination of the group's history as people seek to understand what has happened and why, and what its significance might be within the longer story of the group. Such was the experience of the Jewish people during the Babylonian captivity, and of the first Christians in the months and years after the death and resurrection of Jesus. Likewise, as interviewees were asked to reflect on the first ten years of women's priesting in the Church of England, their accounts were underpinned by a variety of assumptions or observations about where the inclusion of women in the Anglican priesthood was to be located within a much wider historical trajectory. How much did the 1992 decision owe to wider cultural and historical trends, and how much to the prompting of God's Spirit to the Church in this age? Did women's priesting represent the regaining of a true and more Christlike path that had been lost to the Church for some centuries, or a wandering into the wilderness away from God? Charting popular understandings of history and teleology holds a natural curiosity for historians and anthropologists, but is also of crucial importance to the Church, since assumptions of this kind prompted Christians to address the question of women's priesting in quite different ways. If it was remarkably easy for the different viewpoints to 'speak past each other' in the debate on women and priesthood, this was to a very large extent due to the conflicting assumptions about history and teleology that underlay the arguments themselves. The importance of history and story have increasingly been recognized by theologians from across the whole spectrum,[5] and so it would seem valuable for participants in the debate to begin to explore and articulate some of their own assumptions, and listen to the assumptions of others, in order that the ongoing discussions on theology, gender and priesthood can be more constructively held. In particular, the research suggested a real ambivalence amongst clergy towards the idea of a 'period of reception' over women's ordination as priests. It may be that the Church of England can live without a 'doctrine of reception' as such, but it cannot do without a theological understanding of social change, and a preparedness to try and discern the hand of God in the midst of it.

This calls for further reflection on the much more general question of the relationship between the 'sacred' and the 'secular'. In Chapter 3 it was noted that a minority regarded women's ordination as priests as a capitulation to secular fashion. Others believed that in calling for equality of opportunity between men and women, the secular world was teaching the religious an important lesson. Others saw women's priesting as a development supported by both 'sacred' and 'secular' values. All of these perspectives assumed a particular construction of the boundary between the religious and the non-religious. This was not merely a question of whether an idea or a particular cultural artefact was to be placed on the 'sacred' or 'secular' side of the line, but also about how porous or impervious the boundary was. In the twenty-first century West at least, that boundary was often very sharply drawn, with clear differentiation of the 'sacred' and 'secular' spheres. Many of the conflicts of opinion in the debate on women's priesting can be traced to differing understandings of where those boundaries lay. If, as Richard Niebuhr has written, the dialogue between 'Christ' and 'culture' is inherent in the Christian faith,[6] a more frank and open discussion about how we see the intersection of these two spheres might lead us to greater understanding of the differing views on a variety of subjects; not just gender and priesthood.

Next, although the decision to ordain women to the priesthood was most often regarded as a major *change* in the life of the Church, it should also be emphasized that many historically important aspects of Anglican identity continued to exert their influence in the post-1992 context. For one thing, the Church of England remains an astonishingly diverse organization even despite the loss of some of its more Conservative Evangelical and Anglo-Catholic elements over women's priesting, and more threatened losses over female bishops and the ordination of practising homosexuals. And although it is not unproblematic to conceive of the Church of England having evangelical, Catholic and liberal 'wings' to it,[7] it remains the case that no one tradition has managed to achieve a position of hegemony – probably to the enrichment of the whole. The attempt to forge some kind of Anglican middle way between competing interest groups has also been the characteristic response of many bishops over the past few decades – and continued to be a feature of the House of

---

[5] See for example: James F. Hopewell, *Congregation: Stories and Structures* (Fortress Press, Philadelphia, 1987); Russ Parker, *Healing Wounded History* (Darton, Longman and Todd, London, 2001).

[6] H. Richard Niebuhr, *Christ and Culture* (Harper Torchbooks, New York, 1951).

[7] This implies some sort of neutral centre ground not tainted by any of these 'extremes'. Whilst it is possible to identify some kind of historic Anglican 'middle of the road' it is much more difficult to define, and does not take into account the way in which each of the three traditions listed here would see themselves to be the inheritors of an authentic Anglican mainstream.

Bishops' response to the ordination of women debate. Bishops themselves were amongst the first to recognize a tension in this, speaking of the need to resist governance by lobby group, whilst also avoiding the 'greyness' that could result from trying to 'manage' the different constituencies, which risked producing a cautious form of oversight that completely satisfied no one.

The first decade of women's priesting showed further continuities with the past in the re-emergence of much older debates (dating back to the Reformations) on the identity of the Church of England itself. Whilst the ecumenical implications of the 1992 decision did not go unnoticed, the majority of clergy and churchgoers seemed happy to accept that the Church of England had broken with Rome some centuries ago, and whilst it still shared many common features, it had the right and responsibility to make important decisions by itself. (It was widely thought that Rome and the Orthodox Churches would eventually follow in ordaining women anyway.) Some Anglo-Catholic clergy felt that the Church of England had now given up its Catholic heritage to join 'the Protestants' as yet another dissenting sect. However, neither overt Protestantism nor Anti-Catholicism played much of a part in the self-descriptions of interview participants[8] and the questionnaire suggested few wished women to be priested simply because it would strengthen ties with (mainly free church) denominations that also ordained women. A significant proportion of clergy and lay respondents to the questionnaires designated themselves 'Catholic' in some sense, and amongst the first generation of women to be priested there was a marked interest in the riches of the Anglican Catholic liturgical tradition. Nevertheless, the Catholic culture to which many participants in the study were clearly attracted was of a discernibly Anglican kind. This offers a further reason why, in 1992, the Roman option was not taken up by Anglicans (particularly the laity) to the extent that some had predicted.

A third important continuity was in popular attitudes to what priesthood meant. Some have argued that women's ordination as priests created a crisis in ordained ministry. In some respects this is true, but in other ways the debates of the 1980s and 1990s merely reignited some much older debates (never fully resolved) about the nature of ordained ministry and its place in society; for example, whether priesthood was to be understood functionally or ontologically; whether ordained ministry was a profession or a vocation. However, whilst these questions were important, it was also possible to spend *too* long discussing then, at the expense of worship, mission and pastoral care. Some interviewees even complained that the Church of England was 'obsessed with ministry'. Indeed, despite the continued theological debate about the nature of ordained ministry, many of those surveyed seemed to have had remarkably settled expectations of their clergy. Moreover, as already suggested, one of the key reasons why many found it comparatively easy to accept the incorporation of women into the priesthood was because it fitted neatly with (and even strengthened) what many worshippers had been expecting of their clergy for years.

Indeed, the experience of the last ten years suggests that the Church of England is perhaps a much more resilient body than many had expected.[9] It is worth remembering that in the weeks and months surrounding the vote, many outside (and a number within it) had prophesied a schism of such severity that the Church of England itself would barely survive. This is not in any way to deny the seriousness of the division and tension resulting from the ordination of women debate and its practical outworking; however, the impact of ordaining

---

[8] Except in the case of the small number of reformed (and usually Reform) evangelicals who were proud of the Church of England's Protestant credentials.

[9] The idea that 'resilience' is one of the chief characteristics of mainstream organized Christianity in contemporary society is put forward in: Martyn Percy, *Salt of the Earth: Religious Resilience in a Secular Age* (Continuum, London, 2001).

women has resulted in less serious division (particularly at grass roots level) than many had expected. 'It really wasn't the most momentous thing ever to have happened in the Church of England', one vicar liked to tell his congregation; 'it just felt like that'.[10] Much to the exasperation of some and the encouragement of others, popular Christian belief and practice in England has tended to a 'dogged ambivalence' towards figures and structures of ecclesiastical authority: church provides the locus and occasion for the working out of life and belief, to some extent regardless of official church policy or the views of the incumbent. Of course, for the largest proportion of respondents, accepting women's priesting presented no great difficulties anyway. But even amongst those who found the 1992 decision problematic, a majority were able to remain active in the Church of England and find new routes around anything they found difficult to accept. For some, this meant changing churches (there is a some evidence of increasing difference over women's priesting between congregations, and less within congregations, over the last ten years). For others, it meant staying put, safe in the knowledge that it would not be too many years before they had a new vicar who would be different to their predecessor. However, if this reflected a certain resilience in popular Anglican spirituality, the Church should not sit back and assume that this must necessarily continue. Patterns of religious belonging are changing fast (particularly amongst the generations growing up since the mid-1950s) and it is by no means clear how long a residue of loyal but independent-spirited popular Anglicanism will remain. Meanwhile, the first ten years of women's priesting suggested that at the end of the twentieth century, the grass roots of the Church of England retained a remarkable ability to absorb far-reaching change much more easily than its formal structures.

---

[10] Int. cs1:3:233.

Appendices

Appendix I

Ordination of women to the priesthood – Questionnaire for clergy

This questionnaire asks your views on the ordination of women to the priesthood and episcopacy, and about your experiences of living and working in the Church of England since the vote to ordain women to the priesthood in 1992. Please expand on the answers you have given on the back of the questionnaire, or on a separate sheet if necessary: anything else you wish to add will be gratefully received. All your answers will be treated in confidence. Thanks for taking part!

Section 1: About you and your ordained ministry

Q.1.1 Are you ☐ Female? ☐ Male? *(please tick appropriate box)*

Q.1.2 What is/are your current post(s)?

    Q.1.2a) If you are in parish ministry, please state how many churches you have full or shared responsibility for:

    Q.1.2b) If you are in parish ministry, please indicate if your parish has passed:
    (please appropriate tick box(es). Leave blank any that do not apply)
    ☐ Resolution A ☐ Resolution B ☐ Petition for PEV

    Q.1.2c) In your parish or other post, have you ever worked as part of a clergy team that contains both men and women? *(please tick all that apply)*
    ☐ Yes, in the past ☐ Yes, currently ☐ No

Q.1.3 Are you: *(please tick appropriate box)*
☐ Full stipend   ☐ Part stipend   ☐ House for duties
☐ Non-stipendiary   ☐ Other *(please state)* ---------------------------------

Q.1.4 What is your current diocese? --

Q.1.5 Which of the following phrases *most nearly* describes your theological orientation?
(please tick one box only)
☐ (Anglo-)Catholic   ☐ Liberal-Catholic   ☐ Liberal
☐ Liberal-Evangelical   ☐ Evangelical   ☐ Charismatic-Evangelical
☐ Catholic-Evangelical   ☐ Conservative Evangelical

Do you wish to expand on this answer in any way?

Q.1.6 Where did you train for ordained ministry? *(please give the name of the college, or ordination training scheme)*

Q.1.7 In what year were you ordained **a)** Deacon? _____ **b)** Priest?_____

Q.1.8 What is your age? *(please tick appropriate box, below)*
☐ 20-29   ☐ 30-39   ☐ 40-49   ☐ 50-59
☐ 60-69   ☐ 70-79   ☐ 80+

Section 2: Your views on the ordination of women to the priesthood

Q.2.1	Strongly agreed	Agreed	Was not certain	Disagreed	Strongly disagreed
Please think back to 1992, and to your views *at that time* on the ordination of women to the priesthood. Overall, how far did you agree with the opening up of the priesthood to women *at that time*?	1	2	3	4	5

Q.2.2 Please give the three reasons that were most important for you, in coming to that judgement *at that time*.

1. --

----

2. --

----

3. --

Q.2.3	Strongly agree	Agree	Am not certain	Disagree	Strongly disagree
Thinking about your *current* views, overall, how far do you agree, *at the present time*, with the ordination of women to the priesthood?	1	2	3	4	5

Q.2.4 Have your views changed at all over the period since 1992? *(delete as appropriate)*
YES / NO

Q.2.4a) If your views have changed, please say *how/why*, and if your views have not changed, please say *why* (and please continue on an extra sheet if necessary):

Q.2.5	Strongly agree	Agree	Am not certain	Disagree	Strongly disagree
Overall, how far do you agree that the Church of England should allow women to become bishops?	1	2	3	4	5

Q.2.6 Please give the three reasons that are most important for you, in coming to that judgement:

1. --

----

2. --

----

3. --

Q.2.7 It has sometimes been said that we are currently going through a 'period of reception' over the ordination of women to the priesthood. What does this phrase mean for you?

Q.2.8   Below are a series of statements that reflect some possible understandings of what a 'period of reception' over the ordination of women to the priesthood might mean. How far do you agree with each of them? *(please circle appropriate number)*

A 'period of reception' over the ordination of women to the priesthood is:	Strongly agree	Agree	Neither agree nor disagree	Disagree	Strongly disagree
a) Sufficient time and space in which those who have misgivings about the Church's decision to ordain women to the priesthood can be reconciled to what was decided in 1992.	1	2	3	4	5
b) An acknowledgement that we cannot yet be sure that ordaining women to the priesthood is definitely the will of God for the Church.	1	2	3	4	5
c) A concept created by theologians to justify the currently divided nature of the Church of England.	1	2	3	4	5
d) A period in which we wait to see whether the Roman Catholic and Orthodox Churches also move towards ordaining women to the priesthood.	1	2	3	4	5
e) A theological/theoretical framework to allow people of different positions on the ordination of women to remain within the same Church.	1	2	3	4	5
f) An acknowledgement that the final decision over the ordination of women to the priesthood can only be made as part of a wider process of discernment by the whole Church; not just Anglicans.	1	2	3	4	5
g) An acknowledgement that the ordination of women to the priesthood may well be reversible.	1	2	3	4	5
h) An acknowledgement that ideas on faith and order that begin life as minority opinions may gradually come to be recognized as the will of God for the Church.	1	2	3	4	5
i) A concept with no useful meaning whatsoever.	1	2	3	4	5

Section 3: Your experiences

At present, the stated intention within the Church of England is that those with differing views on the ordination of women to the priesthood should be enabled to continue to coexist in the same church, and be treated with integrity.

Q.3.1 Overall, in which aspect of your ministry has this situation been most evident? Why?

....

....

Q.3.2 Overall, in which aspect of your ministry has this situation been least evident? Why?

....

....

Q.3.3 Below are some statements relating to some possible aspects of ministry within a church containing a variety of beliefs and positions on women's ordination to the priesthood. Please fill in:

- **(Box A)** if you have ever experienced this yourself **(tick for YES, cross for NO)**.
- **(Box B)** if you have experienced this within the last six months **(tick for YES, cross for NO)**.

	A	B
Q.3.3a Communion *(Questions i-iv for women only. Men should go to part v of this question)*		

i) Have you known a fellow member of the clergy refuse communion from you because they do not accept your priesthood as a woman? ☐ ☐

ii) Have you known a lay person refuse communion from you because they do not accept your priesthood as a woman? ☐ ☐

iii) Have you known a fellow member of the clergy take communion from you *even though* they disagree with the ordination of women as priests? ☐ ☐

iv) Have you known a lay person take communion from you *even though* they disagree with the ordination of women as priests? ☐ ☐

(Questions v-viii for men only. Women should go on to Q.3.3b)

v) Have you known a fellow member of the clergy refuse communion from you because of your views on the ordination of women as priests? ☐ ☐

vi) Have you known a lay person refuse communion from you because of your views on the ordination of women as priests? ☐ ☐

vii) Have you known a fellow member of the clergy take communion from you *despite* your differences of opinion on the ordination of women as priests? ☐ ☐

viii) Have you known a lay person take communion from you *despite* your differences of opinion on the ordination of women as priests? ☐ ☐

	A	B
Q.3.3b Church membership		

(All parts of this question apply to both men and women)

i) Have you ever known anyone join your church because it has a woman as priest? *(write 'n/a' if no women work as priests in the parish)* ☐ ☐

ii) Have you known anyone leave your church because it has a woman as priest? *(write 'n/a/' if no women work as priests in the parish)* ☐ ☐

iii) Have you known anyone remain with your church despite disagreeing with its official/majority position on the ordination of women (either for or against)? ☐ ☐

	A	B
Q.3.3c Appointments		

(All parts of this question apply to men and women)

i) Would you say your gender has been:
a) A positive factor? ☐ ☐
b) A negative factor? ☐ ☐
in obtaining a suitable position in ordained ministry? *(leave blank if neither apply)*

ii) Would you say your views on the ordination of women have been:
a) A positive factor? ☐ ☐
b) A negative factor? ☐ ☐
in obtaining a suitable position in ordained ministry? *(leave blank if neither apply)*

	A	B
Q.3.3d Working relationships with others in the Church		

(Part i of this question is for both men and women)

i) Do you think *any* gender-related issues have made more difficult your working relationships with:
a) Senior clergy? ☐ ☐
b) Fellow/junior clergy? ☐ ☐
c) Lay people? ☐ ☐

(Questions ii-iii for women only. Men should go to part iv of this question)

ii) Would you say that any of your working relationships with senior clergy have been made more difficult because they did not believe women should be priests? ☐ ☐

iii) Have you ever been ignored or treated rudely by:
a) Fellow/junior clergy? ☐ ☐
b) Lay people? ☐ ☐
because they did not believe women should be priests?

(Questions iv-v for men only. Women should go on to question 3.4)

iv) Would you say that any of your working relationships with senior clergy have been made more difficult because you held different positions on the ordination of women as priests? ☐ ☐

v) Have you ever been ignored or treated rudely by:
a) Fellow/junior clergy? ☐ ☐
b) Lay people? ☐ ☐
because you held differing positions on the ordination of women as priests?

Q.3.4 How far do you agree that: *(please circle appropriate number).*	Strongly agree	Agree	Neither agree nor disagree	Disagree	Strongly disagree
a) In the great majority of cases, I enjoy *good* working relationships with *senior clergy* who differ from me on the question of the ordination of women.	1	2	3	4	5
b) In the great majority of cases, I enjoy *good* working relationships with *fellow clergy in general* who differ from me on the ordination of women.	1	2	3	4	5
c) In the great majority of cases, I enjoy *good* working relationships with lay people who differ from me on the question of the ordination of women.	1	2	3	4	5

(please expand on your answers on the back cover, or a separate sheet if necessary)*

Q.3.5 If you would like to expand on any of the answers you have given in questions 3.3 or 3.4 above (on your own experiences), please do so here, and continue at the end if you need to:

Q.3.6 Provisions for those who do not accept the ordination of women as priests

The 1992 Priests (Ordination of Women) Measure and the 1993 Episcopal Ministry Act of Synod contain provisions enabling parishes where a majority cannot accept the ordination of women to the priesthood to pass resolutions:

a) preventing a woman from celebrating the Eucharist or pronouncing absolution in the Parish (Resolution A, in the 1992 Measure);

b) preventing a woman acting as incumbent in that parish (Resolution B, in the 1992 Measure);

c) enabling a parish to petition for extended pastoral and sacramental care from a Provincial Episcopal Visitor (in the 1993 Act of Synod, popularly known as 'Resolution C').[1]

How far do you agree that: *(please circle appropriate number)*.	Strongly agree	Agree	Neither agree nor disagree	Disagree	Strongly disagree
a) The safeguards offered by the 1992 Priests (Ordination of Women) Measure were an acceptable consequence of the decision to ordain women as priests?	1	2	3	4	5
b) The safeguards offered by the 1993 Episcopal Ministry Act of Synod were an acceptable consequence of the decision to ordain women as priests?	1	2	3	4	5
c) The safeguards offered by the 1992 Priests (Ordination of Women) Measure discriminate against women?	1	2	3	4	5
d) The safeguards offered by the 1993 Episcopal Ministry Act of Synod discriminate against women?	1	2	3	4	5
e) The safeguards offered by the 1993 Episcopal Ministry Act of Synod discriminate against those who ordain women, or support their ordination?	1	2	3	4	5
f) The Measure and the Act discriminate against those who do not accept, or are uncertain about, ordaining women as priests?	1	2	3	4	5
g) It is appropriate that there are provisions in the Measure and Act that maintain a measure of distance between those who accept women's ordination as priests and those who do not?	1	2	3	4	5
h) There are good pastoral grounds for having provisions in the Measure and the Act, for those who do not accept/are uncertain about the ordination of women as priests	1	2	3	4	5
i) There are good theological grounds for having provisions in the Measure and the Act, for those who do not accept/are uncertain about the ordination of women as priests	1	2	3	4	5

(Please expand upon your answers on the back cover, or on a separate sheet, if you wish)

---

[1] In the case of the Petition for extended episcopal oversight, this requires a two-thirds majority in the PCC and the agreement of the minister in charge.

Q.3.7 If you circled **1** or **2** in Q.3.6g, please indicate how you have sought to establish/maintain this distance in your own ministry.

If you circled **4** or **5** in Q.3.6g, please indicate how you have sought to overcome any distance you might have encountered.

Q.3.8 This question asks how you think these provisions (for those who cannot accept women as priests) have been working out *in practice* (rather than about the principles or justifications behind the legislation itself).

How far do you agree that: *(please circle appropriate number)*.	Strongly agree	Agree	Neither agree nor disagree	Disagree	Strongly disagree
a) Overall, on balance, the provisions are working well.	1	2	3	4	5
b) The provisions are vital to enabling those who have difficulty with the ordination of women to remain within the C of E.	1	2	3	4	5
c) The provisions are placing damaging restrictions on the ability of women to minister fully as priests.	1	2	3	4	5
d) The provisions do not produce disharmony if they are implemented with good will on all sides.	1	2	3	4	5
e) The provisions are *occasionally* being abused to extend the power of one constituency over another.	1	2	3	4	5
f) The provisions are *regularly* being abused to extend the power of one constituency over another.	1	2	3	4	5

(Please expand on your answers on the back cover, or on a separate sheet if you wish)

Section 4: The impact of the ordination of women to the priesthood

Q.4.1 Thinking of the Church of England as a whole since the vote to ordain women to the priesthood in 1992, what would you say have been the main consequences of the opening up of the priesthood to women? *(Please list what you would consider to be the most important three)*

1. ....

....

....

2. ....

....

....

3. ....

....

....

Q.4.2 Below are some statements giving different possible views of the impact of the ordination of women to the priesthood in the Church of England.

How far do you agree that: *(please circle appropriate number)*.	Strongly agree	Agree	Neither agree nor disagree	Disagree	Strongly disagree
a) The ordination of women to the priesthood has 'had a detrimental effect on the C of E's relationship with the Roman Catholic Church'.	1	2	3	4	5
b) The opening up of the priesthood to women has enriched ordained ministry through the gifts and experiences that women have brought to it.	1	2	3	4	5
c) The ordination of women has done nothing to change the over-institutionalized nature of the Church.	1	2	3	4	5
d) The ordination of women has 'strengthened the relationship with other churches in Britain that already ordain women'.	1	2	3	4	5
e) The opening up of the priesthood to women has strengthened ordained ministry by creating a truly representative priesthood.	1	2	3	4	5

f) The ordination of women to the priesthood has been a setback for the development of a permanent diaconate.	1	2	3	4	5
g) The ordination of women to the priesthood has raised the credibility of the C of E in the eyes of the general public.	1	2	3	4	5
h) The opening up of the priesthood to women has weakened ordained ministry by bringing doubt about the validity of orders.	1	2	3	4	5
i) The ordination of women has brought about a more relational/collaborative style of pastoral leadership.	1	2	3	4	5
j) The opening up of the priesthood to women has undermined the authority of the ordained ministry by going against biblical principles of male headship.	1	2	3	4	5
k) The ordination of women has led to a less hierarchical style of priesthood.	1	2	3	4	5
l) The ordination of women has led to an empowerment of the laity.	1	2	3	4	5

If you would like to expand upon any of the answers you have given, either above or anywhere in the rest of the questionnaire, please do so here (and continue on a separate sheet if need be):

I would like to find a number of people who would be willing to take part in a follow-up interview, lasting about an hour, at some mutually convenient point.
If you would be happy to be interviewed on a number of issues relating to the research, please provide your contact details below. Thanks.

Name: ....

Address: ....

....

Telephone number: ....

Email address: ....

Thank you very much for your time, in completing this questionnaire!
Please post it back in the envelope provided, by ***[DATE]***

Note:
Question 4.2 and part of question 3.6 adapted from Leslie J. Francis and Mandy Robbins, *The Long Diaconate, 1987–1994* (Gracewing, 1999).
Questions 1.2–3, 1.5, and parts of Q.3.3 and 4.2 adapted from Helen Thorne, *Journey into Priesthood* (University of Bristol, 2000).

Appendix II

Women priests in the Church of England – Questionnaire for congregations

This questionnaire forms an important part of a much wider study on the Church of England since the vote to ordain women to the priesthood, back in 1992. Your help is much appreciated in taking part in this survey, and it is intended that the results will be included in a report, to be published by the Lincoln Theological Institute, University of Sheffield.

The questionnaire is anonymous, and all answers will be treated in confidence. However, if you would be prepared to participate in a short, informal follow-up interview at a mutually convenient time, please provide your name and contact details in the space provided at the end. (If you want to add your own thoughts/opinions at the end, or write more about any of the answers you have given in the questionnaire, this would be very welcome). Thanks again for taking part!

Section 1: About your involvement in the Church

Q.1.1 From which church did you pick up this questionnaire?

Q.1.2 Is this the church you usually attend? *(please tick appropriate box)*
☐ Yes   ☐ No
(If no: please say which church you usually attend:_____)

Q.1.3 About how long have you attended this church? *(to the nearest year)*

Q.1.4 How often have you attended a service here in the last four weeks? *(tick one)*
    ☐ Once   ☐ Twice   ☐ Three times
    ☐ Four times   ☐ More than four times

Q.1.5 Do you live within the parish, of the main church you attend?   **YES / NO**

Q.1.6 What were the *most important reasons* why you decided to attend *this* church, rather than any other church?

Q.1.7 How far do you agree that: *(please circle appropriate number)*.	Strongly agree	Agree	Neither agree nor disagree	Disagree	Strongly disagree
My attitude to the ordination of women was influential in my *current choice of church*?	1	2	3	4	5
My attitude to the ordination of women would be influential in any choice of church I make *in the future*?	1	2	3	4	5

Q.1.8 Do you have any other church involvement, besides attending services? **YES/NO**

(If 'yes', please say briefly what this is. This may be, for example, a position of responsibility in your own congregation, membership of a church group, or taking part in a wider church event, festival or organization outside your congregation)

Section 2: Your experiences of women's ordained ministry

In the Church of England, women were first ordained deacons in 1987, and in 1992, the Church of England voted to allow women to become priests, or 'presbyters' (i.e., that they could celebrate communion, and pronounce the forgiveness of sins in the service). The first women were ordained priests in 1994. Women cannot currently become bishops in the Church of England.

Because the ordination of women has taken place comparatively recently, it is useful to find out about the amount of contact you have had with women in priesthood, so far, and how you have viewed this experience:

Q.2.1 Below is a list of possible ways in which someone might experience the ministry of a woman in priesthood. Please say:

a) whether or not you have experienced this;

b) how far you felt/would feel comfortable with this.
(If you have experienced something, circle 'yes', and answer how far you felt comfortable with it at the time.)
*(If you have not experienced something, circle 'no', and answer how far you **think** you would feel comfortable with this.)*

	Have you experienced this?	How far did you/would you feel comfortable with it? *(please circle appropriate number)*				
		Very	Quite	Not sure	Not very	Not at all
a) Having a woman as vicar/rector of your church	Yes / No	1	2	3	4	5
b) Having a woman as curate of your church	Yes / No	1	2	3	4	5
c) Having a woman as deacon of your church	Yes / No	1	2	3	4	5
d) Having a woman as a lay reader at your church	Yes / No	1	2	3	4	5
e) Women clergy occasionally preaching at your church	Yes / No	1	2	3	4	5

f) Visiting women clergy occasionally presiding at communion in your church	**Yes / No**	1	2	3	4	5
g) Receiving a visit from an ordained woman chaplain at work, in hospital, etc.	**Yes / No**	1	2	3	4	5
h) Being present at a service led by a priest who is a woman	**Yes / No**	1	2	3	4	5
i) Taking communion from a priest who is a woman	**Yes / No**	1	2	3	4	5
j) Being baptized (either you or your children) by a priest who is a woman	**Yes / No**	1	2	3	4	5
k) Meeting women in priesthood regularly through mutual involvement in a church group or organization	**Yes / No**	1	2	3	4	5
l) Having a female friend who is a priest/training for the priesthood	**Yes / No**	1	2	3	4	5
m) Your new vicar having been ordained by a woman bishop	**Yes / No**	1	2	3	4	5

Q.2.2 Please think back over the period since 1992, to **the first time you encountered the ministry of a woman as a priest/presbyter. How did you** *feel* **about this at the time?**

Q.2.3   Did your reaction surprise you? Please say why (not):

Section 3: Your views on the ordination of women to the priesthood

Q.3.1 Overall, how far do you agree with the Church of England's decision of 1992 to allow women to become priest? *(please circle appropriate number).*	Strongly agree	Agree	Neither agree nor disagree	Disagree	Strongly disagree
	1	2	3	4	5

Q.3.2 What is the *most convincing* reason, for you, why you have come to this opinion?

....

....

Q.3.3 What is the *least convincing* argument you have heard, from those who would disagree with you over women's ordination to the priesthood?

....

....

Q.3.4 Overall, how far would you agree with the idea of the Church of England allowing women to become bishops? *(please circle appropriate number).*	Strongly agree	Agree	Neither agree nor disagree	Disagree	Strongly disagree
	1	2	3	4	5

Q.3.5 What is the *most convincing* reason, for you, why you have come to this opinion?

....

....

Q.3.6 Have you changed your opinion on the ordination of women to the priesthood, since the first women were ordained? **YES / NO.** If 'yes', please say why you think this was:

....

....

....

Q.3.7 Below are some common arguments that have been put for and against the ordination of women to the priesthood.

How far do you agree that: *(please circle appropriate number)*.	Strongly agree	Agree	Neither agree nor disagree	Disagree	Strongly disagree
a) The ordination of women in the Church of England was right because it enables us to move closer to other churches that have ordained women for many years.	1	2	3	4	5
b) The Bible speaks of the man being the head of the woman, just as Christ is head of the Church. Therefore it is not appropriate for ordained women to have seniority over men.	1	2	3	4	5
c) Men and women are fundamentally the same, and therefore it was right to allow women to become priests.	1	2	3	4	5
d) Women do not have the necessary character attributes and psychological attributes to be priests.	1	2	3	4	5
e) The Bible speaks of how in Christ, there is neither Jew nor Greek, neither slave nor free, neither male nor female. Therefore it is just as appropriate for women to be ordained to the priesthood as it is for men.	1	2	3	4	5
f) The ordination of women in the Church of England was wrong because it distances us from other churches that do not currently ordain women.	1	2	3	4	5
g) Were Jesus Christ alive on earth today, he would surely have included women amongst his apostles, therefore women should also be priests today.	1	2	3	4	5
h) Many women feel called to be priests, but their understanding of their calling must have been mistaken.	1	2	3	4	5
i) For a priest to truly represent Christ at the altar, the priest must share Christ's humanity; gender is not important to the function of the priest.	1	2	3	4	5
j) Whilst the whole church is still in the process of deciding whether women can be priests, it was wrong for the C of E to go ahead and ordain women unilaterally	1	2	3	4	5

231

Section 4: The impact of the ordination of women to the priesthood

(please circle appropriate number).	Great effect	Some effect	Not much effect	No effect at all
Q.4.1 How far would you say the Church of England's decision to ordain women to the priesthood has affected the week-by-week life of *your congregation?*	1	2	3	4
Q.4.2 How far would you say the Church of England's decision to ordain women to the priesthood has affected the life of *the Church of England as a whole?*	1	2	3	4
(If you would like to expand on the answers you have given above, please use the space provided on the back of the questionnaire)				

Q.4.3 What, for you, have been the most significant results of the Church of England's decision to ordain women?

Q.4.4 How far do you agree that, *as a result* of the ordination of women to the priesthood in the Church of England?

How far do you agree that: *(please circle appropriate number).*	Strongly agree	Agree	Neither agree nor disagree	Disagree	Strongly disagree
a) Chances of unity with the Roman Catholic Church have been badly damaged?	1	2	3	4	5
b) We now have a more representative clergy?	1	2	3	4	5
c) Women's distinctive style of ministry has led to a less clericalized church?	1	2	3	4	5
d) The Church of England has become badly divided?	1	2	3	4	5
e) Fairness has been achieved, and equal opportunities have been advanced?	1	2	3	4	5
f) Doubt has been introduced into the validity of Anglican priestly orders?	1	2	3	4	5
g) Women's gifts have been released for use in ordained ministry?	1	2	3	4	5
h) The Church of England has turned itself into a sect by acting unilaterally on this issue	1	2	3	4	5
i) The Church now seems more intelligible to the person in the street?	1	2	3	4	5

Section 5: Living with difference in the same Church

Since the first ordinations of women to the priesthood in 1994, the Church of England has made it possible for parishes to pass binding resolutions stating the parish's official position on the ordination of women:

> A parish may sign a resolution:
> i) preventing a woman from celebrating the Eucharist in that church ('Resolution A').
> ii) preventing a woman acting as vicar or rector in that church ('Resolution B').
> iii) allowing the parish to come under the oversight of a Provincial Episcopal Visitor (PEV, or 'flying bishop') if they wish to receive extended pastoral and sacramental care from a bishop who does not ordain women to the priesthood.[1] (This is sometimes known as 'Resolution C').

Q.5.1 Has your church passed one or more of these resolutions? *(tick one only)*
☐ Yes   ☐ No   ☐ Don't know   ☐ Did not know these resolutions existed

Q.5.2 How far do you agree that it should be possible for a church to pass each of the above resolutions if a majority of the PCC are unhappy about the ordination of women?

How far do you agree that: *(please circle appropriate number).*	Strongly agree	Agree	Neither agree nor disagree	Disagree	Strongly disagree
a) Resolution A (as described above)	1	2	3	4	5
b) Resolution B (as described above)	1	2	3	4	5
c) a Petition for a PEV (as described above)	1	2	3	4	5
(If you would like to expand upon the answers you have given in question 5.2, please write in the space provided at the end of the questionnaire)					

Q.5.3 Do you think the decision to pass or not to pass, one or more of the resolutions above, has had any *practical effect* on:

a) The life of your congregation?   ☐ Yes ☐ No   ☐ Don't know

b) Your church's relations with nearby Anglican churches?   ☐ Yes ☐ No   ☐ Don't know

c) Your Diocese as a whole?   ☐ Yes ☐ No   ☐ Don't know

(If you would like to expand upon the answers you have given in question 5.3, please write in the space provided at the end of the questionnaire)

---

[1] Whereas Resolutions A and B can be passed by a simply majority in the PCC, petitioning for the oversight of a PEV ('flying bishop') requires a two-thirds majority, and the agreement of the minister in charge.

Section 6: About you

It would be very helpful if you could provide a little bit of information about yourself, to enable responses to be analysed more effectively. As with the rest of the questionnaire, the confidentiality of your answers is guaranteed.

Q.6.1 Sex   ☐ Female   ☐ Male

Q.6.2 Age   ☐ Under 20   ☐ 20-29   ☐ 30-39   ☐ 40-49   ☐ 50-59
☐ 60-69   ☐ 70-79   ☐ 80+

Q.6.3 Your occupation *(If 'retired', please say what your last or main occupation was)*

Q.6.4 Church orientation
a) Which of the following phrases *most nearly* describes your own tradition? *(tick one box only)*
☐ (Anglo-)Catholic   ☐ Liberal-Catholic   ☐ Liberal
☐ Liberal-Evangelical   ☐ Evangelical   ☐ Charismatic-Evangelical
☐ Catholic-Evangelical   ☐ Conservative Evangelical

b) Do you wish to add anything to this description of your own tradition? *(if so, write it here):*

I am looking for a number of people who would be happy to discuss some of these issues with me in greater depth, in an informal interview. This would be confidential and entirely voluntary. If you would be happy to take part in a short interview, at a mutually convenient time, please give your contact details in the space provided below:

Name: _____

Address: _____

_____

Telephone number: _____

Email address: _____

Thank you very much for your time, in completing this questionnaire!
Please return it to the box provided, or failing that, to: Dr Ian Jones, Lincoln Theological Institute for the Study of Religion and Society, University of Sheffield, 36 Wilkinson Street, Sheffield. S10 2GB. *By: ***DATE****

If you have any more comments on any of the questions or issues in this questionnaire survey, or need to continue any of your answers, please use the space provided here (and on the back) to write more:

Note: **Q.6.4** has been adapted from: Helen Thorne, *Journey into Priesthood* (University of Bristol, 2000).

Appendix III

The 14 deanery
case study congregations

For the nine main diocesan case study congregations,
see Table 1iv (Introduction) and Chapter 4 section 4.2.

Church 10 is a parish church in the Anglo-Catholic tradition in an urban area of Deanery D. Its congregation is predominantly middle-aged and elderly, but with a few young families coming into the church from a community project on site. Resolution B is in force, but the incumbent supports women's ordination as priests and the church current has a female curate.

Church 11 is a charismatic evangelical congregation in the same town in Deanery D. It attracts a wide range of age groups across a variety of services. The male incumbent is married to an ordained woman who works elsewhere in the deanery. No resolutions are in place.

Church 12 is a large congregation in a suburban part of Deanery D. Services are classical evangelical in style with a firm emphasis on biblical exegesis. The all-male clergy describe themselves as 'conservative evangelical' and both have reservations over women in headship roles in the local church. Women have been invited to preach in church, but have not presided, though no resolutions are in place.

Church 13 is a town centre congregation in the 'central' Anglican tradition. Its clergy team comprises both men and women, although it has not yet had a female incumbent. The church has a strong civic identity.

[*Church 14*: The parish that was supposed to have appeared as Church 14 withdrew from the study at late notice, and it was not possible to find a replacement.]

Church 15 is an Anglo-Catholic parish in the highly urbanized, multicultural Deanery E. Resolutions A and B are in place and the parish also receives extended episcopal oversight. The priest does not agree with women's ordination as priests at this time, and suggests that a significant proportion of the regular congregation are attracted to the church by its resolution status and its emphasis on Anglo-Catholic liturgy.

Church 16 is in fact two congregations in an urban, multicultural area of Deanery E. Both congregations are in the evangelical tradition, and both have experience of women's priestly ministry, although at present the clergy team is all-male. No resolutions are in place, and a female member of one of the congregations was about to go forward for ordination training at the time of the research.

Church 17 is a small congregation in the Catholic tradition, located in a multicultural city suburb of Deanery E. The congregation has struggled over the question of women's ordination to the priesthood, but has reached a compromise arrangement whereby the church has a male vicar, and does not pass any resolutions. It has yet to experience a woman's priestly ministry.

Church 18 is a large suburban evangelical congregation in Deanery E. The regular congregation, who are predominantly professionals, are drawn from a wide area and include a large spectrum of ages. Church 18 has several years' experience of women's ordained ministry, and currently has a female curate. Up to the present, it has not appointed a female incumbent.

Church 19 is a suburban city parish of liberal-Catholic ethos, not far from Church 16 in Deanery E. It has a long experience of women's ministry as priests, being one of the first in the area to accept a female curate. Current it has a male vicar.

Church 20 is located on the edge of a small town in Deanery F, and is part of a group of neighbouring parishes. The congregation combines both traditional Prayer Book Anglicans and a significant number of charismatic evangelicals. For some years the church has had a female priest-in-charge.

Church 21 is also to be found on the edge of a small town in Deanery F. The church is firmly within the Anglo-Catholic tradition, with a strong Roman emphasis under the last vicar. As part of a team the parish cannot pass a resolution or petition for extended episcopal oversight, but received this provision on a semi-formal basis due to an arrangement between the PEV, diocesan bishop and team rector.

Church 22 is located in a small town in Deanery F. Its male vicar is supportive of women's ministry and in the past an ordained woman has worked on the staff there. Female clergy regularly come to preach and celebrate at the church, which is in the central Anglican tradition.

Church 23 is found in a rural part of Deanery F. It is part of a larger group of parishes looked after by a team of clergy who are currently all men. No resolutions are in place and, to my knowledge, the congregation has yet to experience a woman's priestly ministry.

Bibliography

Abbott, Pamela and Claire Wallace, *An Introduction to Sociology: Feminist Perspectives* (Routledge, London, 2nd edition 1997).

After November; Some Possible Responses in the Event of the Failure of the Draft Priests (Ordination of Women) Measure and its Associated Canons – A Report by the Women Deacons of the Ely Diocese (1992).

Aldridge, Alan, 'Discourse on Women in the Clerical Profession: The Diaconate and Language-games in the Church of England', *Sociology* 26 (1) February 1992, pp. 45–57.

Aldridge, Alan, *Religion in the Contemporary World: A Sociological Introduction* (Polity Press, Cambridge, 2002).

Archbishops' Council Ministry Division, *Statistics of Licensed Ministers; Some Facts and Figures as at 31ˢᵗ December 1999* (General Synod GS Misc. 616, London, 2001).

Archbishops' Council Ministry Division, *Statistics of Licensed Ministers 2001* (General Synod GS Misc 673, London, 2002).

Archbishops' Council Ministry Division, *Statistics of Licensed Ministers 2002* (General Synod GS Misc 721, London, 2003).

Avis, Paul, *The Anglican Understanding of the Church* (SPCK, London, 2000).

Avis, Paul (ed.), *Seeking the Truth of Change in the Church: Reception, Communion and the Ordination of Women* (T & T Clark, London, 2004).

Avis, Paul, 'Reception: Towards an Anglican Understanding' in Paul Avis (ed.), *Seeking the Truth of Change in the Church: Reception, Communion and the Ordination of Women* (T & T Clark, London, 2004), pp. 19-39.

Avis, Paul, 'The Act of Synod: A "Bearable Anomaly"?' in Paul Avis (ed.), *Seeking the Truth of Change in the Church: Reception, Communion and the Ordination of Women* (T & T Clark, London, 2004), pp. 152–170.

Baber, Harriet, 'What the Ordination of Women Entails: A Logical Investigation', *Theology*, vol. CII, No. 806, March/April 1999, pp. 112–121.

Badone, Ellen (ed.), *Religious Orthodoxy and Popular Faith* (Princeton University Press, Princeton N.J., 1990.

Baker, John Austin, *The Right Time; A Lecture Delivered at the First Annual Conference of the Movement for the Ordination of Women* (MOW, London, 1981).

Barking Episcopal Area Working Group, 'Proclaim Afresh in Each Generation: A Submission to the Rochester Commission on Women Bishops' (October 2001).

Barr, Andrew and Liz, *Jobs for the Boys? Women who Became Priests* (Hodder and Stoughton, London, 2001).

Baumann, Zygmunt, 'Morality in the Age of Contingency' in Paul Heelas, Scott Lash and Paul Morris (eds), *Detraditionalisation* (Blackwell, Oxford, 1996), pp. 49–58.

Baxter, Christina, 'Women in the Church: Some Personal Reflections on 1985–2000', *Crucible*, January–March 2001, pp. 14–24.

Beckwith, Roger, 'The Bearing of Holy Scripture' in Peter Moore (ed.), *Man, Woman and Priesthood* (SPCK, London, 1978), pp. 45–62.

Bentley, Lesley, 'At the Grass Roots: The Act in the Parishes' in Monica Furlong (ed.), *Act of Synod: Act of Folly?* (SCM Press, London, 1998), pp. 101–114.

Bentley, Lesley 'Two-clergy Couples' in Gordon Kuhrt (ed.), *Ministry Issues in the Church of England: Mapping the Trends* (Church House Publishing, London, 2001), pp. 208–10.

Berners-Wilson, Angela, 'Pilgrimage to Priesthood' in Christina Rees (ed.), *Voices of this Calling: Experiences of the First Generation of Women Priests* (Canterbury Press, Norwich, 2002), pp. 181–4.

Bloor, David, *Wittgenstein; A Social Theory of Knowledge* (Macmillan, London and Basingstoke, 1983), pp. 140–45.

Blum, Georg Gunter, 'The Office of Woman in the New Testament' in Michael Bruce and G.E. Duffield (eds), *Why Not? Priesthood and the Ministry of Women* (Marcham Manor Press, Abingdon, 1972), pp. 63–77.

Bocock, Robert, *Ritual in Industrial Society; A Sociological Analysis of Ritualism in Modern England* (Allen and Unwin, London, 1974).

Boyd, Ian R., 'What are the Clergy For? Clerical Role Uncertainty and the State of Theology', *Theology* xcviii (783) May/June 1995, pp. 196–8.

Bracegirdle, Wendy, 'Priesthood and Society' in Rees, Christina (ed.), *Voices of this Calling: Experiences of the First Generation of Women Priests* (Canterbury Press, Norwich, 2002), pp. 132–4.

Brown, Callum G., *The Death of Christian Britain: Understanding Secularisation, 1800–2000* (Routledge, London, 2001).

Bruce, Michael and G.E. Duffield (eds), *Why Not? Priesthood and the Ministry of Women* (Marcham Manor Press, Abingdon, 1972).

Bruce, Michael, 'Heresy, Equality and the Rights of Women' in Michael Bruce and G.E. Duffield (eds), *Why Not? Priesthood and the Ministry of Women* (Marcham Manor Press, Abingdon, 1972), pp. 40–55.

Burkill, Mark, *Women's Ordination: Why is this a Crisis for the Church of England?* (Reform Discussion Paper No. 2 Sheffield, 1993).

Burkill, Mark, *The What and Why of the Reform Covenant* (Reform Discussion Paper, No. 20, Sheffield, 1998).

Burkill, Mark, *Reform Survey on Women's Ministry* (Reform Discussion Paper No. 22, Sheffield, 2000).

Calvert, Ellie, 'The Sources of Opposition to Women in the Ordained Ministry among Clergy, Undergraduates and Public Figures' (Cambridge SPS Dissertation, 1997).

Carroll, Jackson W., Barbara Hargrove and Adair T. Lummis, *Women of the Cloth: A New Opportunity for the Churches* (Harper and Row, San Francisco, 1983).

Chaves, Mark, *Ordaining Women; Culture and Conflict in Religious Organisations* (Harvard University Press, London, 1997).

Church of England Newspaper, October 2000 to September 2003.

Church Times, October 2000 onwards.

Clutterbuck, Ivan, *Marginal Catholics: Anglo-Catholicism – A Further Chapter of Modern Church History* (Gracewing, Leominster, 1993).

Collins, Jean, 'Phoebe's Legacy' (unpublished paper, 2000).

Cornell, Jean, 'Kairos Comes Too Soon: Are Women Priests in Retreat in the Church of England?', *Feminist Theology* 12 (1) September 2003, pp. 43–51.

Cost of Conscience [prepared by Geoffrey Kirk], *Alternative Episcopal Oversight: The Agreed Statement* (Cost of Conscience, London, 1990).

Countryman, William, *Dirt, Greed and Sex* (SCM, London, 1989).

Crawford, Patricia, *Women and Religion in England, 1500–1720* (Routledge, London, 1993).

Cross, F.L. and E.A. Livingstone (eds), *The Oxford Dictionary of the Christian Church* (Oxford University Press, Oxford, 1997).

Davies, Douglas, Charles Watkins and Michael Winter, *Church and Religion in Rural England* (T & T Clark, Edinburgh, 1991).

Doe, Norman, 'Ecclesiastical Quasi-legislation', in Norman Doe, Mark Hill and Robert Ombres (eds), *English Canon Law; Essays in Honour of Bishop Eric Kemp* (University of Wales Press, Cardiff, 1998), pp. 93–103.

Douglas, Mary, *Purity and Danger* (Routledge and Kegan Paul, London, 1966).

Douglas, Mary, *Natural Symbols* (Barrie and Rockliff/The Cresset, London, 1970).

Douglas, Mary, 'The Debate on Women Priests' in Mary Douglas, *Risk and Blame: Essays in Cultural Theory* (Routledge, London and New York, 1992), pp. 271–94.

Dowell, Susan and Jane Williams, *Bread, Wine and Women; The Ordination of Women Debate in the Church of England* (Virago, London, 1994).

Duffield, G.E., 'Feminism and the Church', in Michael Bruce and G.E. Duffield (eds), *Why Not? Priesthood and the Ministry of Women* (Marcham Manor Press, Abingdon, 1972), pp. 9–25.

Eames Monitoring Group Report, August 1997 [http://www.anglicancommunion.org/lambeth/reports/report10.htm, downloaded 2 October 2003].

Evans, G.R., *The Reception of the Faith; Reinterpreting the Gospel for Today* (SPCK, London, 1997).

Faith and Heritage (a journal of the Prayer Book Society – various issues from Spring 1992 onwards).

Faith and Worship; A Half-yearly Review Published by the Prayer Book Society (various issues from Autumn 1985 onwards).

Field-Bibb, Jacqueline, *Women towards Priesthood: Ministerial Politics and Feminist Praxis* (Cambridge University Press, Cambridge, 1991), pp. 67–162.

Forward in Faith, 'The Case for a Free Province in the Church of England' (December 1998).

Forward! Plus [Forward in Faith parish newspaper] (various issues from Autumn 2000 onwards).

Francis, Leslie J., 'The Personality Characteristics of Anglican Ordinands: Feminine Men and Masculine Women', *Personality and Individual Differences* 12 (11) 1991, pp. 1133–40.

Francis, Leslie J. and T.H. Thomas, 'Are Anglo-Catholic Priests more Feminine? A Study among Male Anglican Clergy', *Pastoral Sciences* 15 (1996), pp. 15–22.

Francis, Leslie J. and Mandy Robbins, *The Long Diaconate, 1987–1994: Women Deacons and the Delayed Journey to Priesthood* (Gracewing, Leominster, 1999).

Furlong, Monica, *A Dangerous Delight; Women and Power in the Church* (SPCK, London, 1991).

Furlong, Monica (ed.), *Act of Synod: Act of Folly?* (SCM Press, London, 1998).

Futers, Michael, *A Legitimate Development; An Anglican Catholic Case for the Ordination of Women to the Priesthood* (MOW, London, 1988).

Gassmann, Gunther, 'From Reception to Unity: The Historical and Ecumenical Significance of the Concept of Reception' in Colin Podmore (ed.), *Community – Unity – Communion; Essays in Honour of Mary Tanner* (Church House Publishing, London, 1998), pp. 117–29.

Geertz, Clifford, 'Thick Description: Toward an Interpretive Theory of Culture' in Clifford Geertz, *The Intrepretation of Cultures* (Hutchinson, London, 1975 edition), pp. 3–32.

General Synod GS104a, The Ordination of Women to the Priesthood; A Summary of the Consultative Document presented to the Anglican Consultative Council (Church Information Office, London, 1973).

General Synod GS104b, *Supplementary Report on the Ordination of Women to the Priesthood* (CIO, London, 1975).

General Synod GS Misc 252, *The Ordination of Women: Report of the Standing Committee on the Reference to the Dioceses* (CIO, London, 1975).

General Synod GS 738, *The Ordination of Women to the Priesthood: The Scope of the Legislation* (Church House, London, April 1986).

General Synod GS Misc 336, *The Ordination of Women to the Priesthood; Reference of Draft Legislation to the Diocesan Synods, 1990* (Church House, London, 1990).

General Synod November Group of Sessions 1989, *Report of Proceedings No. 20 Vol. 3* (General Synod, London, 1989).

General Synod GS833Y, *General Synod Draft Priests (Ordination of Women) Measure, Draft Canon C4B and Draft Amending Canon no. 13 – Revision Committee Report* (Church House, London, n.d. [?1990]).

General Synod GS Misc 418, *Being in Communion* (Church House, London, 1993).

General Synod, *The Ordination of Women to the Priesthood: The Synod Debate, 11 November 1992: The Verbatim Record* (Church House Publishing, London, 1993).

General Synod Episcopal Ministry Act of Synod 1993.

Gill, Sean, *Women and the Church of England, from the Eighteenth Century to the Present* (SPCK, London, 1994).

GRAS Newsletter, December 2000 onwards.

GRAS, 'The Scandal of the Blackburn Report' (GRAS, London, 2001).

Hammersley, Martyn, *The Politics of Social Research* (Sage, London, 1995).

Handy, Charles, *Understanding Organisations* (Penguin, London, 4th edition 1993).

Hastings, Adrian, *A History of English Christianity, 1920–1990* (SCM Press, London, 3rd edition 1991).

Hauke, Manfred, *Women in the Priesthood? A Systematic Analysis in the Light of the Order of Creation and Redemption* (Ignatius Press, San Francisco, 1988 [first German edition 1986]).

Hayter, Mary, *The New Eve in Christ; The Use and Abuse of the Bible in the Debate about Women in the Church* (SPCK, London, 1987).

Healy, Nicholas M., *Church, World and the Christian Life* (Cambridge University Press, Cambridge, 2000).

Heelas, Paul, Scott Lash and Paul Morris (eds), *Detraditionalisation* (Blackwell, Oxford, 1996).

Hind, John, 'Women Bishops in Ecumenical Perspective' in G.R. Evans and Martyn Percy (eds), *Managing the Church; Order and Organisation in a Secular Age* (Sheffield Academic Press, Sheffield, 2000), pp. 191–215.

HMSO, *Priests (Ordination of Women) Measure 1993 (No. 2)* (HMSO, London, 1993) [http://www.hmso.gov.uk/measures/Ukcm_19930002_en_1.htm, downloaded 20 November 2003].

HMSO, *Ordination of Women (Financial Provisions) Measure 1993, No. 3* (HMSO, London, 1993) [http://www.hmso.gov.uk/measures/Ukcm_19930003_en2.htm#mdiv1, downloaded 4 December 2003].

Hoggart, Richard, *The Uses of Literacy* (Chatto and Windus, London, 1957).

Hopewell, James F., *Congregation: Stories and Structures* (Fortress Press, Philadelphia, 1987).

House of Bishops, 'Statement by the House Following its Meeting in Manchester', 11–14 January 1993.

House of Bishops, 'Guidelines for the Testing and Discernment of Vocation and the Preparation for Ordination to the Priesthood of Women already in Deacons' Orders' in *Ordination of Women to the Priesthood: Pastoral Arrangements – A Report by the House of Bishops* GS 1074 (Church House, London, 1993).

House of Bishops, 'Bonds of Peace: Arrangements for Pastoral Care following the Ordination of Women to the Priesthood in the Church of England' GS 1074 (Church House, London, 1993).

House of Bishops, 'Priests (Ordination of Women) Measure 1993: Code of Practice' (Church House, London, 1994).

House of Bishops 'Episcopal Ministry Act of Synod 1993: Guidelines for Good Practice Emanating from the Working Party of the House of Bishops Chaired by the Bishop of Blackburn ("The Blackburn Report")', GS1395 (7 March 2001).

House of Bishops Standing Committee, 'Episcopal Ministry Act of Synod 1993: Guidelines for Good Practice Emanating from the Report of the Working Party of the House of Bishops Chaired by the Bishop of Blackburn ("The Blackburn Report")', GS1395 (7 March 2001).

House of Bishops, *Working Party on Women in the Episcopate: A Progress Report from the House of Bishops* General Synod GS1457 (Church House, London, 2002).

Howard, Christian, *Women in Society and the Church* (MOW Occasional Papers No. 3, MOW, London, 1983).

Jacob, W.M., *Lay People and Religion in the Early Eighteenth Century* (Cambridge University Press, Cambridge, 1996).

Jones, Serene, *Feminist Theory and Christian Theology; Cartographies of Grace* (Fortress Press, Minneapolis, 2000).

Jones, Ian, 'The "Mainstream" Churches in Birmingham, c. 1945–1998; The Local Church and Generational Change' (University of Birmingham PhD Thesis, 2000).

Jones, Ian, 'Earrings Behind the Altar? Anglican Expectations of the Ordination of Women as Priests', *Dutch Review of Church History Vol. 83 (2003)*, pp. 462–76.

Kirk, Geoffrey, 'A New Province for the Anglican Communion' (paper presented to the Conference 'A Free Province? A Third Province?', Pusey House, Oxford, 22–23 September 2003) [available online at: http://www.forwardinfaith.com/artman/publish/03-09-26-kirk.shtml, downloaded 15 October 2003].

Kuhrt, Gordon W. (ed.), *Ministry Issues in the Church of England; Mapping the Trends* (Church House Publishing, London, 2001).

Kühnis, Anna-Thekla, 'The Ordination of Women: A Contribution from Jungian Depth-Psychology', *Anglican Theological Review* 84 (3) Summer 2002, pp. 689–702.

Kuhrt, Gordon W., and Lesley Bentley, 'Women and Ordained Ministry' in Gordon W. Kuhrt (ed.) *Ministry Issues in the Church of England; Mapping the Trends* (Church House Publishing, London, 2001), pp. 234–49.

Lee, Raymond M., *Doing Research on Sensitive Topics* (Sage, London, 1993).

Lehman jnr, Edward C., *Gender and Work: The Case of the Clergy* (State University of New York Press, Albany, 1993).

Leonard, Graham, 'The Priesthood of Christ' in James Tolhurst (ed.), *Man, Woman and Priesthood* (Gracewing Fowler Wright Books, Leominster, 1989), pp. 1–22.

Low, Robbie and Francis Gardom, *Believe it or Not! What Church of England Clergy Actually Believe* (Christian Research and Cost of Conscience, London, 2003).

Maltby, Judith, 'One Lord, One Faith, One Baptism, but Two Integrities?' in Monica
    Furlong (ed.), *Act of Synod: Act of Folly?* (SCM Press, London, 1998), pp. 42–58.
Mannheim, Karl, *Ideology and Utopia; An Introduction to the Sociology of Knowledge*
    (Routledge and Kegan Paul, London, 1952 edition).
Marwick, Arthur, *The Sixties: Cultural Revolution in Britain, France, Italy and the United
    States, c. 1958–1974* (Oxford University Press, Oxford, 1998).
Mascall, E.L., 'Some Basic Considerations' in Peter Moore (ed.), *Man, Woman and
    Priesthood* (SPCK, London, 1978), pp. 9–26.
Mayland, Jean, 'An Act of Betrayal', in Monica Furlong (ed.), *Act of Synod: Act of Folly?*
    (SCM Press, London, 1998), pp. 59–75.
McGrath, Gavin, 'Will the Circle Be Unbroken? The Crisis Concerning Truth in the Church
    of England' (Reform Discussion Paper No. 4, Sheffield, n.d. [mid-1990s]).
McLeod, Hugh, *Secularisation in Western Europe, 1870–1914* (Macmillan,
    Basingstoke, 2000).
Mead, Margaret, *Male and Female; A Study of the Sexes in a Changing World* (Penguin,
    London, 1962 edition).
Miller, Jeremy, 'A Note on Aquinas and Ordination of Women', *New Blackfriars* 61 (719),
    April 1980, pp. 185–90.
Minnis, A.J., '*De Impedimenta Sexus:* Women's Bodies and Medieval Impediments to
    Female Ordination' in Peter Biller and A.J. Minnis (eds), *Medieval Theology and the
    Natural Body* (York Medieval Press/Boydell and Brewer, York/Woodbridge, Suffolk,
    1997), pp. 109–140.
Moore, Peter (ed.), *Man, Woman and Priesthood* (SPCK, London, 1978).

Nesbitt, Paula D., 'Dual Ordination Tracks: Differential Benefits for Men and Women
    Clergy' in William H. Swatos (ed.), *Gender and Religion* (Transaction Publishers,
    London, 1994), pp. 27–44.
New Directions Magazine, 1 (1) June 1995–6 (102) November 2003.
Niebuhr, H. Richard, *Christ and Culture* (Harper Torchbooks, New York, 1951).
Nolan, Michael, 'The Defective Male: What Aquinas Really Said', *New Blackfriars* 75
    (880), March 1994, pp. 156–66.
Norman, Ralph, 'ARCIC III, Episcopal Authority and Establishment' (unpublished
    paper, 2000).
Norris, Richard, *The Ordination of Women and the Maleness of Christ* (MOW Occasional
    Papers No. 2, MOW, London, 1982).

Oakley, Ann, 'People's Ways of Knowing: Gender and Methodology' in Suzanne Hood,
    Berry Mayall and Sandy Oliver (eds), *Critical Issues in Social Research; Power and
    Prejudice* (Open University Press, Buckingham, 1999), pp. 154–70.
Obelkevich, James, *Religion and Rural Society: South Lindsey, 1825–1875* (Oxford
    University Press, Oxford, 1976).
O'Day, Rosemary, 'The Men from the Ministry', in Gerald Parsons (ed.), *Religion in
    Victorian Britain* vol. II: Controversies (MUP/Open University, Manchester, 1988),
    pp. 258–79.
Oddie, William, *The Roman Option: Crisis and the Realignment of English-speaking
    Christianity* (HarperCollins, London, 1997).
Outlook (Journal of Women and the Church), no. 2, Autumn 1997 onwards.

Parker, Russ, *Healing Wounded History* (Darton, Longman and Todd, London, 2001).
Parliamentary Debates (Hansard), *House of Commons Official Report* Vol. 230, no. 235,
    Friday 29 October 1993 (HMSO, London, 1993).

Parliamentary Debates (Hansard), *House of Lords: Official Report* Vol. 549, No. 194, Tuesday 2 November 1993 (HMSO, London, 1993).

Parliamentary Ecclesiastical Committee 203rd and 204th Reports, *Reports by the Ecclesiastical Committee upon the Priests (Ordination of Women) Measure and the Ordination of Women (Financial Provisions) Measure, laid before both Houses of Parliament pursuant to Section 4 of the Church of England Assembly (Powers) Act 1919* (HMSO, London, 1993).

Parsons, Gerald, 'Between Law and Licence: Christianity, Morality and "Permissiveness"', in Gerald Parsons (ed.), *The Growth of Religious Diversity; Britain from 1945* Vol. II: *Issues* (Open University/Routledge, London, 1994), pp. 231–66.

Peberdy, Alyson S., *A Part of Life; A Study of Lay People's Response to Women's Ministry in the Church of England* (MOW, London, 1985).

Penhale, Francis, *Catholics in Crisis* (Mowbray, London and Oxford, 1986).

Percy, Martyn, 'The Doctrine of Reception and Division in the Church' (unpublished paper, n.d.).

Percy, Martyn, *Salt of the Earth: Religious Resilience in a Secular Age* (Continuum, London, 2001).

Petre, Jonathan, *By Sex Divided; The Church of England and Women Priests* (HarperCollins, London, 1994).

Pickering, W.S.F., *Anglo-Catholicism; A Study in Religious Ambiguity* (Routledge, London, 1989).

Radner, Ephraim, 'Bad Bishops: A Key to Anglican Ecclesiology', *Anglican Theological Review* 82 (2) Spring 2000, pp. 321–41.

Ransom, Stuart, Alan Bryman and C. Robin Hinings, *Clergy, Ministers and Priests* (Routledge and Kegan Paul, London, 1977).

Reed, John Shelton, *Glorious Battle: The Cultural Politics of Victorian Anglo Catholicism* (Vanderbilt University Press, Nashville, 1996).

Rees, Christina (ed.), *Voices of this Calling: Experiences of the First Generation of Women Priests* (Canterbury Press, Norwich, 2002).

Reform Newspaper, 1994 onwards.

Reform, *Dogged by the Collar? Getting Women's Ministry Right in the Church of England* (Reform Discussion Paper 13, Sheffield, 1996).

Renzetti, Claire M. and Raymond M. Lee (eds), *Researching Sensitive Topics* (Sage, London, 1993).

Report of the Archbishop of Canterbury's Commission on Communion and Women in the Episcopate Part II: October 1989 and March 1990 (Anglican Consultative Council, London, 1990).

Review Group of the Archbishop's Council, *Working with the Spirit: Choosing Diocesan Bishops* (General Synod GS 1405, Church House Publishing, London, 2001).

Robbins, Mandy and Leslie J. Francis, 'Role Prioritisation amongst Clergywomen: The Influence of Personality and Church Tradition', *British Journal of Theological Education* 11 (1), August 2000, pp. 7–23.

Roberts, Richard H., *Theology, Religion and the Human Sciences* (Cambridge University Press, Cambridge, 2002).

Ruether, Rosemary Radford (ed.), *Religion and Sexism: Images of Woman in the Jewish and Christian Traditions* (Simon and Schuster, New York, 1974).

Rusch, William G., 'The Landscape of Reception' in Paul Avis (ed.), *Seeking the Truth of Change in the Church: Reception, Communion and the Ordination of Women* (T & T Clark, London, 2004), pp. 1–18.

Russell, Anthony, *The Clerical Profession* (SPCK, London, 1984).

Sacred Congregation for the Doctrine of the Faith, 'Declaration on the Admission of Women to the Ministerial Priesthood' in Austin Flannery (ed.) *Vatican Council II: More Post-Conciliar Documents* (Vatican Collection Vol. II, Fowler Wright Books, Leominster, 1982), pp. 331–45.

Sagovsky, Nicholas, *Ecumenism, Christian Origins and the Practice of Communion* (Cambridge University Press, Cambridge, 2000).

Sani, Fabio and Steve Reicher, 'Contested Identities and Schisms in Groups: Opposing the Ordination of Women as Priests in the Church of England', *British Journal of Social Psychology* 39 (2000), pp. 95–112.

Selby, Peter, 'The Male Tribe' in Peter Selby, *Belonging: Challenge to a Tribal Church* (SPCK, London, 1991), pp. 35–46.

Selby, Peter, 'Working the Act' in Monica Furlong (ed.), *Act of Synod: Act of Folly?* (SCM Press, London, 1998), pp. 59–86.

Sheils, W.J. and Diana Wood (eds), *The Ministry: Clerical and Lay,* Studies in Church History 26 (Blackwell, Oxford, 1989).

Speller, Lydia, *Theological Objections?* (MOW, London, 1980).

Spencer, Jonathan, 'Action Anthropology' in Alan Barnard and Jonathan Spencer (eds) *Encyclopaedia of Social and Cultural Anthropology* (Routledge, London, 1996), pp. 535–59.

Stendahl, Brita, *The Force of Tradition; A Case Study of Women Priests in Sweden* (Fortress Press, Philadelphia, 1985).

St George's Windsor Consultation on 'Changing Perceptions of Ministry', January 1993.

Stroud, Ernest, *Legislating for Schism; Ordination of Women (Financial Provisions) Measure* (Church in Danger, n.d. [?early 1990s]).

Swanson, R.N. (ed.), *Gender and Christian Religion,* Studies in Church History 34 (Boydell and Bewer, London, 1998).

Sykes, Stephen W., *The Integrity of Anglicanism* (Mowbrays, London and Oxford, 1978).

Sykes, Stephen W. (ed.), *Authority in the Anglican Communion: Essays Presented to Bishop John Howe* (Anglican Book Centre, Toronto, 1987).

Sykes, Stephen W., 'The Christian Faith and the Ordination of Women to the Priesthood' (unpublished address, 18 September 1990).

Tanner, Mary, 'Women in the Church of England: The Ecumenical Challenge', *Crucible*, January–March 2001, pp. 4–14.

Tanner, Mary, 'The Episcopal Ministry Act of Synod in Context' in Paul Avis (ed.), *Seeking the Truth of Change in the Church: Reception, Communion and the Ordination of Women* (T & T Clark, London, 2004), pp. 58–74.

Thompson, R.H.T., *The Church's Understanding of Itself; A Study of Four Birmingham Parishes*, Studies in Ministry and Worship (London, 1957).

Thorne, Helen, *Journey to Priesthood: An In-depth Study of the First Women Priests in the Church of England* (University of Bristol, Bristol, 2000).

Threlfall-Holmes, M., 'Diocesan Equal Opportunities League Table 2001' (GRAS, 2002).

Tiger, Lionel, *Men in Groups* (Nelson, London, 1969).

Tolhurst James (ed.), *Man, Woman and Priesthood* (Gracewing Fowler Wright Books, Leominster, 1989).

Towler, Robert, 'The Social Status of the Anglican Minister', in Roland Robertson (ed.), *Sociology of Religion* (Penguin, London, 1969).

Wakeman, Hilary (ed.), *Women Priests; The First Years* (Darton, Longman and Todd, London, 1996), pp. 1–26.

Walrond-Skinner, Sue, *Crossing the Boundary: What Will Women Priests Mean?* (Mowbray, London, 1994).

Walrond-Skinner, Sue, *Double Blessing: Clergy Marriage since the Ordination of Women as Priests* (Mowbray, London, 1998).

Walsh, Clare, *Gender and Discourse: Language and Power in Politics, the Church and Organisations* (Pearson Education/Longman, London, 2001).

Walter, Tony and Grace Davie, 'The Religiosity of Women in the Modern West', *British Journal of Sociology* 49 (4), December 1998, pp. 640–60.

Ware, Kallistos, 'Man, Woman and the Priesthood of Christ' in Peter Moore (ed.), *Man, Woman and Priesthood* (SPCK, London, 1978), pp. 68–90.

'WATCH response to the Blackburn Review', ts.

Webster, Margaret, *A New Strength, A New Song; The Journey to Women's Priesthood* (Mowbray, London, 1994).

Williams, Rowan, 'Authority and the Bishop in the Church' in Mark Santer (ed.), *Their Lord and Ours; Approaches to Authority, Communion and the Unity of the Church* (SPCK, London, 1982), pp. 90–112.

Williams, S.C., *Religious Belief and Popular Culture in Southwark, 1880–1930* (Oxford University Press, Oxford, 1999).

Wiltshire, Susan and Rachel J. Barber/Board of Practice and Procedure, *The Stained Glass Ceiling: The Church of Scotland Gender Attitude Project* (Church of Scotland, Edinburgh, 2001).

Yates, Paul, 'The Priesthood of Women: Resourcing Identity in the Anglican Church', *Oral History* Autumn 1996, pp. 59–65.

Yates, Paul, 'The Social Construction of Priesthood', *Theology* ci (799), January/ February 1998, pp. 13–22.

Index

Note: Page references in italics indicate tables and figures

accommodationism: and women bishops
  195–7, 207
  and women priests 183, *183*, 184, 208
Act of Synod *see* Episcopal Ministry Act
  of Synod 1993
Aldridge, Alan 141, 179, 182–4, *183*,
  193, 198
Anglican Church in Australia, and women
  bishops 187
Anglican Communion: debates on
  women's priesthood 20, 33, 172–3
  and limits of diversity 204
  and women in the episcopate 172, 187,
    192, 195
Anglican Consultative Council 5 n.12
Anglican Group for the Ordination of
  Women into the Historic Ministry of the
  Church 19
Anglo-Catholicism: and biblical witness
  79
  and Draft Ordination of Women
    Measure 40
  and extended episcopal oversight 148
  and feelings of persecution 118–19
  and homosexuality 63
  and nature of the Church of England
    211
  and opposition to women bishops 196
  and opposition to women priests 51–3,
    56, 72–3, 83, 94, 96–7, 204
  and priest as icon of Christ 70–71
  and reactions to the vote 27–30
  and Resolutions A and B 148, 150
  and Roman Catholicism 28, 72, 83,
    88–9
  and support for women bishops 189
  and support for women priests 61, 70
  and tradition 76
  and women clergy 51–2, 118–19
  see also traditionalism
anomaly, responses to 181–5, *183*, 193–4,
  195–200
anthropology, theological 18–19
appointments 6, 53, 103, 107–124, 205
  and chaplaincies 113–14

deployment patterns 2, 108–112, 204,
  205
process 121–2, 140, 205
senior 108, 115–20, 121, 124, 205, 208
  and stained glass ceiling 115–20, 140
stipendiary 88, 112–13
and traditionalist clergy 117–19, 120
Aquinas, St Thomas 18
archdeacons: female 108, 110, 115 n.27,
  140
  and traditionalist clergy 127
Association for Apostolic Ministry 28
Austin, George 29, 173
authority, in Church of England 166,
  207–8
Avis, Paul 182 n.53

Baker, Gilbert 20
Baker, John Austin 202
baptism, as basis for ministry 78–9
Barnes, E.W. 132
Bavin, Timothy 173
Being in Communion (House of Bishops)
  32, 123 n.62, 178
Bennett, Joyce 20, 26
Bentley, Lesley 115
Berners-Wilson, Angela 36
Bible: and three-fold ministry 18
  and women in episcopate 79, 80, 192,
    201
  and women in headship roles 35, 65–6,
    79, 95
  and women priests 29, 60, 65, 67, 76,
    77–9, 80, 95, 204
bishops: appointment 117–18, 124, 164
  and Episcopal Ministry Act of Synod 4,
    31–3
  as focus for unity 33, 118, 125, 135–6,
    192, 194–5, 203
  responses to the vote 30–31, 36
suffragan 22, 118, 136, 164
  and 'taint' 5, 32, 153, 165–7
  and traditionalist clergy 29–30, 127,
    134
  and traditionalist dioceses 109, 117–18,
    163
  see also women in episcopate

Blackburn Report 120 n.52, 122, 137
    n.46, 144–6, 159–60, 162–4
Bloor, David 182
'Bonds of Peace' (House of Bishops) 6,
    32
Bracegirdle, Wendy 25
Broadhurst, John 29, 173
Brown, Margaret 23 n.29
Burgess, Neil 157

calling, women's sense of 60, 61–2, 79,
    80, 95, 204
canons residentiary, female 110, 115 n.27
case studies 8–12, 38, 204–5, 235–6
    and ethnic diversity 13
    and impact of women priests 90–102
Catholicism: case studies 93–4, 99–100
    and Chrism Eucharists 137–8
    and clergy chapters 133–4
    and Eucharist 128
    and nature of priesthood 70–71
    Prayer Book 93–4
    and Resolutions A and B 144–5
    and support for women priests 30, 76–7
    and women clergy 51–2, 211
    and women in episcopate 192
    see also Anglo-Catholicism
catholicity 6, 162, 209
chaplaincy posts: women in 113–14
    and working relationships 138–9
charismatic evangelicals: and support for
    women bishops 189
    and support for women priests 53, 94–5
Chaves, Mark 4 n.5, 67–8
Chesters, Alan 144, *see also* Blackburn
    Report
Chrism Eucharists 136–8
Christendom, and relations with Roman
    Catholic Church 72
Church Assembly, and ordination of
    women 19, 20
Church attendance, effects of women
    incumbents 96, 117
Church of England: and
    congregationalism 162
    as cultural entity 209–211
    debates on women's priesthood 17–18,
        20, 36–7, 172–3
    decision-making processes 207–8
    fears of division 4–6, 27, 30–31, 72–3,
        80, 84, 88–90, 204, 207, 212
    feminization fears 83, 99

    impact of women priests 82–104, 211–
        12
    locus of authority 166, 207–8
    loss of congregations 28, 33, 38, 89
    losses/gains of clergy 21, 27–8, 30, 31–
        3, 38, 42, 84, 97
Church of Sweden 20, 116
Church Union 28 n.66
church shopping 102–3, 205, 212
churchmanship: and attitudes to women
    bishops 189
    and attitudes to women priests 51–3,
        52, 56, 204
    central 51 n.36, 90–92, 95, 97, 118
    and Forward in Faith 94, 97
    liberal 52, 148, 189
    and Resolutions A and B 144–5, 146,
        148
    see also evangelicalism; traditionalism
clergy: age and generational factors *48*,
    49–51, *50*
    attitudes to opt-out provisions 150–57,
        151, 152, 154, 155, 156
    and biblical witness 77–9
    changing attitudes 30, 42–3, *43*, 46, 50,
        52, 53, 55–6
    continuing ministerial education 120
    couples 113, 114, 116
    deployment patterns 2, 108–112, 204
    and Draft Ordination of Women
        Measure 40, *41*
    and experience of women priests 43,
        53–4, *54*, 55, 92
    financial provision 5, 6, 21 n.16,
        22 n.26, 171
    gender and support for women priests
        46–8, *47*, 56
    and impact of women priests 85–6, *85*
    leaving Church of England 21, 27–8,
        30, 31–3, 38, 42, 89, 97, 99, 155–6,
        198 n.47, 210
    in mixed teams 54, 84, 90, 99
    non-stipendiary 110, *110*, 112–15, 116,
        205
    and opposition to women bishops 192,
        197
    ordained local ministers 110
    reactions to the vote 26–31, 38
    and reception process 174–8, *174, 175*,
        186, 210
    and Resolutions A and B 150–51, *151*,
        153, 155–6

and support for women bishops 188–9, *188*, 192, 194, 207
as 'third gender' 86
and tradition 74–5
working relationships 30–31, 100, 126–30, 206
clergy chapters: 'alternative' 2, 29, 133, 141
and working relationships 126, 130–34, 141, 206
clergy conferences 134
communion: and chapter meetings 131, 133–4, 141–2
in diversity 6, 22, 33, 126, 128–30, 153, 172–3
impaired 33, 130, 138, 153, 165, 167, 206
as sign of unity 128, 130
congregationalism 162, 208
congregations: and changing attitudes 45–6, *46*, 129, 146
and division in the Church 73, 89, 91, 93, 97, 101, 102–3
and experience of women priests 53, 54–5, *54*, 56, 85, 88, 90–102, 123 n.61, 190
gender and support for women priests 47–8, 69
and impact of women priests 85–7, *86*
leaving Church of England 28, 33, 38, 89
rural 95–7, 161–2
support for women priests 43–4, *45*, 55–6, 64
and women bishops 189–93, *190*, 207
conservative evangelicals: and nature of priesthood 70
and opposition to women bishops 52 n.40, 192, 196
and opposition to women priests 51–3, 70, 73, 83, 128
and reactions to the vote 29, 51, 52
and Resolutions A and B 144, 148
and support for women bishops 189–90
and support for women priests 53, 56, 97–9
and women in headship roles 29, 53, 93, 144, 192
and women's calling 62
see also Reform
Cost of Conscience 13 n.26, 21, 28, 44, 83 n.5, 188

creation, and divine intention 77–8
curates, stipendiary 109, 110, *110*, 113

data sample 8–12, 188
qualitative data 57–81
quantitative date 39–56
deaconesses 17, 94, 190 n.12
deaneries: and alternative structures 2, 29, 133, 141
and deployment of women clergy 113
and interregna 132–3, 139, 141
and working relationships 130–34, 141, 205–6
deanery synods, votes on legislation 39–40, *41*, 93
deans, female 108, 110, 115 n.27, 140
decision-making, democratic/monarchical 207–8
deployment patterns 2, 108–112, 204, 205
diaconate: ordinations to 135, 136
and women 17, 20, 23, 34–6, 75, 91, 187, 198
Diocesan Advisers for Women's Ministry 125, 139, 140, 208
diocesan synods: and campaign for women bishops 201
votes on legislation 1, 22, 39–40
dioceses: and appointments process 120–21, 122–3, 140, 205
and Chrism Eucharists 137–8, 141, 206
and decision to ordain women 5, 35–6
and deployment patterns 2, 108–111, *109*, *110*, 112, 204
and division 6, 27, 30–31, 100, 103, 117
and ordination services 134–6, 141
and support for women priests 139–41
traditionalist 46
'two-tier' 22
and working relationships 100, 126, 134–8, 163, 205–6
see also oversight, extended episcopal
discernment period 6, 153, 171, 172–8, 195–6
diversity: and communion 6, 22, 33, 126, 128–30, 131, 133, 153, 172–3, 196
limits 186, 193, 203, 204
division in the Church 4–6, 72–3, 75, 80, 84, 88–90, 204, 207, 212
and dioceses 6, 27, 30–31, 100, 117
parish experience 73, 91, 93–4, 97, 99, 101, 102–3, 119

and women in episcopate 186, 192–4, 197

doctrine, and change 172, 173, 210

Doe, Norman 122

Donald, Steve 118 n.46

Douglas, Mary 63 n.27, 65, 182, 193, 196, 197

Dowell, Susan and Williams, Jane 17 n.1

Draft Ordination of Women Measure 1990: deanery and diocesan votes 39–40, *41*

  and General Synod 173

dress, clerical 64, 130, 138

duty, and role of women 209

Eames Commission 153–4, 195

early Church, and role of women 18, 77, 201

ecumenism: and impact of women bishops 193, 194–5

  and impact of women priests 1, 26, 72–3, 83, 84, 88–9, 102, 204, 211

Elizabethan Settlement 7

Episcopal Church of the USA: and deployment of women 114 n.24

  and women bishops 187

  and women priests 20, 22, 153, 177

Episcopal Ministry Act of Synod 1993 5–6, 7, 22, 29–30, 31–4, 143, 186

  as anomalous 181–5, 193–200, 202–3

  and Blackburn Report 120 n.52, 122, 144–5, 159, 162–3

  calls for rescinding 153, 171, 195–200

  clergy attitudes to *151*, 152–7, 180

  as discriminatory 143, 151–3, *152*, 156, 167, 193, 200

  lay attitudes to 148, 149–50

  pastoral justification 153–5, *154*, 156, 167

  theological implications 55 n.51, 153, 165–6

  theological justification *154*, 155, 156, 184

  and women in episcopate 195–201

episcopate: and 1992 Measure 4, 31–3

  and leadership style 191–2, 202, 208

  see also oversight, extended episcopal; women in episcopate

equality, and gender 67–8, 78, 80, 101, 103, 204, 210

Eucharist: and chapter meetings 131, 133–4

  Chrism Eucharists 136–8, 141, 206

Evangelical Lutheran Churches, and women bishops 187

evangelicalism: and biblical witness 77–8, 79, 95, 201

  in case studies 92–3, 97–9

  and changes in lay attitudes 45–6

  liberal/open 51 n.38, 189

  and opposition to women priests 24, 28, 51–2

  and reactions to the vote 28, 29, 52

  and support for women priests 24, 52, 53

  and women in leadership 29, 53, 79, 93, 94–5, 144, 192

  see also charismatic evangelicals; conservative evangelicals

exclusionism: and women bishops 194, 198, 201, 207

  and women priests 183, *183*, 184, 208

experience of women priests 63, 204

  and attitudes of clergy 43, 53–4, *54*, 55, 92

  and attitudes of laity 24, 44, 53, 54–5, *54*, 56, 85, 88, 90–102, 190

  support for 44, 53–5, *54*, 56, 88, 123 n.61

family life, and priesthood 67, 83, 114

feeling: and arguments for women bishops 192

  and arguments for women priests 57–8, 62–4, 80–81, 205

feminization of the Church 99

feminism 23–4, 61–2, 83, 103

'flying bishops' *see* Provincial Episcopal Visitors

Forward in Faith 12, 28–9, 32 n.93, 48 n.24, 100

  and churchmanship 94, 97

  and exclusionism 184

  and female sexuality 63

  and freehold 118

  New Directions 75, 146, 165

  and regional deans 133

  and Resolution C 163

  and Resolutions A and B 146

  and third province movement 196–7

Francis, Leslie J. 66

Francis, Leslie J. and Robbins, Mandy 62, 84–5, 88 n.29, 127 n.10, 152 n.26, 191
freehold, and traditionalist clergy 118
Furlong, Monica 23 n.32, 32, 33 n.99

gender: and attitudes to women bishops 190
    and attitudes to women priests 46–8, *47*, 56
    characteristics 65–6
    and equality 67–8, 78, 80, 101, 103, 204, 210
    in popular beliefs 65–8, 69
    and priest as icon of Christ 70–71
    and priesthood 18–20, 60, 65, 80, 202
    roles 66–7
Gender and Ministry 17
General Synod: authority 72, 192, 208
    and women in episcopate 193
    and women in priesthood 17–18, 20, 24, 25–6, 173
    see also Episcopal Ministry Act of Synod; Priests (Ordination of Women) Measure
gifts, of women 65–6, 80, 87, 91–2, 95, 98, 101, 102, 107, 191, 205
Gill, Sean 25, 40 n.7
Gilmore, Isabella 120 n.51
GRAS (Group for Rescinding the Act of Synod) 14, 111, 115 n.25, 171, 184, 194, 196–8
gut feeling: and arguments for women bishops 192
    and arguments for women priests 57–8, 62–4, 80–81, 205

Habgood, John, Archbishop of York 22, 23, 25, 153, 165, 173, 177–8
Hall, R. O. 20
Hardy, Alison 161
Harris, Barbara 187
Hayter, Mary 77 n.111
Hind, John 118 n.42
history, importance 209–210
homosexuality: and Anglo-Catholicism 63
    and ordination of homosexuals 171, 186, 204
Hope, David 34
House of Bishops: and accommodationism 184, 195

and legislative settlement 21–3, 31, 153, 208, 211
and locus of authority 208
and reception process 173
and women in episcopate 201
    see also Being in Communion; 'Bonds of Peace'; Manchester Statement
Howard, Christian 62
humanity of the priest 60, 68, 70, 80, 102
Hwang, Jane 20

icon of Christ, priest as 70–71
impossibilists 60, 70, 71, 75, 194
incumbents, female 2, 92, 95–6, 97–8, 109, *110*, 115–17
indifference: and women bishops 194, 198
    and women priests 183, *183*, 185
individual, and the Church 208–9
integrities, dual 123–4, 152, 178–80
interregna: and passing of Resolutions 93, 97, 101, 157, 158, 206
    Sections 11 and 12 meetings 159
    and theology of taint 166
    and working relationships 132–3, 139, 141
interviews, in-depth 8–10
'Isabella's List' 120

Jamieson, Penny 187
Julian of Norwich 19
justice, and gender 68, 73, 80, 82, 86, 92, 93, 191, 197, 201

kairos moment 202
Keyfitz, Nathan 39
Kirk, Geoffrey 193, 196–7
Kuhrt, Gordon W. 107 n.1, 115

laity: age and generational factors *48*, 49
    and biblical witness 77–9, 95
    and changing attitudes 45–6, 129, 146
    and choice of church 45–6, *46*
    and church unity 73
    and churchmanship 52–3, *52*
    and common arguments for/against women priests *59*, 60
    and communion 129–30, *129*
    and division in the Church 73, 89, 91, 93, 97, 101, 102–3
    and Draft Ordination of Women Measure 39–40, *41*

empowerment 82–3, 84, 87–8
expectations of women priests 23–4,
    96, 98–9, 103–4
and experience of women priests 24,
    53, 54–5, *54*, 56, 85, 88, 90–102, 190
gender and support for women priests
    47–8, 56
and gut feelings 64
and impact of women priests 85–7, *86*
and opposition to women priests 28, 38,
    60, 64, 75
and relationships with clergy 127, *128*
and Resolutions A and B 147–9, *148*,
    149
and support for women priests 43–4,
    45, 47–8, 55–6, 64, 73, 76, 80, 86,
    205
survey 8, 11–12, 41–4, *45*
and tradition 74, 76
and women bishops 187, 189–93, *190*,
    207
Lambeth Conferences: 1968 5 n.12
    1988 172–3
leadership: democratic/monarchical 207–
8
    evangelical views 29, 53, 79, 93, 94–5,
        144, 192
    and gifts of women 102, 115, 191–2,
        202
Lehman, Edward C. Jnr 53, 66, 123 n.61
'letter of comfort' 162
lobby group culture 31, 73
Lunn, David 145

Maltby, Judith 31 n.85, 165
Manchester Statement 31, 34, 123 n.62,
    131 n.21, 178 n.33
Matthews, Victoria 187
Mayland, Jean 31 n.84
McClean Report (1986) 33 n.96
methodology of study 7–8
    data sample 8–12, 188
    and social research 8, 39
    and underlying beliefs 58
militancy, fears of 23–4, 95
The Mind of Anglicans 13 n.26, 44, 83
    n.5, 188
ministry: continuing ministerial education
    120
    non-stipendiary 110, *110*, 112–15, 116,
        205
    ordained local 110

as profession or vocation 68–70, 211
mission: impact of women priests 74, 80
    versus ministry 24, 73, 203, 211
Monckton, Joanna 38 n.3
Movement for the Ordination of Women
    20–21, 26, 33, 34, 78, 95

NADAWM (National Association of
    Diocesan Advisers for Women's
    Ministry) 208
New Directions 61, 75, 146, 165
Niebuhr, H. Richard 210

Oakley, Richard 173
Oddie, William, *The Roman Option* 27–8,
    29–30
Oi, Florence Li Tim 20
opportunism: and women bishops 194,
    199–200
    and women priests 183, *183*, 184
opposition to women priests 6, 12, 38,
    204–5
    and age and cohort 48
    and appointment of bishops 117–18
    and appointment to parishes 118
    and biblical witness 77–9
    case studies 93–4, 96–7, 99–100
    and changing attitudes 42–3, 56, 146
    and churchmanship 51–2
    contingency plans 21
    and ecumenism 72–3, 83, 84, 88–9, 204
    and equality 68
    and feminization fears 83, 99
    and gender 47
    and gut feeling 63, 81, 205
    and laity 28, 38, 60, 64
    and marginalization 6, 118–19, 123,
        127
    and pastoral oversight 30–31
    and popular beliefs 60, 63–5, 68
    and popular expectations 83–4, 86, 88
    and priest as icon of Christ 70–71
    and relations with other churches 60,
        88–9
    and secularism 19, 23, 74, 210
    and sexuality 63–4
    theological objections 64–5, 159, 204
    and tradition 74–7, 204
    and traditionalists 27–30, 51–2, 63, 70,
        111, 199
    see also Cost of Conscience; Forward
        in Faith; opt-out provisions; Reform

opt-out provisions 5, 6, 21 n.16, 22–3,
31–2, 143–68, 174
abuse of 156, *156*, 157, 206
and avoidance of pastoral
reorganization
160, 163
clergy and lay attitudes to 147–57
and interpretation of legislation 6,
157–8, 206
pastoral justification 153–5, *154*, 156,
167, 206
theological justification *154*, 155, 156,
165–7, 206
time limit 5, 173
and unforeseen circumstances 160–62
and women bishops 200, 201
see also oversight, extended episcopal;
Resolution C; Resolutions A and B
ordination services 134–6, 141, 167
Ordination of Women (Financial
Provisions) Measure 1993 6, 7, 21 n.16,
33, 34, 171, 179
organizations, para-church 12–13
Orthodox Churches: ecumenical
implications of women priests 72, 83,
102, 211
moves to 21, 78, 150 n.18
oversight, extended episcopal 5, 48,
99–100, 119, 143, 206
clergy attitudes to 153, 155
and evangelicals 29 n.70
and House of Bishops 22–3, 32–4
lay attitudes to 148, 149–50
parish uptake 144–7, *145*, 160
petitioning for 21, 162–7
versus diocesan/regional arrangements
32, 136–8, 164, 208

parish profiles 93, 121, 122, 124, 159
n.45
parishes: Anglo-Catholic 27–9, 53, 96–7
and appointments 119, 121
case studies 8–12, 38, 90–102, 205,
235–6
and extended episcopal oversight 5, 32,
38, 99–100, 119, 143, 144, 160
rural 93–4, 95–7, 161–2
team 116–17, 119, 162
and 'yes, but not yet' response 101,
103, 117, 122–3, 124, 146, 205
see also Resolution C; Resolutions A
and B

patriarchy, shift from 62, 82
patronage system 107–8, 119, 123
Peberdy, Alyson 55 n.50, 148
Percy, Martyn 197
Perry Report 117–18, 124
pragmatism: and ordination of women 22,
30, 199, 208
and women in episcopate 195, 198–
201, 207
preferment 6, 115-20, *see also* women in
episcopate
priesthood: functional view 69, 211
and gender 18–20, 60, 65, 80, 202
and hierarchical style 82–3, 87–8, 90,
96
historical overview 18–20
and humanity 60, 68, 70, 80, 102
as more than a job 68–70, 211
nurturing role 91–2
ontological understanding 69–70, 94,
211
in popular belief 57–81
priest as icon of Christ 70–71
and tradition 74–7
Priests (Ordination of Women) Measure
1992 7
Code of Practice 131 n.20, 132 n.29,
135 n.39, 159
drafting of legislation 21–2
ecumenical implications 1, 26, 72, 83,
84, 88–9, 102, 211
interpretation of legislation 6, 157–8,
160
opt-out provisions 2, 4–6, 7, 22–3,
31–2, 143–68
reactions to the vote 25–34, 37, 38–56
and women in episcopate 4, 171
priests-in-charge: female 109, 117
traditionalist 118
Protestantism, and Church of England 72,
83, 211
Provincial Episcopal Visitors 5, 100, 119,
120, 143
and diocesan/regional arrangements 32,
136–8, 164, 208
parish requests for 145, 162
and pastoral care 164
and working relationships 162–3

quasi-legislation 122, 208
questionnaire surveys 8–10
clergy 8–9, 12, 126, 147, 174, 215–26

and common arguments for/against
women priests 58–60, *59*
laity 8, 11–12, 85 n.11, 147, 227–34
response rate 11, 38
quota, withholding 21, 29

Rausch, Thomas 172
Reade, Nicholas 118 n.42
reception period 6, 7, 57–8, 94, 123,
172–4, 185, 195, 207
clergy views 174–8, *174*, *175*, 186, 210
and short-term future 178–81
Reform 12, 52, 53, 62 n.16, 63, 118, 164,
178
and women bishops 193
and women in leadership 29
Reformation, and constructions of
womanhood 19
Resolution C 5, 99–100, 143, 163–4, 206
Resolutions A and B 5, 41–2, 46, 53, 85,
96–7, 99–100, 143, 206
as cause of division 93–4, 97, 100, 101,
103
clergy attitudes to 150–51, *151*, 153,
155–6
and diocesan deployment patterns 109,
118–19
and interpretation of legislation 157–8
and interregnum cover 132–3, 142
n.57,
149, 206
lay attitudes to 44, 147–9, *148*, *149*
and time limits 157–8
and unforeseen circumstances 160–62
uptake 144–7, *145*
voting on 158–60, 167
and 'yes, but not yet' response 101,
103, 117, 122–3, 124, 146, 205
Richardson, John 63 n.26
rights, and ordination of women 209
Ripon Report (1992) 22
Roberts, Richard H. 122
robing 130–31, 138
Rochester working party 186–7, 201, 202
n.61
Rogerson, Barry 35
Roman Catholic Church: and Anglican
orders 72–3
moves to 21, 27, 99, 211
and women bishops 193
and women priests 1, 26, 72–3, 83, 84,
88–90, 102, 211

Rowell, Geoffrey 75
Royden, Maude 19
rural deans: female 128
traditionalist 131, 133
Russell, Anthony 107 n.1

Sandom, Carrie 35 n.110
Scottish Episcopal Church, and women
bishops 187
sector ministry: women in 110, 112, 113
and working relationships 138–9
secularism, and women priests 19, 23, 74,
210
Selby, Peter 34
servers, female 75, 90, 101–2
settlement 1992–4: as anomalous 181–5,
193–4, 195–200, 202–3
and discernment period 6, 153, 171,
172–8, 195–6
future prospects 171–89
impact on the Church 82–104
as interim measure 6
as long-term measure 5–6
and opt-out provisions 5, 6, 7, 22–3,
31–2, 143–68
and short-term future 178–81
unresolved issues 7, 13, 97, 103,
157-67, 179, 204, 206, *see also*
appointments; working relationships
sexuality, and opposition to women
priests
63–4
sisterhoods, reintroduction 17
Society of the Holy Cross (SSC) 28 n.66
sociology, and research methods 8, 39
'stained glass ceiling' effect 115–20, 140
stipends: and clergy couples 113
women in stipendiary posts 88, 112–15,
116
suffragan bishops 22, 118, 136, 164,
see also Provincial Episcopal Visitors
suffrage, female 19
support for women priests: and age and
cohort 48–51
and biblical witness 77–9, 95
case studies 90–98, 101–2, 204
changing attitudes 30, 42–3, *43*, 46, 50,
52, 53, 55–6, 63
and church tradition 51–3, *52*, 56
and clergy 41–3, 46–7, 52, 55, 64–5,
110, 163, *188*
and deployment patterns 108, 110, 205

and equality 67–8, 101, 103, 204, 210
and experience of women priests 53–5,
54, 56, 88, 123 n.61
and gender 47–8, *47*, 56
and gut feeling 62–3, 205
and laity 43–4, *45*, 47–8, 55, 64, 86–7,
205
organized 139–41
and popular beliefs 58–68, 77–9, 80
and popular expectations 82–3, 86–7,
96, 98–9, 103–4
and tradition 74, 76–7

taint, theology of 5, 32, 55 n.51, 153,
165–7
Tanner, Mary 5 n.12, 178 n.33
theology, and opposition to women
priests
64–5, 159
Third Province Movement 2, 171, 184,
186, 193–4, 196–9
Thompson, R.H.T. 69 n.68
Thorne, Helen 4, 13 n.26, 35, 38, 62, 67,
139 nn.51-2, 152
and appointment of women clergy 112
n.12, 113–14
and impact of women priests 84, 85,
96, 104
questionnaire 127 n.7, 128 n.14, 181
tradition: and women bishops 192
and women priests 74–7, 204
traditionalism: and age and generational
factors 48 n.24, 50
and alternative chapters 2, 29, 133, 141
and appointments 111, 117–19, 120,
205
case studies 96–7
and Chrism Eucharists 137–8, 141, 206
and dioceses 109, 117–18, 163
and extended episcopal oversight 22–3,
30–31
and hierarchical style 90 n.43
and opposition to women priests 22,
27–30, 51–3, 63, 70, 72–3, 159, 173,
186, 198
options open to 27–30
and ordination services 134–5, 167
and priest as icon of Christ 71
and Roman Catholic Church 72, 83,
88–9
and settlement as anomalous 182,
193–4, 196

and support for women priests 46
and women in episcopate 193–4, 196,
200
and working relationships 127, 130–31
see also Forward in Faith; Resolutions
A and B; Third Province Movement
triumphalism 26–7
Trott, Stephen 7 n.17

Ultra-Montanism 88

vocation: discerning 32, 35
and functional view of ministry 69
and sense of calling 21, 60, 61–2, 79,
80, 95, 204

Wakeman, Hilary 4, 38
Walrond-Skinner, Sue 26 n.50, 108
WATCH (Women and the Church) 12,
34, 164 n.59, 178
Webster, Margaret 26
Whitehead, Neil 161
Williams, Rowan 186, 195
women, in early Church 18
Women against the Ordination of Women
28
Women and the Church (WATCH) 12,
34, 163 n.59, 178
women deacons 17, 20, 23, 75, 91, 101
and preferment 116
and preparation for priesthood 34–6
women in episcopate 186, 187–95
and 1992 Measure 4, 171, 184
and biblical witness 79, 80
campaigning for 34, 186–7, 192,
200–201
and leadership styles 103, 191–2, 202
opposition to 189, 192–3, 196
reservations expressed 93, 95, 100, 103
support for 2, 55, 111, 188–92, *188*,
193–4, 196–201, 207
and theological arguments 191, 192,
201, 202, 207
and timing 193, 194, 196, 199–200,
202
see also Episcopal Ministry Act of
Synod
women priests: acceptance 3–4, 13, 26–7,
37–56, 57–8, 171, 197, 204–5
and discernment of vocation 32, 35
and family commitments 67, 83, 114

General Synod debates 17–18, 20,
    25–6, 173
historical setting 17–20
impact 4, 6, 23, 82–104, 211–12
mentoring 120
mutual support 125, 139–41
numbers 108–110, *109*, *110*
particular gifts 65–6, 80, 87, 91–2, 95,
    98, 101, 102, 107, 205
in popular beliefs 57–81
popular expectations 82–90, *85*, 96,
    98–9, 103–4
preparation for priesthood 34–6
public response 1, 25–6, 89
reception 6, 7, 57–8, 94, 123, 172–8,
    186, 195, 207, 210
as role models 98
and social expectations 73–4
theological objections 64–5
and working relationships 126–7, *127*
working styles 82, 84, 87–8, 90, 96,
    103
see also opposition to women priests;
    support for women priests
working relationships 125–42, 180, 205–6
    and communion 128–30, 131
    in deaneries 130–34, 141
    in dioceses 30–31, 100, 134–8, 141
    and interregnum cover 132–3, 139, 141
    and laity 127, *128*
    and Provincial Episcopal Visitors 136,
        162–3
    and senior clergy 127
*Working with the Spirit: Choosing
    Diocesan Bishops* 117–18, 124